MICHAEL CHABON

PRESENTS

WRITER

BRIAN K. VAUGHAN

ARTISTS

STEVE ROLSTON
JASON SHAWN ALEXANDER
PHILIP BOND
EDUARDO BARRETO

COLORISTS

DAVE STEWART
MATTHEW HOLLINGSWORTH
PAUL HORNSCHEMEIER
DAN JACKSON

LETTERER

TOM ORZECHOWSKI

COVER ARTIST

ALEX ROSS

PRESTIDIGITATOR

MICHAEL CHABON

INSPIRED BY
The Amazing Adventures of Kavalier & Clay
by MICHAEL CHABON

DARK HORSE BOOKS®

INTRODUCTION

BY MICHAEL CHABON

ONE WEEKEND TOWARD the end of his public life, as he and his ex-wife plied their yearly course along the circuit of comic book conventions, bickering, bantering, holding each other up when the sidewalks were icy or the stairs steep, Sam Clay found himself in Cleveland, Ohio, as a guest of honor at the 1986 ErieCon. ErieCon was a mid-sized regional show held in the ballroom of a Euclid Avenue hotel that stood, until it was demolished, across the street from a grand old movie palace that soon after also succumbed to the wrecking ball, during one of the spasms of redevelopment that have tormented Cleveland's slumber for the past forty years.

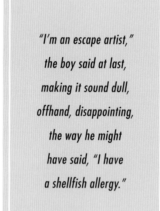

"I'm an escape artist," the boy said at last, making it sound dull, offhand, disappointing, the way he might have said, "I have a shellfish allergy."

People who saw them making the con scene in those years were often touched by the steadfast way that Rosa Kavalier—born Rosa Luxemburg Saks in New York City in 1919 and known to the world, if at all, as Rose Saxon, a queen of the romance comics—kept hold of the elbow of one of her ex-husband's trademark loud blazers as they moved from curb to counter, from ballroom to elevator, from bar to dining room. They were, people said, devoted to each other. And undoubtedly this was the case. They had known each other for more than forty-five years, and though no one ever quite untangled the complicated narrative of their various creative and romantic partnerships over the years, mutual devotion was certainly part of the story. But the truth of the tight grip that Rosa kept on Sam was that, after a series of unsuccessful operations to repair his damaged retinas, the man could barely see a foot in front of his face.

"She's my seeing-eye dog," he would say, and then he would wait, wearing a short-sighted grin, as if daring his ex-wife to find no humor in his witticism, a challenge she was always ready to accept.

But to the people who knew Sam—old-timers, friends, and enemies from the Golden and Silver Ages, the beaming young (or formerly young) protégés who regularly radiated from the formless warmth of the Kavalier-Clay ménage—it was obvious how humiliating he found his poor vision, his lousy teeth, the hobbled, foot-dragging gait that had resulted from the surprise return, when he hit his sixties, of the polio that crippled him as a boy. Sam Clay was a professionally (if not always convincingly) fierce man whose mighty shoulders and Popeye forearms attested to a lifelong regimen of pushups, dumbbells, and the punching of speed bags. You could see that he hated every moment he had to spend "hanging around Rosa," in his own formulation, "like a persistent fart."

On this particular Saturday afternoon in Cleveland, Ohio, in 1986, therefore, when it came time for Sam to transfer custody, from his plumbing system to the hotel's, of the Dr. Pepper-and-orange-juice cocktail (mixed by a secret formula known and palatable only to him) that he been swilling from a thermos all morning, Sam got up from the "Kavalier & Clay" table in Artists' Alley and set forth alone to find the men's room, which, according to the guy at the next table, lay just a few steps outside and to the left of the Cuyahoga Ballroom's gilded doors. How hard could it be? Rosa was off somewhere having a confab with some skinny little thing named Diana from Comico, and Sam's new assistant Mark Morgenstern (later known for his work on the DC/Vertigo revival of the old Pharaoh Comics title *Earthman*) was attending the Klaus Nordling tribute panel. And Sammy, Sam decided, could goddamn well find his own goddamn way to the toilet.

As it turned out, there was no bathroom just outside and to the left of the ballroom's gilded doors; or perhaps the ballroom had more doors than Sam knew about, or featured less gilding than he had been led to expect; or maybe, he thought bitterly, he was just so addled-pated and purblind that he no longer knew his left from his right. He spent ten minutes blundering around the elevator lobby, responding with cheerful irritation to greetings and good wishes from blurred faces and voices that sounded as though he ought to know them. But his attention was wholly occupied with the effort it cost him not to appear to be lost, blind, and in desperate need of a pee, so that he might as well have been in a crowd of strangers. There was an unpleasant incident with a large potted fern and a compromising entanglement with the legs of a display easel. Sam's dignity—an attribute with which, until quite recently, he had never been unduly burdened—would not, it appeared, permit him to admit that he was in need of assistance.

At one point he found himself in an intimate, metallic space whose acoustics suggested a washroom or stall, and he knew a horrible instant of hope and relief before realizing that he was in fact riding an elevator. He got off at some floor and walked in some direction, trailing his right hand against the dark-red softness of the hallway's flocked wallpaper because once, many years before, in an issue of *Astounding*, he had read that you could always count on finding your way in and out of any labyrinth as long as, from the moment you entered it, you kept one hand in continuous contact with one wall. This expedient may, or may not, have had something to do with the fact that, twenty-five minutes after setting out from Artists' Alley full of piss and confidence, he succeeded, not without effort, in locking himself inside a broom closet.

Like most grave mistakes, his became apparent more or less upon commission. The bright, burgundy, flocked-velvet blur of the hallway went black. The door shut behind him with the decisive click of some instrument of execution snapping to. There was an acrid bubblegum stink of disinfectant and the damp-bedsheet smell of old mop heads. Sammy knew a moment of pure infantile dread. Then in the darkness he smiled.

"At least," he pointed out to himself, unzipping his fly, "there'll be a bucket."

With a chiming like some liquid carillon he relieved himself into the rolling mop bucket whose contours his shoetips then fingertips had revealed to him. Bliss, fulfillment through evacuation. He zipped up and began, with fresh dread, to contemplate the impossible task that lay before him, which consisted of shouldering the now almost unendurable and infinitely imperiled burden of his dignity while pounding on the door of the broom closet and screaming for help until he was hoarse, all the while enjoying the piscine bouquet of his own urine. He opened his mouth, ready to scream. Then he closed his mouth, experiencing second thoughts about this course. When, after all, they finally discovered his corpse, or perhaps his skeleton, in this closet, huddled over a bucket of ancient pee, that would perhaps be embarrassing for *some* people—but not for him, because he would be dead. He slapped the door once, twice with

the flat of his hand. He leaned against a steel shelf stacked with rolls of toilet paper in their paper wrappers, and readied himself for the final indignity, and sighed.

There was a rattle—the doorknob—and then an insect scratching, wire feelers. And then a burst of light and air.

"I saw you go in," said a boy. "Then I heard knocking." A boy in a red baseball cap. An open mouth, maybe some kind of dirt around the mouth. Sammy leaned forward to get a better look. About ten years old, a standard-issue little American kid but with something sly in his eyes and an overall air of injury or grievance. He was wearing a red jersey with the word LIONS running in old-timey script across the front, and in his hand he held an open Swiss army knife. The grime on his lips a streak of chocolate, a chocolate crumb or two. A Hostess cupcake, or perhaps a Ding Dong.

"It smells kind of like pee in there," the boy said.

"God, you're right!" said Sam, waving his hand back and forth in front of his face. "This hotel really is a dump."

He stepped out of the closet and shut the door behind him.

"Hey, thanks, kid. Guess I—" But what was the point of lying? Would he ever see this kid again? *Guess I just wandered into a closet.* "Guess I had the wrong room. Thanks." He and the boy shook hands, the boy's boneless and reluctant in his. He gestured with his chin to the little red knife. "Pretty handy with that. What are you, the world's youngest second-story man? Hotel dick know about you?"

The boy blinked, as if doubting his own reply or the wisdom of even making it. His breathing came wheezy through congested nostrils.

"I'm an escape artist," the boy said at last, making it sound dull, offhand, disappointing, the way he might have said, "I have a shellfish allergy."

"That so?" Sam felt his heart squeeze at the sound of the words *escape artist*, the deviated-septum rasp, the eyes that sought to slip free of the enforced deadpan manner of a ten-year-old boy. "Good with locks?"

The kid shrugged.

"Yours was easy." The boy refolded the pick blade into his knife and returned it to the pocket of his jeans. "I'm actually not really all that good."

In his semi-blindness it took a moment for Sam to realize that the boy was crying, softly, and had been crying possibly for a long time before he took it upon himself to rescue the old guy in the closet.

"Hmm," he said. "So what are you doing, wandering around the hotel, freeing strange geezers from broom closets? Where are your mother and father?"

The kid shrugged.

"I'm supposed to be downstairs. At the league award lunch."

"You like baseball?"

Another shrug.

"I take it they aren't handing you any awards."

The boy reached into the pocket of his blue jeans again and took out a crumpled wad of paper. He handed it wordlessly to Sammy with an expression on his face of utter disdain for the paper and its contents. Sammy unfolded and smoothed it out and then pressed it right up to his right eye, the stronger, to read it.

"'Nice Try Citation,'" he said.

The boy leaned back against the far wall of the corridor and sank slowly to the ground until his forehead touched his knees.

"Long season?" Sammy said, after a moment.

"Ninth place," the boy said, his voice muffled and small. "Out of nine. Also I have personal problems I don't care to discuss."

Sam considered pressing, but decided that when you were ten, all your problems were more or less personal.

"Look at me," Sam said. "I just peed into a bucket."

This seemed to make the boy feel better about himself.

"Listen. I don't know what the trouble is. I'm going to, uh, respect your privacy there. But I appreciate your helping me. I'd like to pay you back." He reached into the hip pocket of his suit pants and then remembered that his wallet was in the breast pocket of his jacket, hanging over the back of the chair in Artists' Alley. "Only I'm, uh, busted." He rubbed at the stubble on his chin. "So I guess I need to find somebody else who's stuck in a jam and do the same for them like you did for me. Creed of the League of the Golden Key."

"Huh?"

"Forget about it. What's your name?"

"Hey, dickhead!" A gang of boys, wearing red Lions jerseys and red caps tumbled into the hallway from the elevator and stood. "Vaughan!" The voice, cracking with mockery or pubescence, seemed to be issuing from the largest among them. "What the hell are you doing up here? Coach is looking everywhere for you! He called your *mommy*, dickhead!"

"You best get your ass downstairs!"

"Hey, Vaughan, who's the old guy?"

Sammy took a step toward the boy, Vaughan, and lowered his voice.

"They want to give you another certificate?"

"A trophy. But I saw mine. The head was missing. I guess maybe somebody, well. Broke it off. When I saw that, that's when I left."

"Come *on*, Vaughan!"

"Hey," Sam told the boys, flexing his Popeye arms, and putting as much Brooklyn into his voice as he could muster. It was, still, a decent amount. "Whyn't you punks get the hell out of here and leave the kid alone?"

The red mass hung a moment in the hallway, wavering like the afterimage of a bright flash on his damaged retinas. Then a moment later it was gone.

"You ever read comic books?" Sam asked the boy.

"Not really. Like, Archies?"

"Archies. No, well, Archie has his place. But—"

Sam reached a hand down and offered to help the boy to his feet.

"Look, they got a big show going on downstairs. Cuyahoga Ballroom. A comics show. You might like it. Take Doctor Strange. He's a magician. You'd like that one, I bet."

"I've heard of him."

"You ought to check it out."

He pulled the boy up and stepped away from him.

"I'd better get back to the banquet," the boy said.

"Suit yourself," Sam said. "'Suit yourself,' that's good advice. I wish somebody'd given it to me when I was your age."

They went to the elevator and the boy pressed the button. They said nothing when it arrived and the doors opened, and nothing until they were halfway down.

"'Suit yourself,'" the boy repeated. "I let you out of a dark, stinky closet where you could've died; you give me some cheap advice."

Sam looked at the boy and saw that sly light in the boy's eyes again.

"Ten-year-olds," Sam said, as he got out of the elevator at the mezzanine. "God help me." The doors started to close on the boy and his chance to redeem himself and repay his debt of freedom. He stuck his arm in and stopped them from closing. "Check out the show," he said. "*That's* my advice to you. Cheap as it may be."

"I can't," the boy said. "I really don't think I can. But, uh, thanks."

"Vaughan. What's the rest of it?"

"Brian K. Vaughan." It came out in a rush, a single word, almost a single syllable.

"Uh-huh. What's the K for?"

"Kellar."

"Like the magician. Self-decapitation, right? Harry Kellar. That the guy?"

Brian K. Vaughan looked shocked, almost put out, as if his middle initial represented a grave and powerful mystery of which he had hitherto believed himself the sole initiate.

"Yeah," he said wonderingly.

Sam stepped back from the doors, and drew back his hand with a Harry Kellar flourish, and the door slid shut on Brian K. Vaughan who, having called home from a pay phone in the lobby, received permission to stay after the league banquet and attend the remainder of the Saturday session of ErieCon '86, at which he purchased a copy of *Strange Tales* number 146 (featuring Baron Mordo, Dormammu, *and* the Ancient One), in Very Good condition, thus altering the entire course of his future life, not to mention the lives of those of us who are fortunate enough to know and appreciate the comic book genius so wildly and thoroughly on display (along with the estimable talents of Steve Rolston, Jason Alexander, Philip Bond, and Eduardo Barreto) in the pages that follow.

He and Sam Clay never saw or spoke to each another again. ⚷

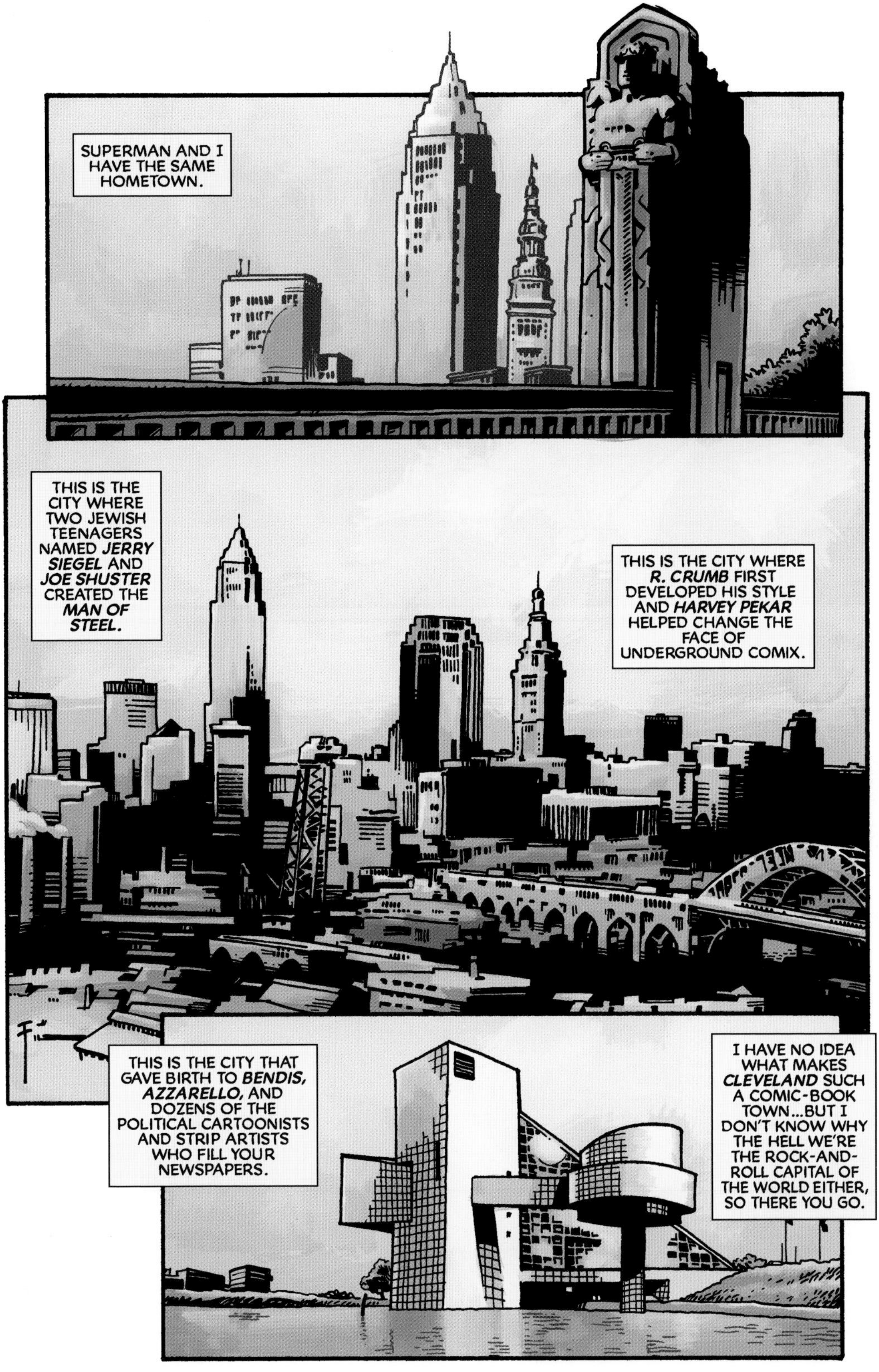
SUPERMAN AND I HAVE THE SAME HOMETOWN.
THIS IS THE CITY WHERE TWO JEWISH TEENAGERS NAMED *JERRY SIEGEL* AND *JOE SHUSTER* CREATED THE *MAN OF STEEL.*
THIS IS THE CITY WHERE *R. CRUMB* FIRST DEVELOPED HIS STYLE AND *HARVEY PEKAR* HELPED CHANGE THE FACE OF UNDERGROUND COMIX.
THIS IS THE CITY THAT GAVE BIRTH TO *BENDIS, AZZARELLO,* AND DOZENS OF THE POLITICAL CARTOONISTS AND STRIP ARTISTS WHO FILL YOUR NEWSPAPERS.
I HAVE NO IDEA WHAT MAKES *CLEVELAND* SUCH A COMIC-BOOK TOWN...BUT I DON'T KNOW WHY THE HELL WE'RE THE ROCK-AND-ROLL CAPITAL OF THE WORLD EITHER, SO THERE YOU GO.

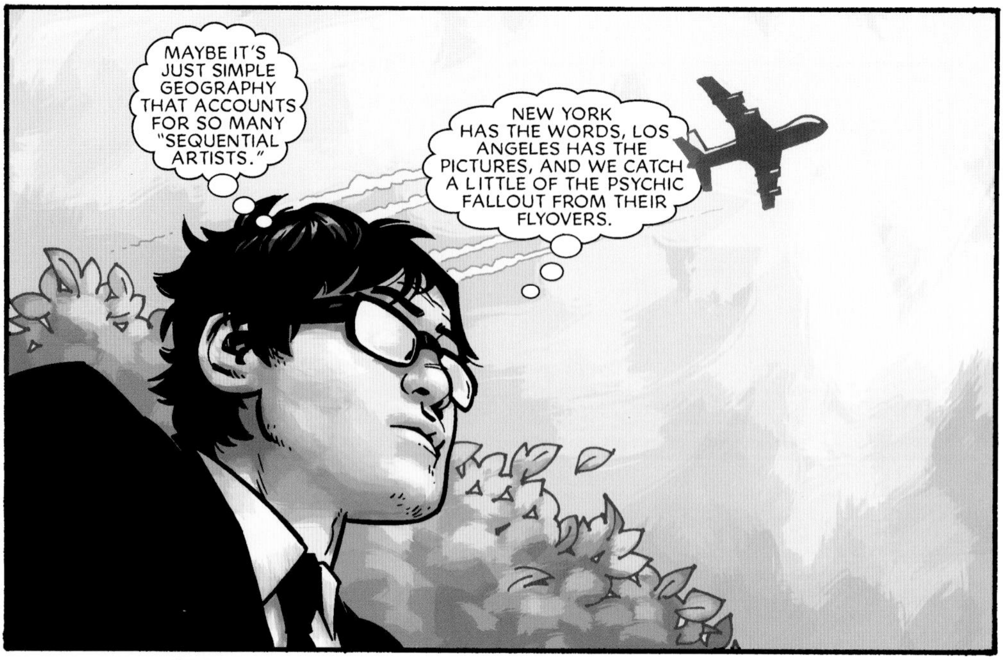
MAYBE IT'S JUST SIMPLE GEOGRAPHY THAT ACCOUNTS FOR SO MANY "SEQUENTIAL ARTISTS."
NEW YORK HAS THE WORDS, LOS ANGELES HAS THE PICTURES, AND WE CATCH A LITTLE OF THE PSYCHIC FALLOUT FROM THEIR FLYOVERS.

OR MAYBE IT'S SOMETHING IN THE WATER...

...NEW CHEMICAL COMPOUNDS PRODUCED IN LAKE ERIE, LIKE THE MAGICAL SERUMS THAT TURNED SO MANY MERE MORTALS OF FICTION INTO GOLDEN AGE DEMIGODS.

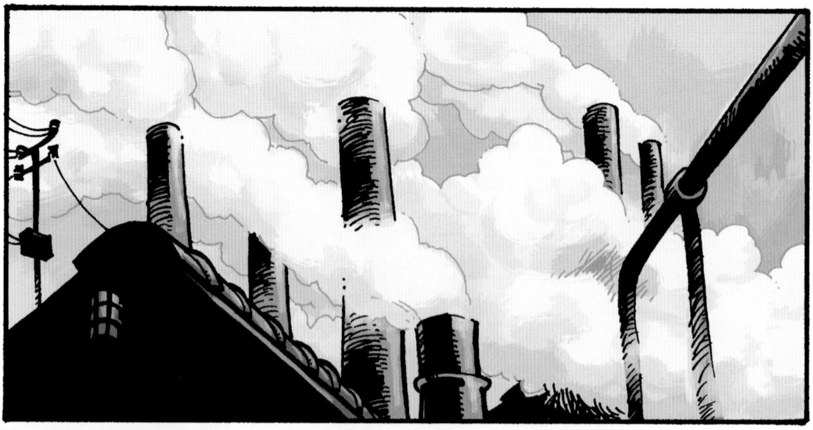

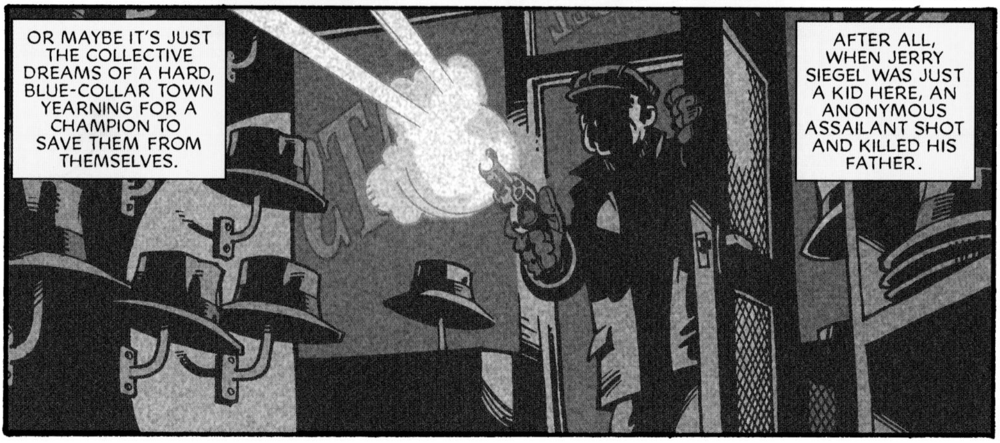
OR MAYBE IT'S JUST THE COLLECTIVE DREAMS OF A HARD, BLUE-COLLAR TOWN YEARNING FOR A CHAMPION TO SAVE THEM FROM THEMSELVES.
AFTER ALL, WHEN JERRY SIEGEL WAS JUST A KID HERE, AN ANONYMOUS ASSAILANT SHOT AND KILLED HIS FATHER.

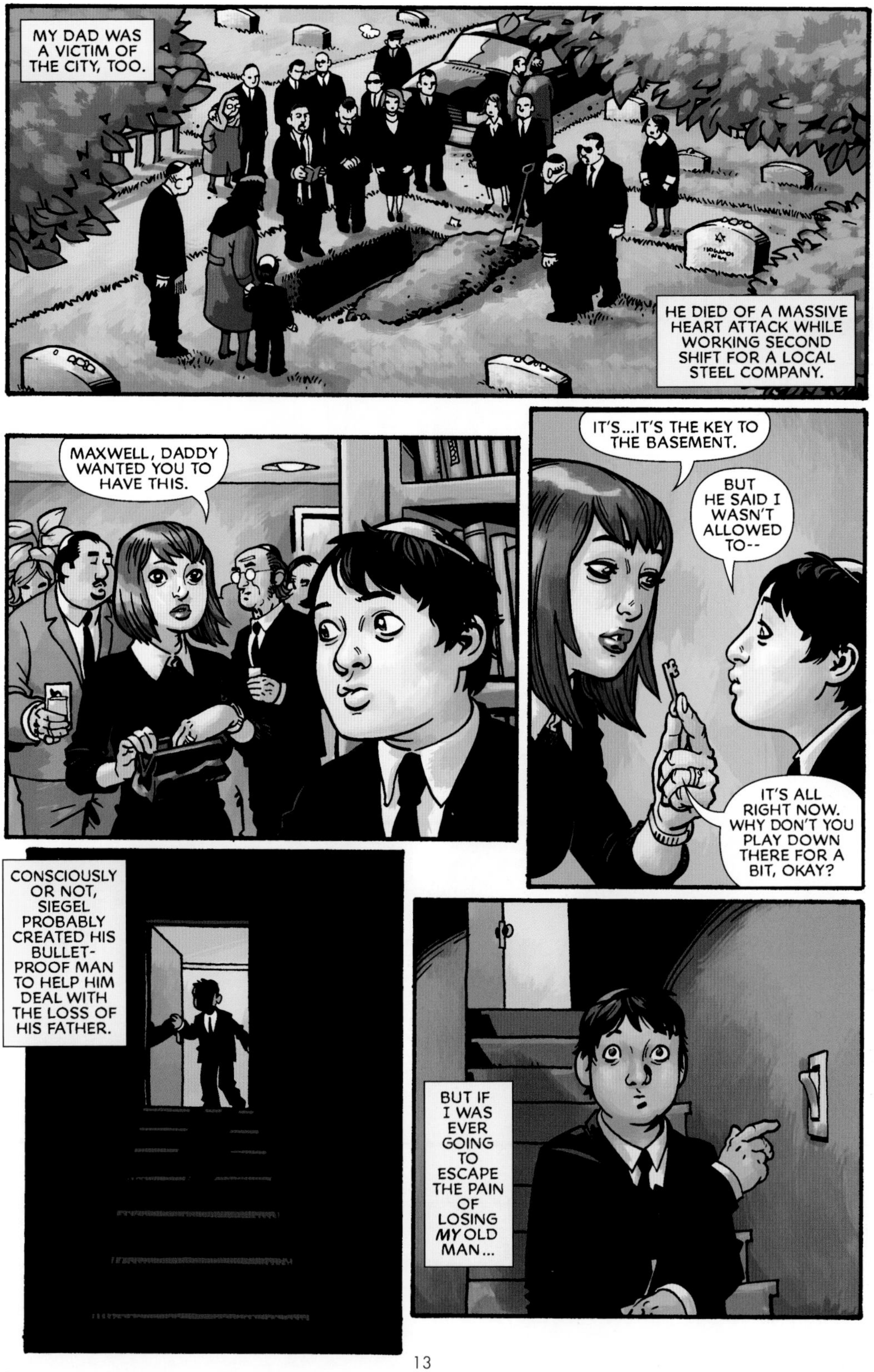
MY DAD WAS A VICTIM OF THE CITY, TOO.
HE DIED OF A MASSIVE HEART ATTACK WHILE WORKING SECOND SHIFT FOR A LOCAL STEEL COMPANY.
MAXWELL, DADDY WANTED YOU TO HAVE THIS.
IT'S...IT'S THE KEY TO THE BASEMENT.
BUT HE SAID I WASN'T ALLOWED TO--
IT'S ALL RIGHT NOW. WHY DON'T YOU PLAY DOWN THERE FOR A BIT, OKAY?
CONSCIOUSLY OR NOT, SIEGEL PROBABLY CREATED HIS BULLET-PROOF MAN TO HELP HIM DEAL WITH THE LOSS OF HIS FATHER.
BUT IF I WAS EVER GOING TO ESCAPE THE PAIN OF LOSING *MY* OLD MAN...

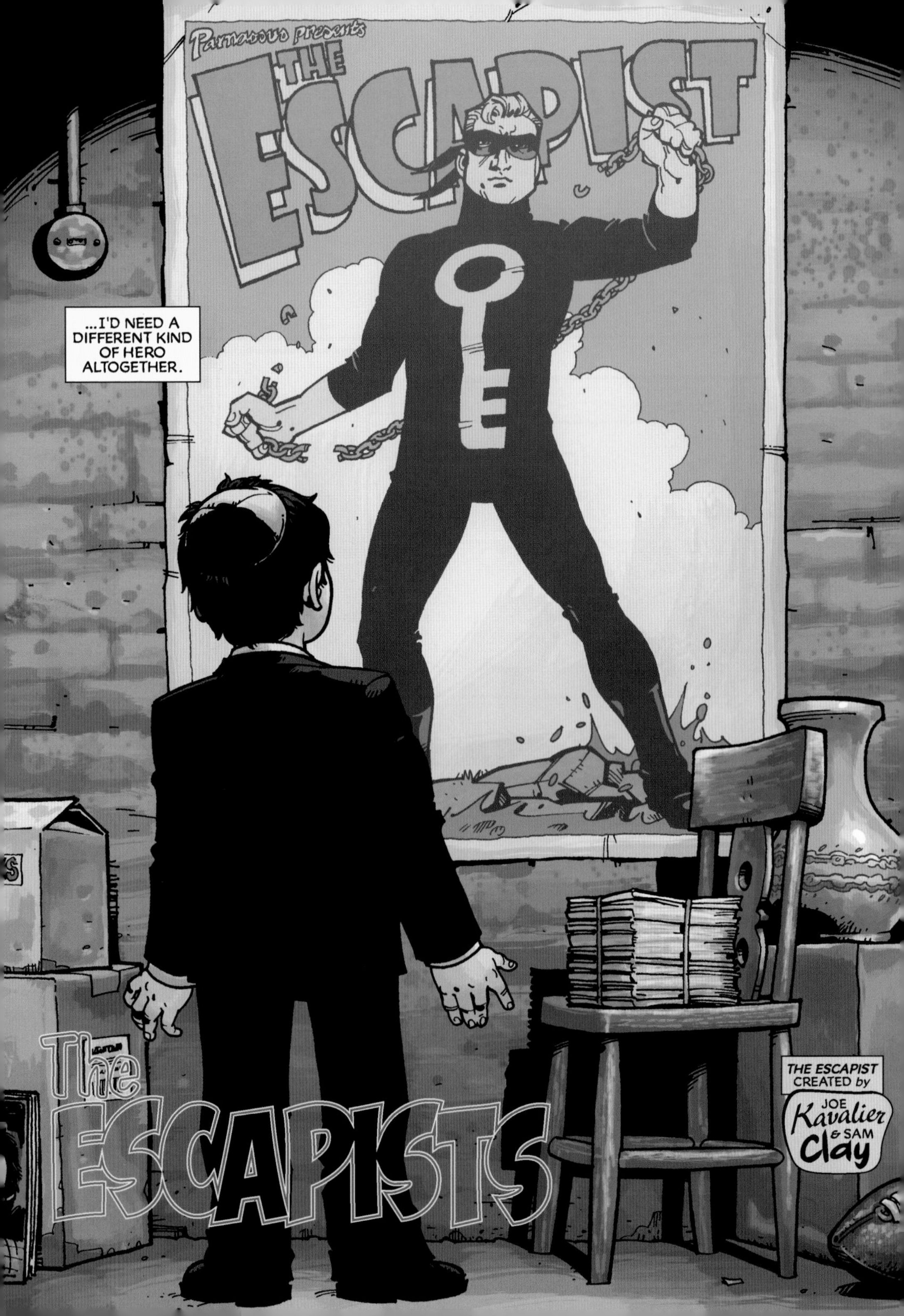
Parnassus presents
THE ESCAPIST
...I'D NEED A DIFFERENT KIND OF HERO ALTOGETHER.
The ESCAPISTS
THE ESCAPIST CREATED by JOE Kavalier & SAM Clay

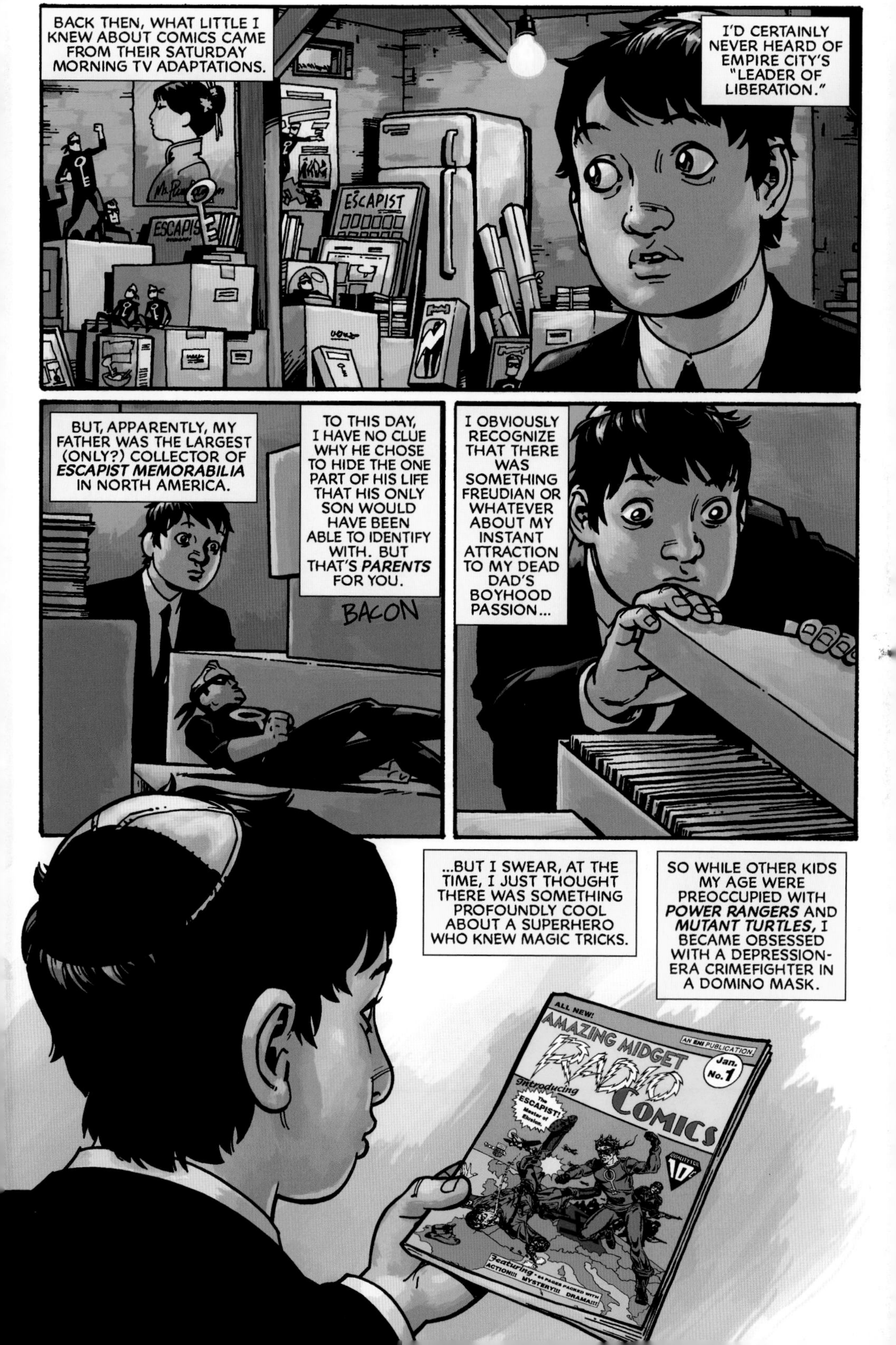

BACK THEN, WHAT LITTLE I KNEW ABOUT COMICS CAME FROM THEIR SATURDAY MORNING TV ADAPTATIONS.
I'D CERTAINLY NEVER HEARD OF EMPIRE CITY'S "LEADER OF LIBERATION."
ESCAPIST
BUT, APPARENTLY, MY FATHER WAS THE LARGEST (ONLY?) COLLECTOR OF *ESCAPIST MEMORABILIA* IN NORTH AMERICA.
TO THIS DAY, I HAVE NO CLUE WHY HE CHOSE TO HIDE THE ONE PART OF HIS LIFE THAT HIS ONLY SON WOULD HAVE BEEN ABLE TO IDENTIFY WITH. BUT THAT'S *PARENTS* FOR YOU.
BACON
I OBVIOUSLY RECOGNIZE THAT THERE WAS SOMETHING FREUDIAN OR WHATEVER ABOUT MY INSTANT ATTRACTION TO MY DEAD DAD'S BOYHOOD PASSION...
...BUT I SWEAR, AT THE TIME, I JUST THOUGHT THERE WAS SOMETHING PROFOUNDLY COOL ABOUT A SUPERHERO WHO KNEW MAGIC TRICKS.
SO WHILE OTHER KIDS MY AGE WERE PREOCCUPIED WITH *POWER RANGERS* AND *MUTANT TURTLES,* I BECAME OBSESSED WITH A DEPRESSION-ERA CRIMEFIGHTER IN A DOMINO MASK.
ALL NEW!
AMAZING MIDGET RADIO COMICS
AN ENI PUBLICATION
Jan. No. 1
Introducing The ESCAPIST! Master of Elusion
10¢
Featuring - 64 PAGES PACKED WITH ACTION!!! MYSTERY!!! DRAMA!!!

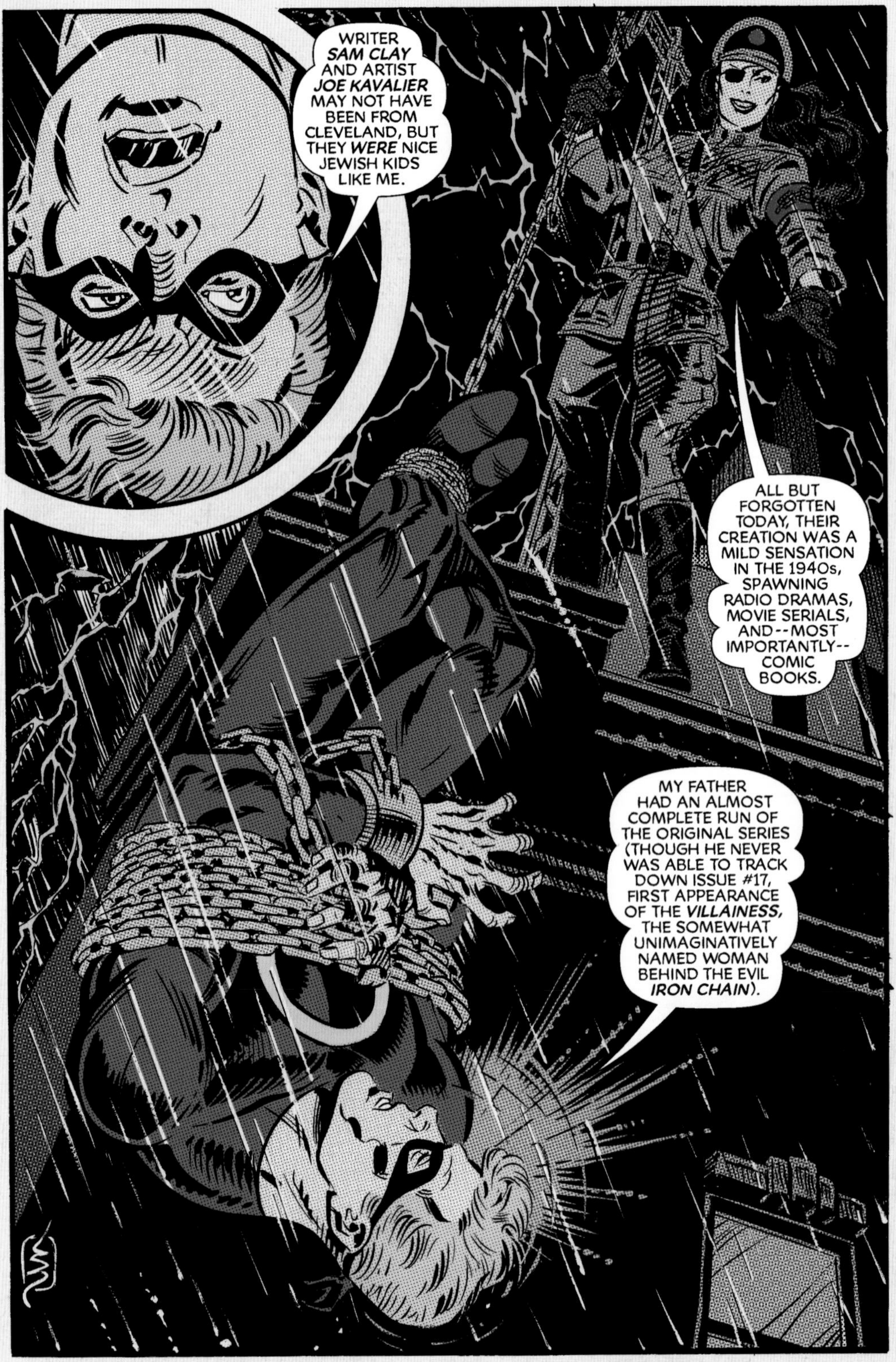
WRITER SAM CLAY AND ARTIST JOE KAVALIER MAY NOT HAVE BEEN FROM CLEVELAND, BUT THEY WERE NICE JEWISH KIDS LIKE ME.
ALL BUT FORGOTTEN TODAY, THEIR CREATION WAS A MILD SENSATION IN THE 1940s, SPAWNING RADIO DRAMAS, MOVIE SERIALS, AND--MOST IMPORTANTLY--COMIC BOOKS.
MY FATHER HAD AN ALMOST COMPLETE RUN OF THE ORIGINAL SERIES (THOUGH HE NEVER WAS ABLE TO TRACK DOWN ISSUE #17, FIRST APPEARANCE OF THE VILLAINESS, THE SOMEWHAT UNIMAGINATIVELY NAMED WOMAN BEHIND THE EVIL IRON CHAIN).

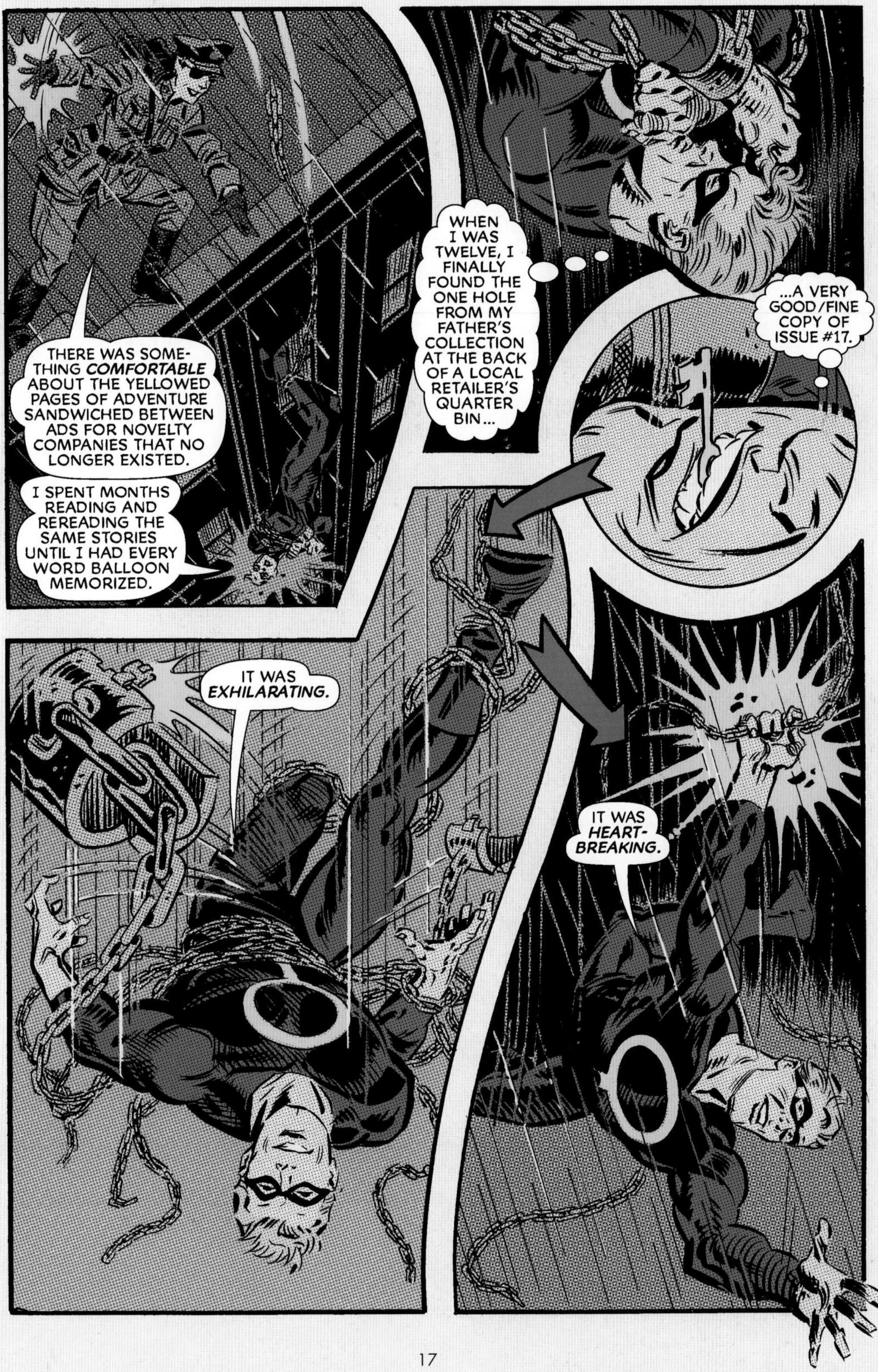
THERE WAS SOMETHING COMFORTABLE ABOUT THE YELLOWED PAGES OF ADVENTURE SANDWICHED BETWEEN ADS FOR NOVELTY COMPANIES THAT NO LONGER EXISTED.
I SPENT MONTHS READING AND REREADING THE SAME STORIES UNTIL I HAD EVERY WORD BALLOON MEMORIZED.
WHEN I WAS TWELVE, I FINALLY FOUND THE ONE HOLE FROM MY FATHER'S COLLECTION AT THE BACK OF A LOCAL RETAILER'S QUARTER BIN...
...A VERY GOOD/FINE COPY OF ISSUE #17.
IT WAS EXHILARATING.
IT WAS HEART-BREAKING.

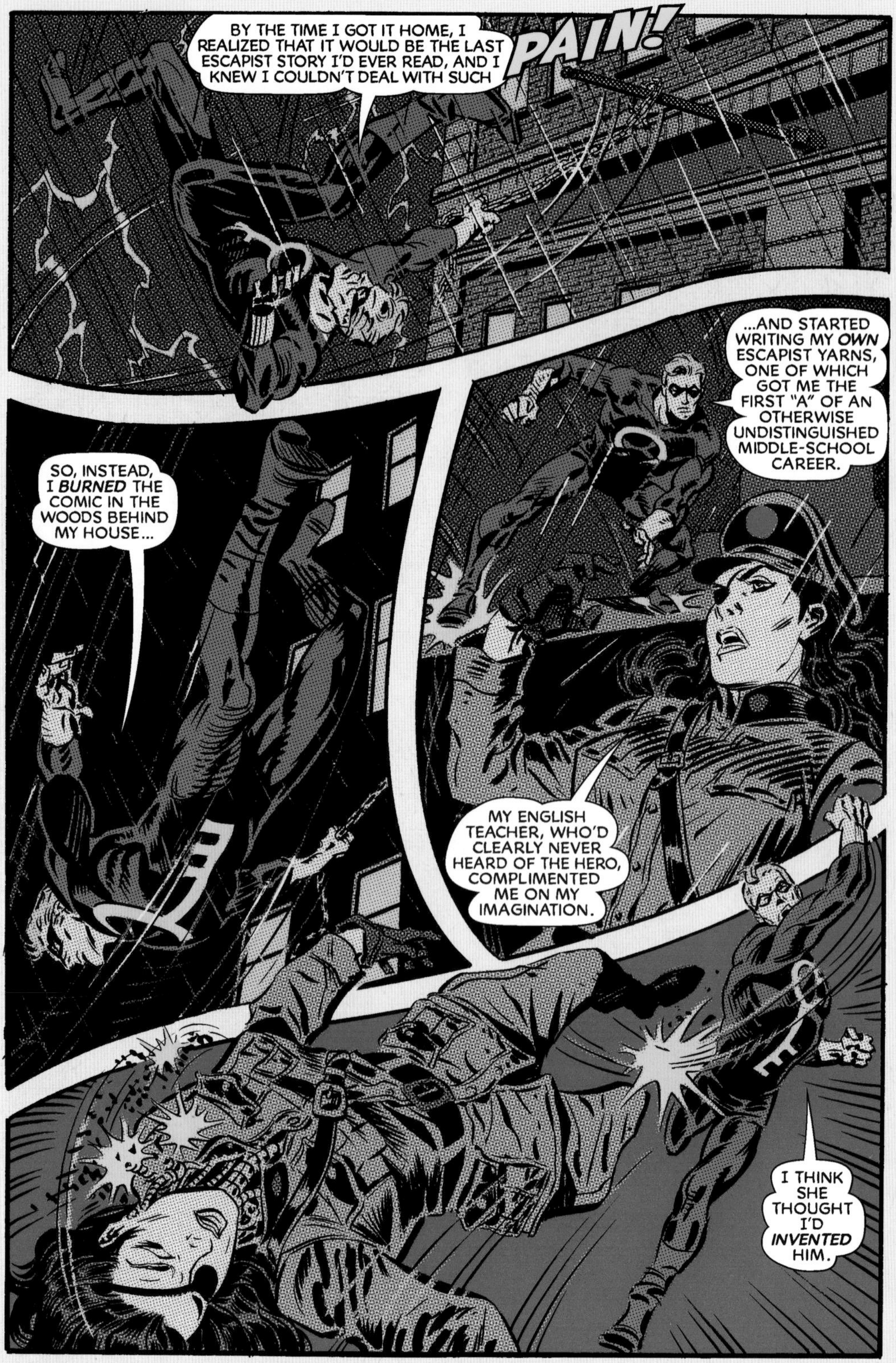
BY THE TIME I GOT IT HOME, I REALIZED THAT IT WOULD BE THE LAST ESCAPIST STORY I'D EVER READ, AND I KNEW I COULDN'T DEAL WITH SUCH
PAIN!
SO, INSTEAD, I *BURNED* THE COMIC IN THE WOODS BEHIND MY HOUSE...
...AND STARTED WRITING MY *OWN* ESCAPIST YARNS, ONE OF WHICH GOT ME THE FIRST "A" OF AN OTHERWISE UNDISTINGUISHED MIDDLE-SCHOOL CAREER.
MY ENGLISH TEACHER, WHO'D CLEARLY NEVER HEARD OF THE HERO, COMPLIMENTED ME ON MY IMAGINATION.
I THINK SHE THOUGHT I'D *INVENTED* HIM.

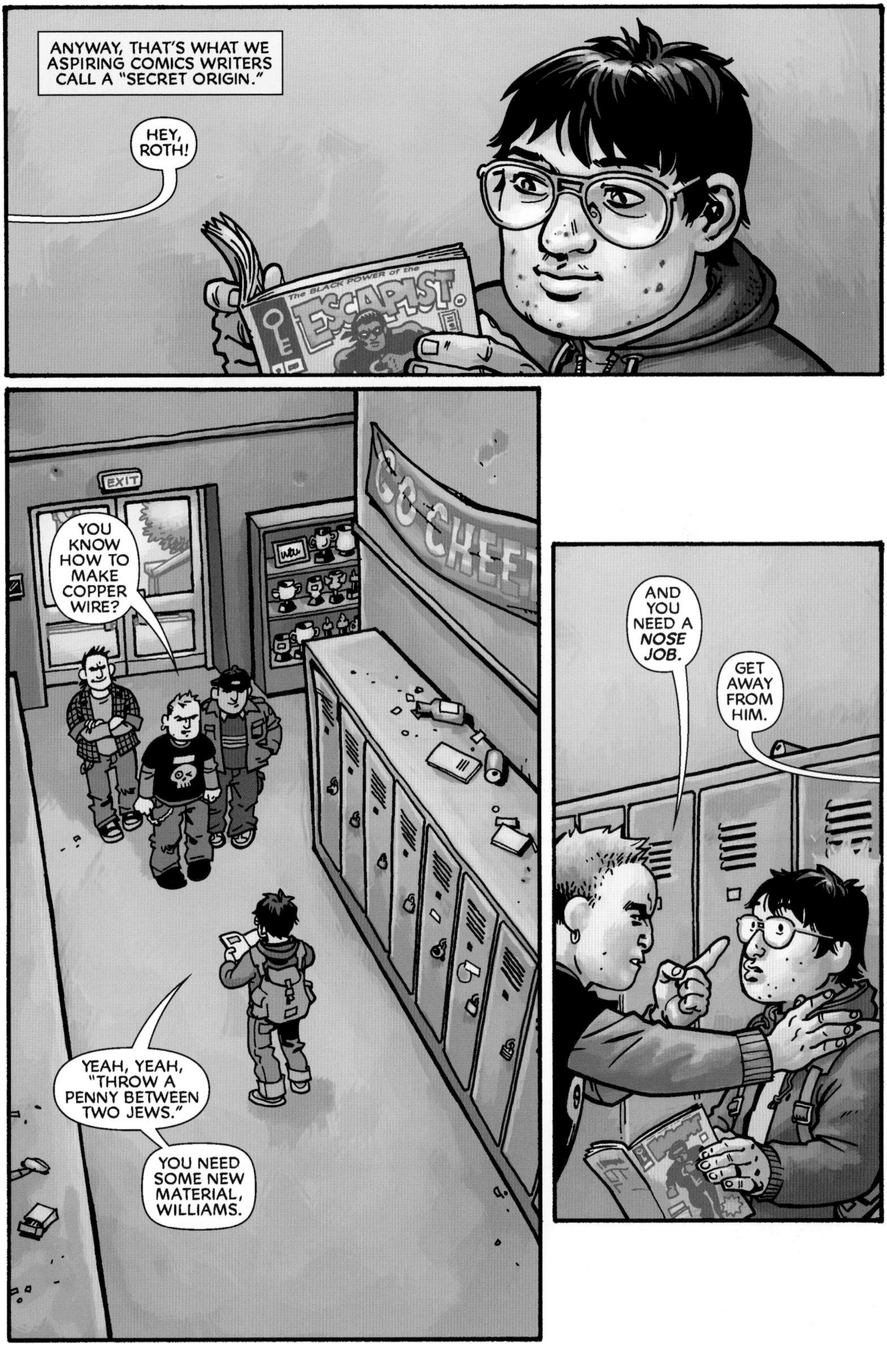
ANYWAY, THAT'S WHAT WE ASPIRING COMICS WRITERS CALL A "SECRET ORIGIN."
HEY, ROTH!
The BLACK POWER of the ESCAPIST
EXIT
GO CHEET
YOU KNOW HOW TO MAKE COPPER WIRE?
YEAH, YEAH, "THROW A PENNY BETWEEN TWO JEWS."
YOU NEED SOME NEW MATERIAL, WILLIAMS.
AND YOU NEED A *NOSE JOB.*
GET AWAY FROM HIM.

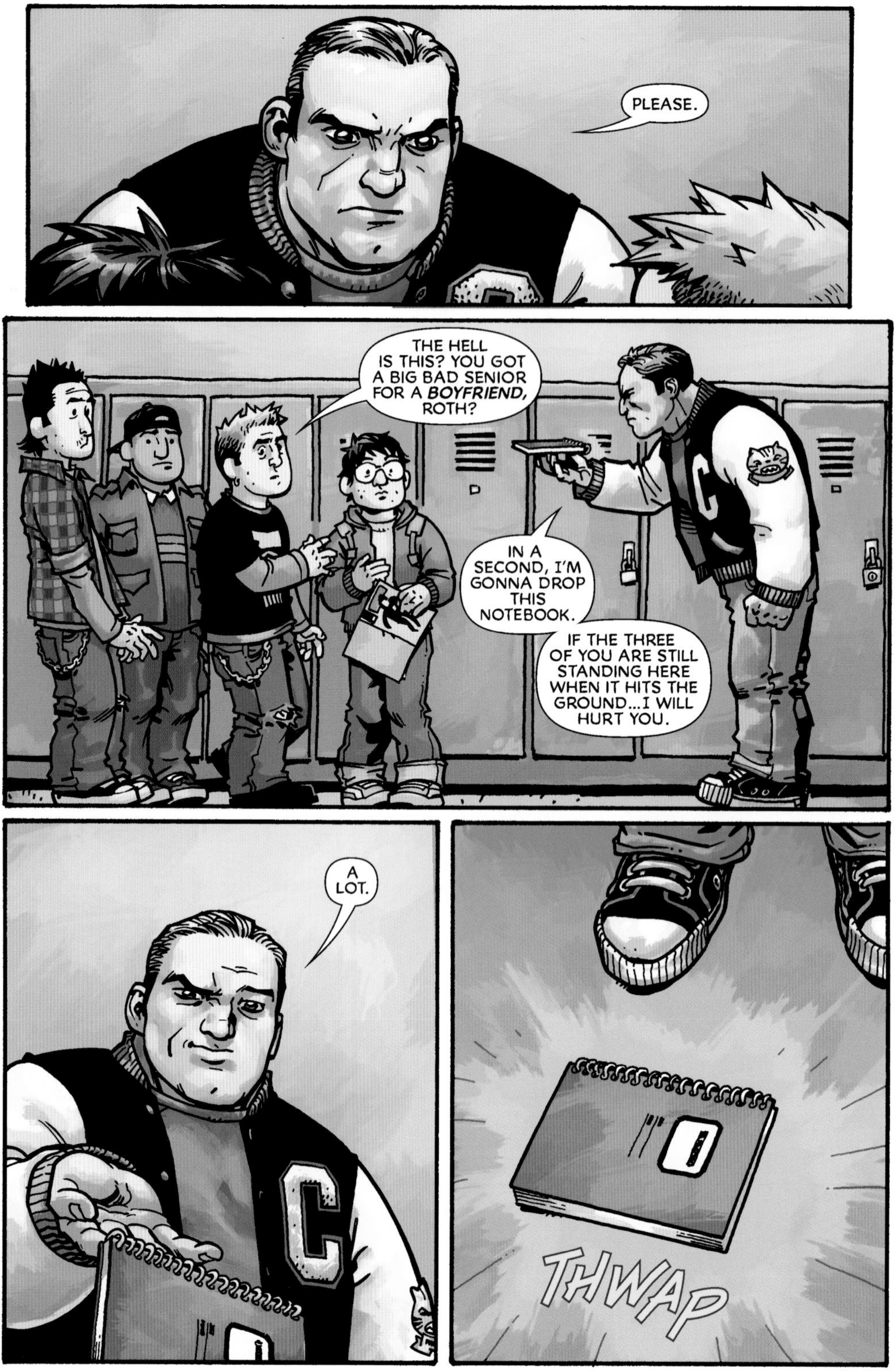
PLEASE.
THE HELL IS THIS? YOU GOT A BIG BAD SENIOR FOR A *BOYFRIEND,* ROTH?
IN A SECOND, I'M GONNA DROP THIS NOTEBOOK.
IF THE THREE OF YOU ARE STILL STANDING HERE WHEN IT HITS THE GROUND...I WILL HURT YOU.
A LOT.
THWAP

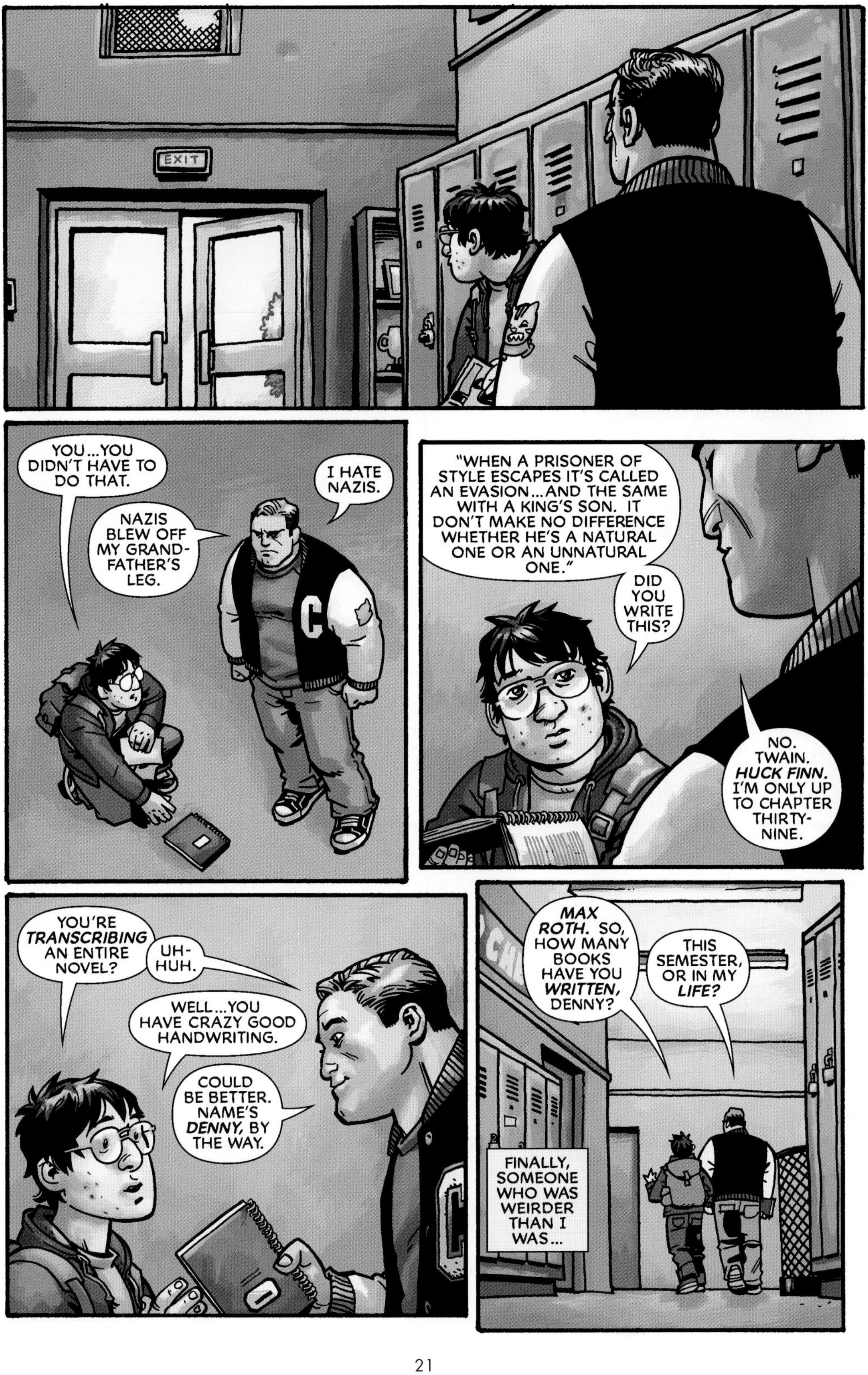
EXIT
YOU...YOU DIDN'T HAVE TO DO THAT.
I HATE NAZIS.
NAZIS BLEW OFF MY GRAND-FATHER'S LEG.
"WHEN A PRISONER OF STYLE ESCAPES IT'S CALLED AN EVASION...AND THE SAME WITH A KING'S SON. IT DON'T MAKE NO DIFFERENCE WHETHER HE'S A NATURAL ONE OR AN UNNATURAL ONE."
DID YOU WRITE THIS?
NO. TWAIN. *HUCK FINN.* I'M ONLY UP TO CHAPTER THIRTY-NINE.
YOU'RE *TRANSCRIBING* AN ENTIRE NOVEL?
UH-HUH.
WELL...YOU HAVE CRAZY GOOD HANDWRITING.
COULD BE BETTER. NAME'S *DENNY,* BY THE WAY.
MAX ROTH. SO, HOW MANY BOOKS HAVE YOU *WRITTEN,* DENNY?
THIS SEMESTER, OR IN MY *LIFE?*
FINALLY, SOMEONE WHO WAS WEIRDER THAN I WAS...

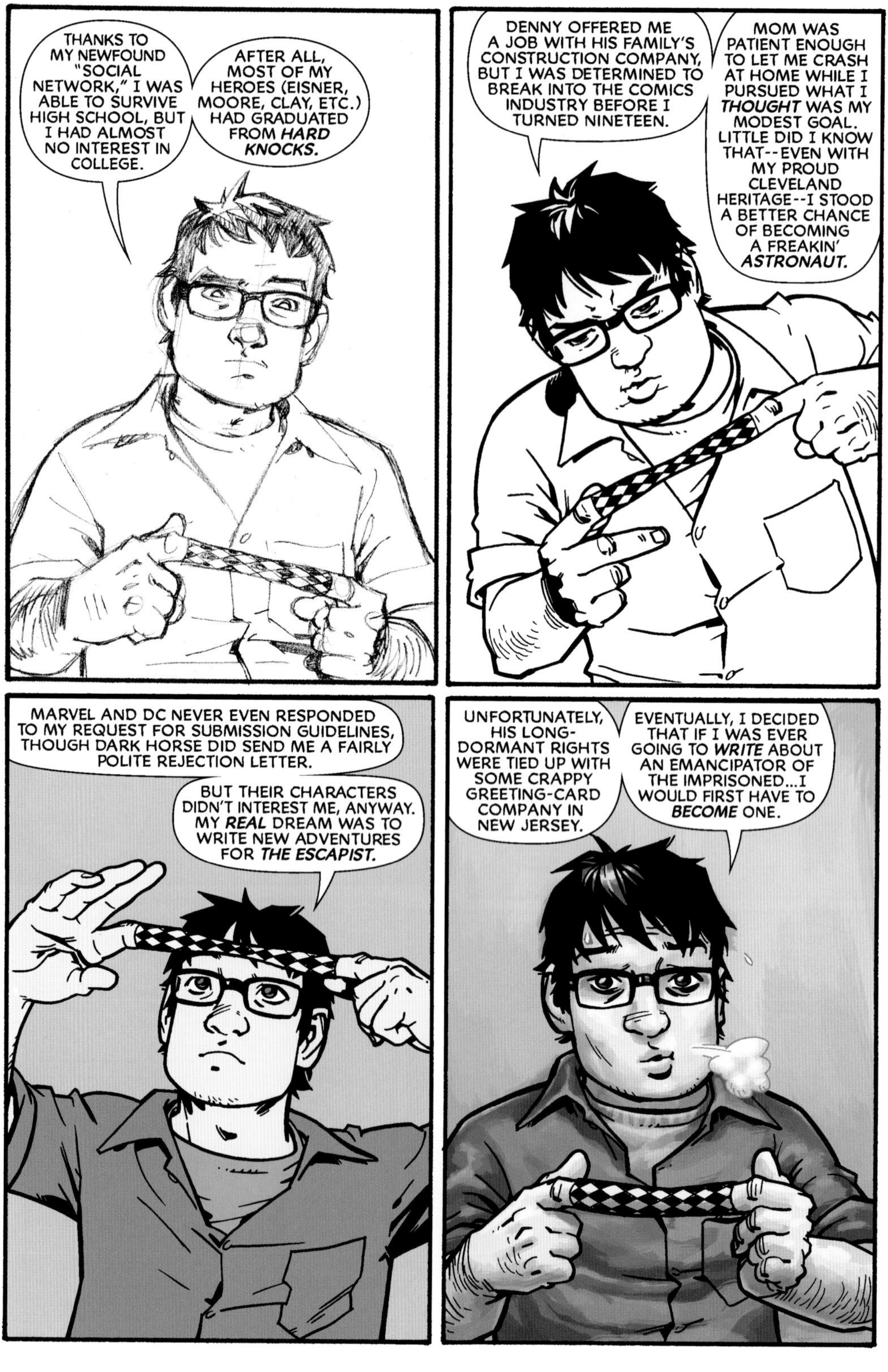
THANKS TO MY NEWFOUND "SOCIAL NETWORK," I WAS ABLE TO SURVIVE HIGH SCHOOL, BUT I HAD ALMOST NO INTEREST IN COLLEGE.
AFTER ALL, MOST OF MY HEROES (EISNER, MOORE, CLAY, ETC.) HAD GRADUATED FROM *HARD KNOCKS.*
DENNY OFFERED ME A JOB WITH HIS FAMILY'S CONSTRUCTION COMPANY, BUT I WAS DETERMINED TO BREAK INTO THE COMICS INDUSTRY BEFORE I TURNED NINETEEN.
MOM WAS PATIENT ENOUGH TO LET ME CRASH AT HOME WHILE I PURSUED WHAT I *THOUGHT* WAS MY MODEST GOAL. LITTLE DID I KNOW THAT--EVEN WITH MY PROUD CLEVELAND HERITAGE--I STOOD A BETTER CHANCE OF BECOMING A FREAKIN' *ASTRONAUT.*
MARVEL AND DC NEVER EVEN RESPONDED TO MY REQUEST FOR SUBMISSION GUIDELINES, THOUGH DARK HORSE DID SEND ME A FAIRLY POLITE REJECTION LETTER.
BUT THEIR CHARACTERS DIDN'T INTEREST ME, ANYWAY. MY *REAL* DREAM WAS TO WRITE NEW ADVENTURES FOR *THE ESCAPIST.*
UNFORTUNATELY, HIS LONG-DORMANT RIGHTS WERE TIED UP WITH SOME CRAPPY GREETING-CARD COMPANY IN NEW JERSEY.
EVENTUALLY, I DECIDED THAT IF I WAS EVER GOING TO *WRITE* ABOUT AN EMANCIPATOR OF THE IMPRISONED...I WOULD FIRST HAVE TO *BECOME* ONE.

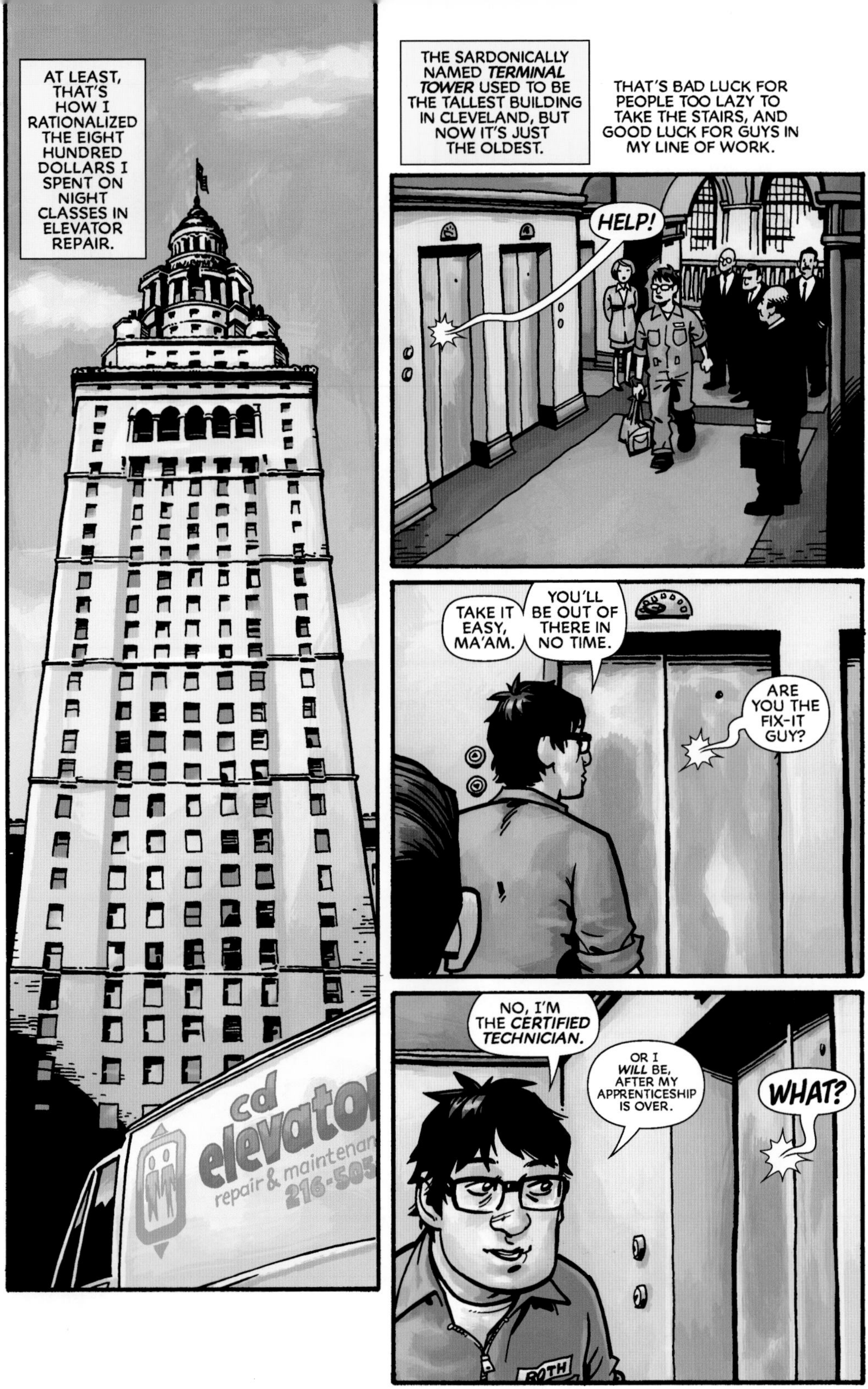
AT LEAST, THAT'S HOW I RATIONALIZED THE EIGHT HUNDRED DOLLARS I SPENT ON NIGHT CLASSES IN ELEVATOR REPAIR.
cd elevator
repair & maintenan
216-505
THE SARDONICALLY NAMED *TERMINAL TOWER* USED TO BE THE TALLEST BUILDING IN CLEVELAND, BUT NOW IT'S JUST THE OLDEST.
THAT'S BAD LUCK FOR PEOPLE TOO LAZY TO TAKE THE STAIRS, AND GOOD LUCK FOR GUYS IN MY LINE OF WORK.
HELP!
TAKE IT EASY, MA'AM.
YOU'LL BE OUT OF THERE IN NO TIME.
ARE YOU THE FIX-IT GUY?
NO, I'M THE *CERTIFIED TECHNICIAN.*
OR I *WILL* BE, AFTER MY APPRENTICESHIP IS OVER.
WHAT?
ROTH

OKAY, COULD YOU PLEASE SET THE EMERGENCY SWITCH AT THE BOTTOM OF YOUR CONSOLE TO THE STOP POSITION?

IS... IS THIS THING GONNA *FALL?*

NAH, THAT'S A REAR-SLUNG CANTILEVER ROPED HYDRAULIC, SO YOU'RE COOL.

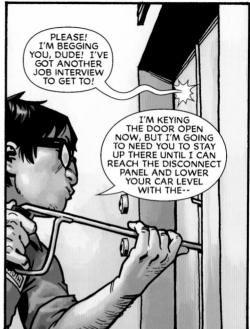

PLEASE! I'M BEGGING YOU, DUDE! I'VE GOT ANOTHER JOB INTERVIEW TO GET TO!

I'M KEYING THE DOOR OPEN NOW, BUT I'M GOING TO NEED YOU TO STAY UP THERE UNTIL I CAN REACH THE DISCONNECT PANEL AND LOWER YOUR CAR LEVEL WITH THE--

FINALLY!

HEY! GET BACK IN THERE! YOU CAN'T JUST...

WOW.

ROTH

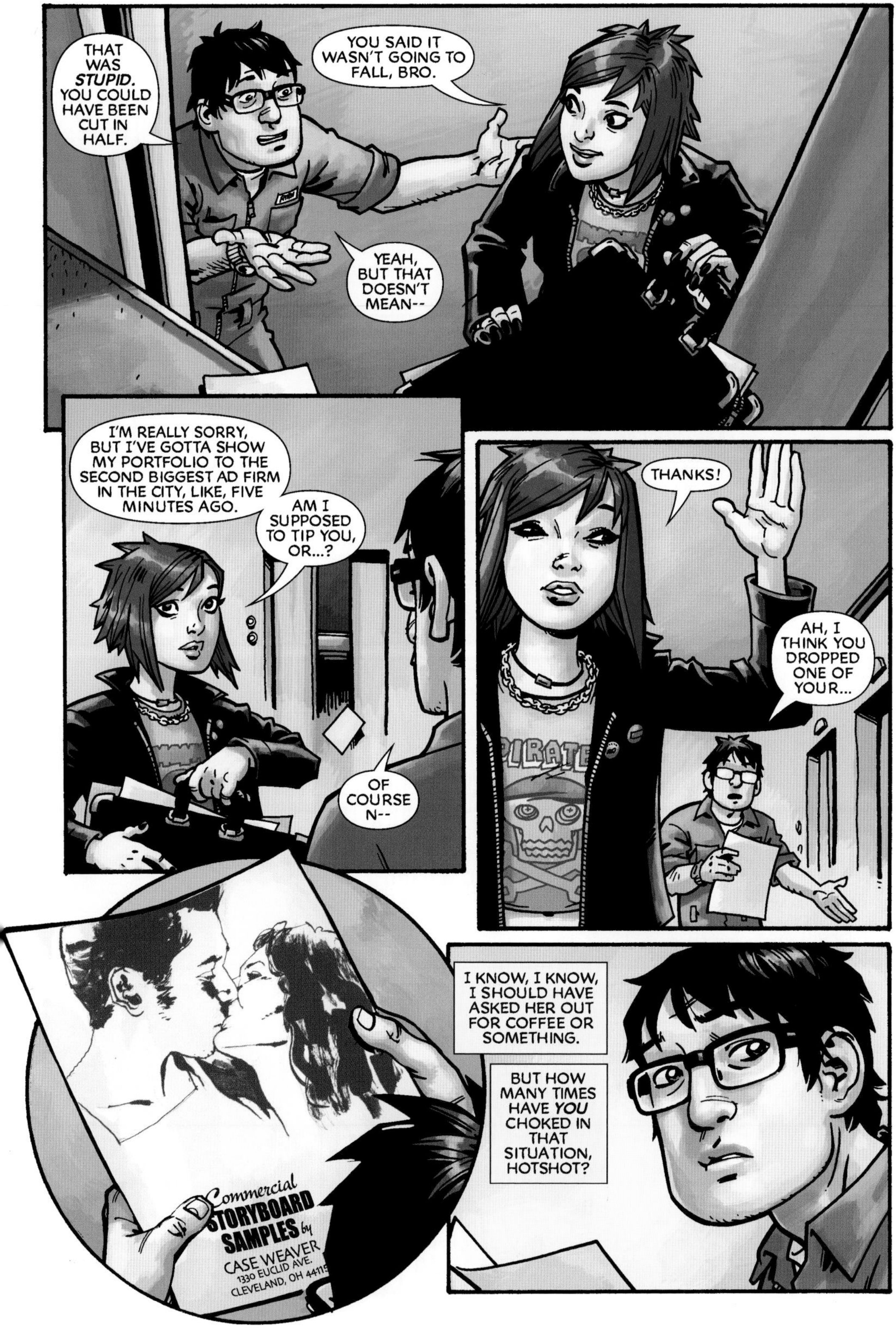
THAT WAS STUPID. YOU COULD HAVE BEEN CUT IN HALF.
YOU SAID IT WASN'T GOING TO FALL, BRO.
YEAH, BUT THAT DOESN'T MEAN--
I'M REALLY SORRY, BUT I'VE GOTTA SHOW MY PORTFOLIO TO THE SECOND BIGGEST AD FIRM IN THE CITY, LIKE, FIVE MINUTES AGO.
AM I SUPPOSED TO TIP YOU, OR...?
OF COURSE N--
THANKS!
AH, I THINK YOU DROPPED ONE OF YOUR...
Commercial STORYBOARD SAMPLES by
CASE WEAVER
1330 EUCLID AVE.
CLEVELAND, OH 44115
I KNOW, I KNOW, I SHOULD HAVE ASKED HER OUT FOR COFFEE OR SOMETHING.
BUT HOW MANY TIMES HAVE YOU CHOKED IN THAT SITUATION, HOTSHOT?

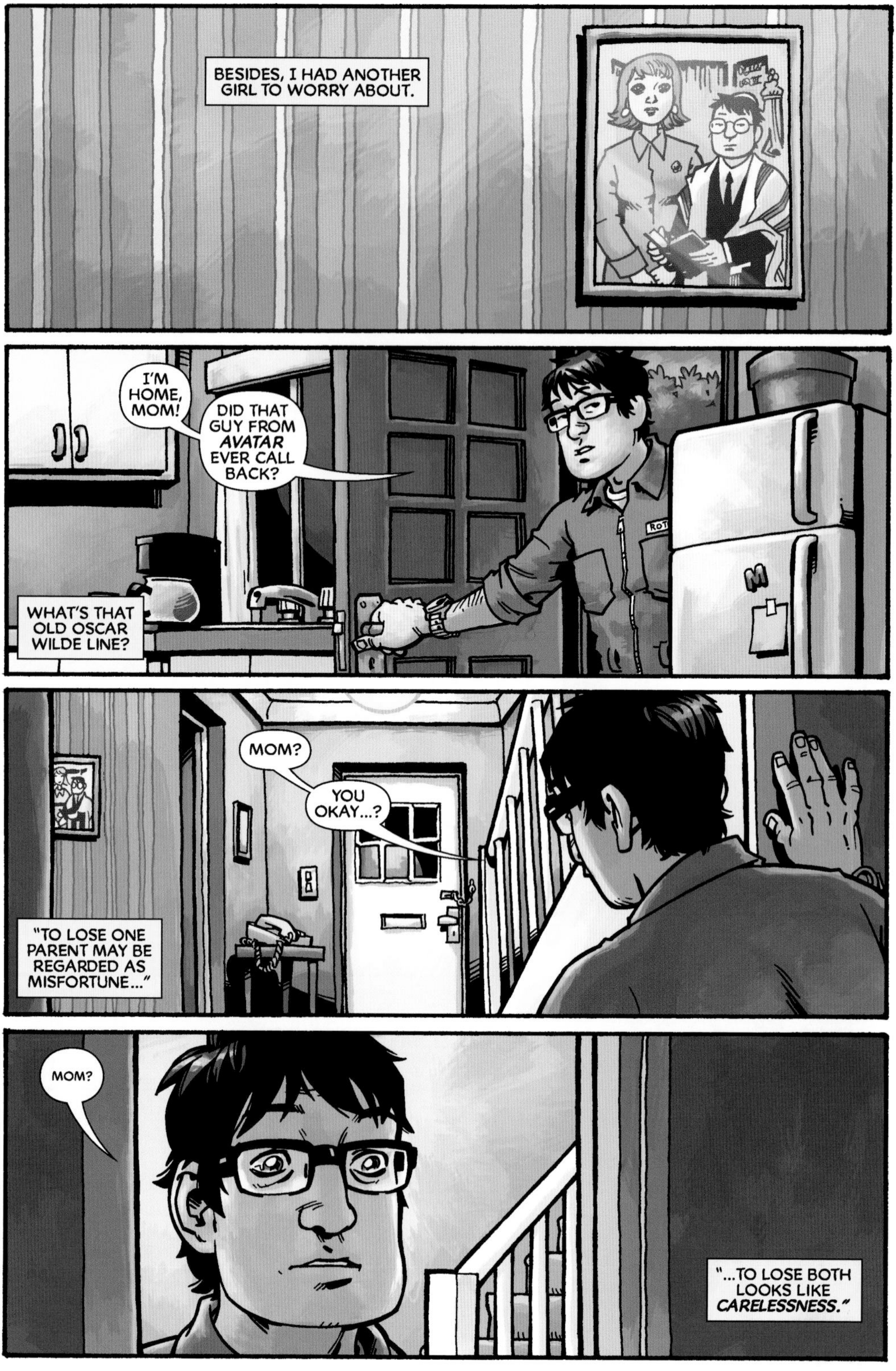

BESIDES, I HAD ANOTHER GIRL TO WORRY ABOUT.
I'M HOME, MOM!
DID THAT GUY FROM AVATAR EVER CALL BACK?
WHAT'S THAT OLD OSCAR WILDE LINE?
MOM?
YOU OKAY...?
"TO LOSE ONE PARENT MAY BE REGARDED AS MISFORTUNE..."
MOM?
"...TO LOSE BOTH LOOKS LIKE CARELESSNESS."

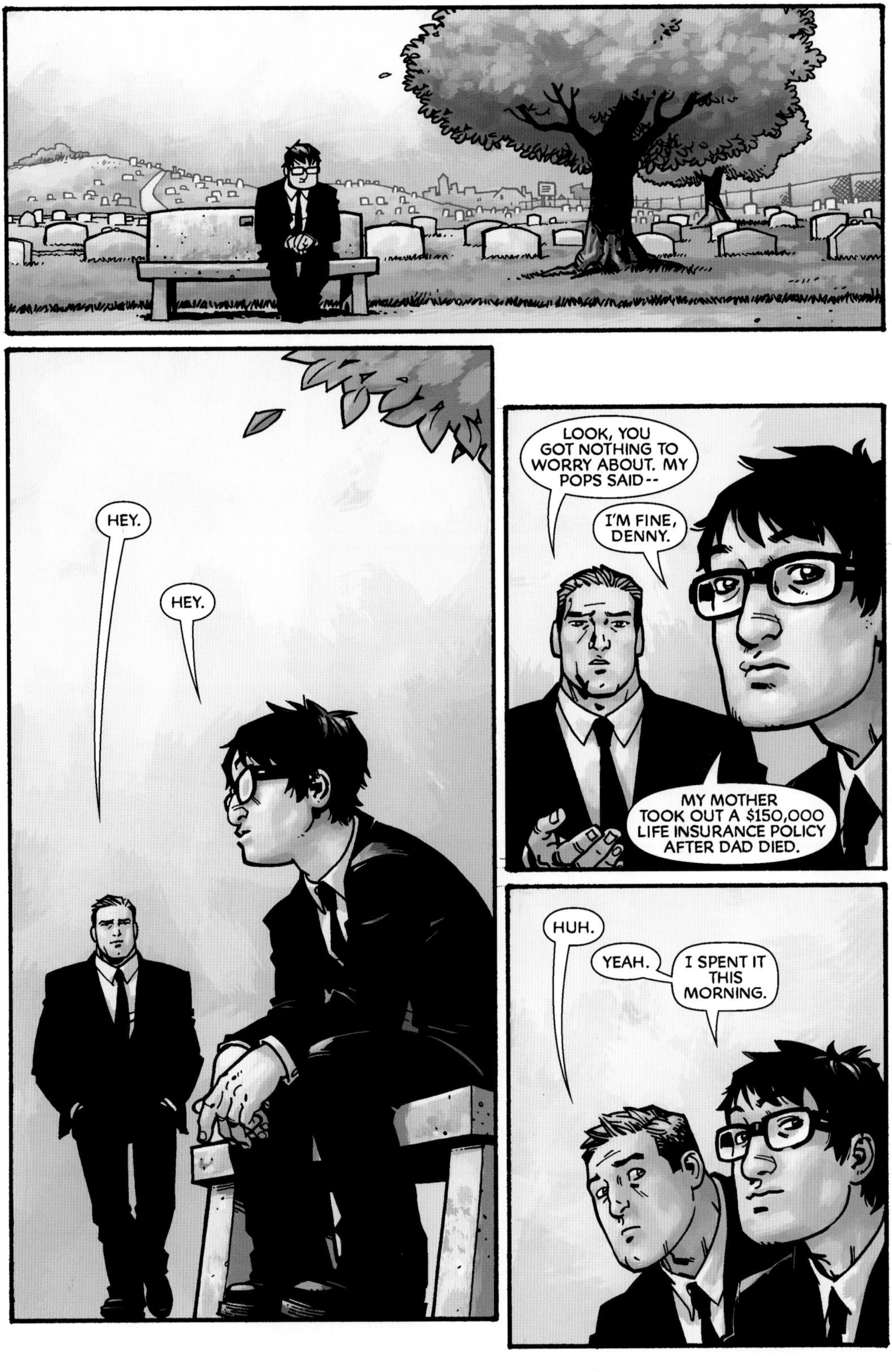
HEY.
HEY.
LOOK, YOU GOT NOTHING TO WORRY ABOUT. MY POPS SAID--
I'M FINE, DENNY.
MY MOTHER TOOK OUT A $150,000 LIFE INSURANCE POLICY AFTER DAD DIED.
HUH.
YEAH.
I SPENT IT THIS MORNING.

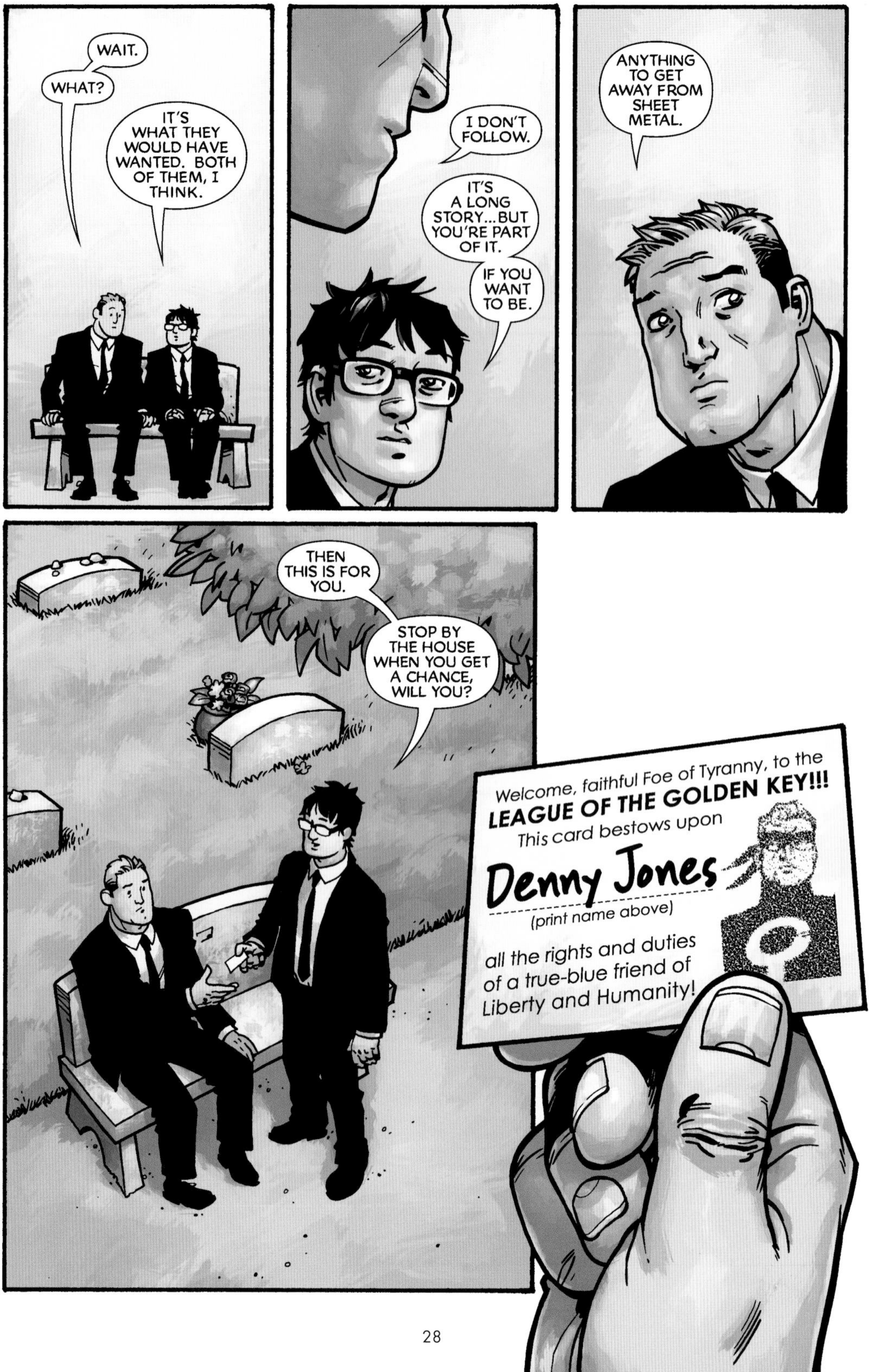
WAIT.
WHAT?
IT'S WHAT THEY WOULD HAVE WANTED. BOTH OF THEM, I THINK.
I DON'T FOLLOW.
IT'S A LONG STORY...BUT YOU'RE PART OF IT.
IF YOU WANT TO BE.
ANYTHING TO GET AWAY FROM SHEET METAL.
THEN THIS IS FOR YOU.
STOP BY THE HOUSE WHEN YOU GET A CHANCE, WILL YOU?
Welcome, faithful Foe of Tyranny, to the
LEAGUE OF THE GOLDEN KEY!!!
This card bestows upon
Denny Jones
(print name above)
all the rights and duties of a true-blue friend of Liberty and Humanity!

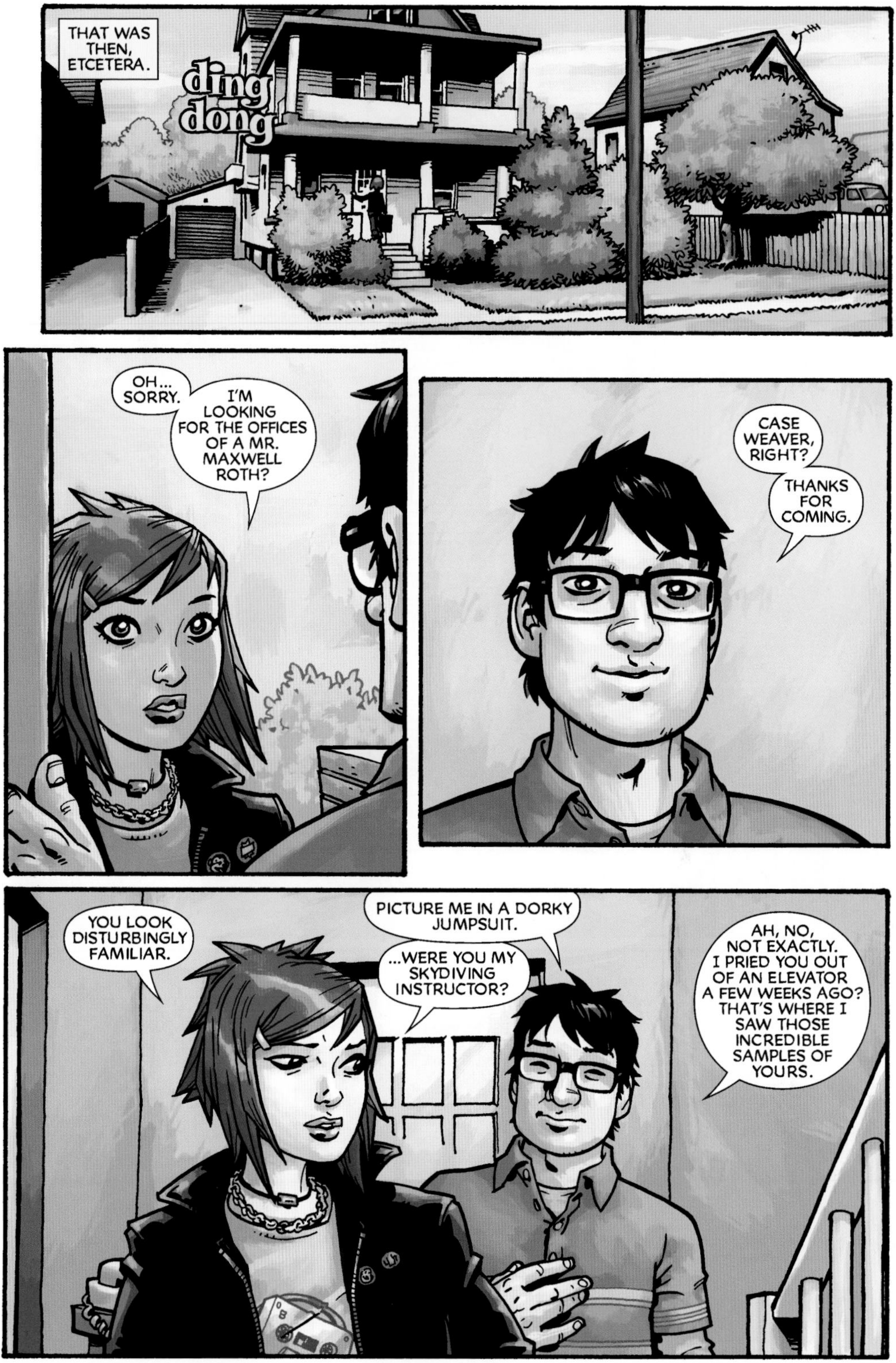
THAT WAS THEN, ETCETERA.
ding dong
OH... SORRY.
I'M LOOKING FOR THE OFFICES OF A MR. MAXWELL ROTH?
CASE WEAVER, RIGHT?
THANKS FOR COMING.
YOU LOOK DISTURBINGLY FAMILIAR.
...WERE YOU MY SKYDIVING INSTRUCTOR?
PICTURE ME IN A DORKY JUMPSUIT.
AH, NO, NOT EXACTLY. I PRIED YOU OUT OF AN ELEVATOR A FEW WEEKS AGO? THAT'S WHERE I SAW THOSE INCREDIBLE SAMPLES OF YOURS.

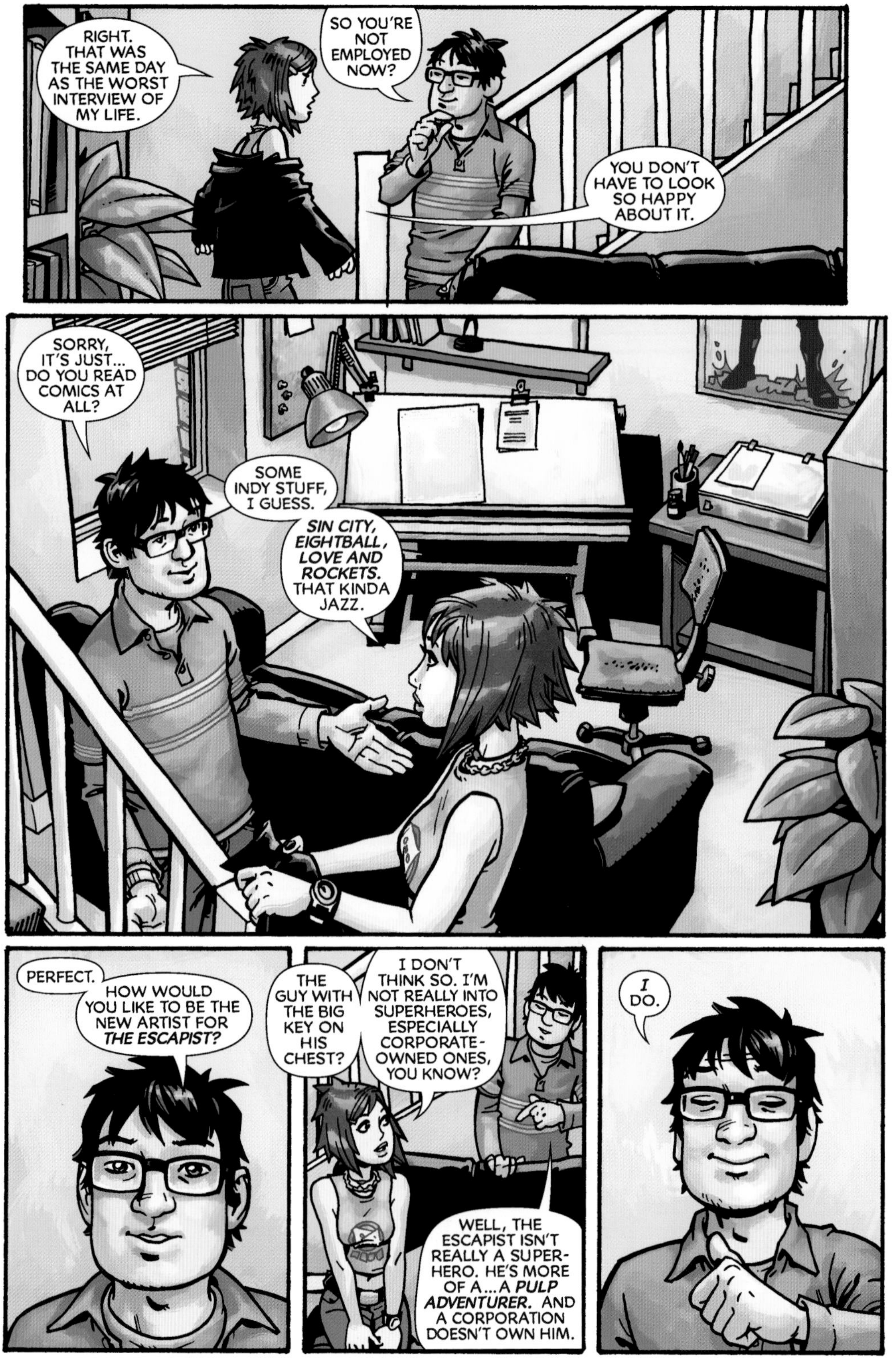
RIGHT. THAT WAS THE SAME DAY AS THE WORST INTERVIEW OF MY LIFE.
SO YOU'RE NOT EMPLOYED NOW?
YOU DON'T HAVE TO LOOK SO HAPPY ABOUT IT.
SORRY, IT'S JUST... DO YOU READ COMICS AT ALL?
SOME INDY STUFF, I GUESS.
SIN CITY, EIGHTBALL, LOVE AND ROCKETS. THAT KINDA JAZZ.
PERFECT.
HOW WOULD YOU LIKE TO BE THE NEW ARTIST FOR THE ESCAPIST?
THE GUY WITH THE BIG KEY ON HIS CHEST?
I DON'T THINK SO. I'M NOT REALLY INTO SUPERHEROES, ESPECIALLY CORPORATE-OWNED ONES, YOU KNOW?
WELL, THE ESCAPIST ISN'T REALLY A SUPER-HERO. HE'S MORE OF A... A PULP ADVENTURER. AND A CORPORATION DOESN'T OWN HIM.
I DO.

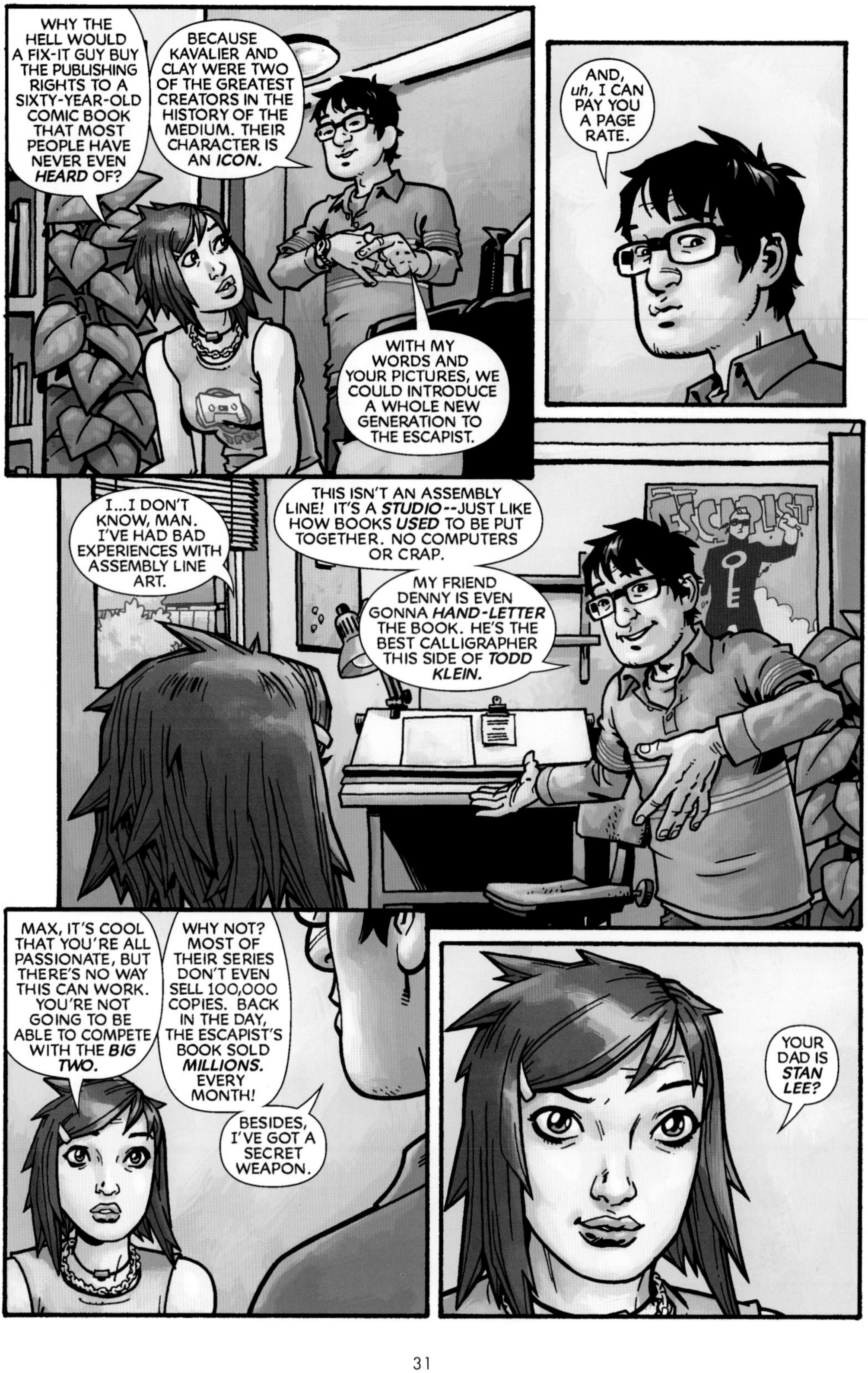
WHY THE HELL WOULD A FIX-IT GUY BUY THE PUBLISHING RIGHTS TO A SIXTY-YEAR-OLD COMIC BOOK THAT MOST PEOPLE HAVE NEVER EVEN *HEARD* OF?
BECAUSE KAVALIER AND CLAY WERE TWO OF THE GREATEST CREATORS IN THE HISTORY OF THE MEDIUM. THEIR CHARACTER IS AN *ICON.*
WITH MY WORDS AND YOUR PICTURES, WE COULD INTRODUCE A WHOLE NEW GENERATION TO THE ESCAPIST.
AND, *uh,* I CAN PAY YOU A PAGE RATE.
I...I DON'T KNOW, MAN. I'VE HAD BAD EXPERIENCES WITH ASSEMBLY LINE ART.
THIS ISN'T AN ASSEMBLY LINE! IT'S A *STUDIO*--JUST LIKE HOW BOOKS *USED* TO BE PUT TOGETHER. NO COMPUTERS OR CRAP.
MY FRIEND DENNY IS EVEN GONNA *HAND-LETTER* THE BOOK. HE'S THE BEST CALLIGRAPHER THIS SIDE OF *TODD KLEIN.*
ESCAPIST
MAX, IT'S COOL THAT YOU'RE ALL PASSIONATE, BUT THERE'S NO WAY THIS CAN WORK. YOU'RE NOT GOING TO BE ABLE TO COMPETE WITH THE *BIG TWO.*
WHY NOT? MOST OF THEIR SERIES DON'T EVEN SELL 100,000 COPIES. BACK IN THE DAY, THE ESCAPIST'S BOOK SOLD *MILLIONS.* EVERY MONTH!
BESIDES, I'VE GOT A SECRET WEAPON.
YOUR DAD IS *STAN LEE?*

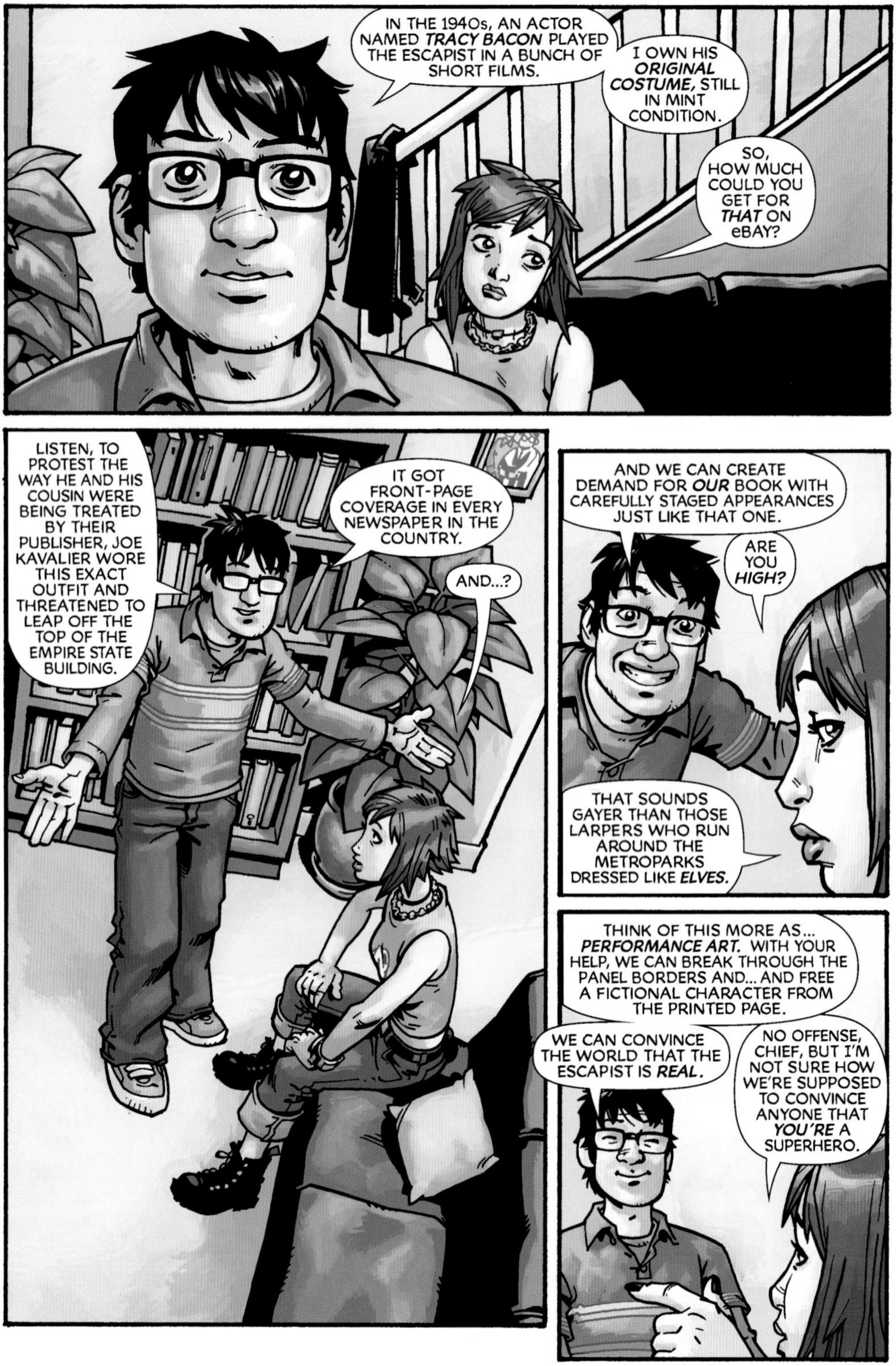
IN THE 1940s, AN ACTOR NAMED TRACY BACON PLAYED THE ESCAPIST IN A BUNCH OF SHORT FILMS.
I OWN HIS ORIGINAL COSTUME, STILL IN MINT CONDITION.
SO, HOW MUCH COULD YOU GET FOR THAT ON eBAY?
LISTEN, TO PROTEST THE WAY HE AND HIS COUSIN WERE BEING TREATED BY THEIR PUBLISHER, JOE KAVALIER WORE THIS EXACT OUTFIT AND THREATENED TO LEAP OFF THE TOP OF THE EMPIRE STATE BUILDING.
IT GOT FRONT-PAGE COVERAGE IN EVERY NEWSPAPER IN THE COUNTRY.
AND...?
AND WE CAN CREATE DEMAND FOR OUR BOOK WITH CAREFULLY STAGED APPEARANCES JUST LIKE THAT ONE.
ARE YOU HIGH?
THAT SOUNDS GAYER THAN THOSE LARPERS WHO RUN AROUND THE METROPARKS DRESSED LIKE ELVES.
THINK OF THIS MORE AS... PERFORMANCE ART. WITH YOUR HELP, WE CAN BREAK THROUGH THE PANEL BORDERS AND... AND FREE A FICTIONAL CHARACTER FROM THE PRINTED PAGE.
WE CAN CONVINCE THE WORLD THAT THE ESCAPIST IS REAL.
NO OFFENSE, CHIEF, BUT I'M NOT SURE HOW WE'RE SUPPOSED TO CONVINCE ANYONE THAT YOU'RE A SUPERHERO.

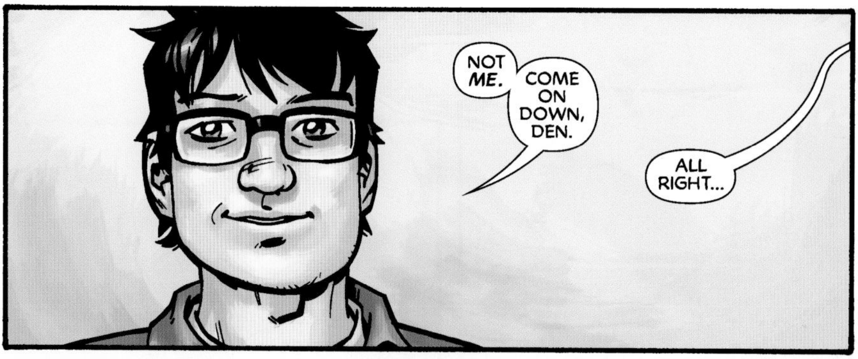
NOT *ME.*
COME ON DOWN, DEN.
ALL RIGHT...

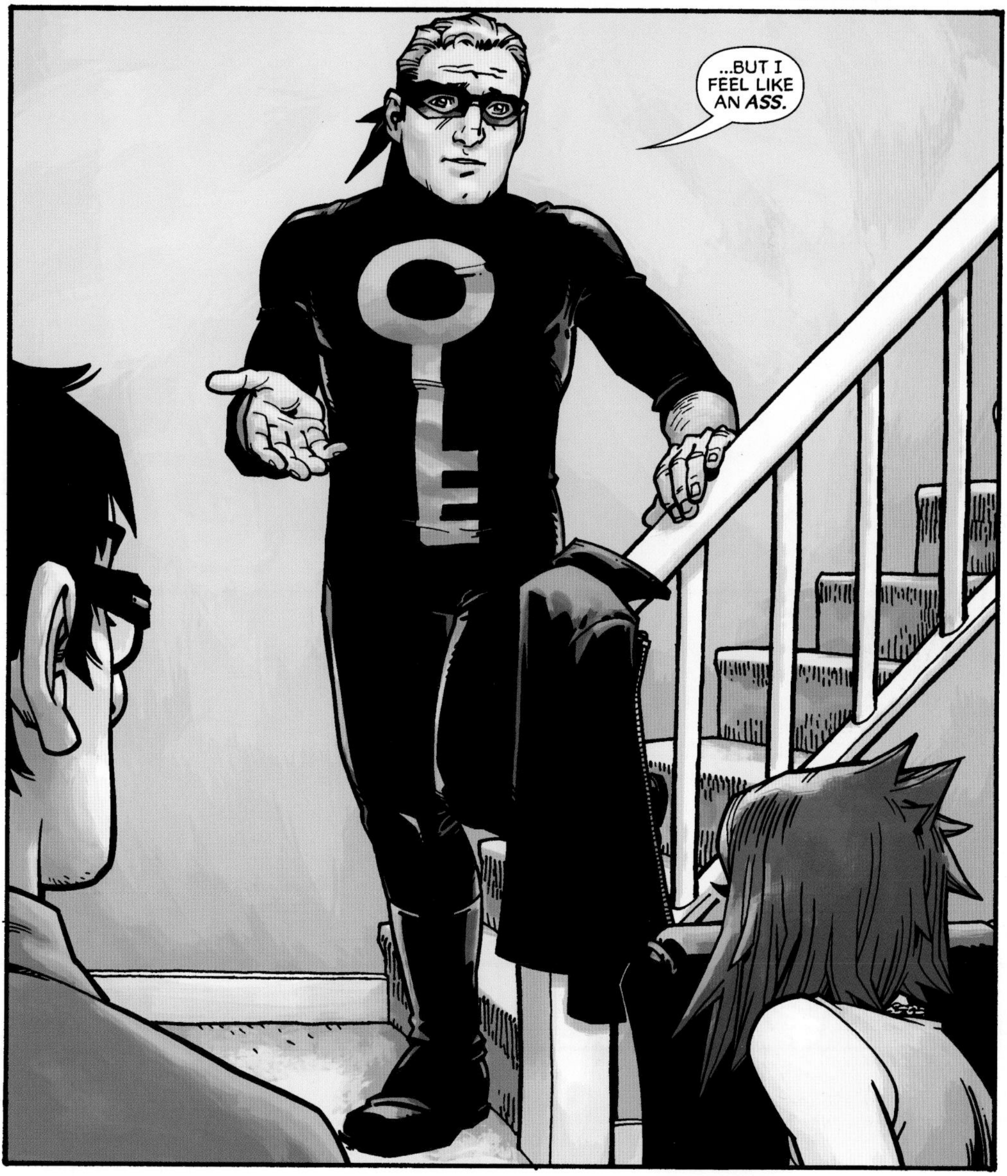
...BUT I FEEL LIKE AN *ASS.*

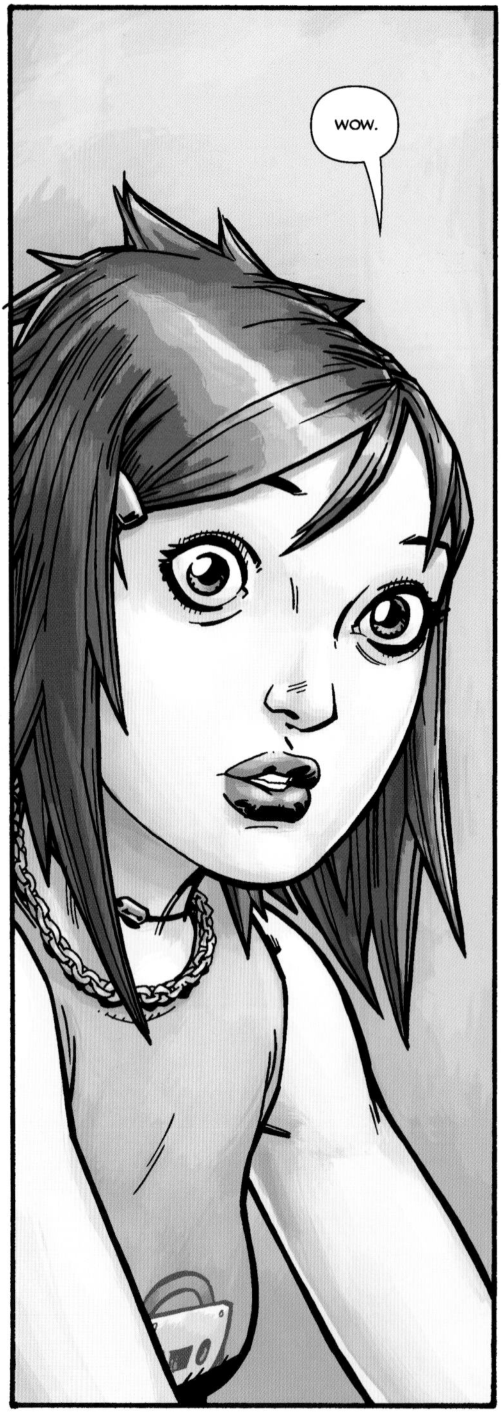
WOW.

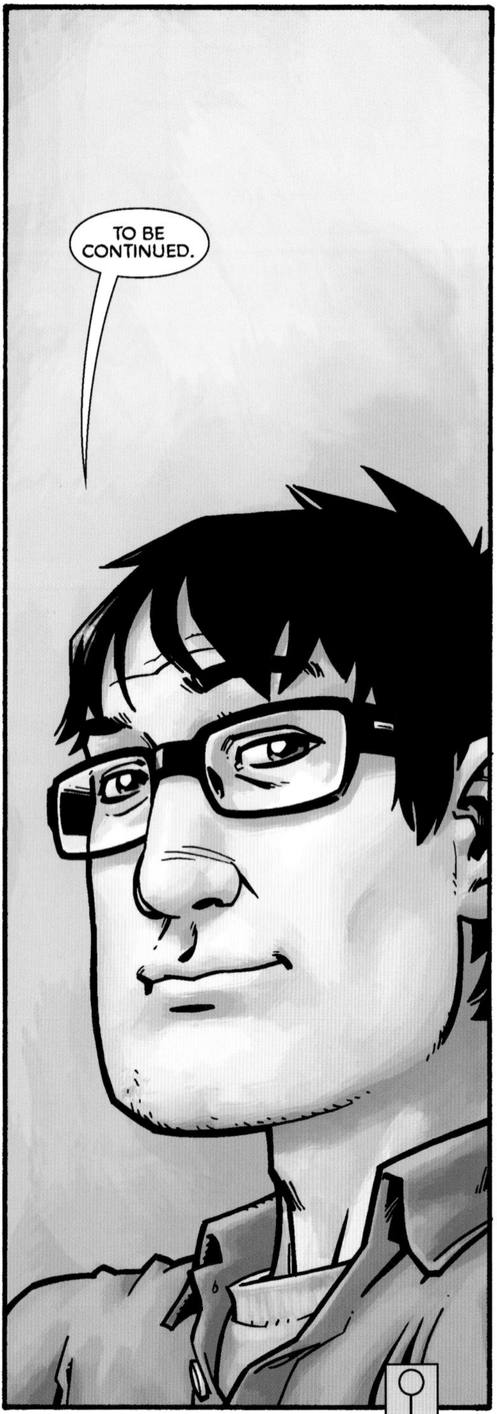
TO BE CONTINUED.

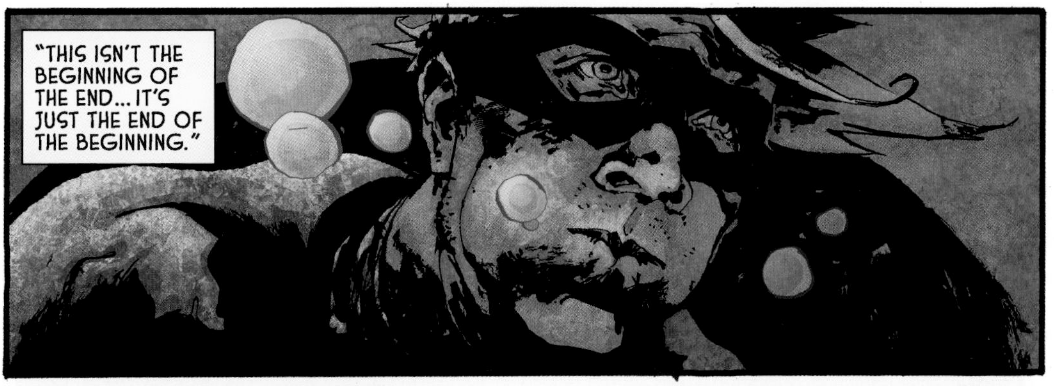
"THIS ISN'T THE BEGINNING OF THE END... IT'S JUST THE END OF THE BEGINNING."

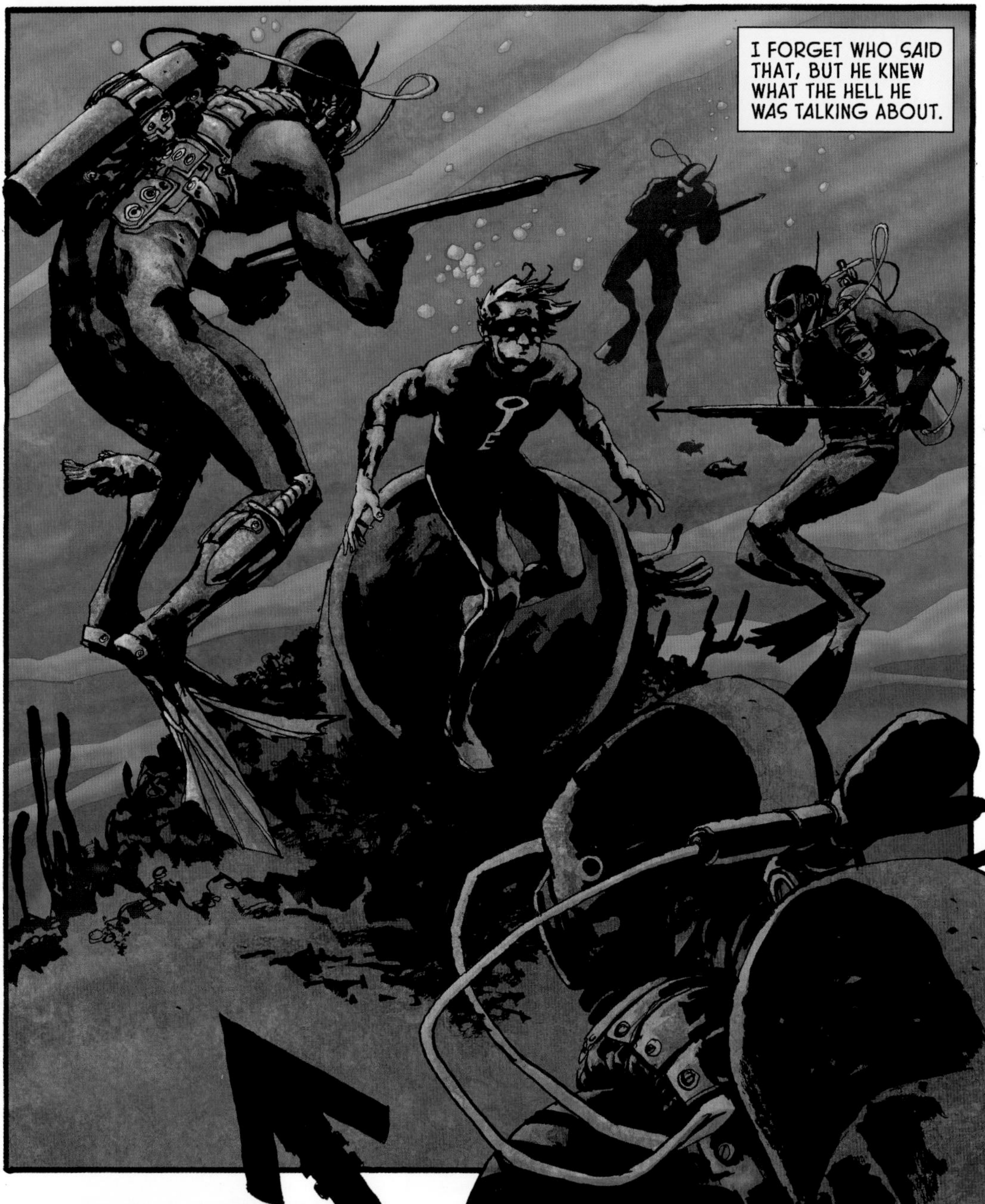
I FORGET WHO SAID THAT, BUT HE KNEW WHAT THE HELL HE WAS TALKING ABOUT.

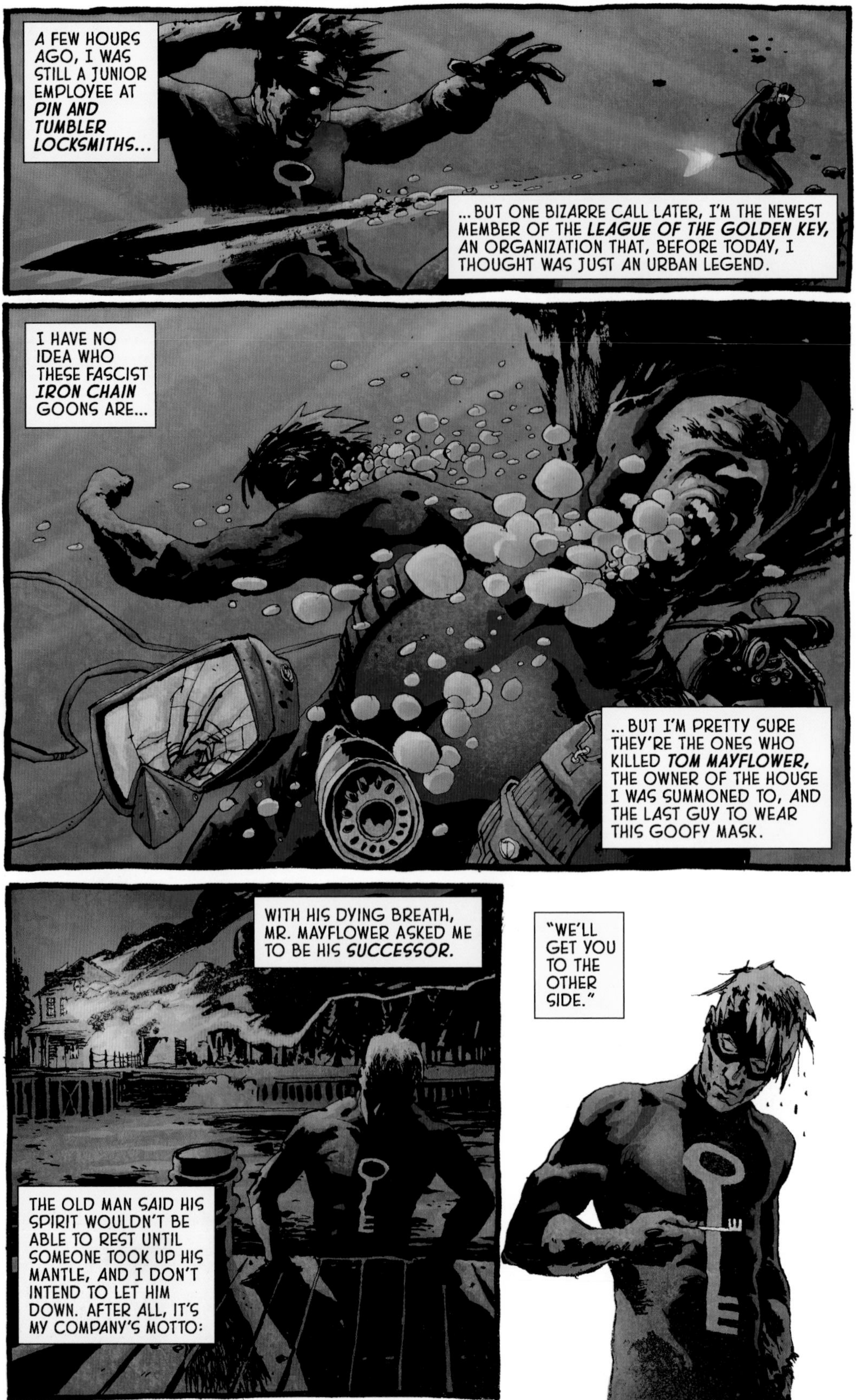
A FEW HOURS AGO, I WAS STILL A JUNIOR EMPLOYEE AT PIN AND TUMBLER LOCKSMITHS...
...BUT ONE BIZARRE CALL LATER, I'M THE NEWEST MEMBER OF THE LEAGUE OF THE GOLDEN KEY, AN ORGANIZATION THAT, BEFORE TODAY, I THOUGHT WAS JUST AN URBAN LEGEND.
I HAVE NO IDEA WHO THESE FASCIST IRON CHAIN GOONS ARE...
...BUT I'M PRETTY SURE THEY'RE THE ONES WHO KILLED TOM MAYFLOWER, THE OWNER OF THE HOUSE I WAS SUMMONED TO, AND THE LAST GUY TO WEAR THIS GOOFY MASK.
WITH HIS DYING BREATH, MR. MAYFLOWER ASKED ME TO BE HIS SUCCESSOR.
THE OLD MAN SAID HIS SPIRIT WOULDN'T BE ABLE TO REST UNTIL SOMEONE TOOK UP HIS MANTLE, AND I DON'T INTEND TO LET HIM DOWN. AFTER ALL, IT'S MY COMPANY'S MOTTO:
"WE'LL GET YOU TO THE OTHER SIDE."

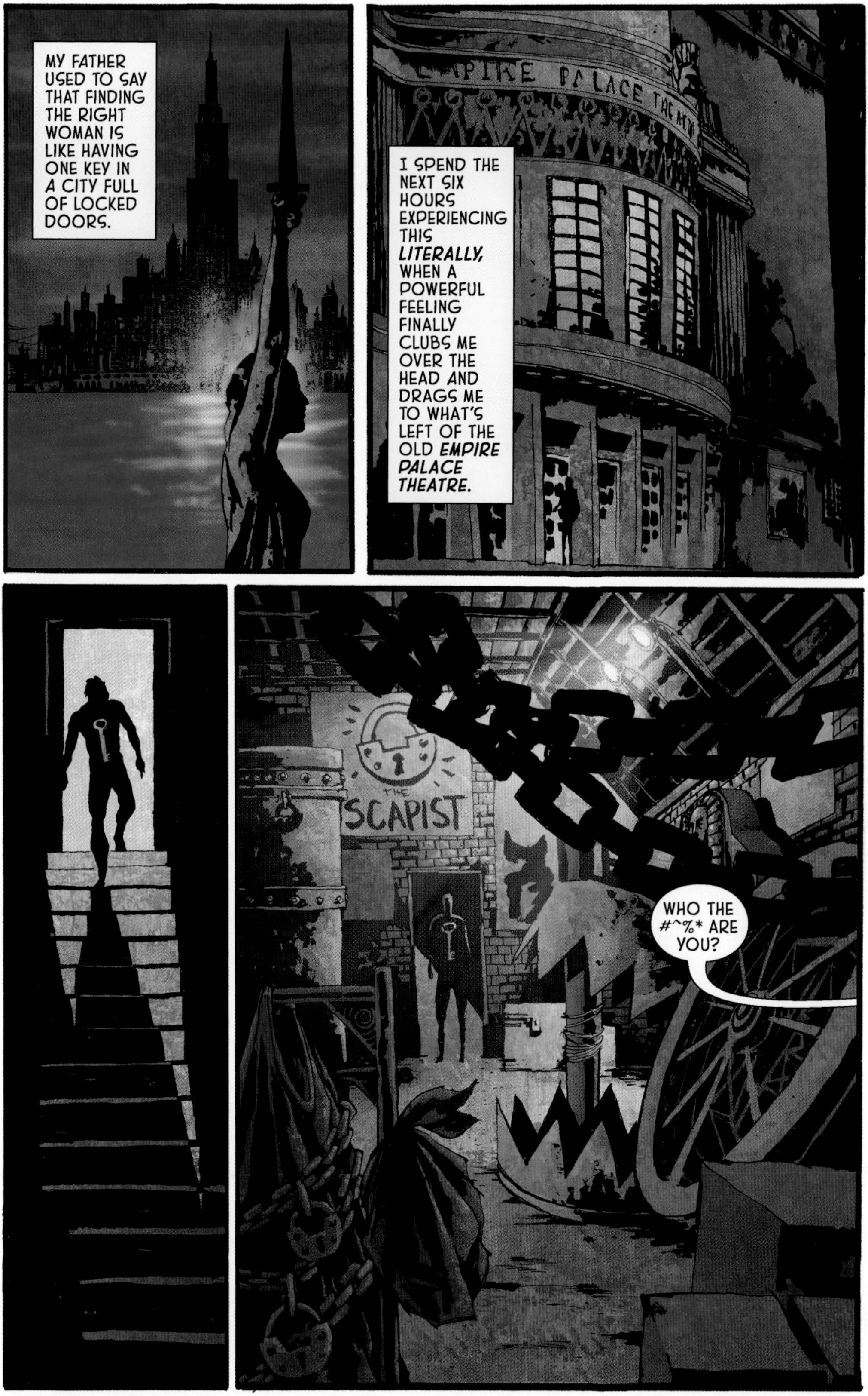
MY FATHER USED TO SAY THAT FINDING THE RIGHT WOMAN IS LIKE HAVING ONE KEY IN A CITY FULL OF LOCKED DOORS.
EMPIRE PALACE THEATRE
I SPEND THE NEXT SIX HOURS EXPERIENCING THIS *LITERALLY,* WHEN A POWERFUL FEELING FINALLY CLUBS ME OVER THE HEAD AND DRAGS ME TO WHAT'S LEFT OF THE OLD *EMPIRE PALACE THEATRE.*
THE SCAPIST
WHO THE #^%* ARE YOU?

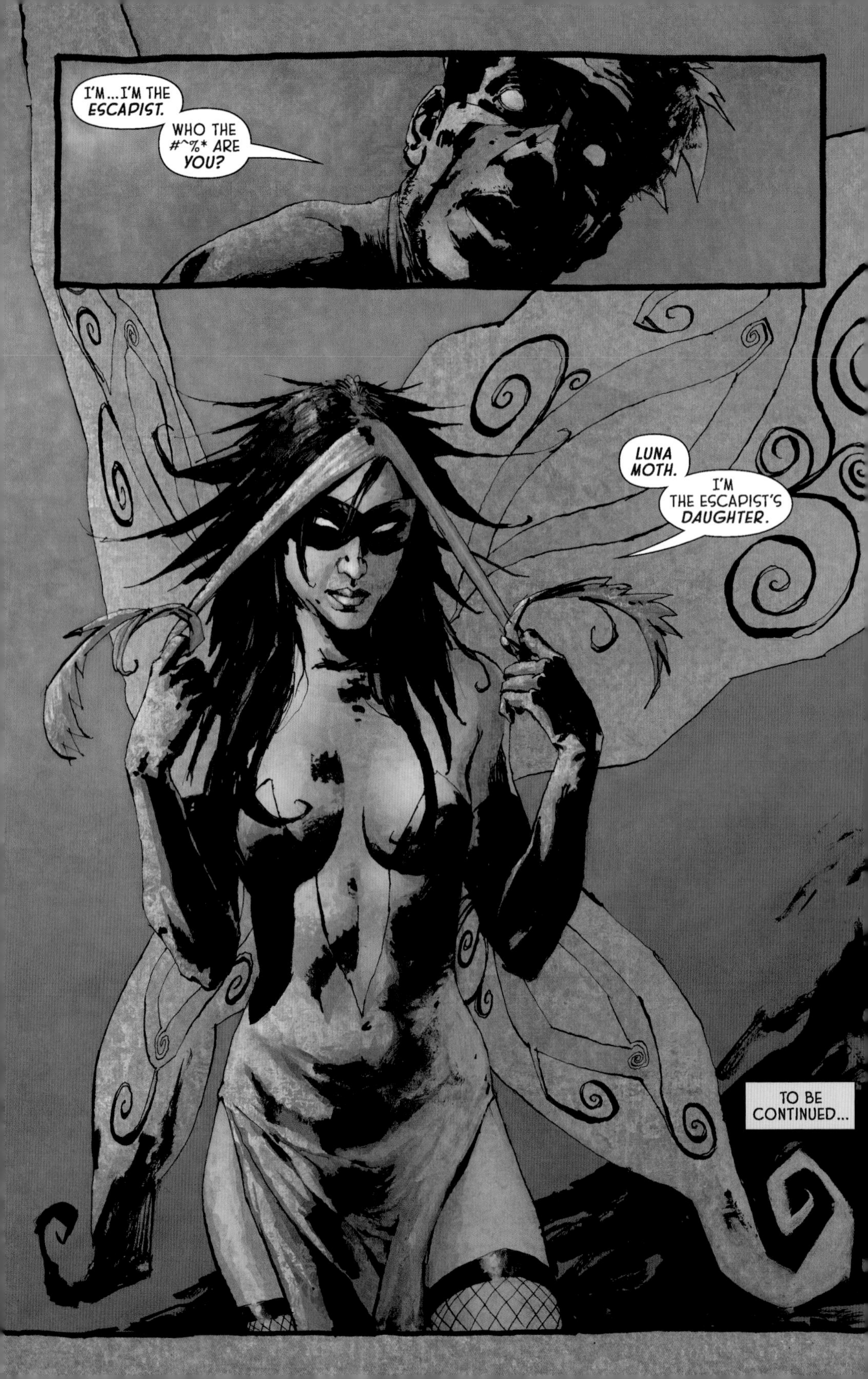
I'M...I'M THE ESCAPIST.
WHO THE #^%* ARE YOU?
LUNA MOTH.
I'M THE ESCAPIST'S DAUGHTER.
TO BE CONTINUED...

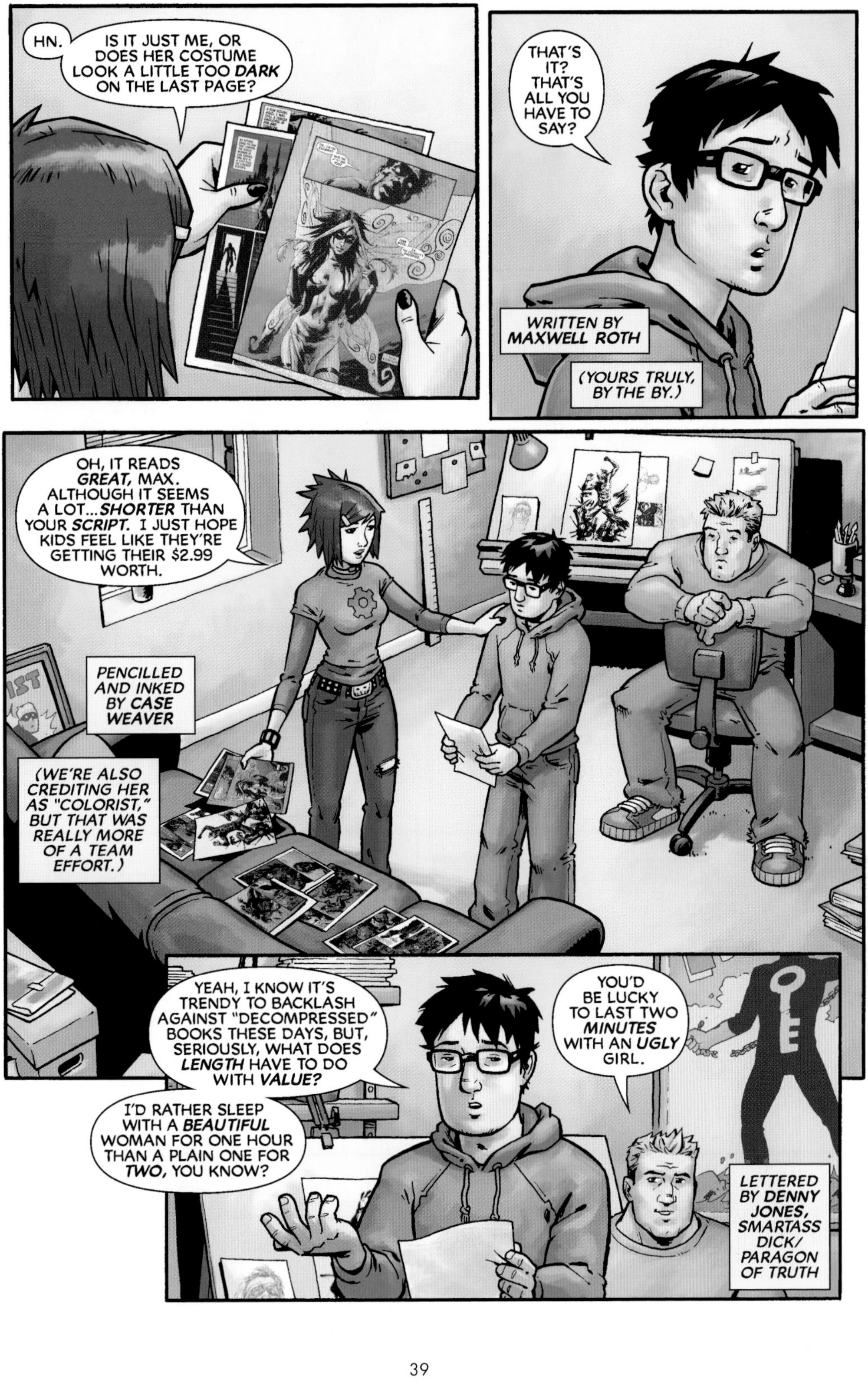
HN.
IS IT JUST ME, OR DOES HER COSTUME LOOK A LITTLE TOO DARK ON THE LAST PAGE?
THAT'S IT? THAT'S ALL YOU HAVE TO SAY?
WRITTEN BY MAXWELL ROTH
(YOURS TRULY, BY THE BY.)
OH, IT READS GREAT, MAX. ALTHOUGH IT SEEMS A LOT...SHORTER THAN YOUR SCRIPT. I JUST HOPE KIDS FEEL LIKE THEY'RE GETTING THEIR $2.99 WORTH.
PENCILLED AND INKED BY CASE WEAVER
(WE'RE ALSO CREDITING HER AS "COLORIST," BUT THAT WAS REALLY MORE OF A TEAM EFFORT.)
YEAH, I KNOW IT'S TRENDY TO BACKLASH AGAINST "DECOMPRESSED" BOOKS THESE DAYS, BUT, SERIOUSLY, WHAT DOES LENGTH HAVE TO DO WITH VALUE?
I'D RATHER SLEEP WITH A BEAUTIFUL WOMAN FOR ONE HOUR THAN A PLAIN ONE FOR TWO, YOU KNOW?
YOU'D BE LUCKY TO LAST TWO MINUTES WITH AN UGLY GIRL.
LETTERED BY DENNY JONES, SMARTASS DICK/ PARAGON OF TRUTH

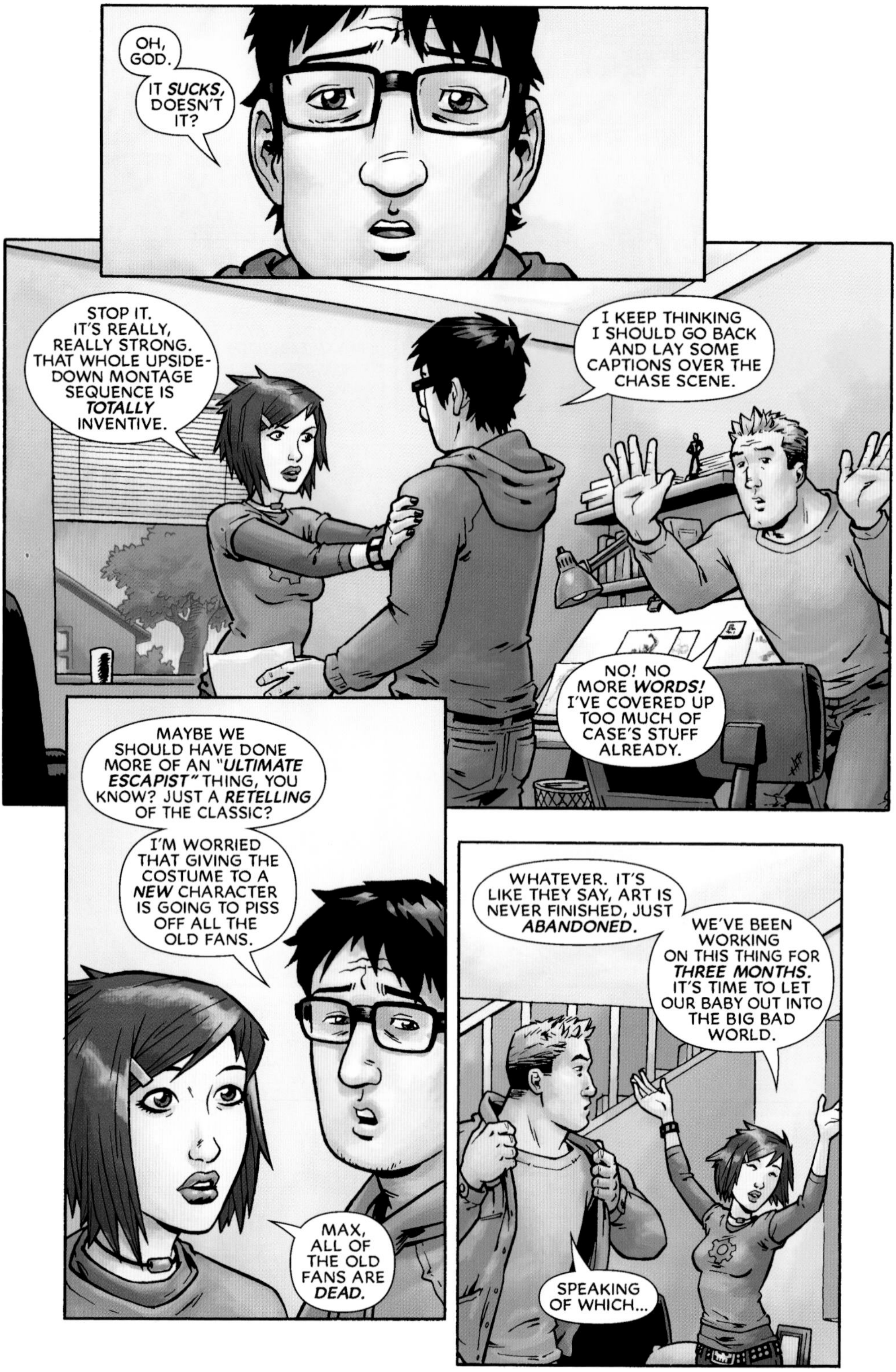
OH, GOD.
IT SUCKS, DOESN'T IT?
STOP IT. IT'S REALLY, REALLY STRONG. THAT WHOLE UPSIDE-DOWN MONTAGE SEQUENCE IS TOTALLY INVENTIVE.
I KEEP THINKING I SHOULD GO BACK AND LAY SOME CAPTIONS OVER THE CHASE SCENE.
NO! NO MORE WORDS! I'VE COVERED UP TOO MUCH OF CASE'S STUFF ALREADY.
MAYBE WE SHOULD HAVE DONE MORE OF AN "ULTIMATE ESCAPIST" THING, YOU KNOW? JUST A RETELLING OF THE CLASSIC?
I'M WORRIED THAT GIVING THE COSTUME TO A NEW CHARACTER IS GOING TO PISS OFF ALL THE OLD FANS.
MAX, ALL OF THE OLD FANS ARE DEAD.
WHATEVER. IT'S LIKE THEY SAY, ART IS NEVER FINISHED, JUST ABANDONED.
WE'VE BEEN WORKING ON THIS THING FOR THREE MONTHS. IT'S TIME TO LET OUR BABY OUT INTO THE BIG BAD WORLD.
SPEAKING OF WHICH...

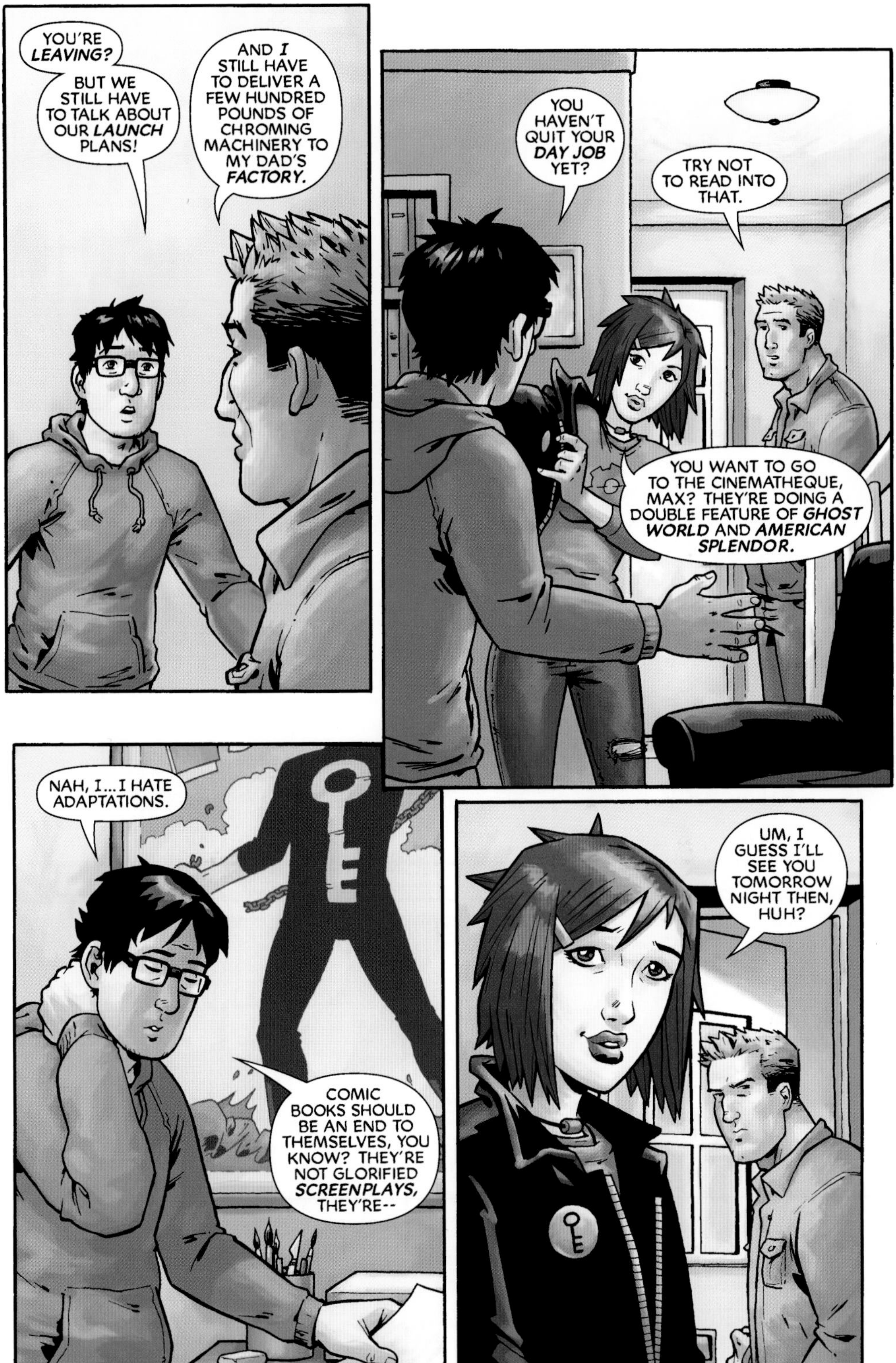
YOU'RE *LEAVING?*
BUT WE STILL HAVE TO TALK ABOUT OUR *LAUNCH* PLANS!
AND *I* STILL HAVE TO DELIVER A FEW HUNDRED POUNDS OF CHROMING MACHINERY TO MY DAD'S *FACTORY.*
YOU HAVEN'T QUIT YOUR *DAY JOB* YET?
TRY NOT TO READ INTO THAT.
YOU WANT TO GO TO THE CINEMATHEQUE, MAX? THEY'RE DOING A DOUBLE FEATURE OF *GHOST WORLD* AND *AMERICAN SPLENDOR.*
NAH, I...I HATE ADAPTATIONS.
COMIC BOOKS SHOULD BE AN END TO THEMSELVES, YOU KNOW? THEY'RE NOT GLORIFIED *SCREENPLAYS,* THEY'RE--
UM, I GUESS I'LL SEE YOU TOMORROW NIGHT THEN, HUH?

YEAH. SURE.

TOMORROW...

WHAT'S *WRONG* WITH YOU?

SHE *LIKES* YOU, DUMMY.

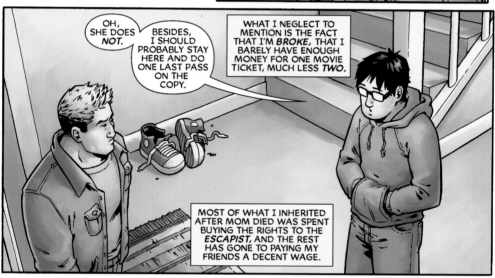

OH, SHE DOES *NOT*.

BESIDES, I SHOULD PROBABLY STAY HERE AND DO ONE LAST PASS ON THE COPY.

WHAT I NEGLECT TO MENTION IS THE FACT THAT I'M *BROKE*, THAT I BARELY HAVE ENOUGH MONEY FOR ONE MOVIE TICKET, MUCH LESS *TWO*.

MOST OF WHAT I INHERITED AFTER MOM DIED WAS SPENT BUYING THE RIGHTS TO THE *ESCAPIST*, AND THE REST HAS GONE TO PAYING MY FRIENDS A DECENT WAGE.

I KEEP TELLING MYSELF THAT I HAVEN'T PISSED AWAY MY PARENTS' LEGACY...THAT I'LL MAKE THEIR INVESTMENT BACK, AND *MORE*, WHEN OUR DEBUT ISSUE FINALLY HITS THE STANDS.

UNTIL THEN, I'M IN A PRISON OF MY OWN MAKING.

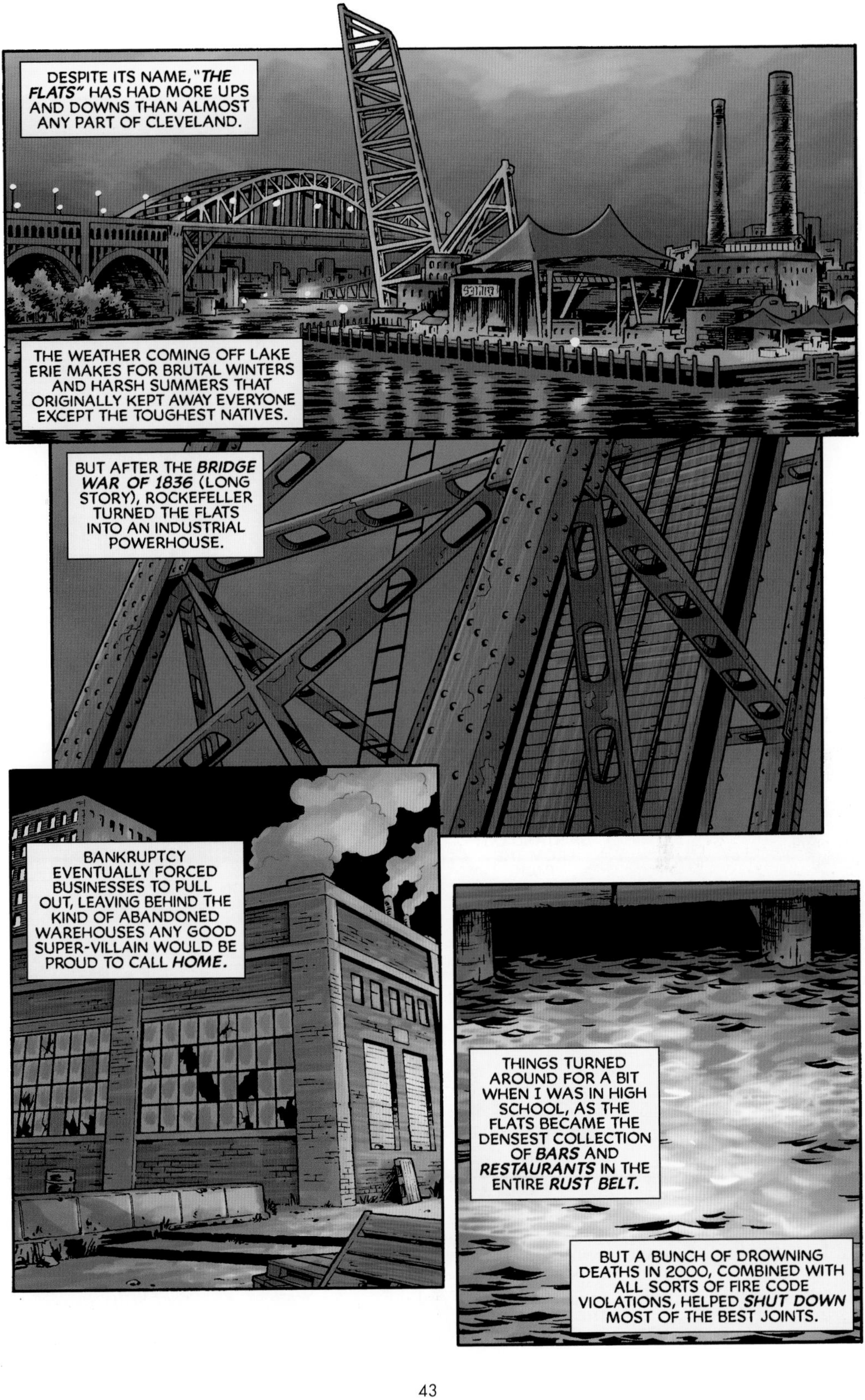
DESPITE ITS NAME, "THE FLATS" HAS HAD MORE UPS AND DOWNS THAN ALMOST ANY PART OF CLEVELAND.
THE WEATHER COMING OFF LAKE ERIE MAKES FOR BRUTAL WINTERS AND HARSH SUMMERS THAT ORIGINALLY KEPT AWAY EVERYONE EXCEPT THE TOUGHEST NATIVES.
BUT AFTER THE BRIDGE WAR OF 1836 (LONG STORY), ROCKEFELLER TURNED THE FLATS INTO AN INDUSTRIAL POWERHOUSE.
BANKRUPTCY EVENTUALLY FORCED BUSINESSES TO PULL OUT, LEAVING BEHIND THE KIND OF ABANDONED WAREHOUSES ANY GOOD SUPER-VILLAIN WOULD BE PROUD TO CALL HOME.
THINGS TURNED AROUND FOR A BIT WHEN I WAS IN HIGH SCHOOL, AS THE FLATS BECAME THE DENSEST COLLECTION OF BARS AND RESTAURANTS IN THE ENTIRE RUST BELT.
BUT A BUNCH OF DROWNING DEATHS IN 2000, COMBINED WITH ALL SORTS OF FIRE CODE VIOLATIONS, HELPED SHUT DOWN MOST OF THE BEST JOINTS.

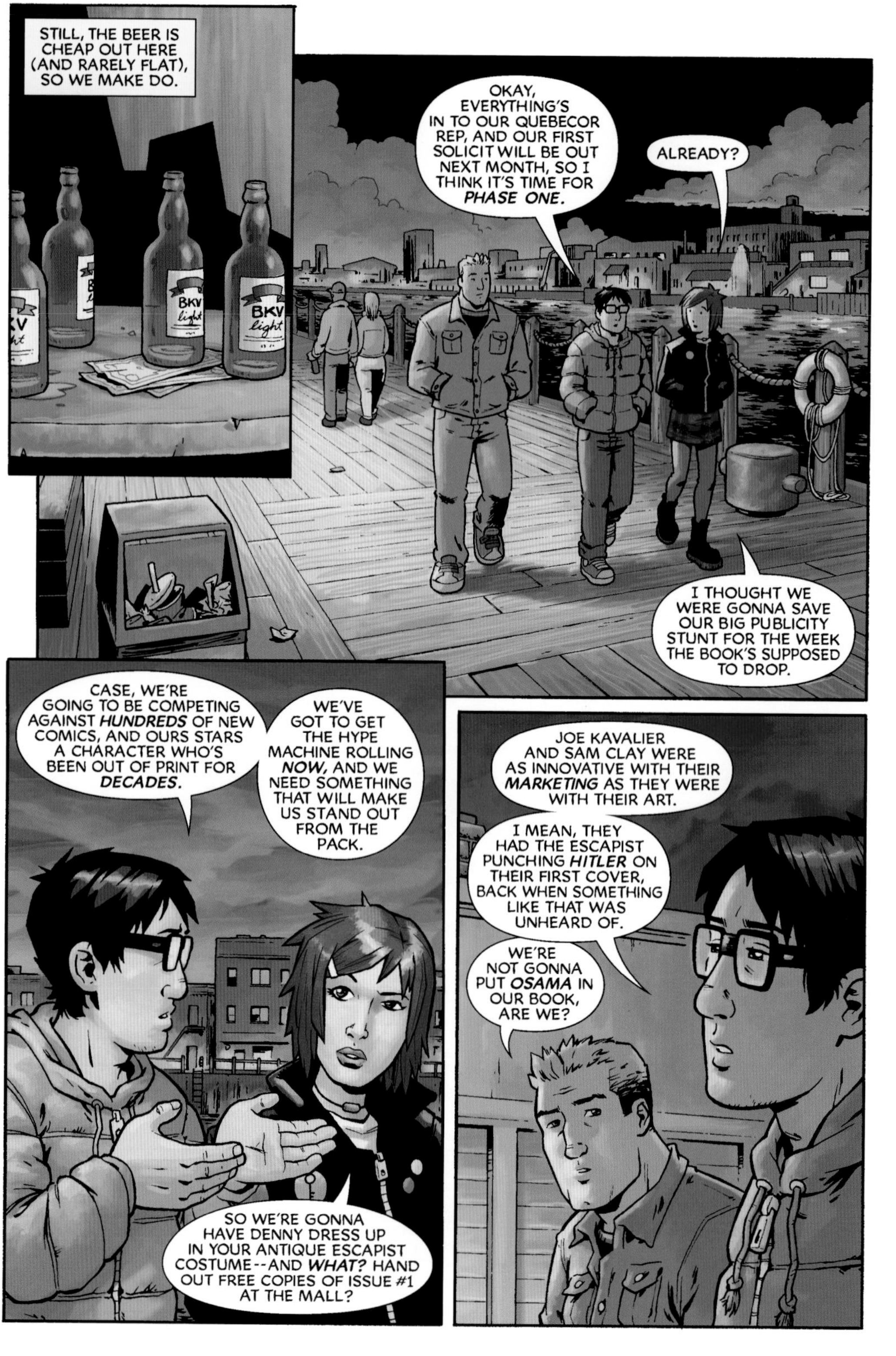
STILL, THE BEER IS CHEAP OUT HERE (AND RARELY FLAT), SO WE MAKE DO.
BKV light
BKV light
OKAY, EVERYTHING'S IN TO OUR QUEBECOR REP, AND OUR FIRST SOLICIT WILL BE OUT NEXT MONTH, SO I THINK IT'S TIME FOR PHASE ONE.
ALREADY?
I THOUGHT WE WERE GONNA SAVE OUR BIG PUBLICITY STUNT FOR THE WEEK THE BOOK'S SUPPOSED TO DROP.
CASE, WE'RE GOING TO BE COMPETING AGAINST HUNDREDS OF NEW COMICS, AND OURS STARS A CHARACTER WHO'S BEEN OUT OF PRINT FOR DECADES.
WE'VE GOT TO GET THE HYPE MACHINE ROLLING NOW, AND WE NEED SOMETHING THAT WILL MAKE US STAND OUT FROM THE PACK.
SO WE'RE GONNA HAVE DENNY DRESS UP IN YOUR ANTIQUE ESCAPIST COSTUME--AND WHAT? HAND OUT FREE COPIES OF ISSUE #1 AT THE MALL?
JOE KAVALIER AND SAM CLAY WERE AS INNOVATIVE WITH THEIR MARKETING AS THEY WERE WITH THEIR ART.
I MEAN, THEY HAD THE ESCAPIST PUNCHING HITLER ON THEIR FIRST COVER, BACK WHEN SOMETHING LIKE THAT WAS UNHEARD OF.
WE'RE NOT GONNA PUT OSAMA IN OUR BOOK, ARE WE?

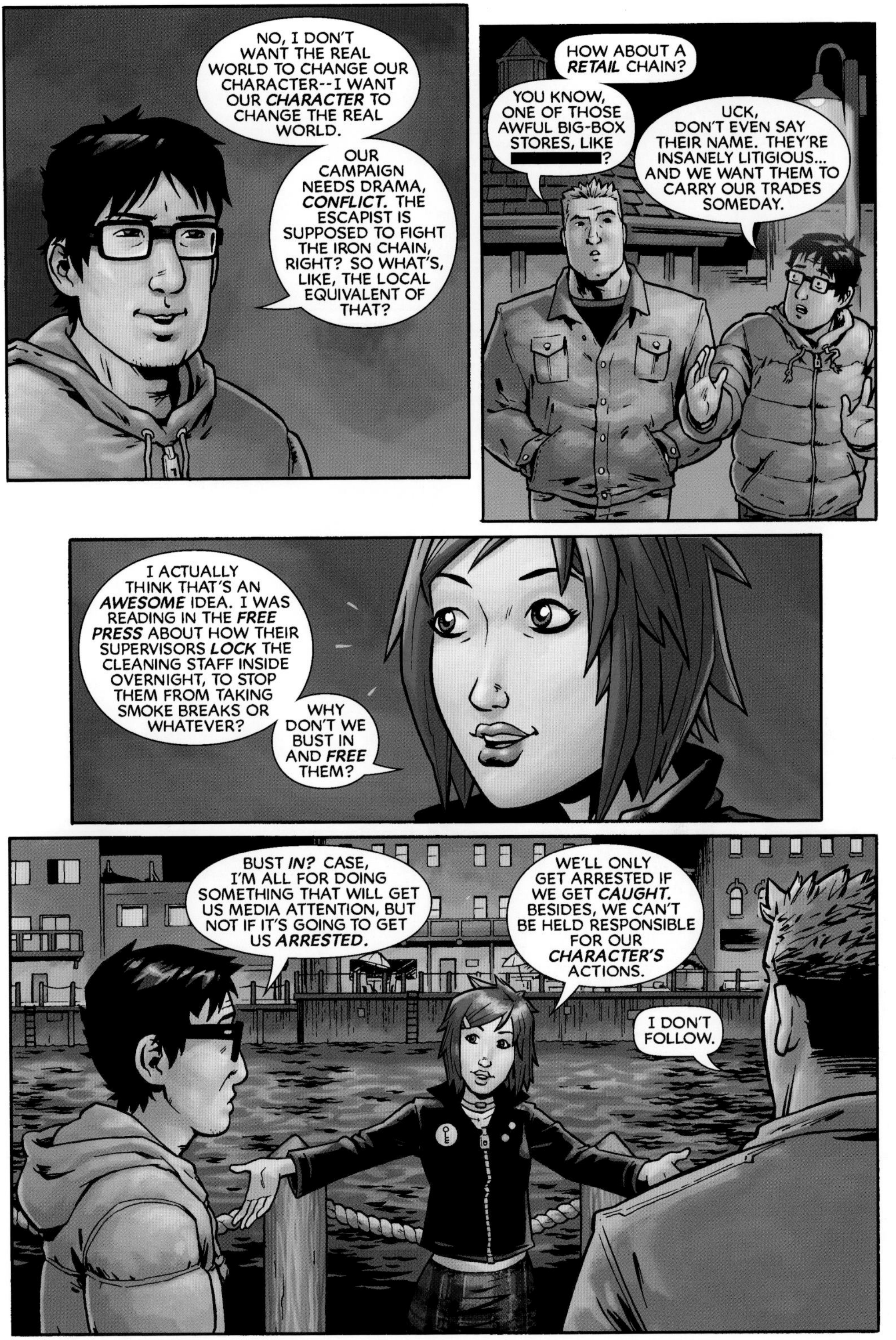
NO, I DON'T WANT THE REAL WORLD TO CHANGE OUR CHARACTER--I WANT OUR *CHARACTER* TO CHANGE THE REAL WORLD.
OUR CAMPAIGN NEEDS DRAMA, *CONFLICT.* THE ESCAPIST IS SUPPOSED TO FIGHT THE IRON CHAIN, RIGHT? SO WHAT'S, LIKE, THE LOCAL EQUIVALENT OF THAT?
HOW ABOUT A *RETAIL* CHAIN?
YOU KNOW, ONE OF THOSE AWFUL BIG-BOX STORES, LIKE [redacted]?
UCK, DON'T EVEN SAY THEIR NAME. THEY'RE INSANELY LITIGIOUS... AND WE WANT THEM TO CARRY OUR TRADES SOMEDAY.
I ACTUALLY THINK THAT'S AN *AWESOME* IDEA. I WAS READING IN THE *FREE PRESS* ABOUT HOW THEIR SUPERVISORS *LOCK* THE CLEANING STAFF INSIDE OVERNIGHT, TO STOP THEM FROM TAKING SMOKE BREAKS OR WHATEVER?
WHY DON'T WE BUST IN AND *FREE* THEM?
BUST *IN?* CASE, I'M ALL FOR DOING SOMETHING THAT WILL GET US MEDIA ATTENTION, BUT NOT IF IT'S GOING TO GET US *ARRESTED*.
WE'LL ONLY GET ARRESTED IF WE GET *CAUGHT.* BESIDES, WE CAN'T BE HELD RESPONSIBLE FOR OUR *CHARACTER'S* ACTIONS.
I DON'T FOLLOW.

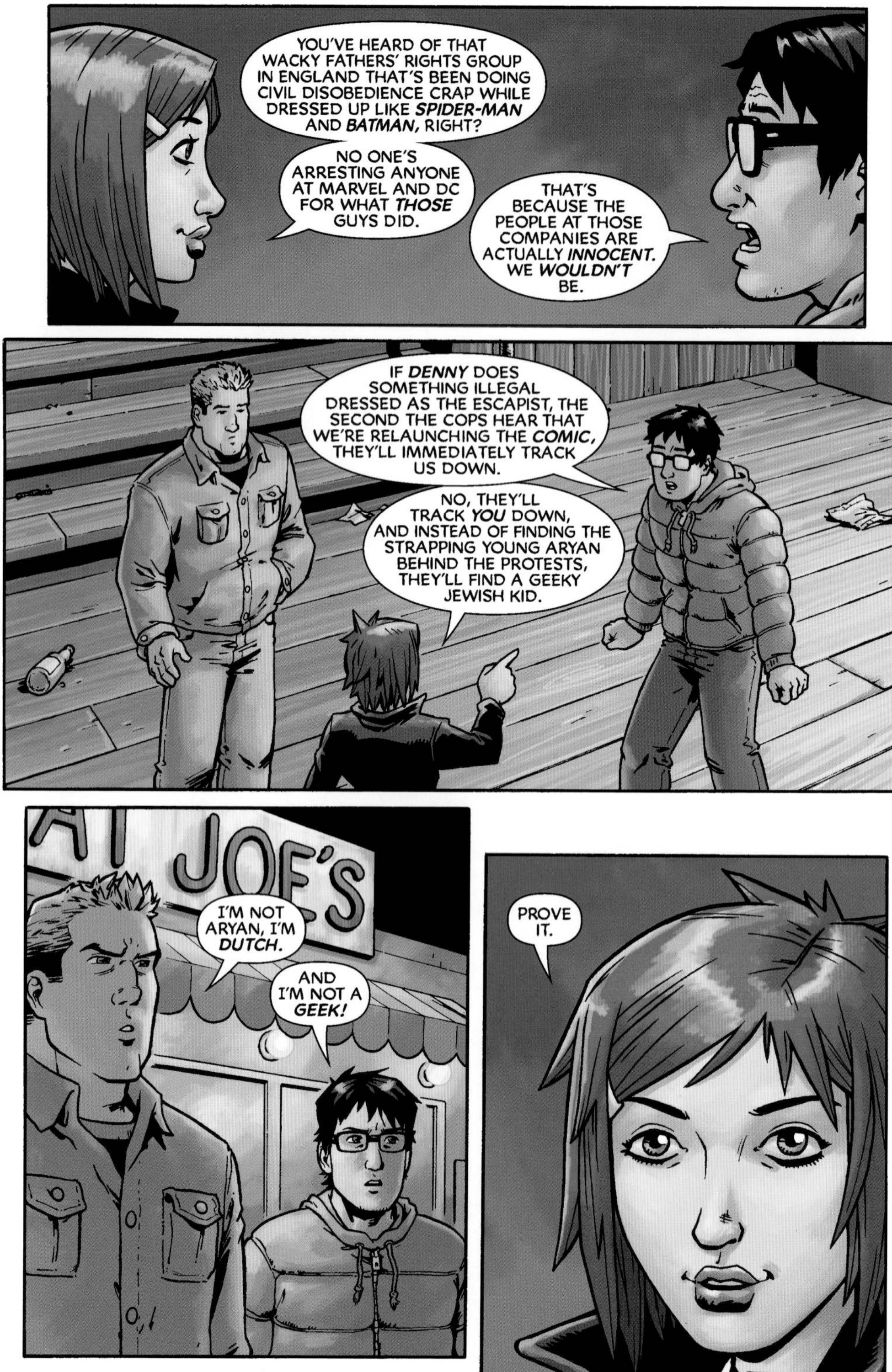
YOU'VE HEARD OF THAT WACKY FATHERS' RIGHTS GROUP IN ENGLAND THAT'S BEEN DOING CIVIL DISOBEDIENCE CRAP WHILE DRESSED UP LIKE *SPIDER-MAN* AND *BATMAN,* RIGHT?
NO ONE'S ARRESTING ANYONE AT MARVEL AND DC FOR WHAT *THOSE* GUYS DID.
THAT'S BECAUSE THE PEOPLE AT THOSE COMPANIES ARE ACTUALLY *INNOCENT.* WE *WOULDN'T* BE.
IF *DENNY* DOES SOMETHING ILLEGAL DRESSED AS THE ESCAPIST, THE SECOND THE COPS HEAR THAT WE'RE RELAUNCHING THE *COMIC,* THEY'LL IMMEDIATELY TRACK US DOWN.
NO, THEY'LL TRACK *YOU* DOWN, AND INSTEAD OF FINDING THE STRAPPING YOUNG ARYAN BEHIND THE PROTESTS, THEY'LL FIND A GEEKY JEWISH KID.
JOE'S
I'M NOT ARYAN, I'M *DUTCH.*
AND I'M NOT A *GEEK!*
PROVE IT.

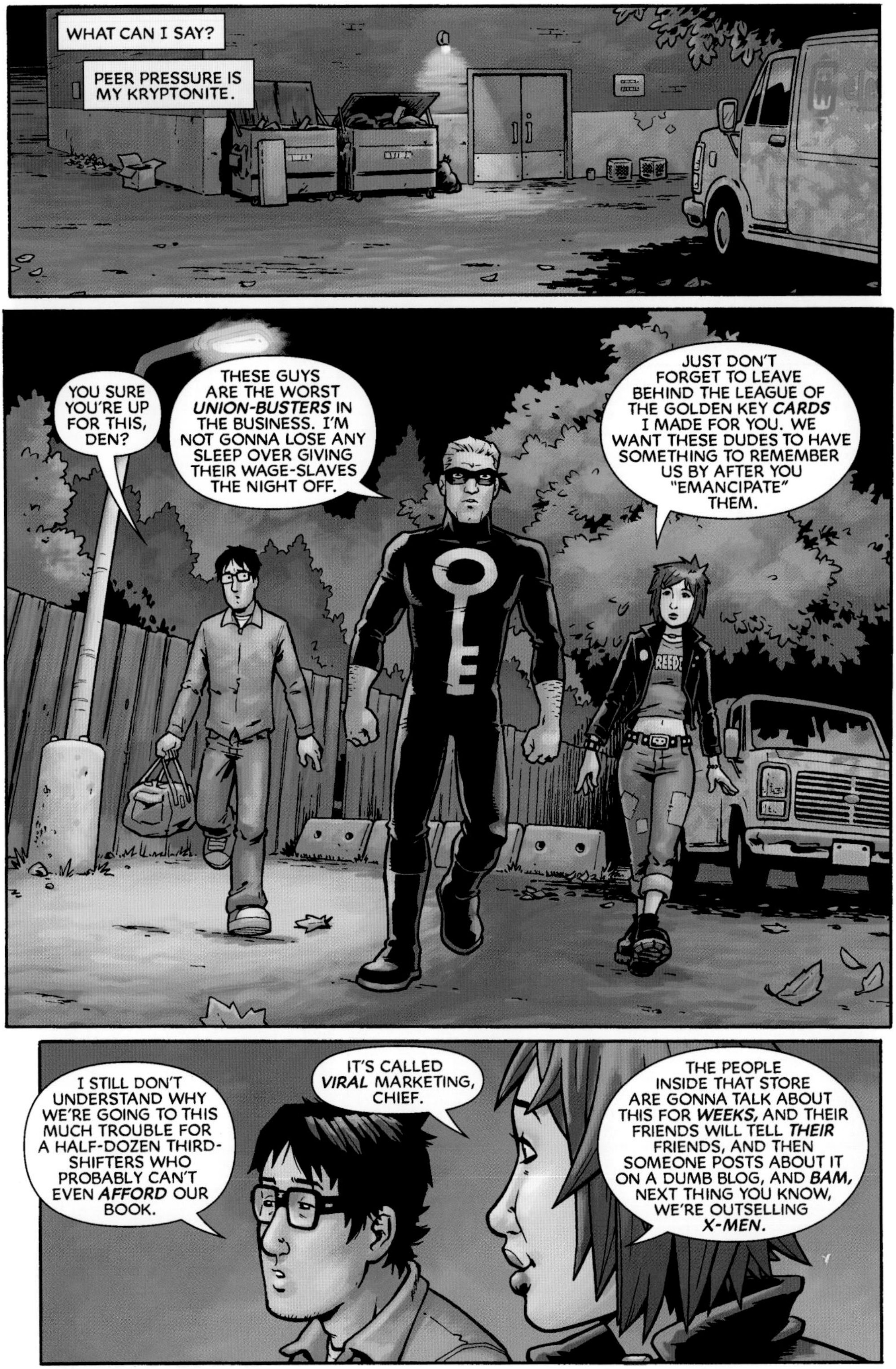
WHAT CAN I SAY?
PEER PRESSURE IS MY KRYPTONITE.
YOU SURE YOU'RE UP FOR THIS, DEN?
THESE GUYS ARE THE WORST *UNION-BUSTERS* IN THE BUSINESS. I'M NOT GONNA LOSE ANY SLEEP OVER GIVING THEIR WAGE-SLAVES THE NIGHT OFF.
JUST DON'T FORGET TO LEAVE BEHIND THE LEAGUE OF THE GOLDEN KEY *CARDS* I MADE FOR YOU. WE WANT THESE DUDES TO HAVE SOMETHING TO REMEMBER US BY AFTER YOU "EMANCIPATE" THEM.
I STILL DON'T UNDERSTAND WHY WE'RE GOING TO THIS MUCH TROUBLE FOR A HALF-DOZEN THIRD-SHIFTERS WHO PROBABLY CAN'T EVEN *AFFORD* OUR BOOK.
IT'S CALLED *VIRAL* MARKETING, CHIEF.
THE PEOPLE INSIDE THAT STORE ARE GONNA TALK ABOUT THIS FOR *WEEKS,* AND THEIR FRIENDS WILL TELL *THEIR* FRIENDS, AND THEN SOMEONE POSTS ABOUT IT ON A DUMB BLOG, AND *BAM,* NEXT THING YOU KNOW, WE'RE OUTSELLING *X-MEN.*

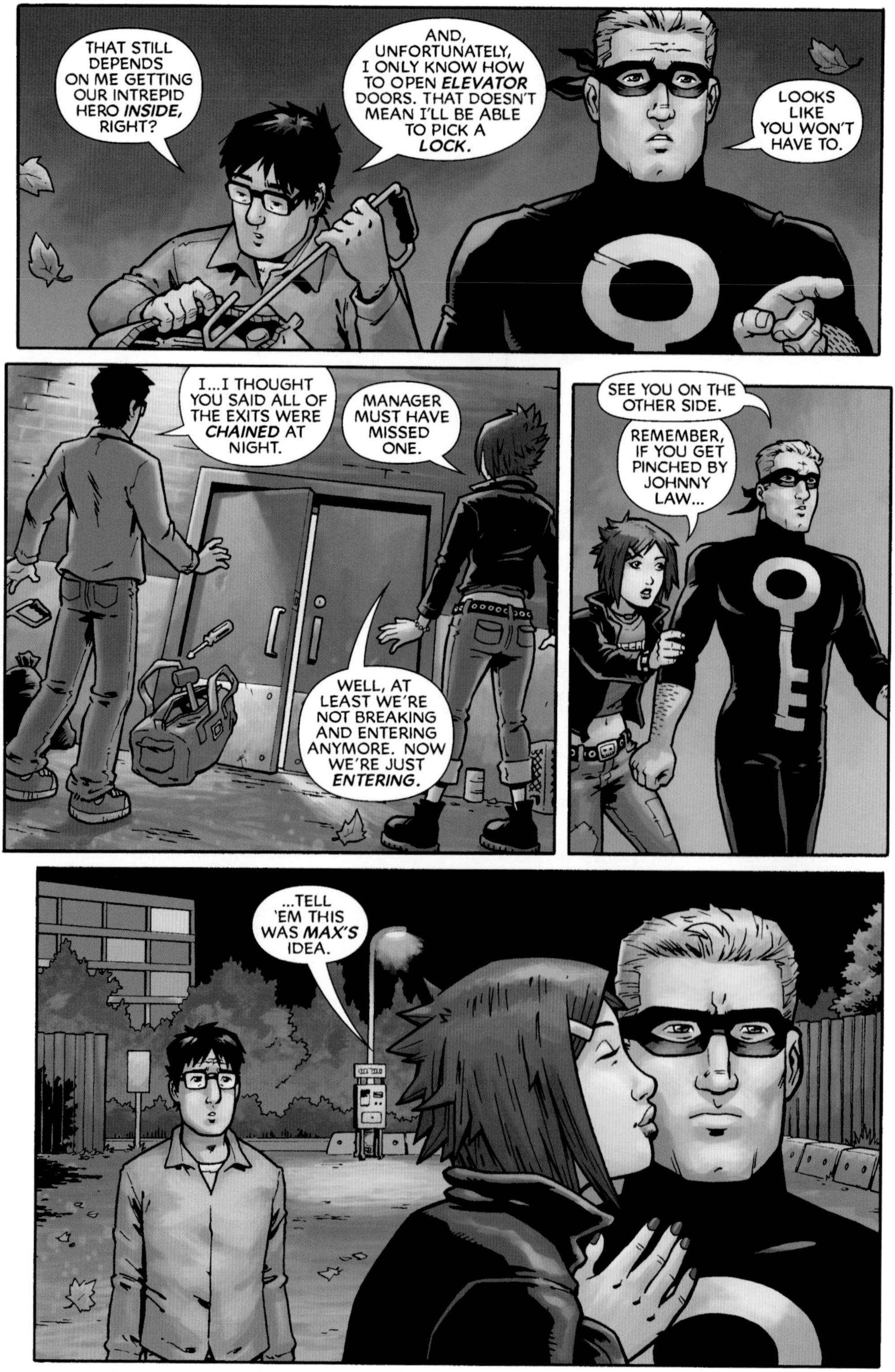
THAT STILL DEPENDS ON ME GETTING OUR INTREPID HERO *INSIDE,* RIGHT?
AND, UNFORTUNATELY, I ONLY KNOW HOW TO OPEN *ELEVATOR* DOORS. THAT DOESN'T MEAN I'LL BE ABLE TO PICK A *LOCK.*
LOOKS LIKE YOU WON'T HAVE TO.
I...I THOUGHT YOU SAID ALL OF THE EXITS WERE *CHAINED* AT NIGHT.
MANAGER MUST HAVE MISSED ONE.
WELL, AT LEAST WE'RE NOT BREAKING AND ENTERING ANYMORE. NOW WE'RE JUST *ENTERING.*
SEE YOU ON THE OTHER SIDE.
REMEMBER, IF YOU GET PINCHED BY JOHNNY LAW...
...TELL 'EM THIS WAS *MAX'S* IDEA.

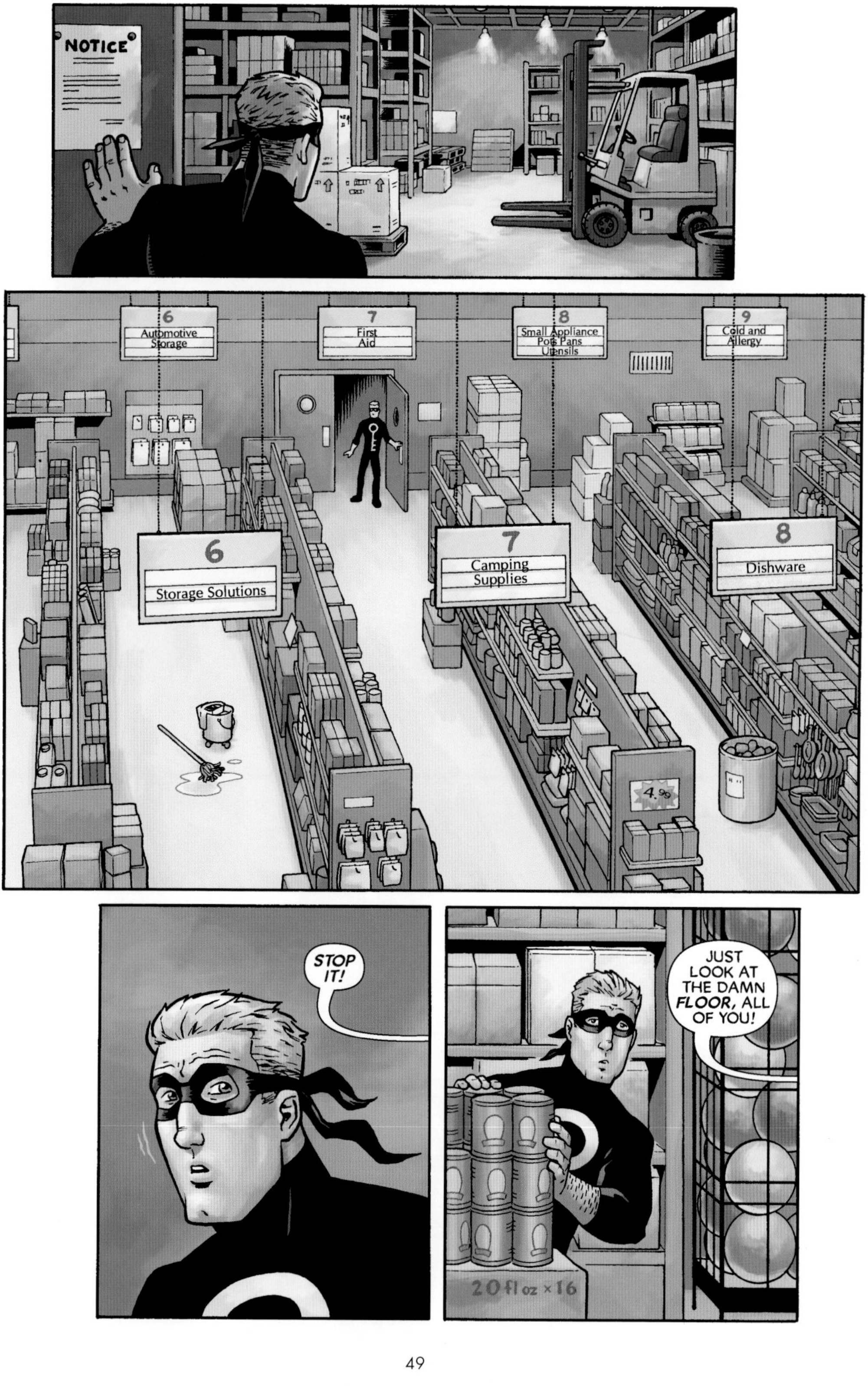
NOTICE
6
Automotive
Storage
7
First
Aid
8
Small Appliance
Pots Pans
Utensils
9
Cold and
Allergy
6
Storage Solutions
7
Camping
Supplies
8
Dishware
4.99
STOP IT!
JUST LOOK AT THE DAMN *FLOOR*, ALL OF YOU!
20 fl oz ×16

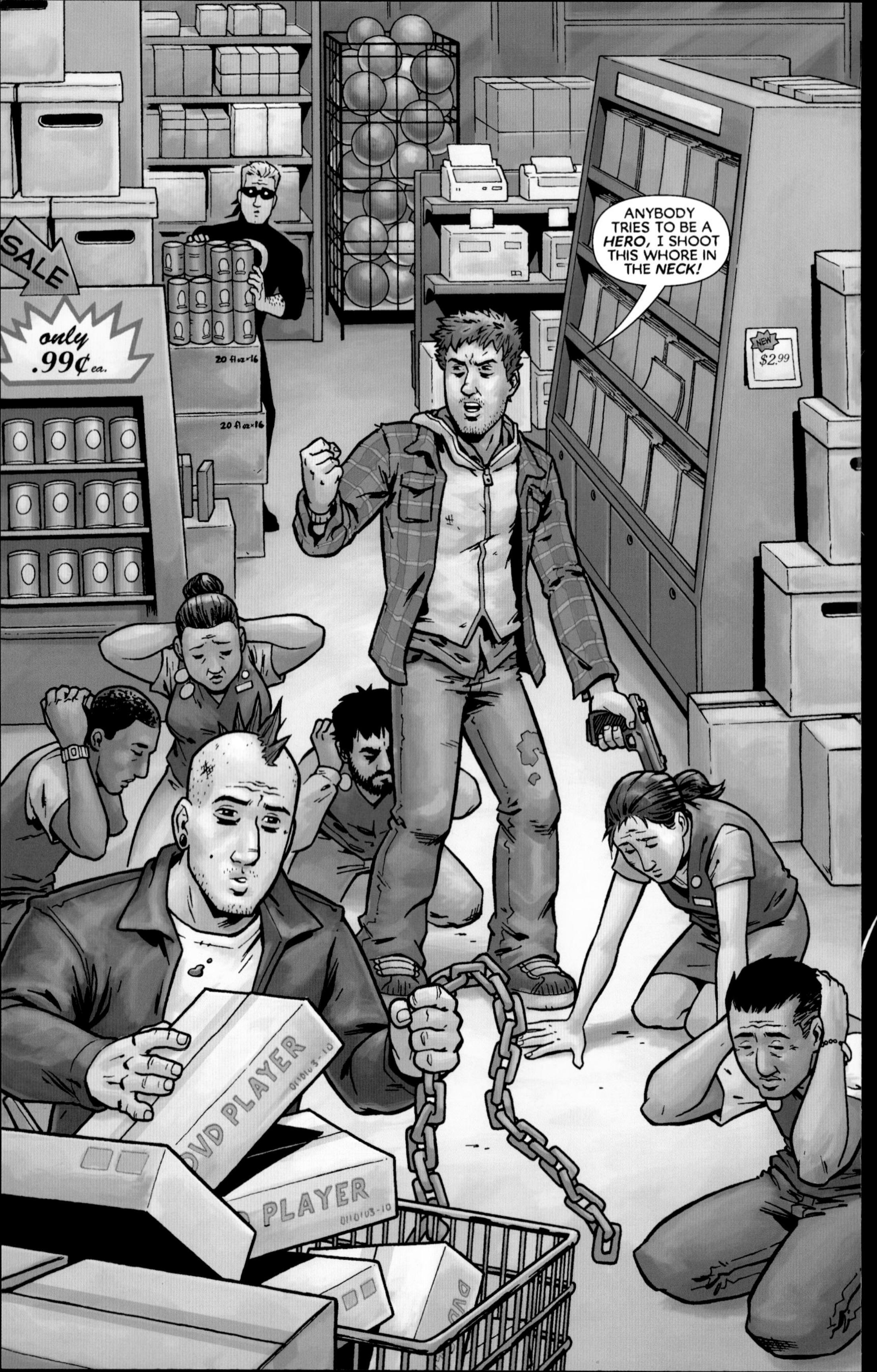
SALE
only .99¢ ea.
20 fl oz×16
20 fl oz×16
ANYBODY TRIES TO BE A *HERO,* I SHOOT THIS WHORE IN THE *NECK!*
NEW $2.99
DVD PLAYER
0110103-10
PLAYER
0110103-10

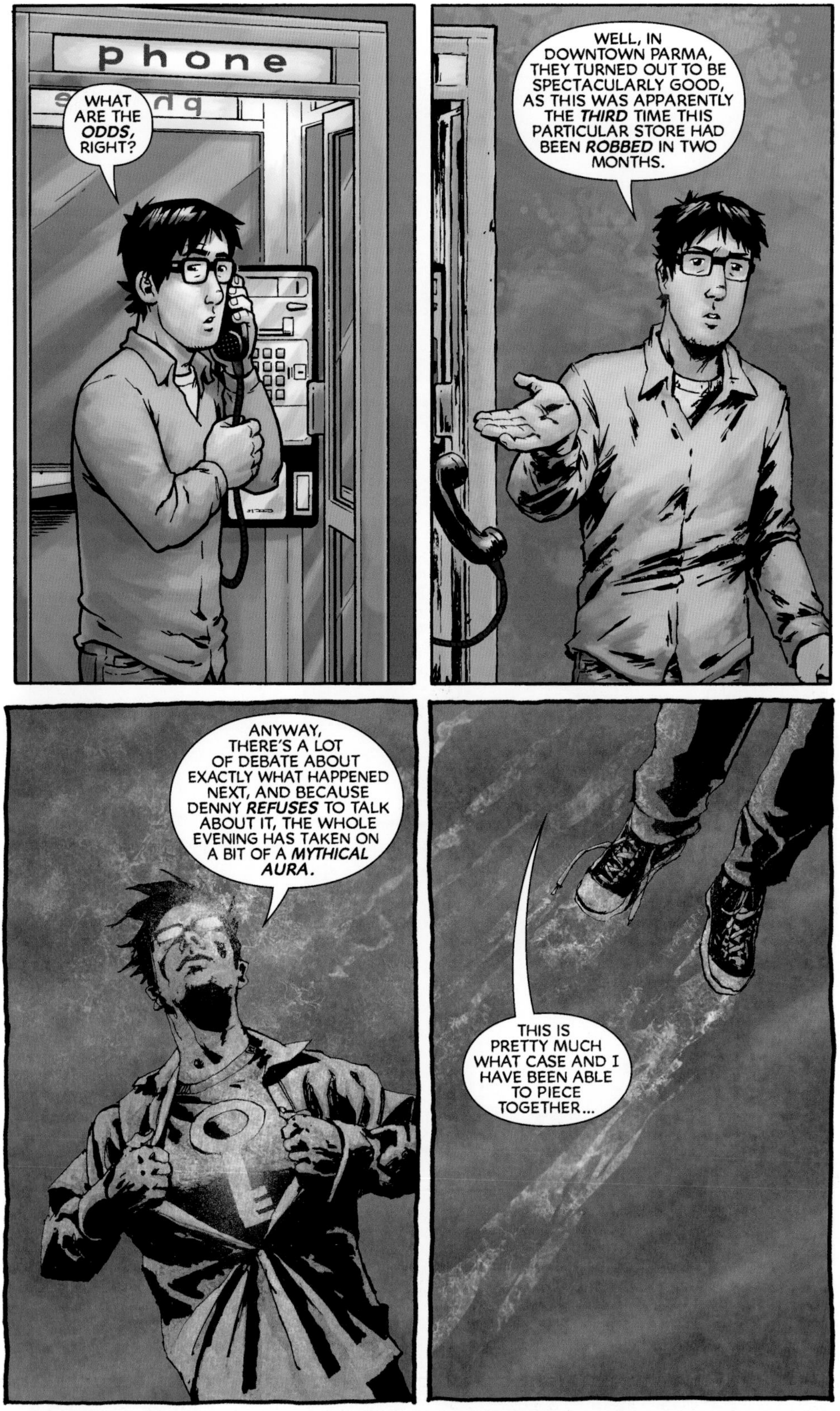
phone
WHAT ARE THE ODDS, RIGHT?
WELL, IN DOWNTOWN PARMA, THEY TURNED OUT TO BE SPECTACULARLY GOOD, AS THIS WAS APPARENTLY THE THIRD TIME THIS PARTICULAR STORE HAD BEEN ROBBED IN TWO MONTHS.
ANYWAY, THERE'S A LOT OF DEBATE ABOUT EXACTLY WHAT HAPPENED NEXT, AND BECAUSE DENNY REFUSES TO TALK ABOUT IT, THE WHOLE EVENING HAS TAKEN ON A BIT OF A MYTHICAL AURA.
THIS IS PRETTY MUCH WHAT CASE AND I HAVE BEEN ABLE TO PIECE TOGETHER...

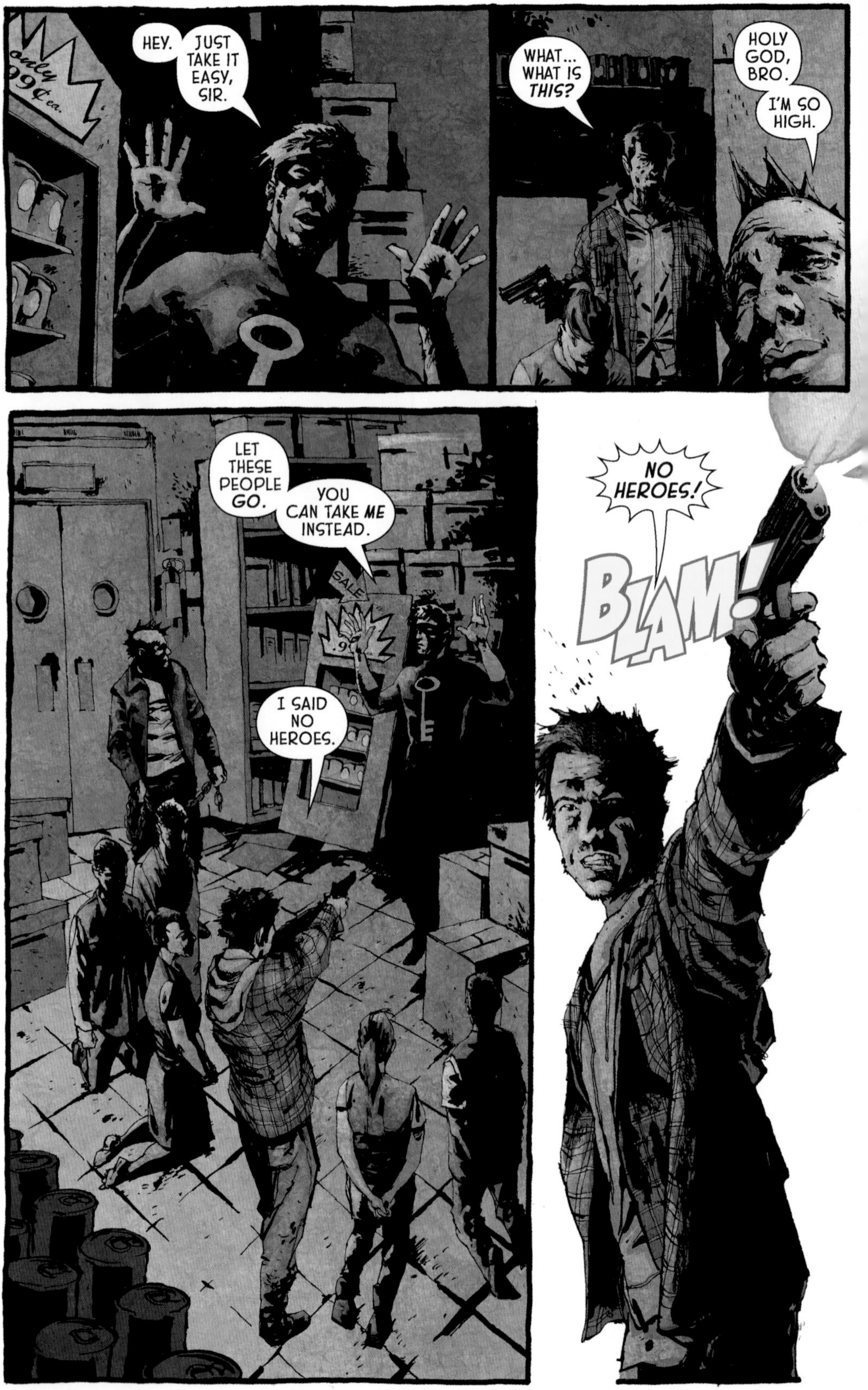
only 99¢ ea.
HEY.
JUST TAKE IT EASY, SIR.
WHAT... WHAT IS THIS?
HOLY GOD, BRO.
I'M SO HIGH.
LET THESE PEOPLE GO.
YOU CAN TAKE ME INSTEAD.
SALE
I SAID NO HEROES.
NO HEROES!
BLAM!

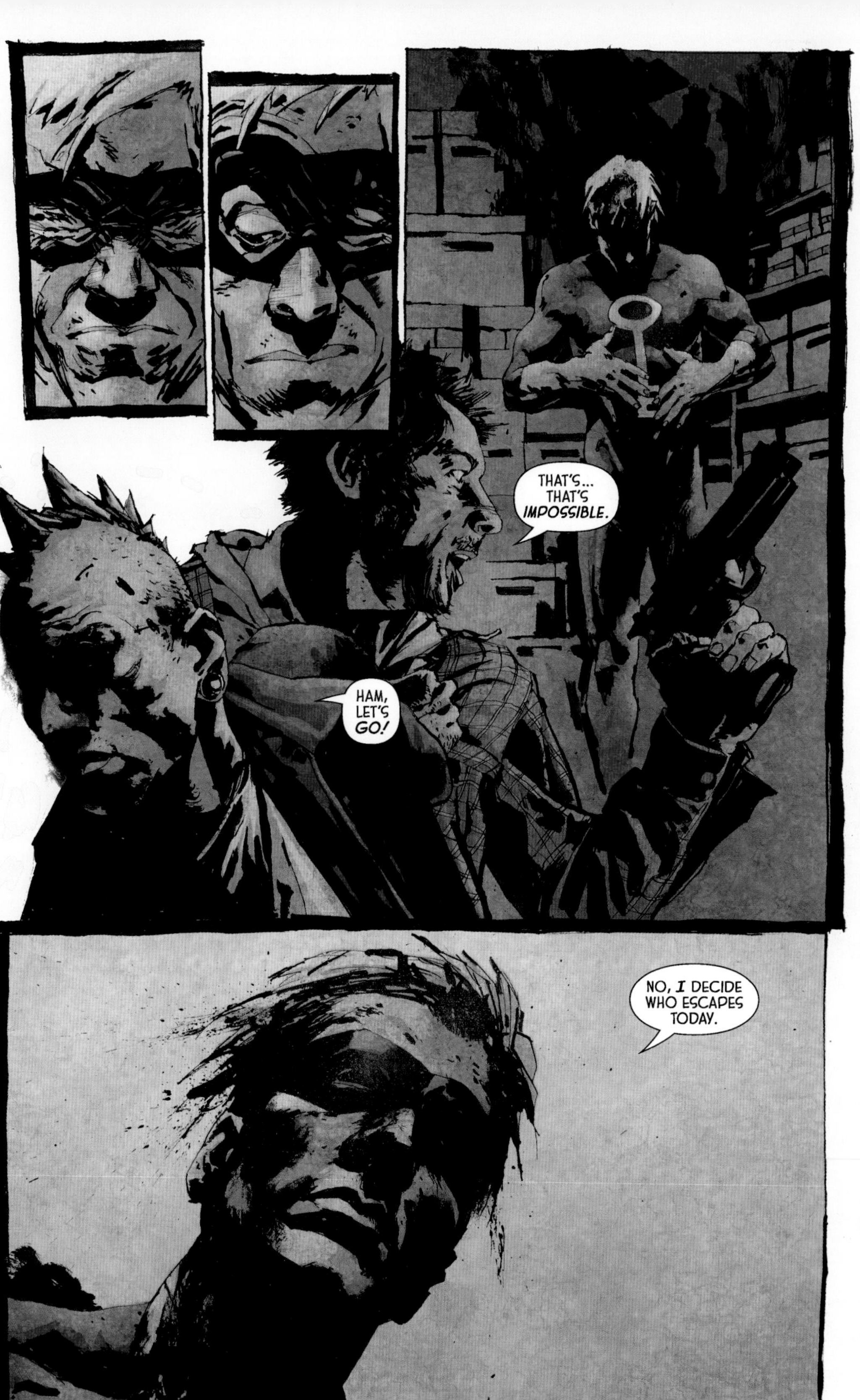
THAT'S... THAT'S IMPOSSIBLE.
HAM, LET'S GO!
NO, I DECIDE WHO ESCAPES TODAY.

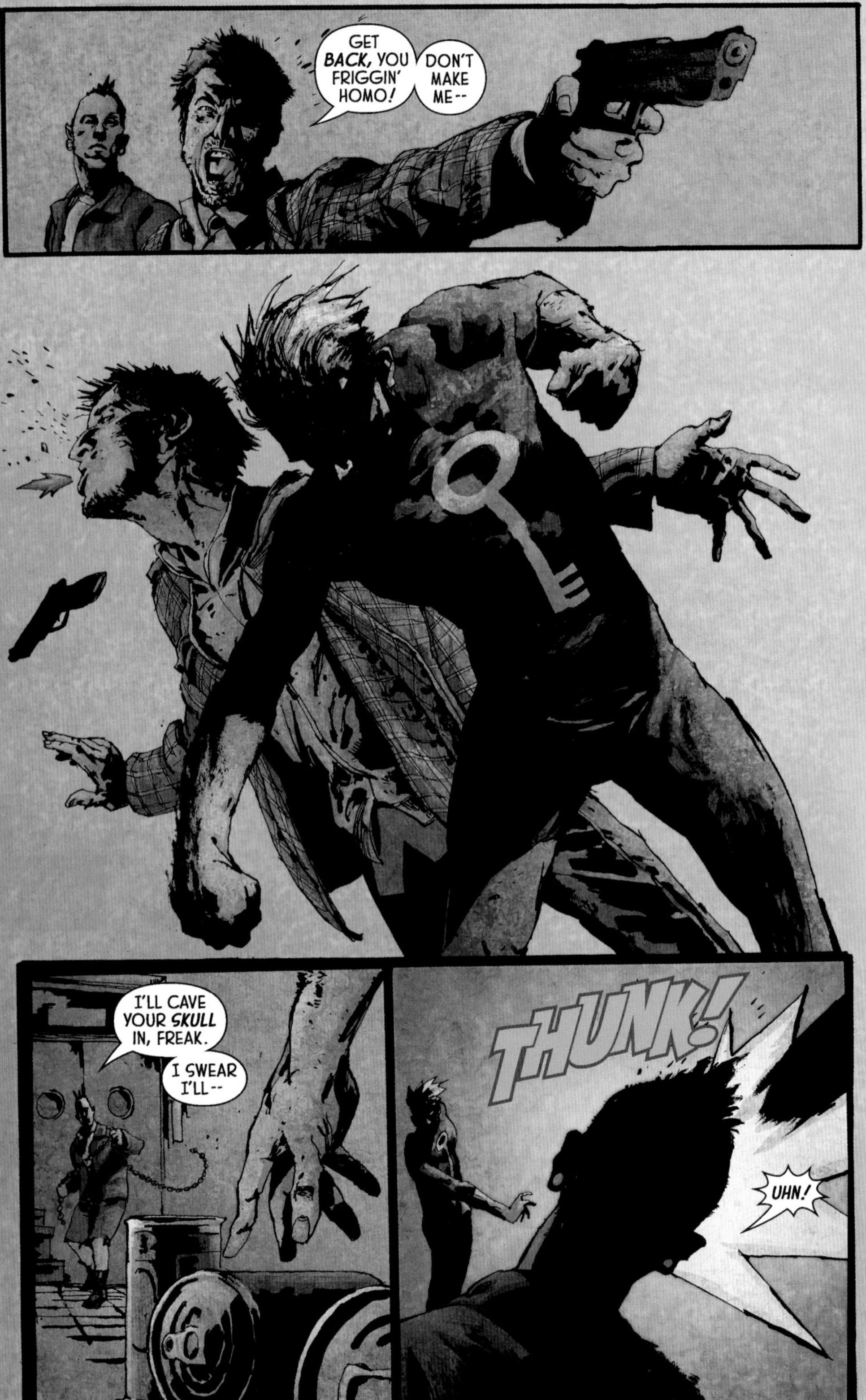
GET BACK, YOU FRIGGIN' HOMO!
DON'T MAKE ME--
I'LL CAVE YOUR SKULL IN, FREAK.
I SWEAR I'LL--
THUNK!
UHN!

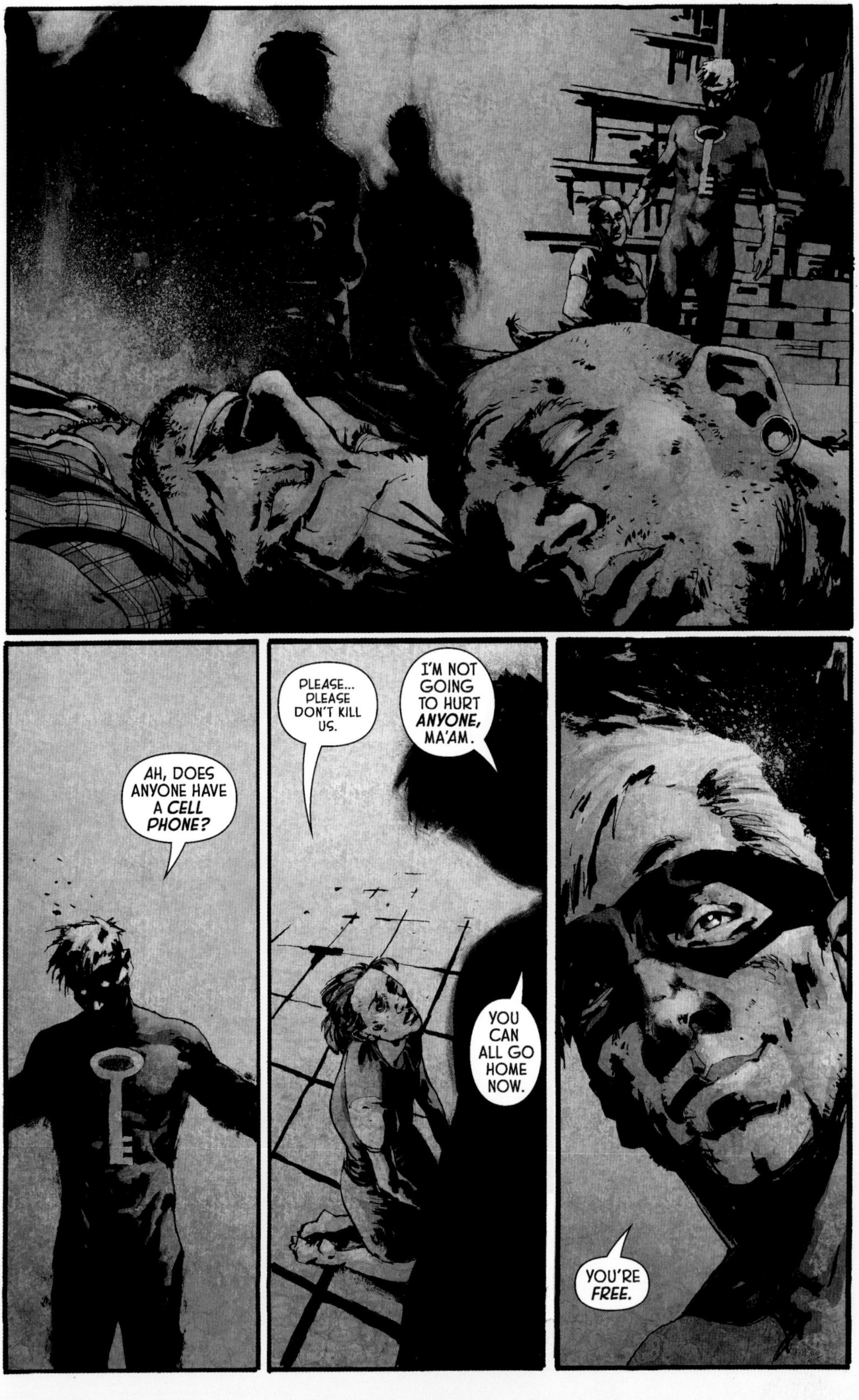
AH, DOES ANYONE HAVE A *CELL PHONE?*
PLEASE... PLEASE DON'T KILL US.
I'M NOT GOING TO HURT *ANYONE,* MA'AM.
YOU CAN ALL GO HOME NOW.
YOU'RE *FREE.*

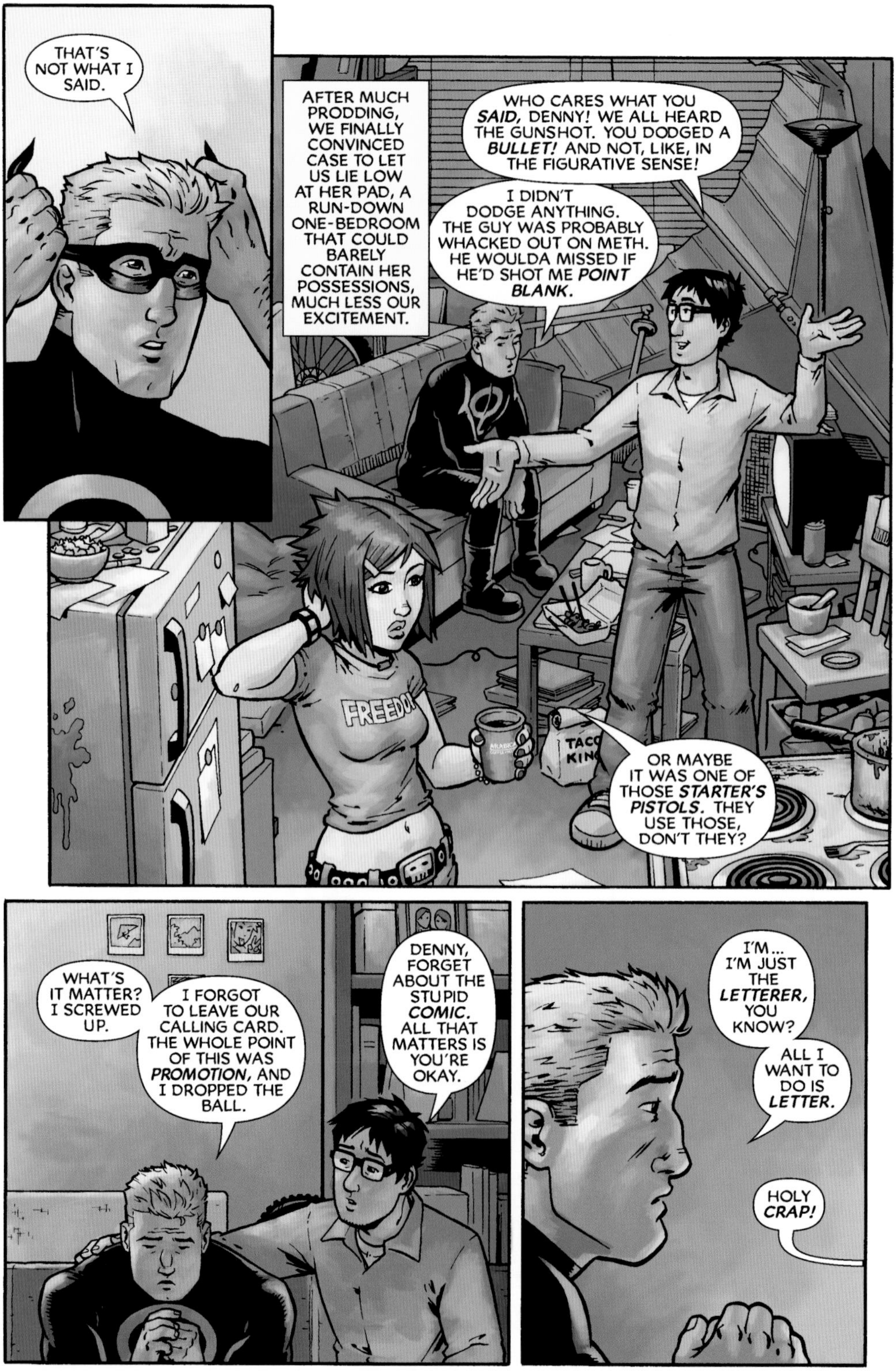

THAT'S NOT WHAT I SAID.
AFTER MUCH PRODDING, WE FINALLY CONVINCED CASE TO LET US LIE LOW AT HER PAD, A RUN-DOWN ONE-BEDROOM THAT COULD BARELY CONTAIN HER POSSESSIONS, MUCH LESS OUR EXCITEMENT.
WHO CARES WHAT YOU SAID, DENNY! WE ALL HEARD THE GUNSHOT. YOU DODGED A BULLET! AND NOT, LIKE, IN THE FIGURATIVE SENSE!
I DIDN'T DODGE ANYTHING. THE GUY WAS PROBABLY WHACKED OUT ON METH. HE WOULDA MISSED IF HE'D SHOT ME POINT BLANK.
OR MAYBE IT WAS ONE OF THOSE STARTER'S PISTOLS. THEY USE THOSE, DON'T THEY?
WHAT'S IT MATTER? I SCREWED UP.
I FORGOT TO LEAVE OUR CALLING CARD. THE WHOLE POINT OF THIS WAS PROMOTION, AND I DROPPED THE BALL.
DENNY, FORGET ABOUT THE STUPID COMIC. ALL THAT MATTERS IS YOU'RE OKAY.
I'M... I'M JUST THE LETTERER, YOU KNOW?
ALL I WANT TO DO IS LETTER.
HOLY CRAP!

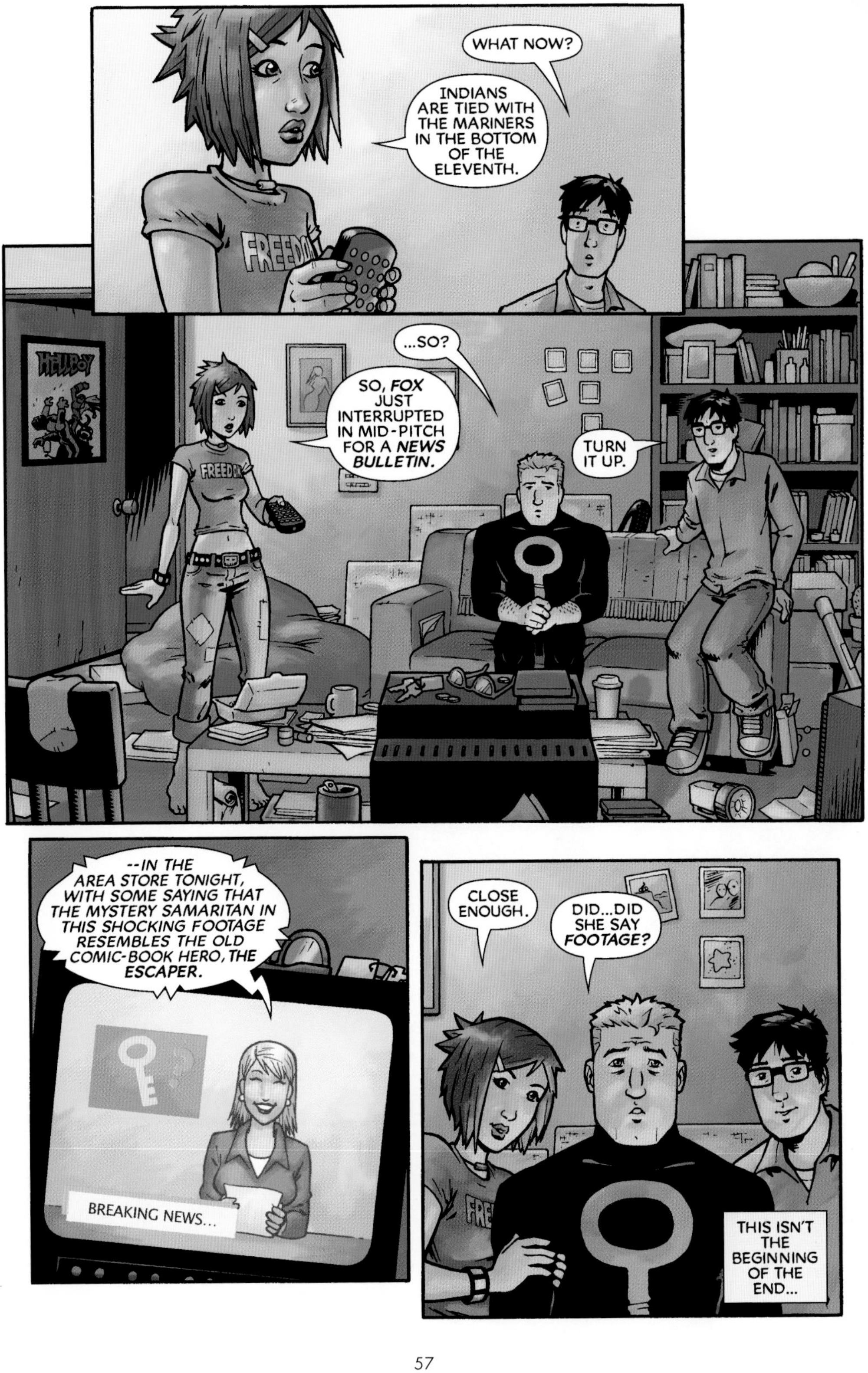
WHAT NOW?
INDIANS ARE TIED WITH THE MARINERS IN THE BOTTOM OF THE ELEVENTH.
HELLBOY
...SO?
SO, *FOX* JUST INTERRUPTED IN MID-PITCH FOR A *NEWS BULLETIN.*
TURN IT UP.
--IN THE AREA STORE TONIGHT, WITH SOME SAYING THAT THE MYSTERY SAMARITAN IN THIS SHOCKING FOOTAGE RESEMBLES THE OLD COMIC-BOOK HERO, THE ESCAPER.
BREAKING NEWS...
CLOSE ENOUGH.
DID...DID SHE SAY *FOOTAGE?*
THIS ISN'T THE BEGINNING OF THE END...

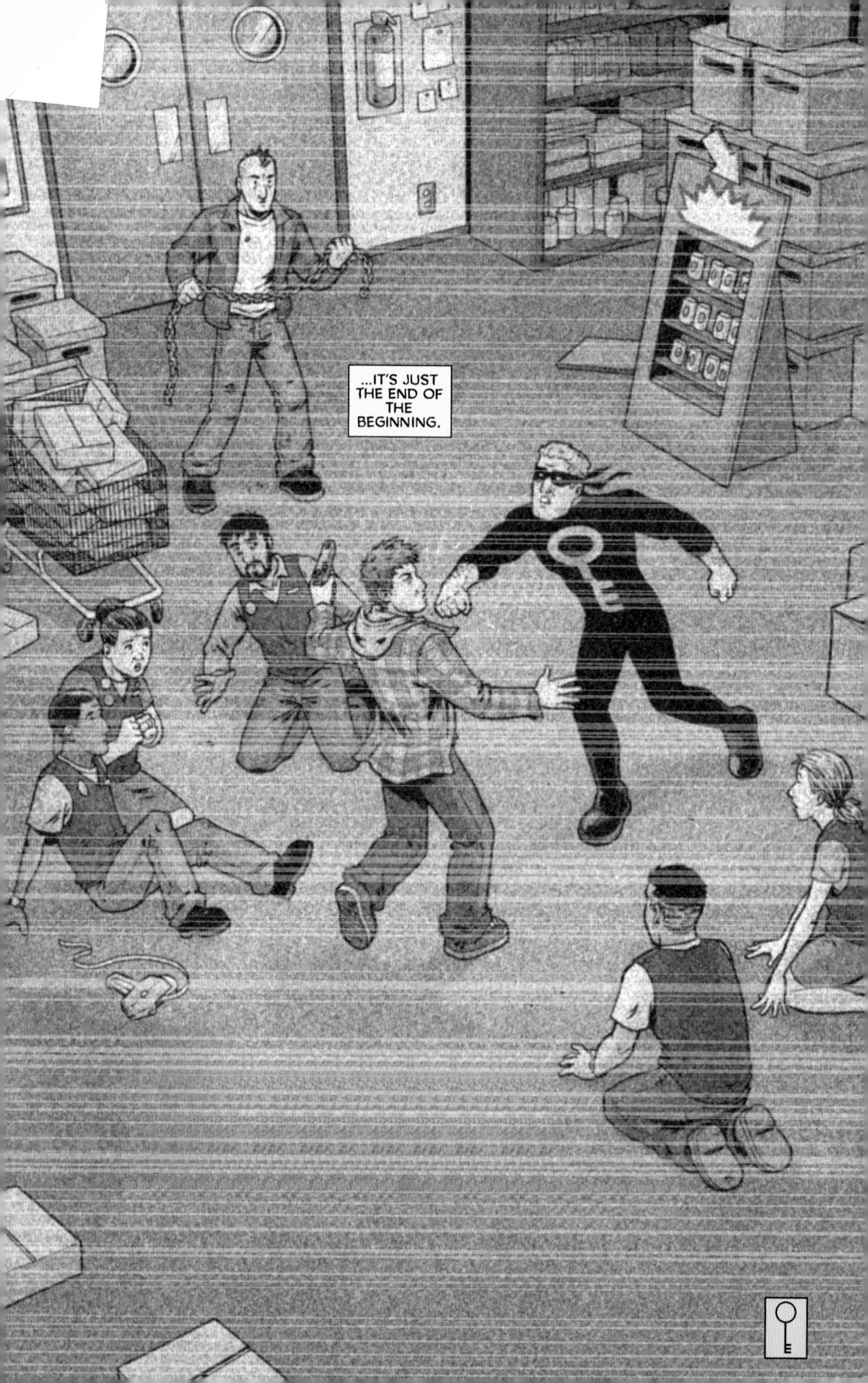
...IT'S JUST THE END OF THE BEGINNING.

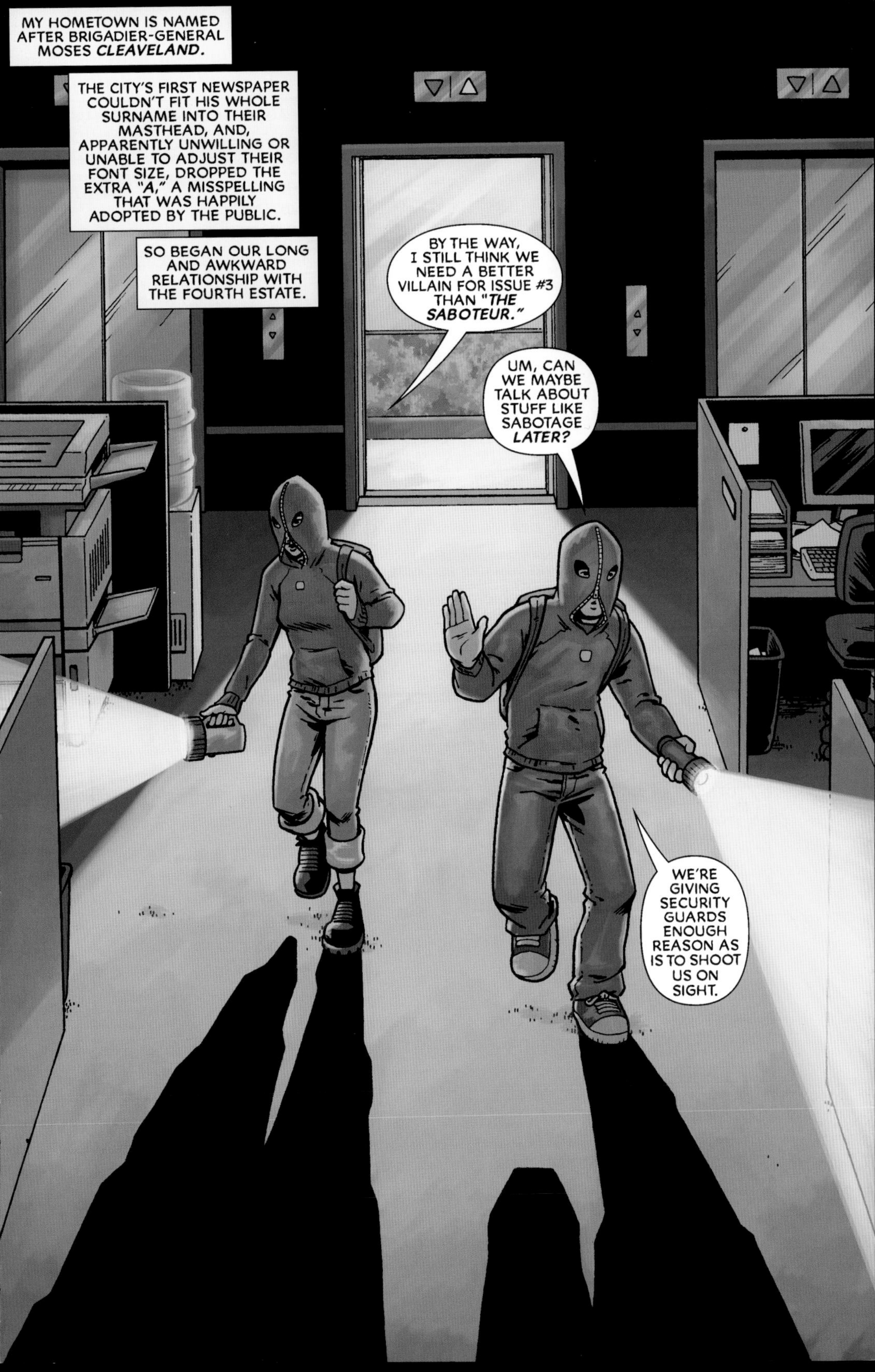

MY HOMETOWN IS NAMED AFTER BRIGADIER-GENERAL MOSES *CLEAVELAND.*
THE CITY'S FIRST NEWSPAPER COULDN'T FIT HIS WHOLE SURNAME INTO THEIR MASTHEAD, AND, APPARENTLY UNWILLING OR UNABLE TO ADJUST THEIR FONT SIZE, DROPPED THE EXTRA *"A,"* A MISSPELLING THAT WAS HAPPILY ADOPTED BY THE PUBLIC.
SO BEGAN OUR LONG AND AWKWARD RELATIONSHIP WITH THE FOURTH ESTATE.
BY THE WAY, I STILL THINK WE NEED A BETTER VILLAIN FOR ISSUE #3 THAN *"THE SABOTEUR."*
UM, CAN WE MAYBE TALK ABOUT STUFF LIKE SABOTAGE *LATER?*
WE'RE GIVING SECURITY GUARDS ENOUGH REASON AS IS TO SHOOT US ON SIGHT.

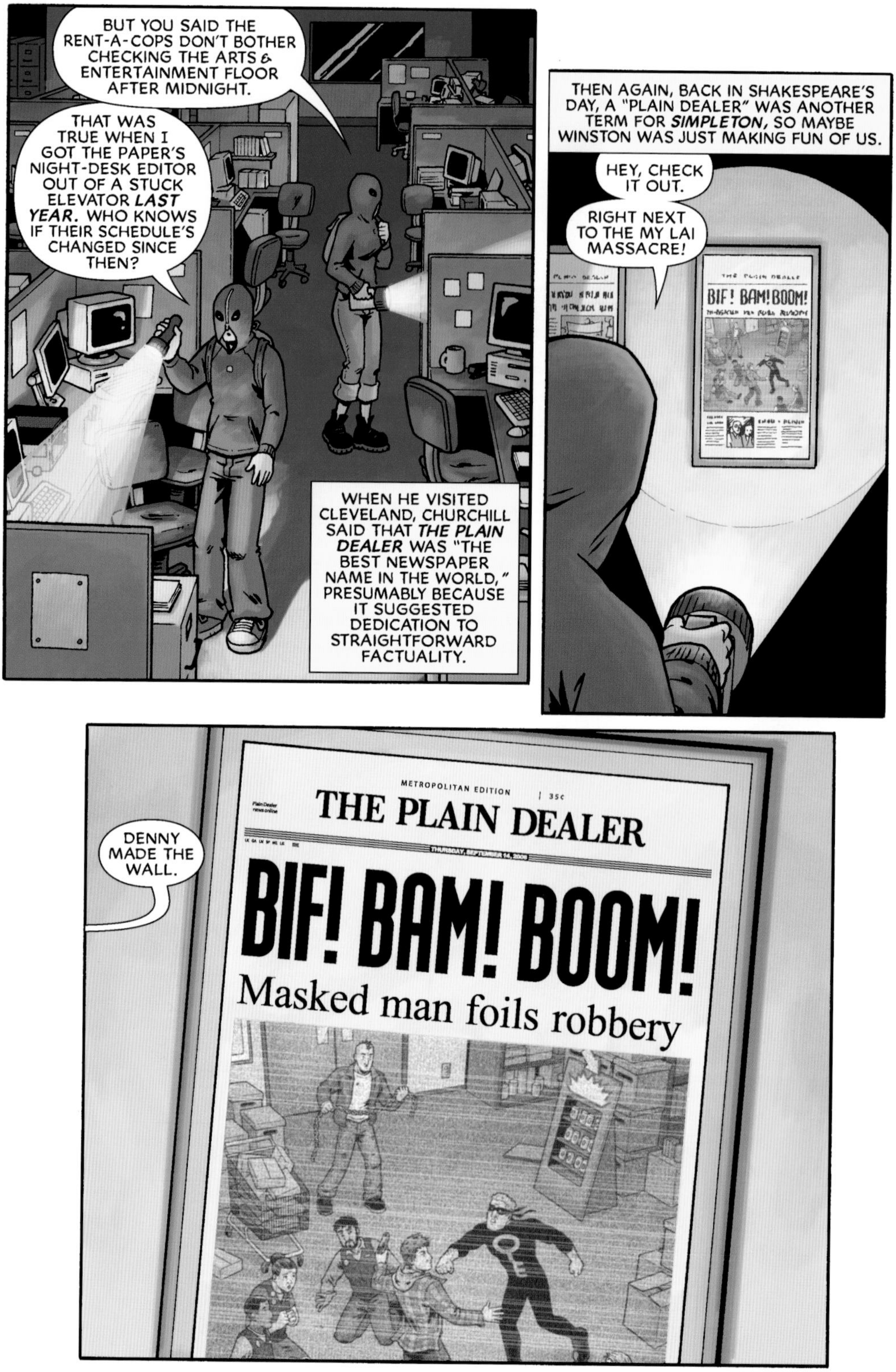
BUT YOU SAID THE RENT-A-COPS DON'T BOTHER CHECKING THE ARTS & ENTERTAINMENT FLOOR AFTER MIDNIGHT.
THAT WAS TRUE WHEN I GOT THE PAPER'S NIGHT-DESK EDITOR OUT OF A STUCK ELEVATOR *LAST YEAR.* WHO KNOWS IF THEIR SCHEDULE'S CHANGED SINCE THEN?
WHEN HE VISITED CLEVELAND, CHURCHILL SAID THAT *THE PLAIN DEALER* WAS "THE BEST NEWSPAPER NAME IN THE WORLD," PRESUMABLY BECAUSE IT SUGGESTED DEDICATION TO STRAIGHTFORWARD FACTUALITY.
THEN AGAIN, BACK IN SHAKESPEARE'S DAY, A "PLAIN DEALER" WAS ANOTHER TERM FOR *SIMPLETON,* SO MAYBE WINSTON WAS JUST MAKING FUN OF US.
HEY, CHECK IT OUT.
RIGHT NEXT TO THE MY LAI MASSACRE!
BIF! BAM! BOOM!
METROPOLITAN EDITION | 35¢
THE PLAIN DEALER
DENNY MADE THE WALL.
BIF! BAM! BOOM!
Masked man foils robbery

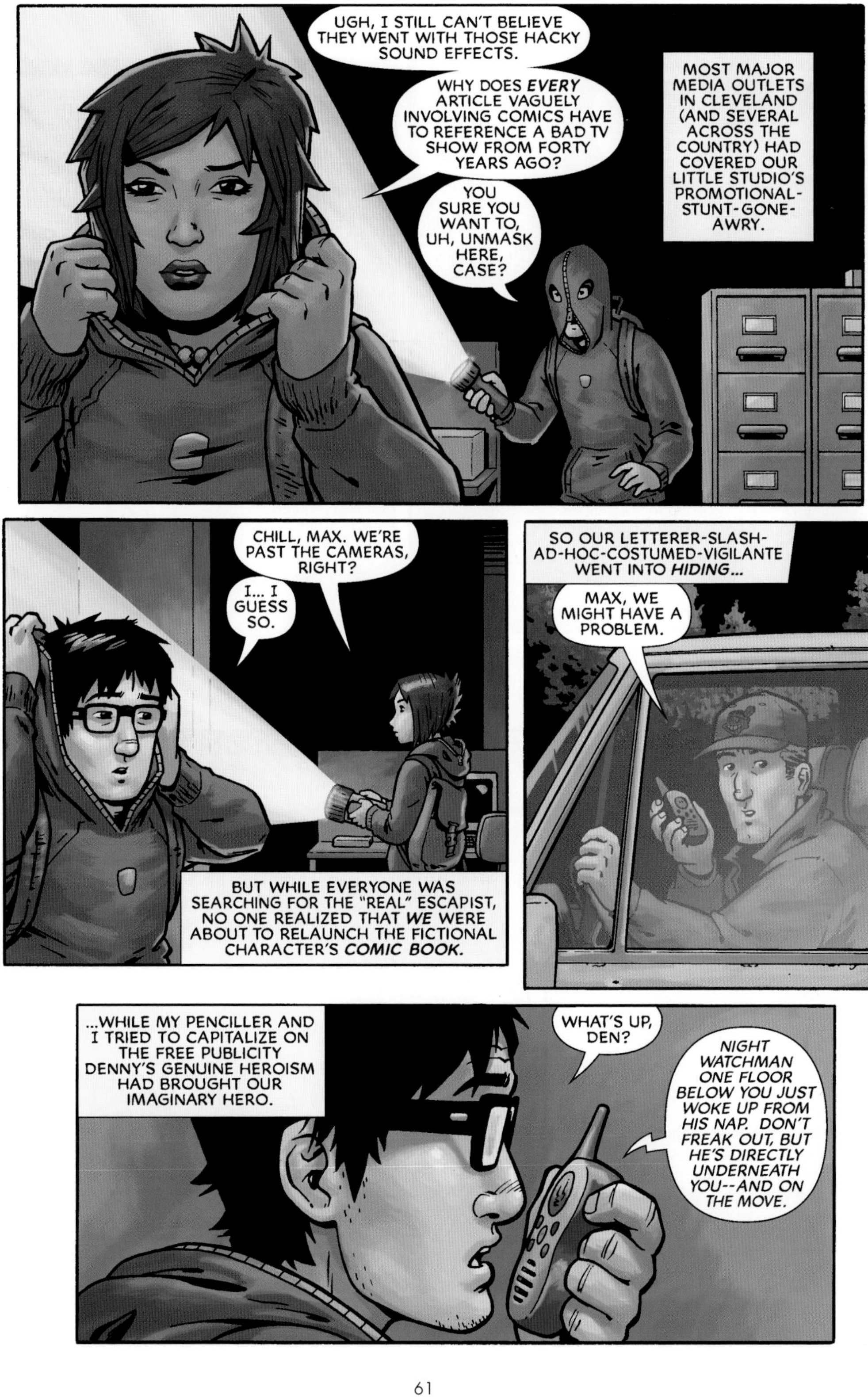
UGH, I STILL CAN'T BELIEVE THEY WENT WITH THOSE HACKY SOUND EFFECTS.
WHY DOES *EVERY* ARTICLE VAGUELY INVOLVING COMICS HAVE TO REFERENCE A BAD TV SHOW FROM FORTY YEARS AGO?
MOST MAJOR MEDIA OUTLETS IN CLEVELAND (AND SEVERAL ACROSS THE COUNTRY) HAD COVERED OUR LITTLE STUDIO'S PROMOTIONAL-STUNT-GONE-AWRY.
YOU SURE YOU WANT TO, UH, UNMASK HERE, CASE?
CHILL, MAX. WE'RE PAST THE CAMERAS, RIGHT?
I... I GUESS SO.
BUT WHILE EVERYONE WAS SEARCHING FOR THE "REAL" ESCAPIST, NO ONE REALIZED THAT *WE* WERE ABOUT TO RELAUNCH THE FICTIONAL CHARACTER'S *COMIC BOOK.*
SO OUR LETTERER-SLASH-AD-HOC-COSTUMED-VIGILANTE WENT INTO *HIDING...*
MAX, WE MIGHT HAVE A PROBLEM.
...WHILE MY PENCILLER AND I TRIED TO CAPITALIZE ON THE FREE PUBLICITY DENNY'S GENUINE HEROISM HAD BROUGHT OUR IMAGINARY HERO.
WHAT'S UP, DEN?
NIGHT WATCHMAN ONE FLOOR BELOW YOU JUST WOKE UP FROM HIS NAP. DON'T FREAK OUT, BUT HE'S DIRECTLY UNDERNEATH YOU--AND ON THE MOVE.

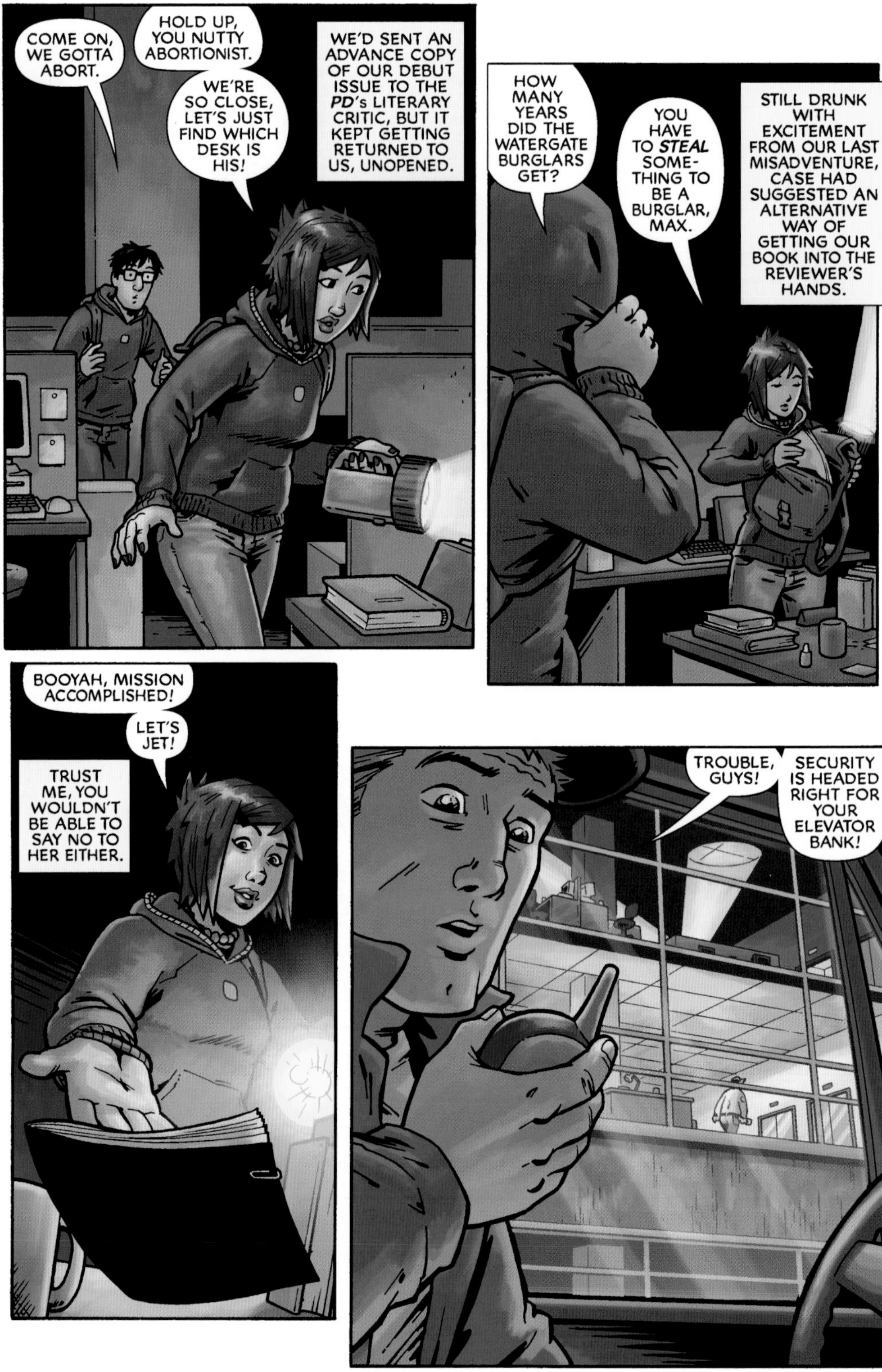
COME ON, WE GOTTA ABORT.
HOLD UP, YOU NUTTY ABORTIONIST.
WE'RE SO CLOSE, LET'S JUST FIND WHICH DESK IS HIS!
WE'D SENT AN ADVANCE COPY OF OUR DEBUT ISSUE TO THE PD's LITERARY CRITIC, BUT IT KEPT GETTING RETURNED TO US, UNOPENED.
HOW MANY YEARS DID THE WATERGATE BURGLARS GET?
YOU HAVE TO STEAL SOME-THING TO BE A BURGLAR, MAX.
STILL DRUNK WITH EXCITEMENT FROM OUR LAST MISADVENTURE, CASE HAD SUGGESTED AN ALTERNATIVE WAY OF GETTING OUR BOOK INTO THE REVIEWER'S HANDS.
BOOYAH, MISSION ACCOMPLISHED!
LET'S JET!
TRUST ME, YOU WOULDN'T BE ABLE TO SAY NO TO HER EITHER.
TROUBLE, GUYS!
SECURITY IS HEADED RIGHT FOR YOUR ELEVATOR BANK!

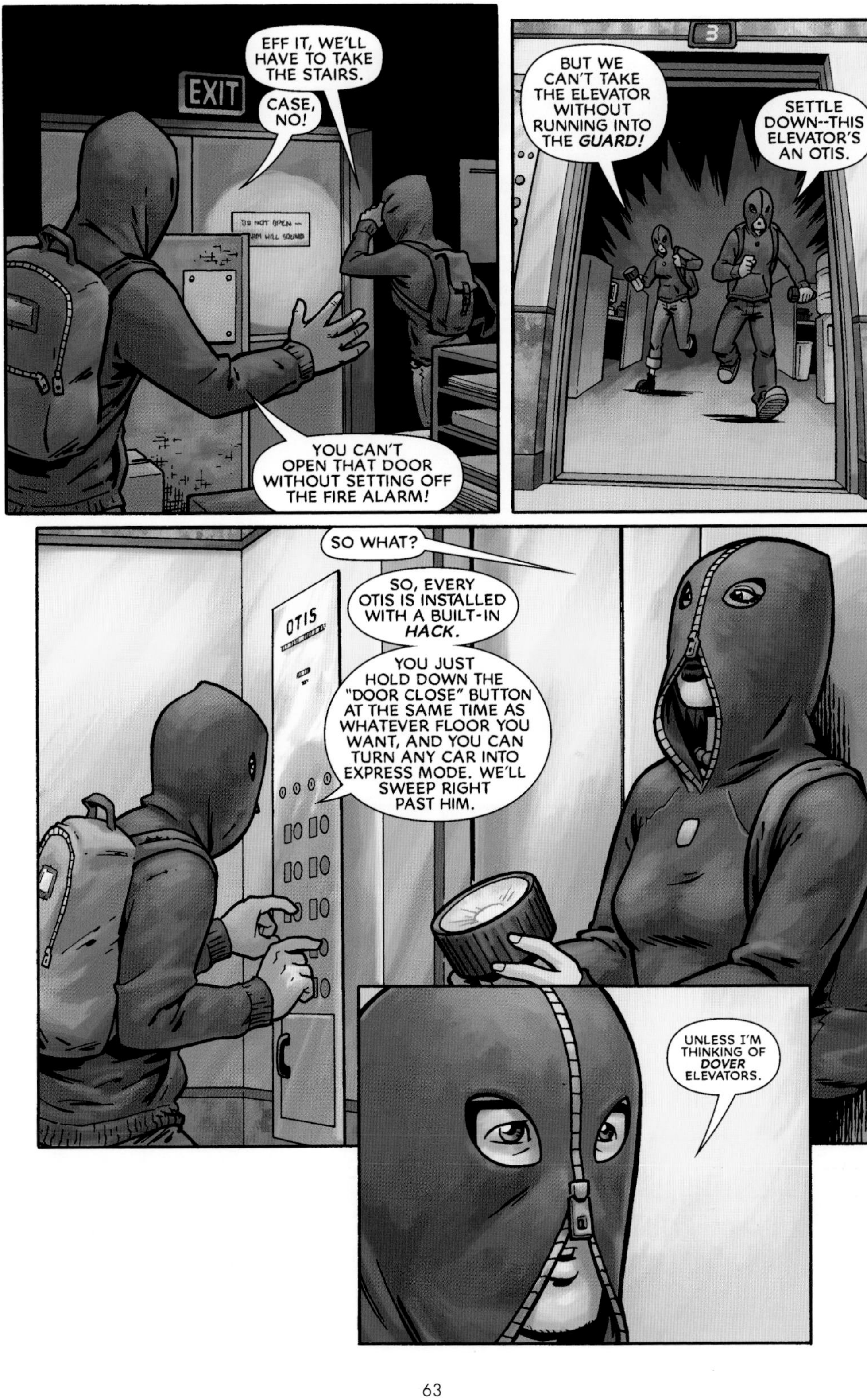
EFF IT, WE'LL HAVE TO TAKE THE STAIRS.
EXIT
CASE, NO!
YOU CAN'T OPEN THAT DOOR WITHOUT SETTING OFF THE FIRE ALARM!
3
BUT WE CAN'T TAKE THE ELEVATOR WITHOUT RUNNING INTO THE *GUARD!*
SETTLE DOWN--THIS ELEVATOR'S AN OTIS.
SO WHAT?
SO, EVERY OTIS IS INSTALLED WITH A BUILT-IN *HACK.*
YOU JUST HOLD DOWN THE "DOOR CLOSE" BUTTON AT THE SAME TIME AS WHATEVER FLOOR YOU WANT, AND YOU CAN TURN ANY CAR INTO EXPRESS MODE. WE'LL SWEEP RIGHT PAST HIM.
OTIS
UNLESS I'M THINKING OF *DOVER* ELEVATORS.

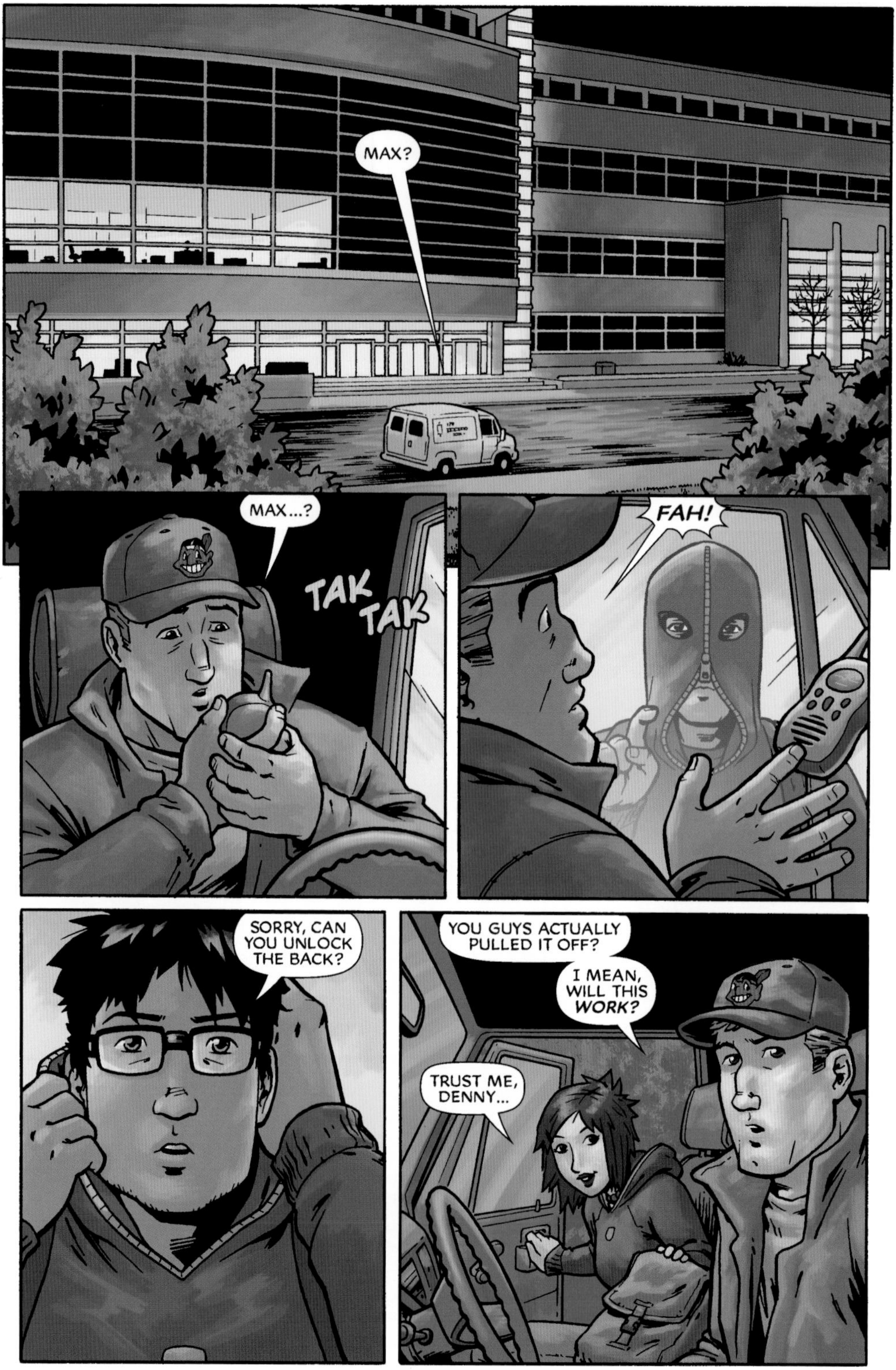
MAX?
MAX...?
TAK TAK
FAH!
SORRY, CAN YOU UNLOCK THE BACK?
YOU GUYS ACTUALLY PULLED IT OFF?
I MEAN, WILL THIS *WORK?*
TRUST ME, DENNY...

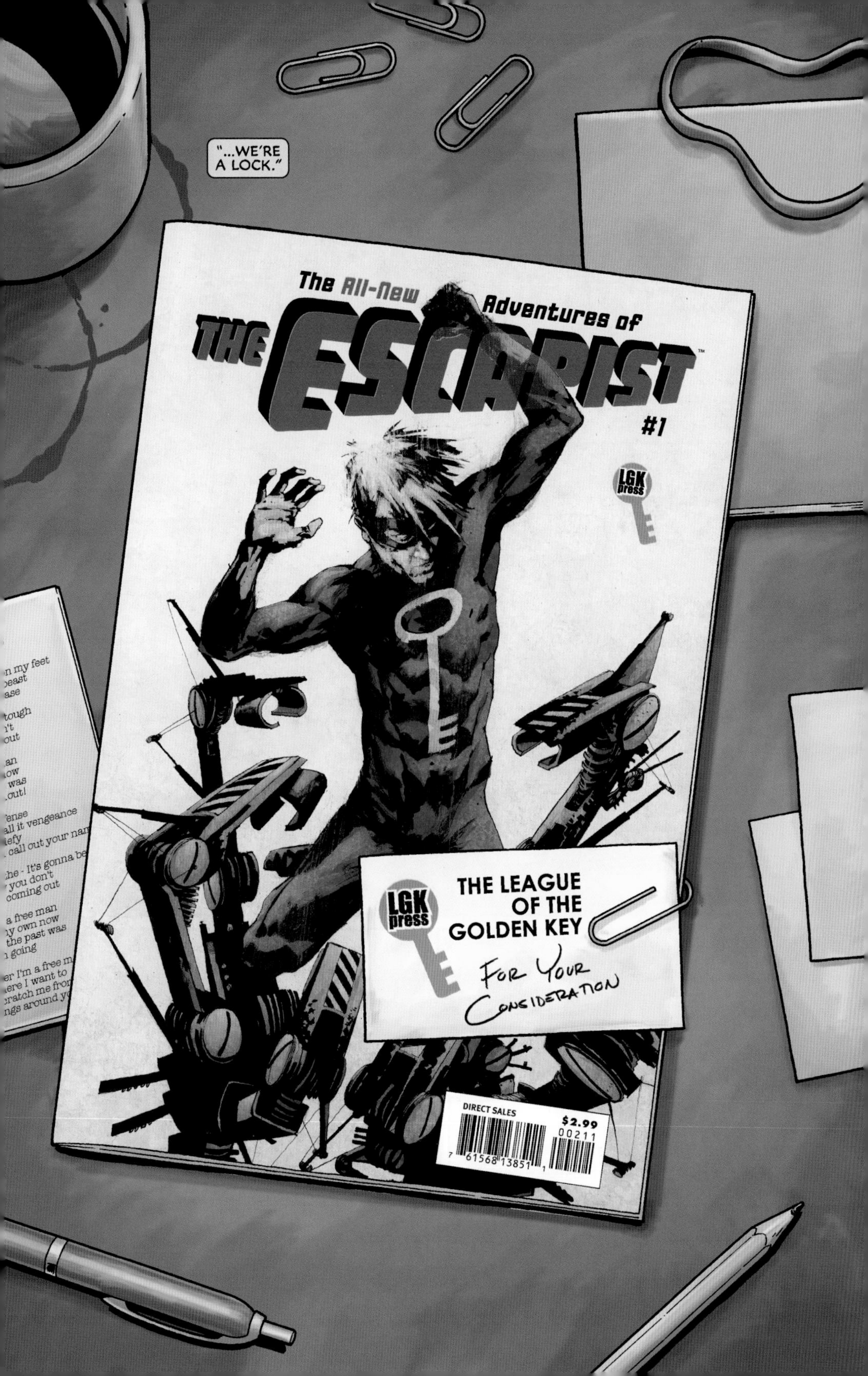
"...WE'RE A LOCK."
The All-New Adventures of THE ESCAPIST™
#1
LGK press
THE LEAGUE OF THE GOLDEN KEY
For Your Consideration
DIRECT SALES
$2.99

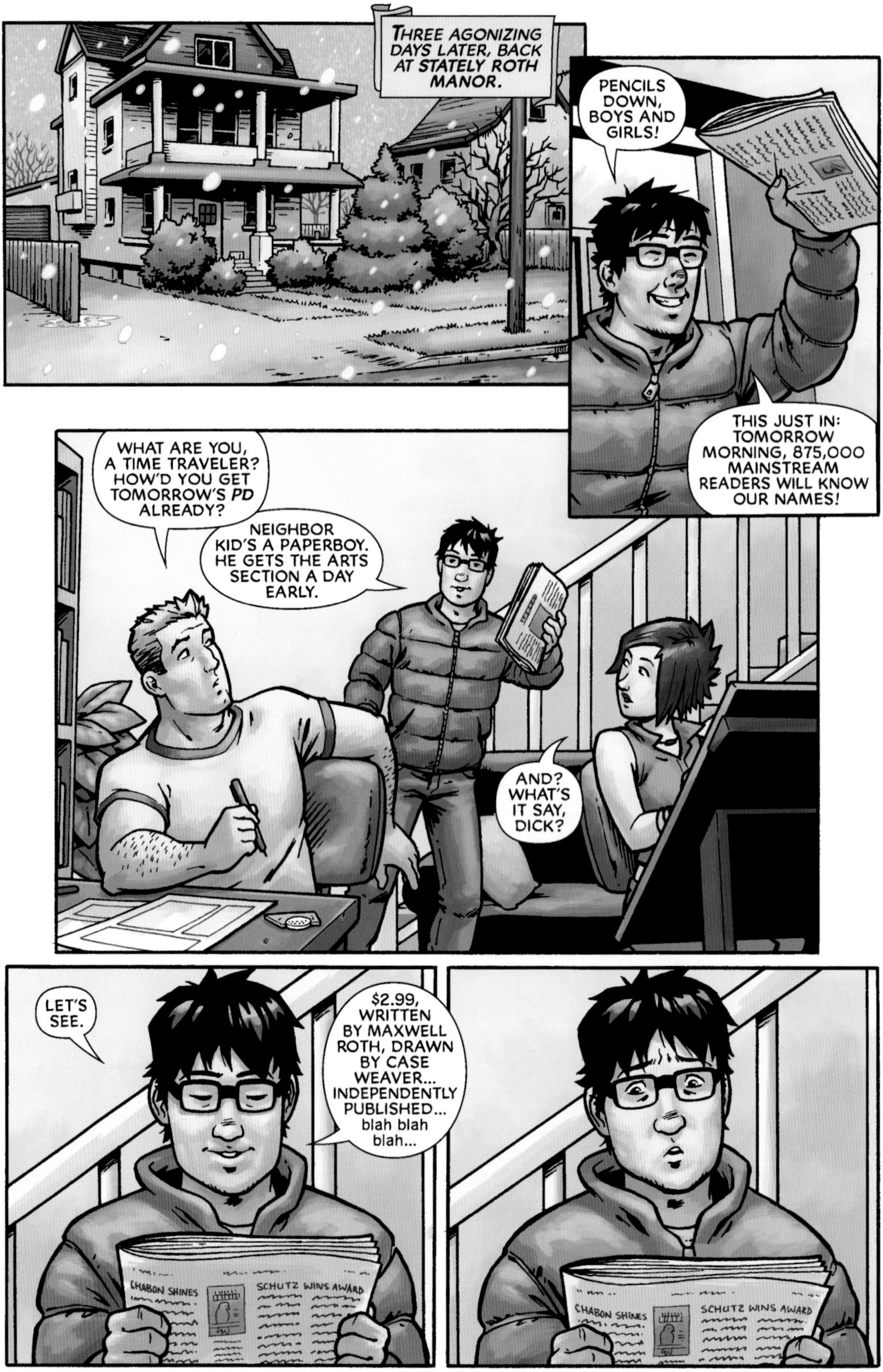
THREE AGONIZING DAYS LATER, BACK AT STATELY ROTH MANOR.
PENCILS DOWN, BOYS AND GIRLS!
THIS JUST IN: TOMORROW MORNING, 875,000 MAINSTREAM READERS WILL KNOW OUR NAMES!
WHAT ARE YOU, A TIME TRAVELER? HOW'D YOU GET TOMORROW'S *PD* ALREADY?
NEIGHBOR KID'S A PAPERBOY. HE GETS THE ARTS SECTION A DAY EARLY.
AND? WHAT'S IT SAY, DICK?
LET'S SEE.
$2.99, WRITTEN BY MAXWELL ROTH, DRAWN BY CASE WEAVER... INDEPENDENTLY PUBLISHED... blah blah blah...
CHABON SHINES
SCHUTZ WINS AWARD
CHABON SHINES
SCHUTZ WINS AWARD

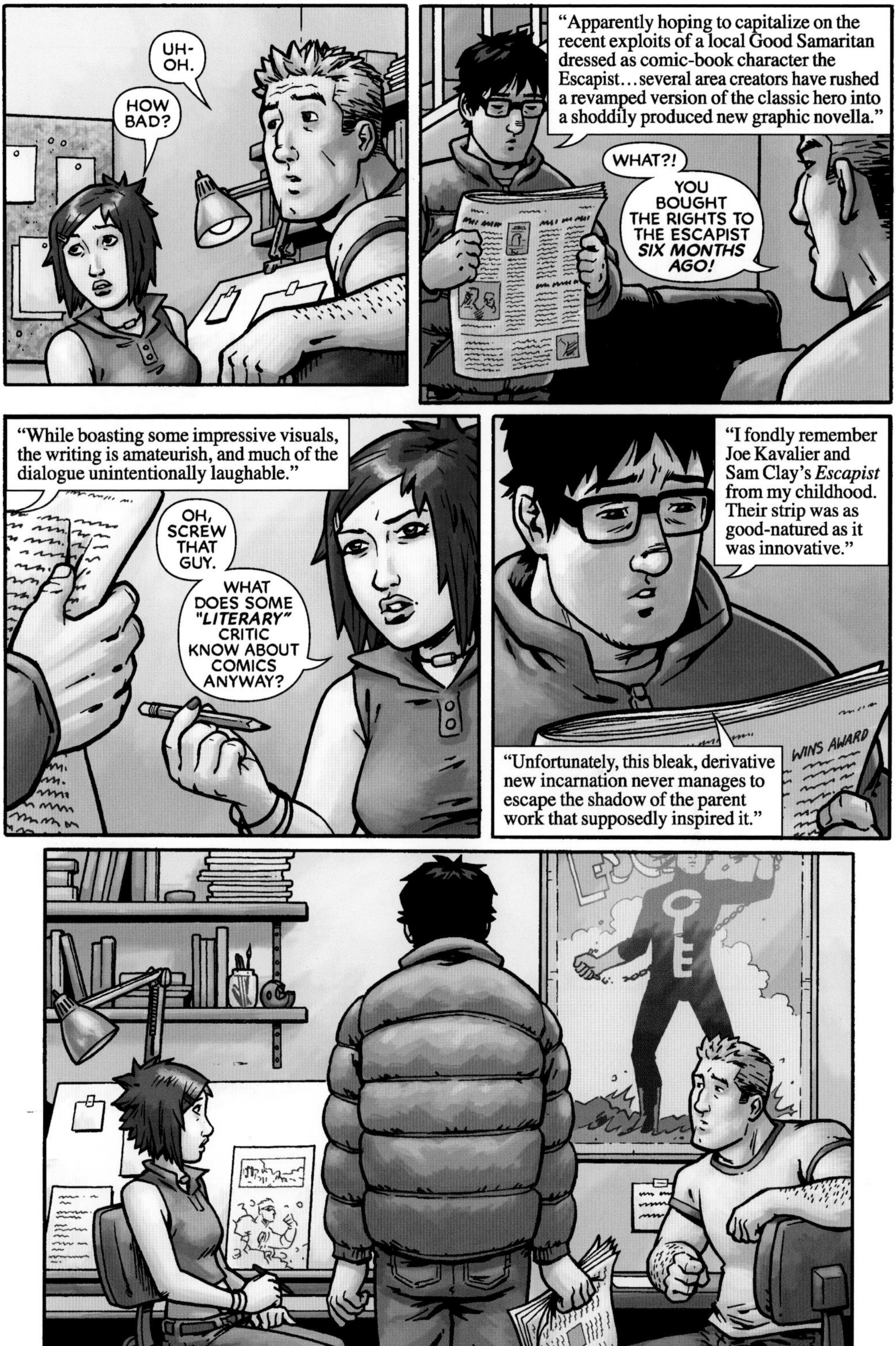
UH-OH.
HOW BAD?
"Apparently hoping to capitalize on the recent exploits of a local Good Samaritan dressed as comic-book character the Escapist... several area creators have rushed a revamped version of the classic hero into a shoddily produced new graphic novella."
WHAT?!
YOU BOUGHT THE RIGHTS TO THE ESCAPIST *SIX MONTHS AGO!*
"While boasting some impressive visuals, the writing is amateurish, and much of the dialogue unintentionally laughable."
OH, SCREW THAT GUY.
WHAT DOES SOME *"LITERARY"* CRITIC KNOW ABOUT COMICS ANYWAY?
"I fondly remember Joe Kavalier and Sam Clay's *Escapist* from my childhood. Their strip was as good-natured as it was innovative."
"Unfortunately, this bleak, derivative new incarnation never manages to escape the shadow of the parent work that supposedly inspired it."
WINS AWARD

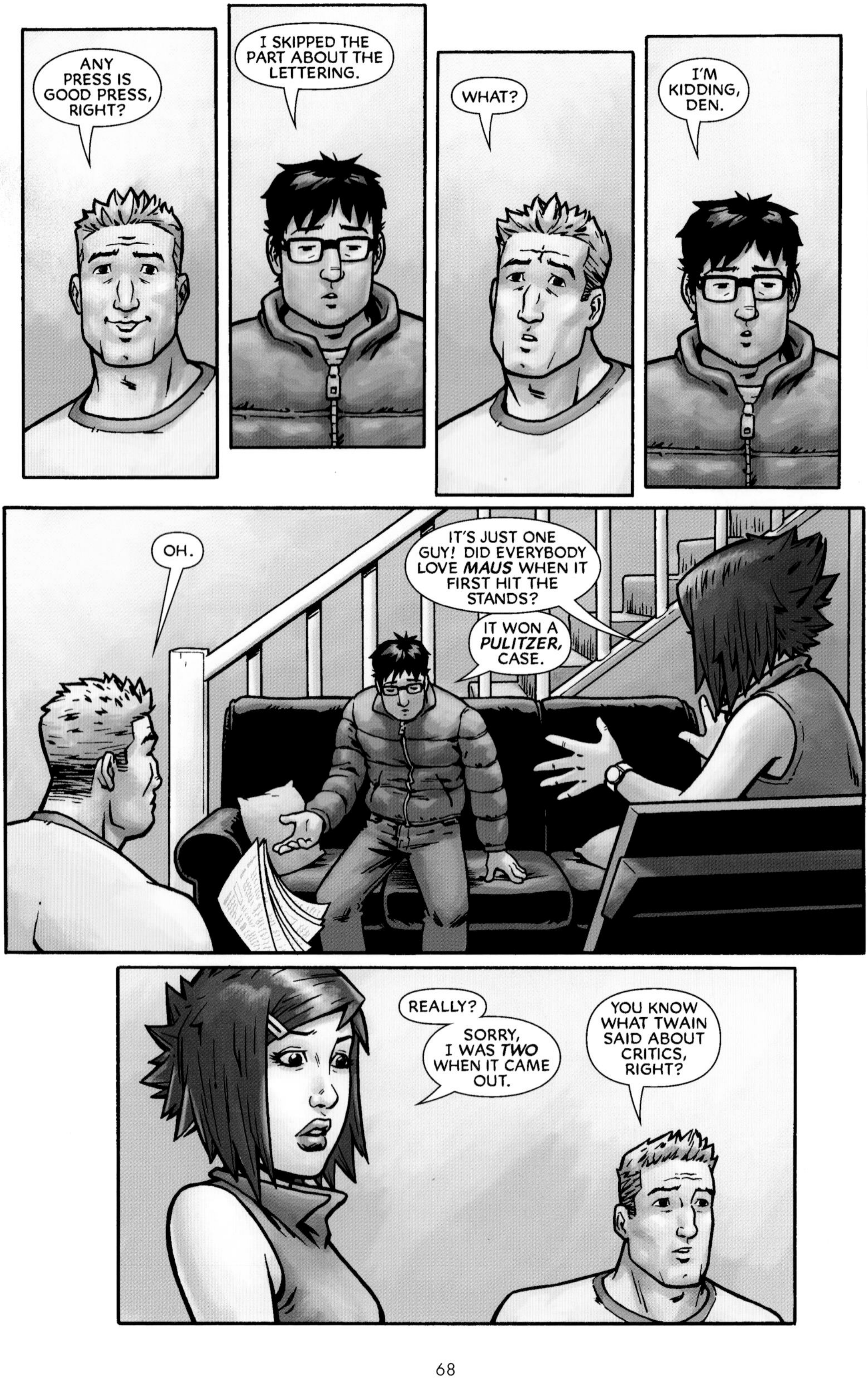
ANY PRESS IS GOOD PRESS, RIGHT?
I SKIPPED THE PART ABOUT THE LETTERING.
WHAT?
I'M KIDDING, DEN.
OH.
IT'S JUST ONE GUY! DID EVERYBODY LOVE MAUS WHEN IT FIRST HIT THE STANDS?
IT WON A PULITZER, CASE.
REALLY?
SORRY, I WAS TWO WHEN IT CAME OUT.
YOU KNOW WHAT TWAIN SAID ABOUT CRITICS, RIGHT?

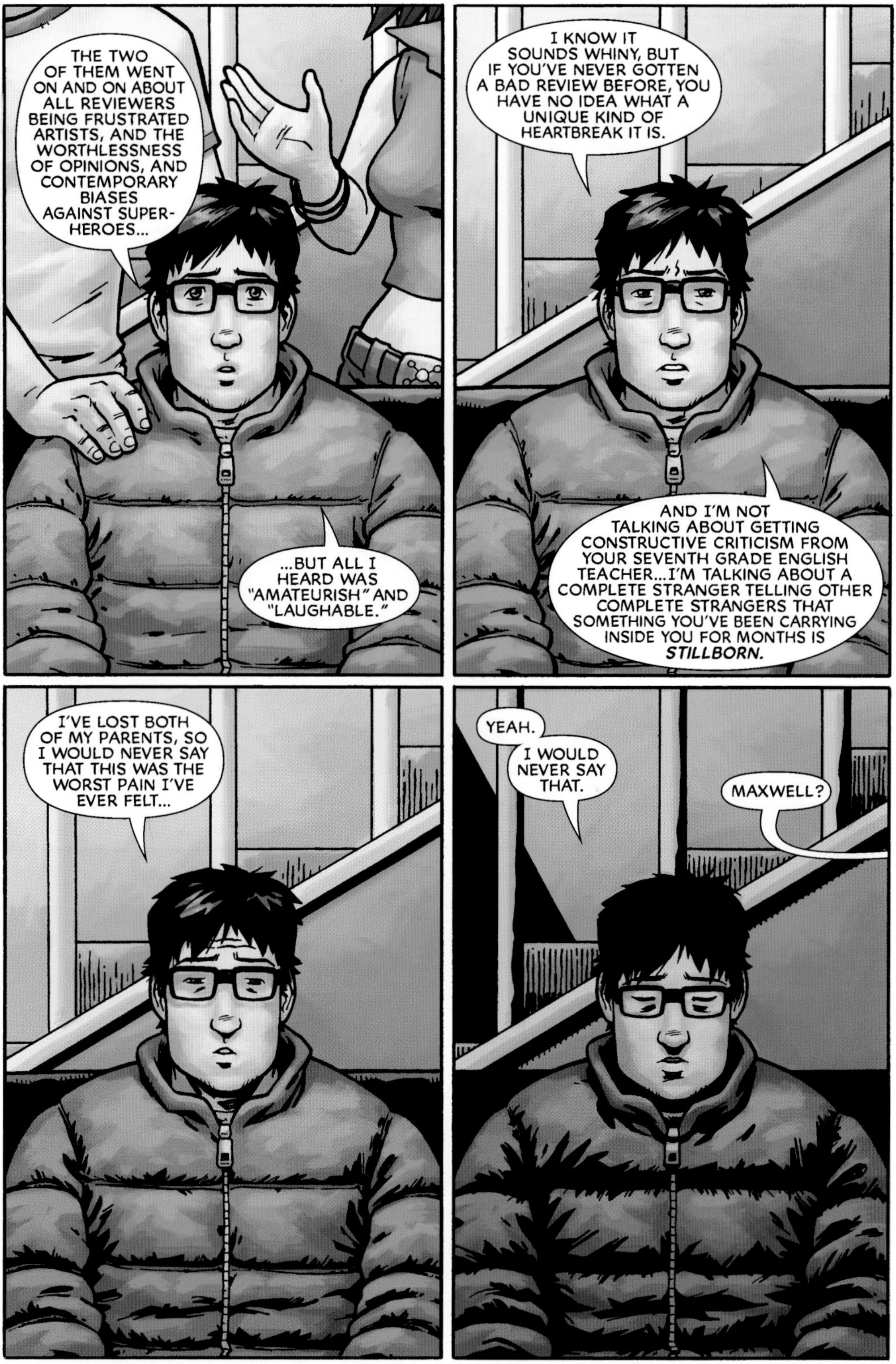
THE TWO OF THEM WENT ON AND ON ABOUT ALL REVIEWERS BEING FRUSTRATED ARTISTS, AND THE WORTHLESSNESS OF OPINIONS, AND CONTEMPORARY BIASES AGAINST SUPER-HEROES...
...BUT ALL I HEARD WAS "AMATEURISH" AND "LAUGHABLE."
I KNOW IT SOUNDS WHINY, BUT IF YOU'VE NEVER GOTTEN A BAD REVIEW BEFORE, YOU HAVE NO IDEA WHAT A UNIQUE KIND OF HEARTBREAK IT IS.
AND I'M NOT TALKING ABOUT GETTING CONSTRUCTIVE CRITICISM FROM YOUR SEVENTH GRADE ENGLISH TEACHER...I'M TALKING ABOUT A COMPLETE STRANGER TELLING OTHER COMPLETE STRANGERS THAT SOMETHING YOU'VE BEEN CARRYING INSIDE YOU FOR MONTHS IS ***STILLBORN.***
I'VE LOST BOTH OF MY PARENTS, SO I WOULD NEVER SAY THAT THIS WAS THE WORST PAIN I'VE EVER FELT...
YEAH.
I WOULD NEVER SAY THAT.
MAXWELL?

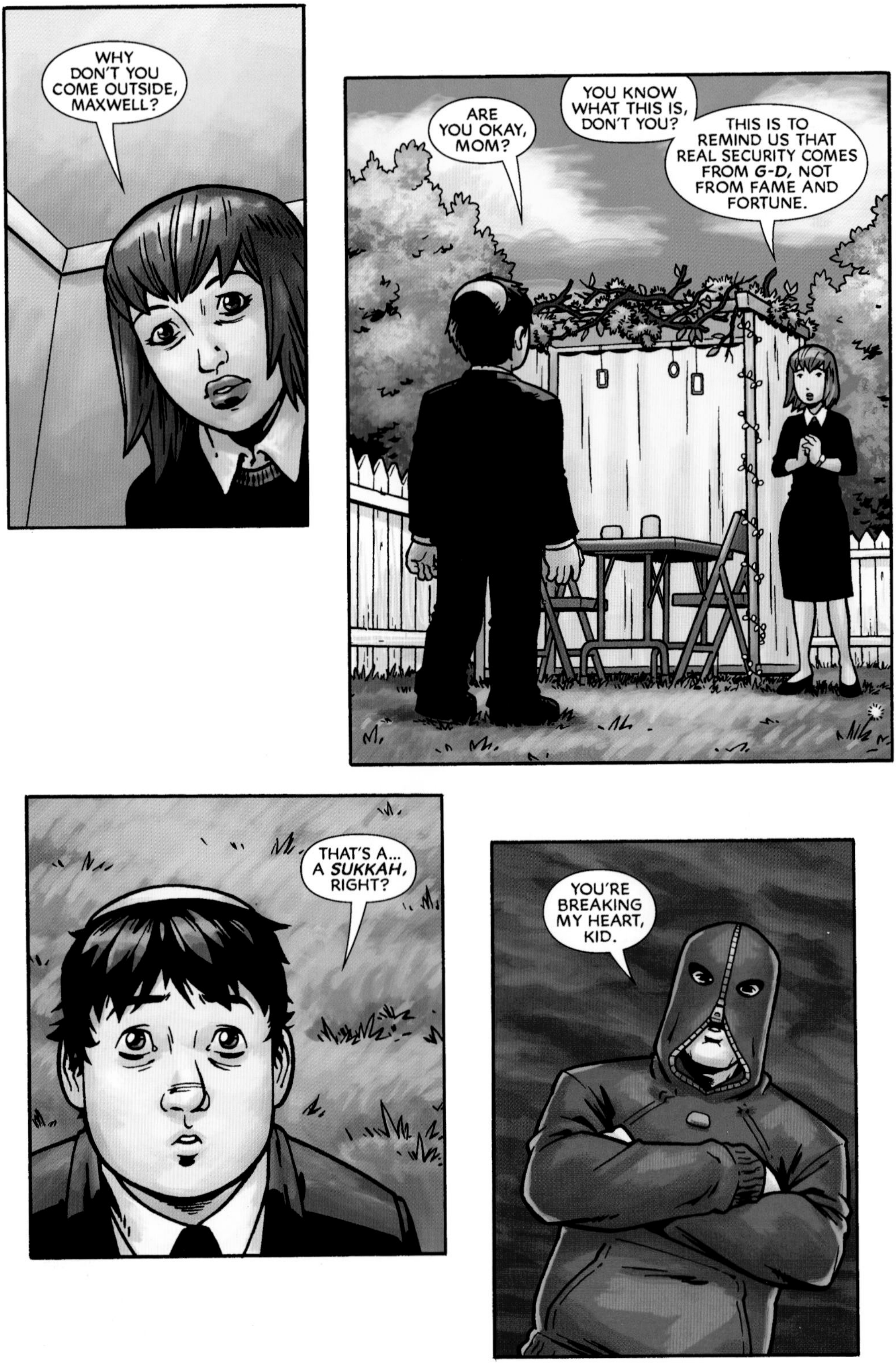
WHY DON'T YOU COME OUTSIDE, MAXWELL?
ARE YOU OKAY, MOM?
YOU KNOW WHAT THIS IS, DON'T YOU?
THIS IS TO REMIND US THAT REAL SECURITY COMES FROM *G-D,* NOT FROM FAME AND FORTUNE.
THAT'S A... A *SUKKAH,* RIGHT?
YOU'RE BREAKING MY HEART, KID.

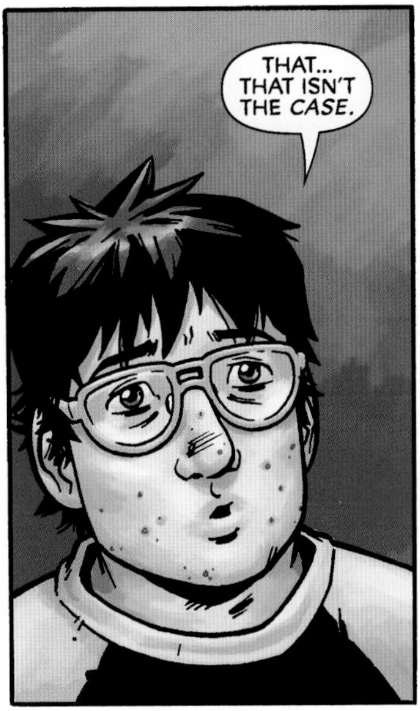
THAT... THAT ISN'T THE *CASE.*

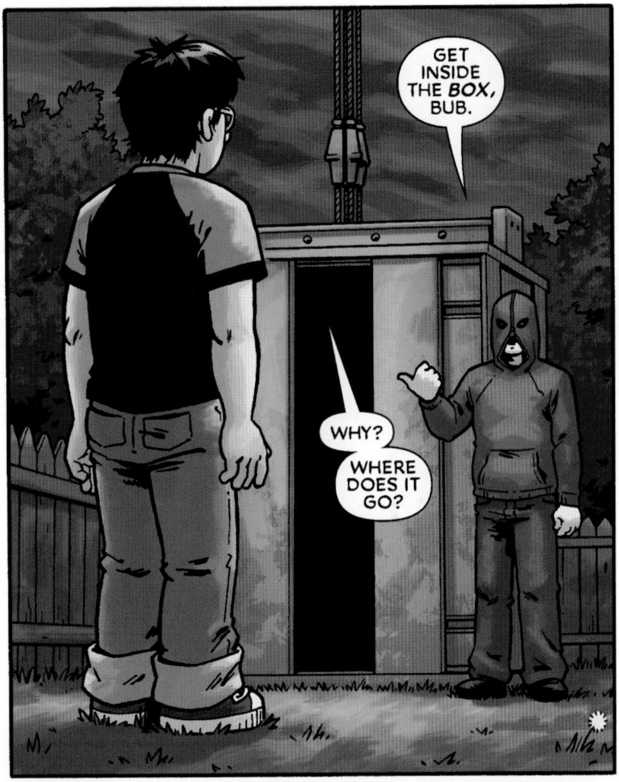
GET INSIDE THE *BOX,* BUB.
WHY?
WHERE DOES IT GO?

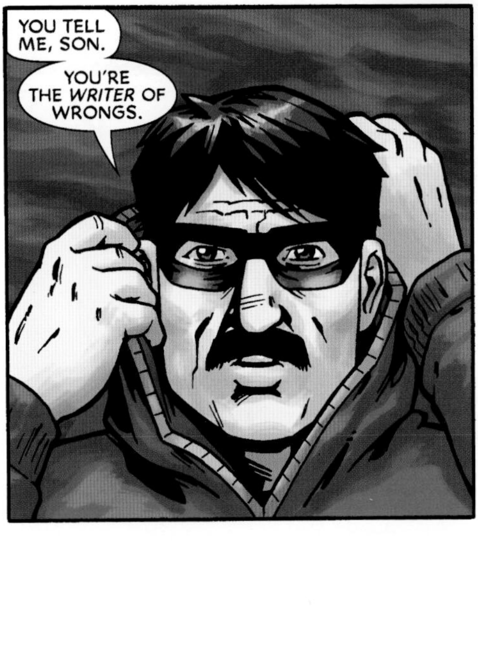
YOU TELL ME, SON.
YOU'RE THE *WRITER* OF WRONGS.

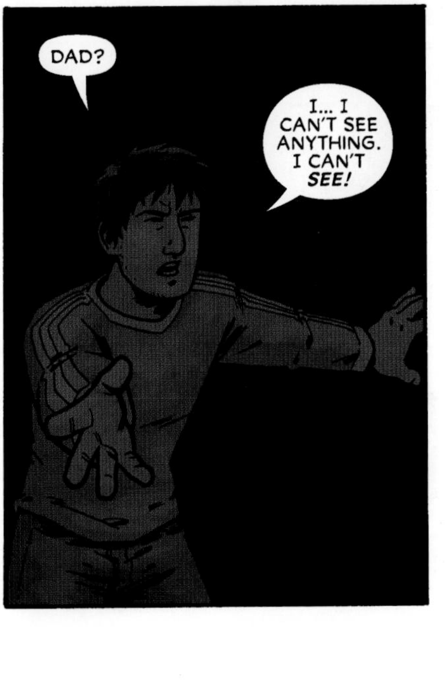
DAD?
I... I CAN'T SEE ANYTHING. I CAN'T *SEE!*

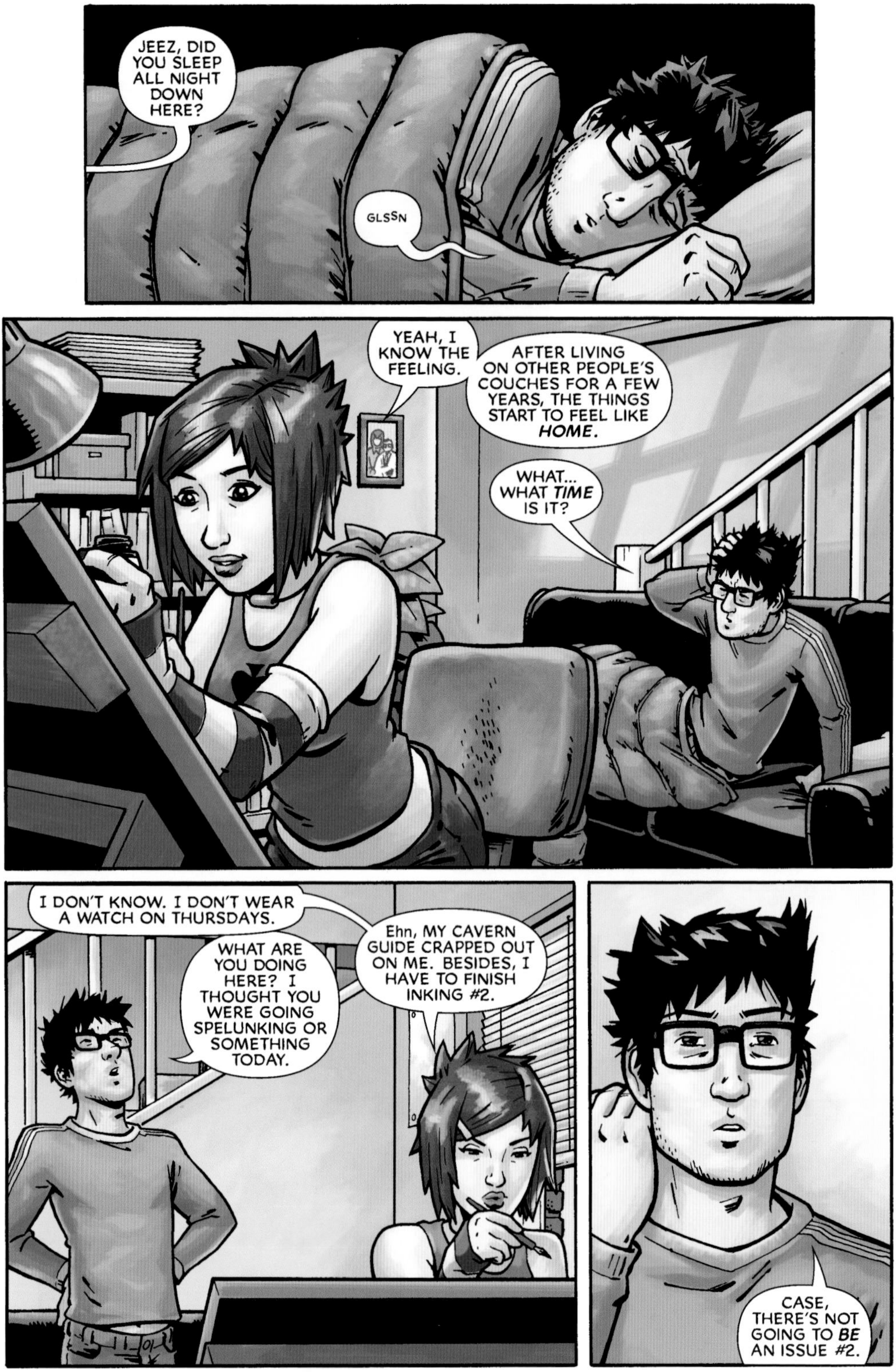
JEEZ, DID YOU SLEEP ALL NIGHT DOWN HERE?
GLSSN
YEAH, I KNOW THE FEELING.
AFTER LIVING ON OTHER PEOPLE'S COUCHES FOR A FEW YEARS, THE THINGS START TO FEEL LIKE *HOME*.
WHAT... WHAT *TIME* IS IT?
I DON'T KNOW. I DON'T WEAR A WATCH ON THURSDAYS.
WHAT ARE YOU DOING HERE? I THOUGHT YOU WERE GOING SPELUNKING OR SOMETHING TODAY.
Ehn, MY CAVERN GUIDE CRAPPED OUT ON ME. BESIDES, I HAVE TO FINISH INKING #2.
CASE, THERE'S NOT GOING TO *BE* AN ISSUE #2.

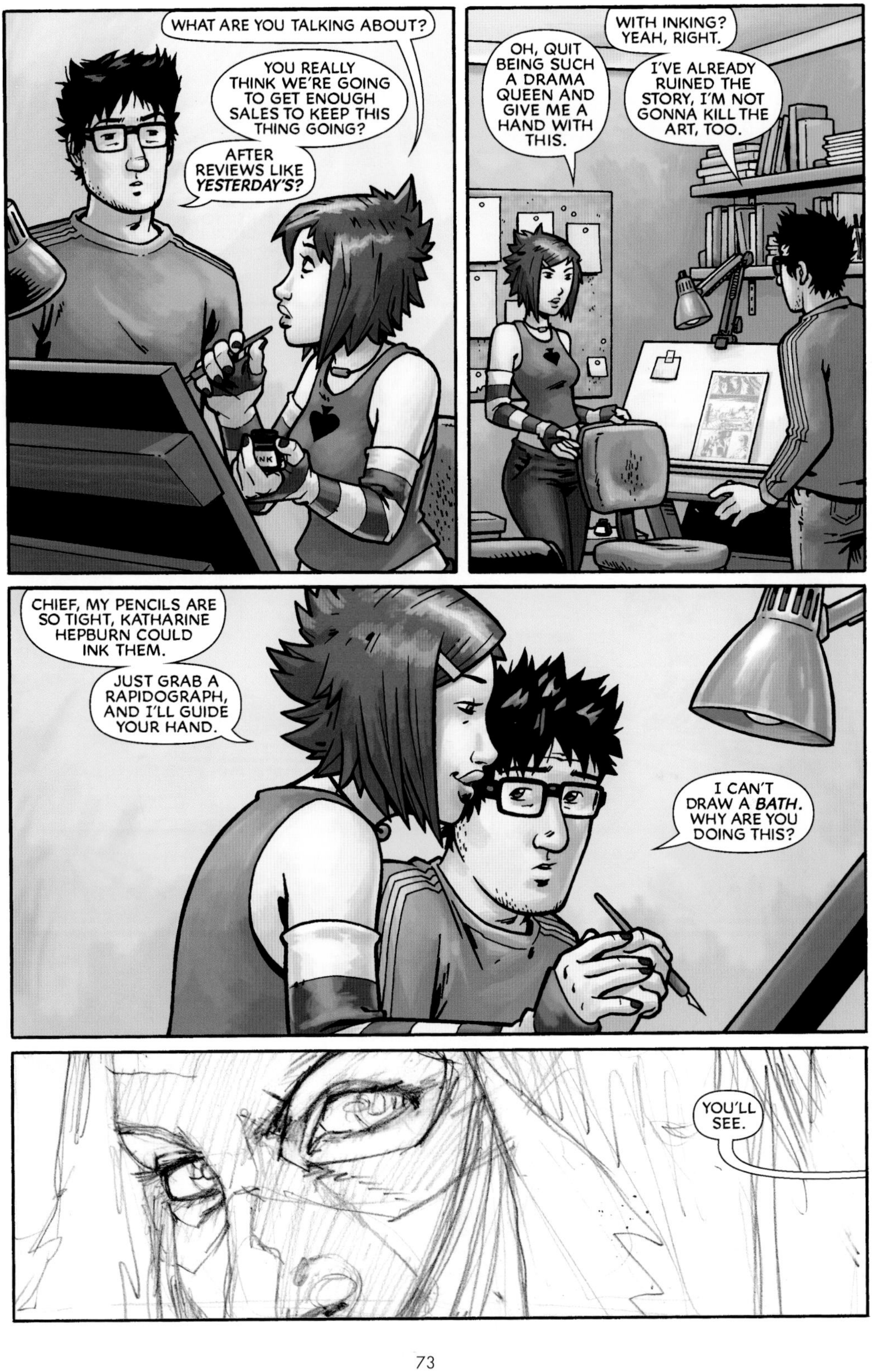

WHAT ARE YOU TALKING ABOUT?
YOU REALLY THINK WE'RE GOING TO GET ENOUGH SALES TO KEEP THIS THING GOING?
AFTER REVIEWS LIKE *YESTERDAY'S?*
INK
OH, QUIT BEING SUCH A DRAMA QUEEN AND GIVE ME A HAND WITH THIS.
WITH INKING? YEAH, RIGHT.
I'VE ALREADY RUINED THE STORY, I'M NOT GONNA KILL THE ART, TOO.
CHIEF, MY PENCILS ARE SO TIGHT, KATHARINE HEPBURN COULD INK THEM.
JUST GRAB A RAPIDOGRAPH, AND I'LL GUIDE YOUR HAND.
I CAN'T DRAW A *BATH*. WHY ARE YOU DOING THIS?
YOU'LL SEE.

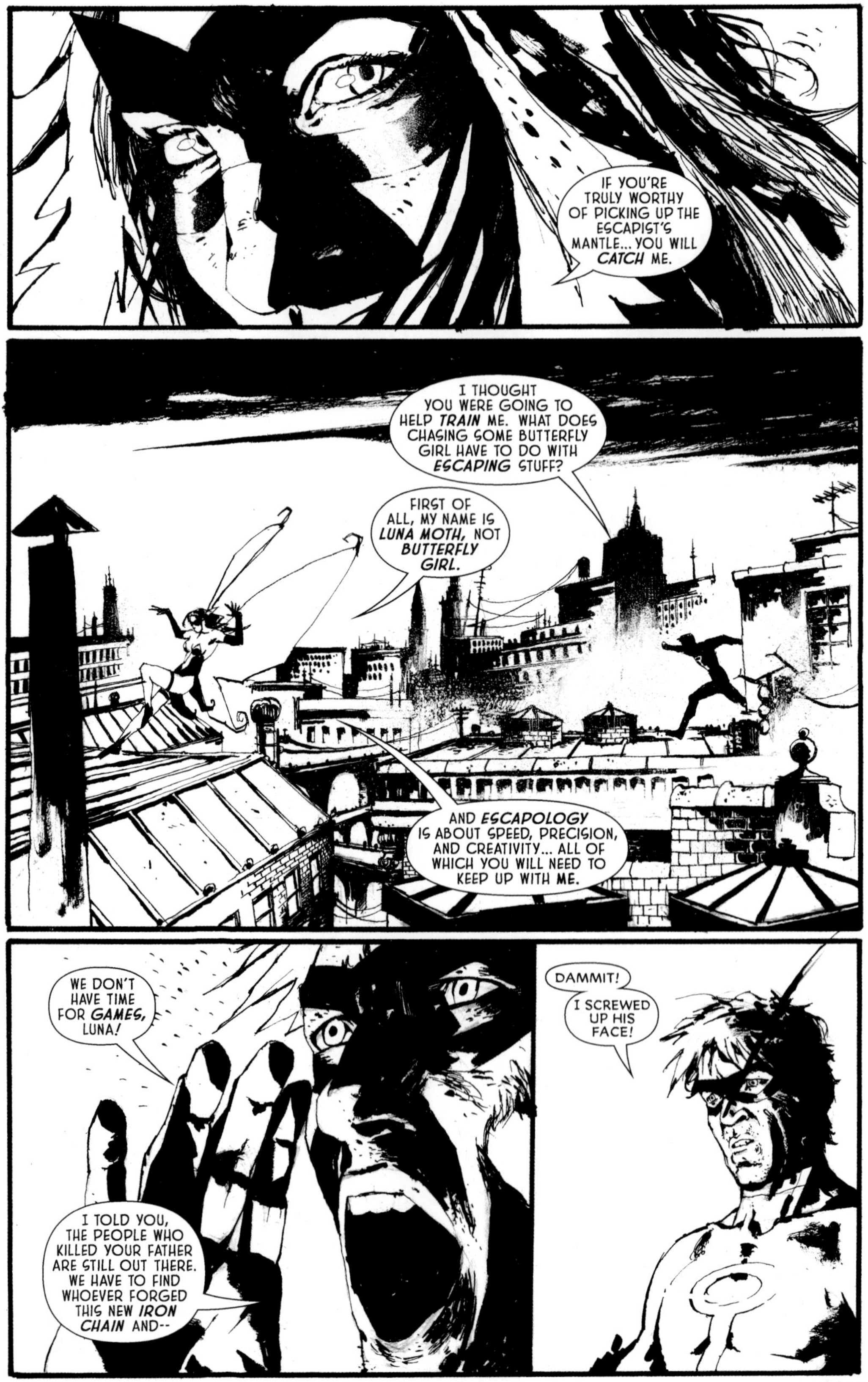

IF YOU'RE TRULY WORTHY OF PICKING UP THE ESCAPIST'S MANTLE... YOU WILL *CATCH* ME.
I THOUGHT YOU WERE GOING TO HELP *TRAIN* ME. WHAT DOES CHASING SOME BUTTERFLY GIRL HAVE TO DO WITH *ESCAPING* STUFF?
FIRST OF ALL, MY NAME IS ***LUNA MOTH,*** NOT ***BUTTERFLY GIRL.***
AND ***ESCAPOLOGY*** IS ABOUT SPEED, PRECISION, AND CREATIVITY... ALL OF WHICH YOU WILL NEED TO KEEP UP WITH **ME.**
WE DON'T HAVE TIME FOR ***GAMES,*** LUNA!
I TOLD YOU, THE PEOPLE WHO KILLED YOUR FATHER ARE STILL OUT THERE. WE HAVE TO FIND WHOEVER FORGED THIS NEW ***IRON CHAIN*** AND--
DAMMIT!
I SCREWED UP HIS FACE!

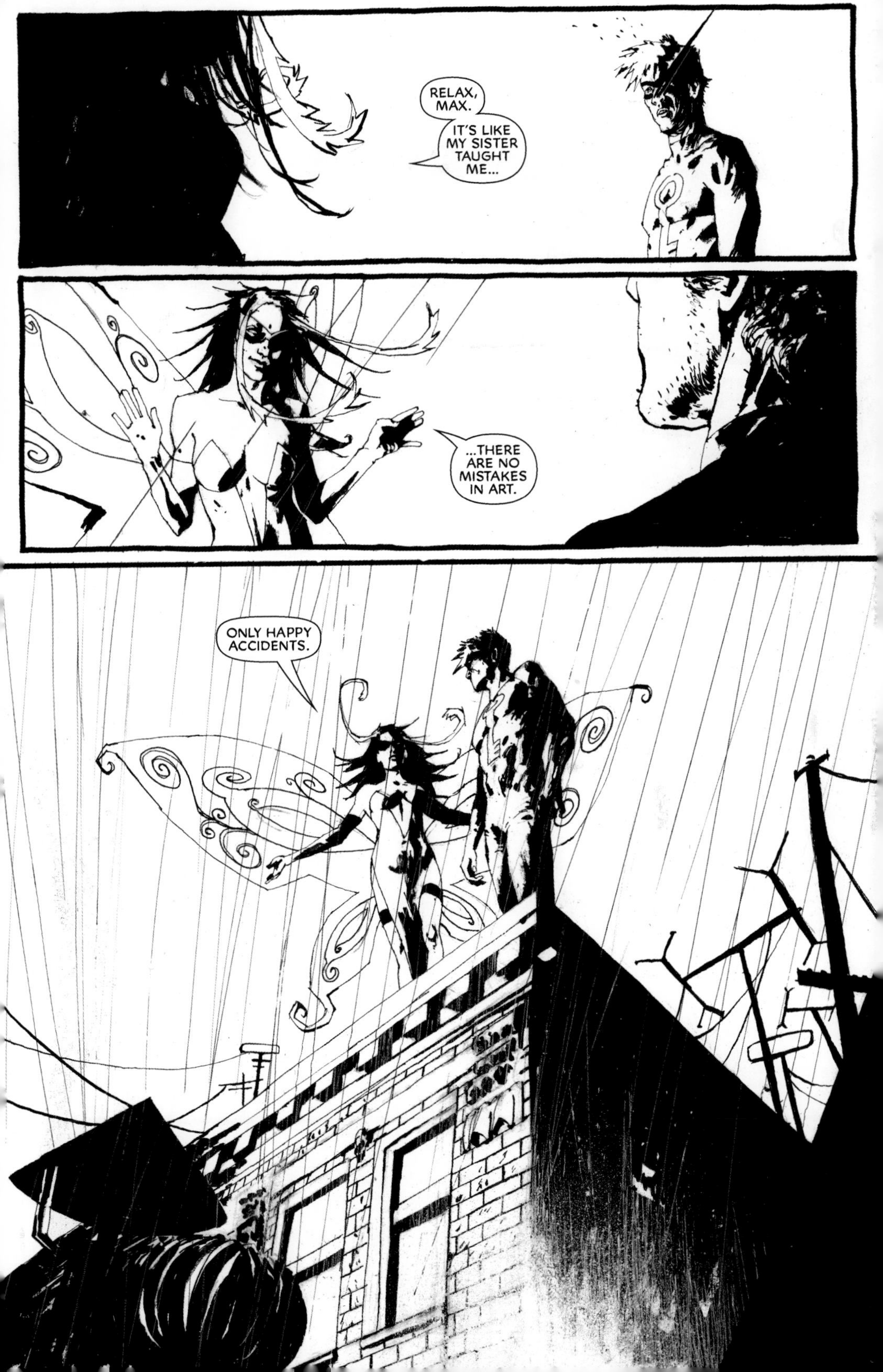
RELAX, MAX.
IT'S LIKE MY SISTER TAUGHT ME...
...THERE ARE NO MISTAKES IN ART.
ONLY HAPPY ACCIDENTS.

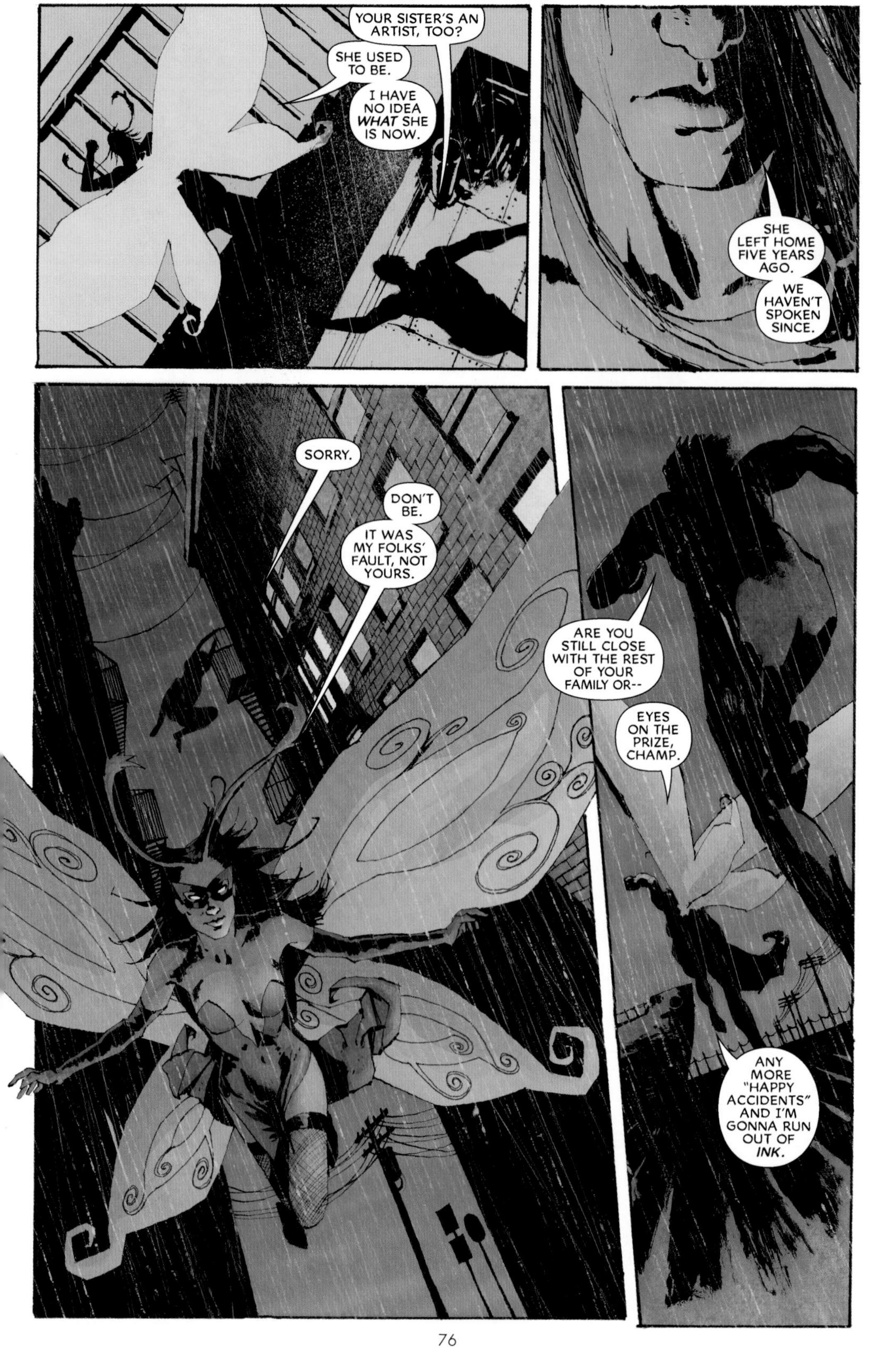
YOUR SISTER'S AN ARTIST, TOO?
SHE USED TO BE.
I HAVE NO IDEA *WHAT* SHE IS NOW.
SHE LEFT HOME FIVE YEARS AGO.
WE HAVEN'T SPOKEN SINCE.
SORRY.
DON'T BE.
IT WAS MY FOLKS' FAULT, NOT YOURS.
ARE YOU STILL CLOSE WITH THE REST OF YOUR FAMILY OR--
EYES ON THE PRIZE, CHAMP.
ANY MORE "HAPPY ACCIDENTS" AND I'M GONNA RUN OUT OF *INK*.

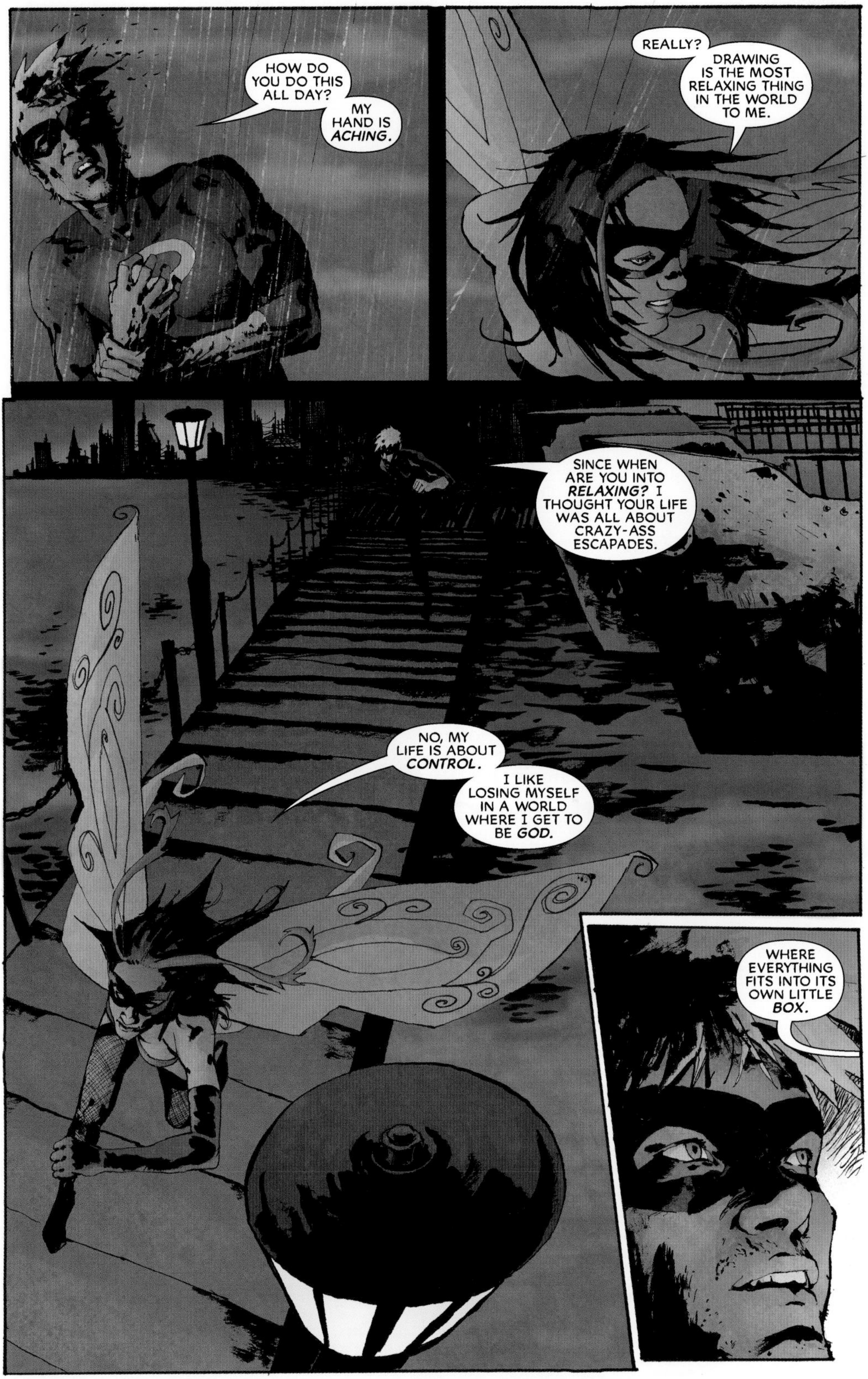
HOW DO YOU DO THIS ALL DAY?
MY HAND IS *ACHING.*
REALLY?
DRAWING IS THE MOST RELAXING THING IN THE WORLD TO ME.
SINCE WHEN ARE YOU INTO *RELAXING?* I THOUGHT YOUR LIFE WAS ALL ABOUT CRAZY-ASS ESCAPADES.
NO, MY LIFE IS ABOUT *CONTROL.*
I LIKE LOSING MYSELF IN A WORLD WHERE I GET TO BE *GOD.*
WHERE EVERYTHING FITS INTO ITS OWN LITTLE *BOX.*

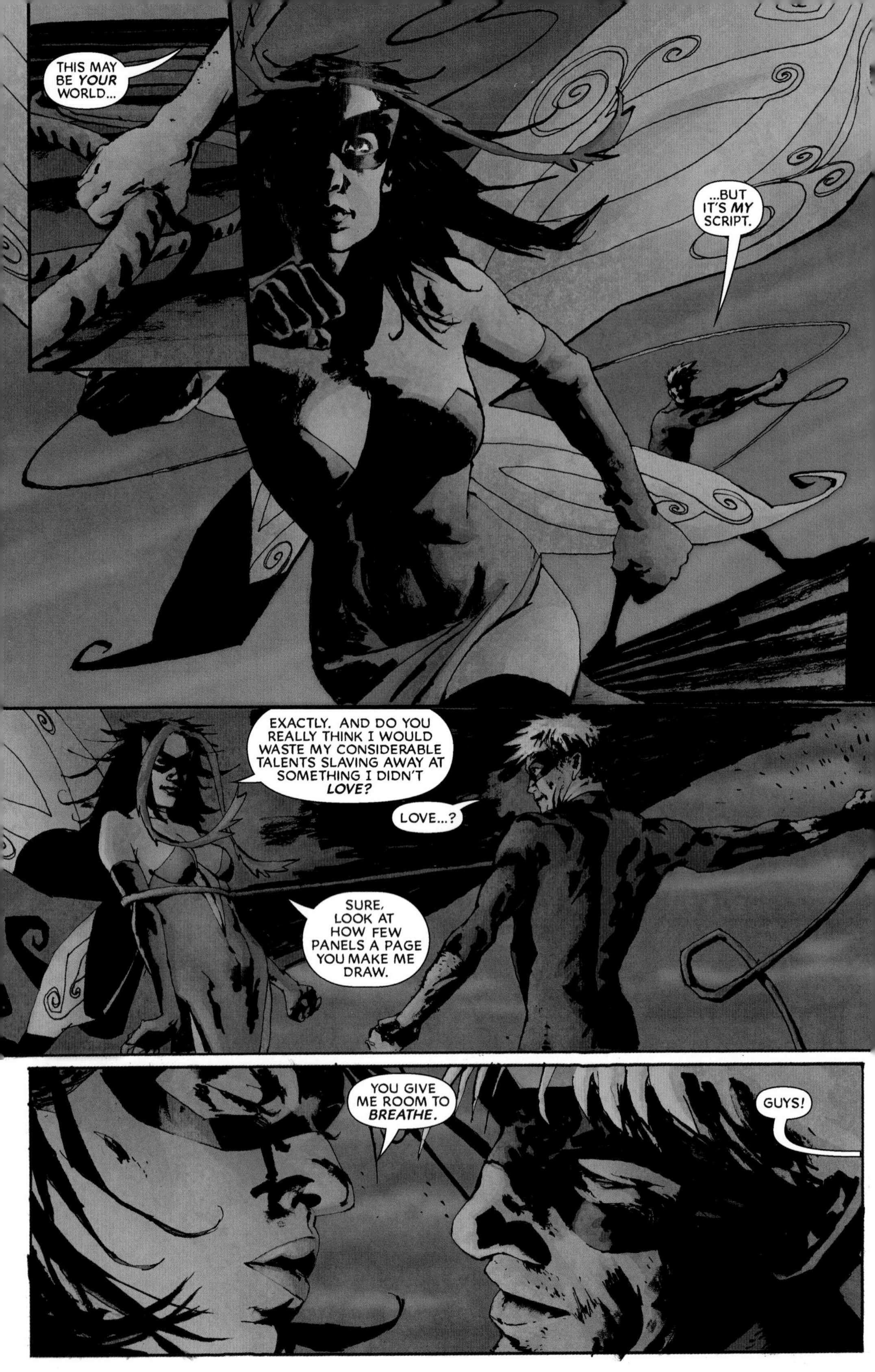
THIS MAY BE *YOUR* WORLD...
...BUT IT'S *MY* SCRIPT.
EXACTLY. AND DO YOU REALLY THINK I WOULD WASTE MY CONSIDERABLE TALENTS SLAVING AWAY AT SOMETHING I DIDN'T *LOVE?*
LOVE...?
SURE, LOOK AT HOW FEW PANELS A PAGE YOU MAKE ME DRAW.
YOU GIVE ME ROOM TO *BREATHE*.
GUYS!

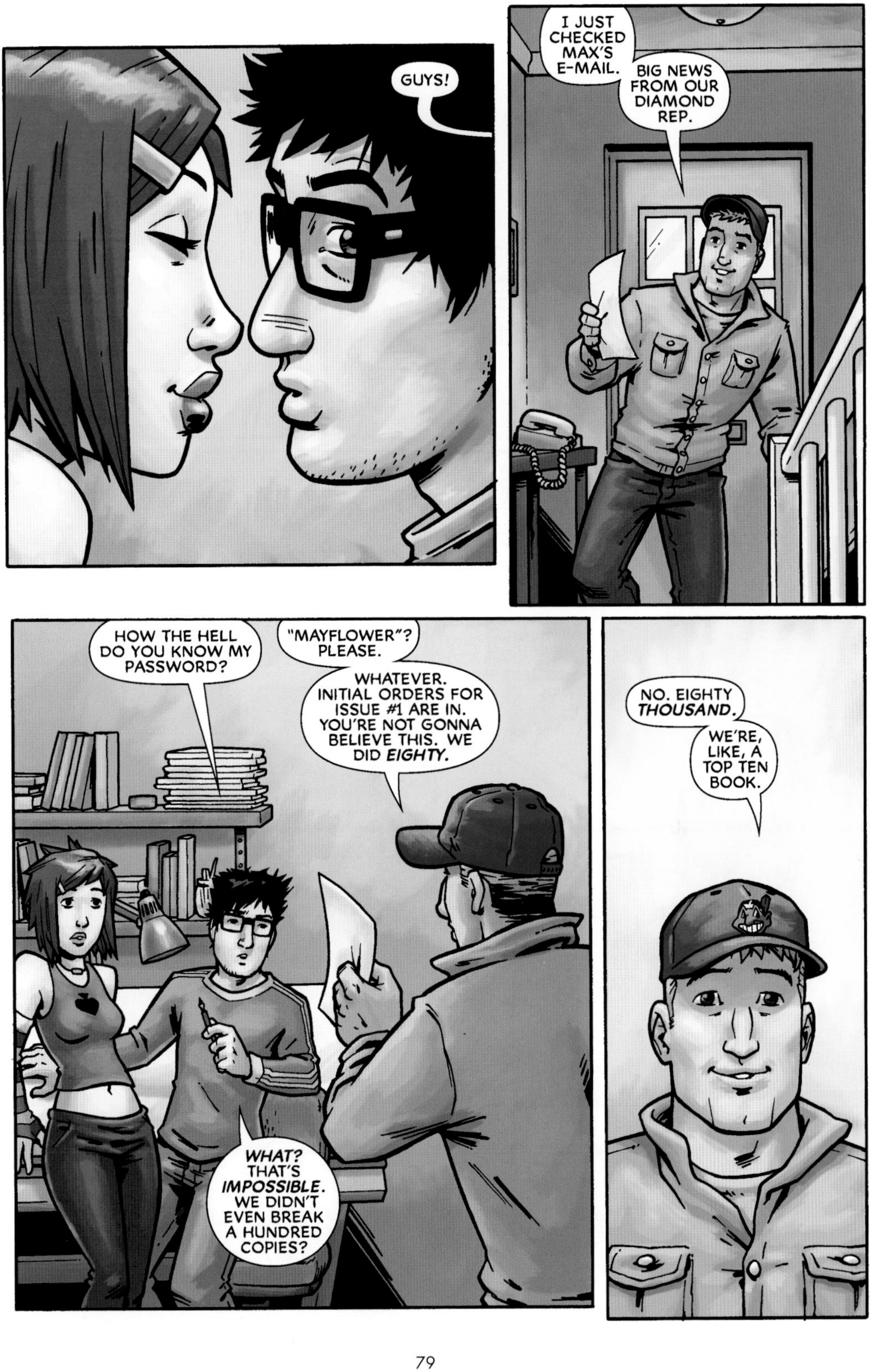

GUYS!
I JUST CHECKED MAX'S E-MAIL.
BIG NEWS FROM OUR DIAMOND REP.
HOW THE HELL DO YOU KNOW MY PASSWORD?
"MAYFLOWER"? PLEASE.
WHATEVER. INITIAL ORDERS FOR ISSUE #1 ARE IN. YOU'RE NOT GONNA BELIEVE THIS. WE DID *EIGHTY.*
WHAT? THAT'S *IMPOSSIBLE*. WE DIDN'T EVEN BREAK A HUNDRED COPIES?
NO. EIGHTY *THOUSAND.*
WE'RE, LIKE, A TOP TEN BOOK.

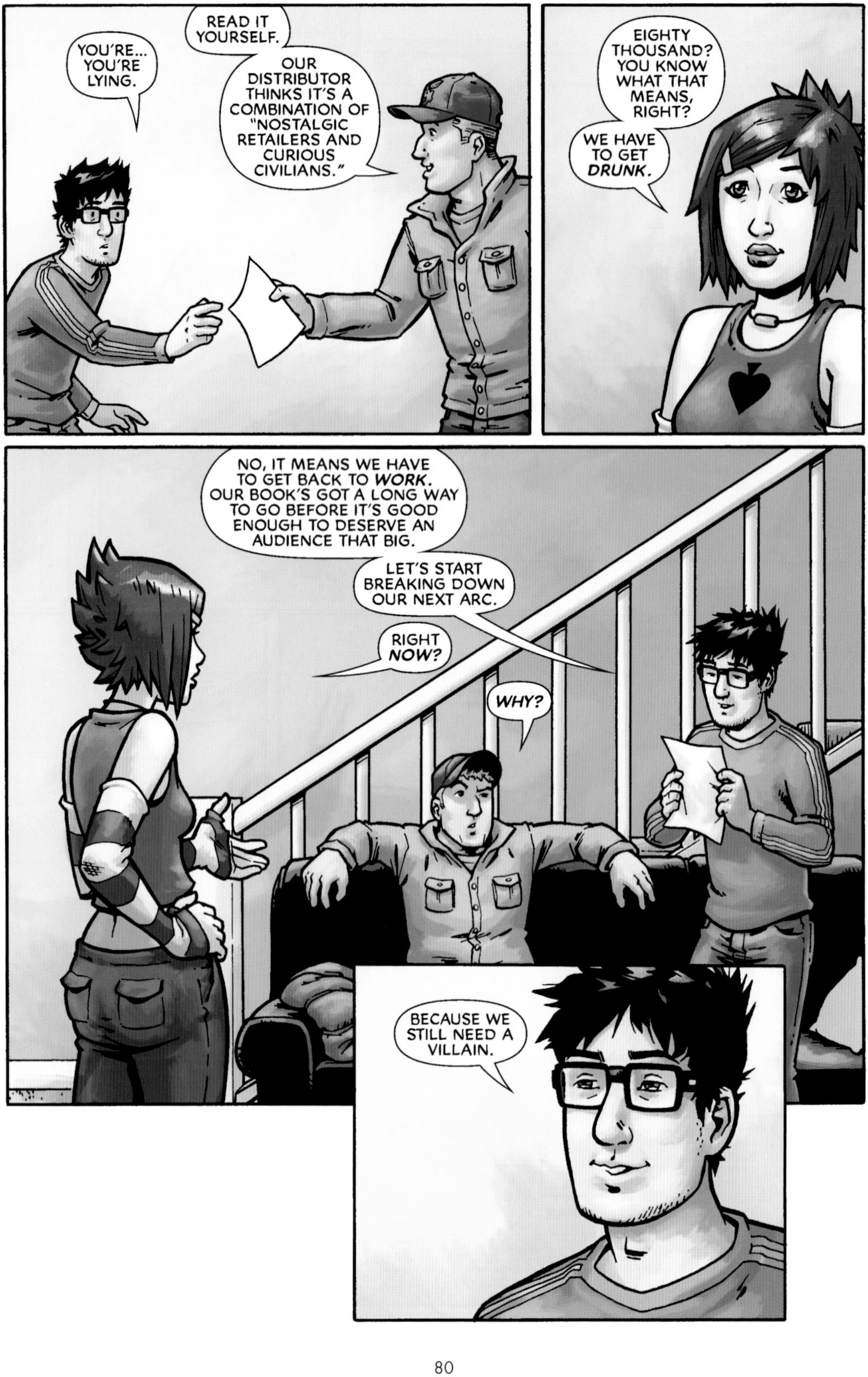
YOU'RE... YOU'RE LYING.
READ IT YOURSELF.
OUR DISTRIBUTOR THINKS IT'S A COMBINATION OF "NOSTALGIC RETAILERS AND CURIOUS CIVILIANS."
EIGHTY THOUSAND? YOU KNOW WHAT THAT MEANS, RIGHT?
WE HAVE TO GET *DRUNK.*
NO, IT MEANS WE HAVE TO GET BACK TO *WORK.* OUR BOOK'S GOT A LONG WAY TO GO BEFORE IT'S GOOD ENOUGH TO DESERVE AN AUDIENCE THAT BIG.
LET'S START BREAKING DOWN OUR NEXT ARC.
RIGHT *NOW?*
WHY?
BECAUSE WE STILL NEED A VILLAIN.

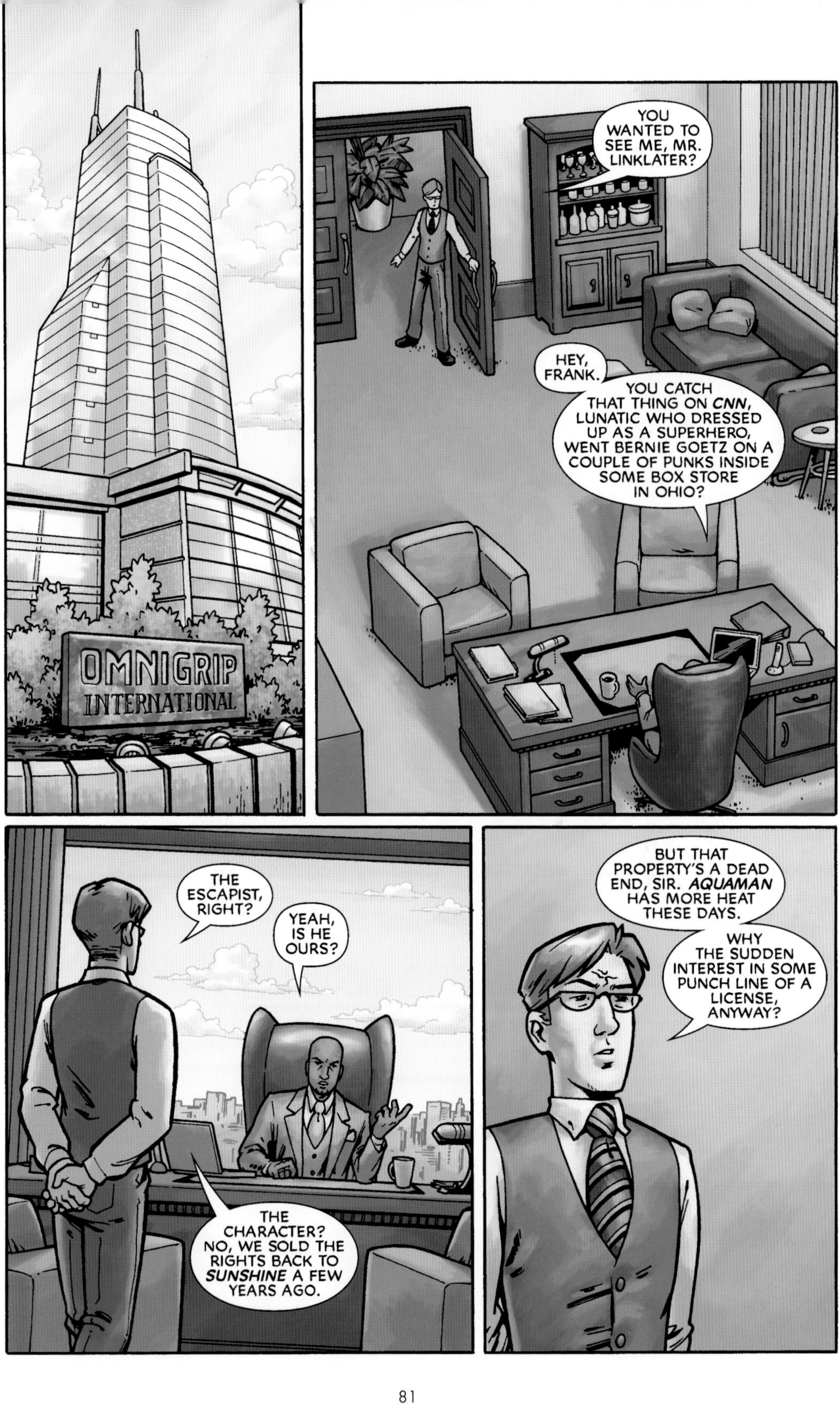
OMNIGRIP
INTERNATIONAL
YOU WANTED TO SEE ME, MR. LINKLATER?
HEY, FRANK.
YOU CATCH THAT THING ON *CNN*, LUNATIC WHO DRESSED UP AS A SUPERHERO, WENT BERNIE GOETZ ON A COUPLE OF PUNKS INSIDE SOME BOX STORE IN OHIO?
THE ESCAPIST, RIGHT?
YEAH, IS HE OURS?
THE CHARACTER? NO, WE SOLD THE RIGHTS BACK TO *SUNSHINE* A FEW YEARS AGO.
BUT THAT PROPERTY'S A DEAD END, SIR. *AQUAMAN* HAS MORE HEAT THESE DAYS.
WHY THE SUDDEN INTEREST IN SOME PUNCH LINE OF A LICENSE, ANYWAY?

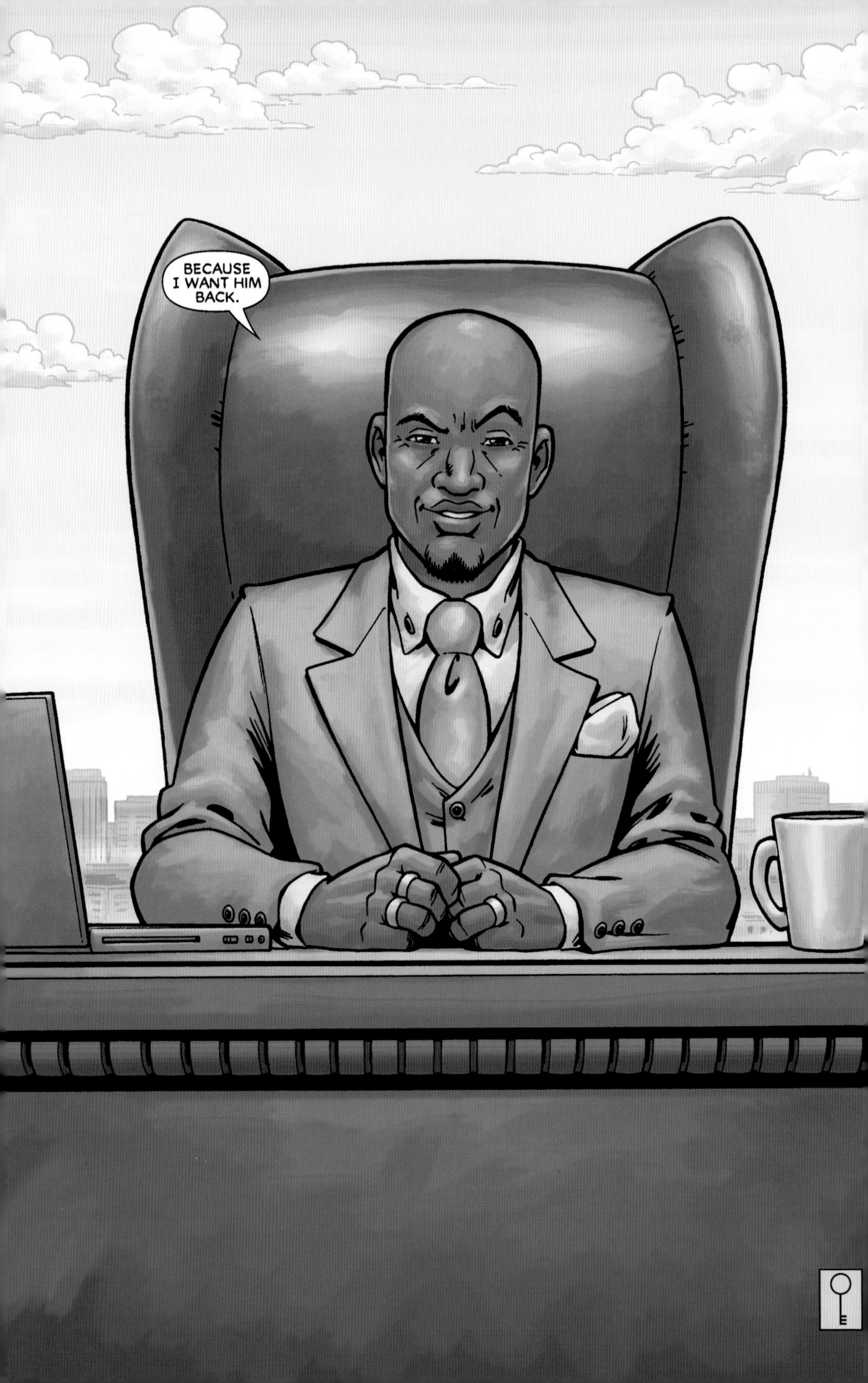
BECAUSE I WANT HIM BACK.

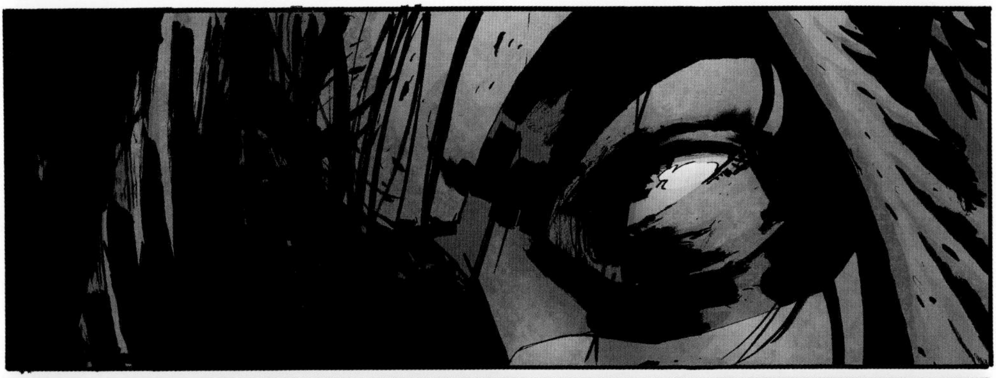

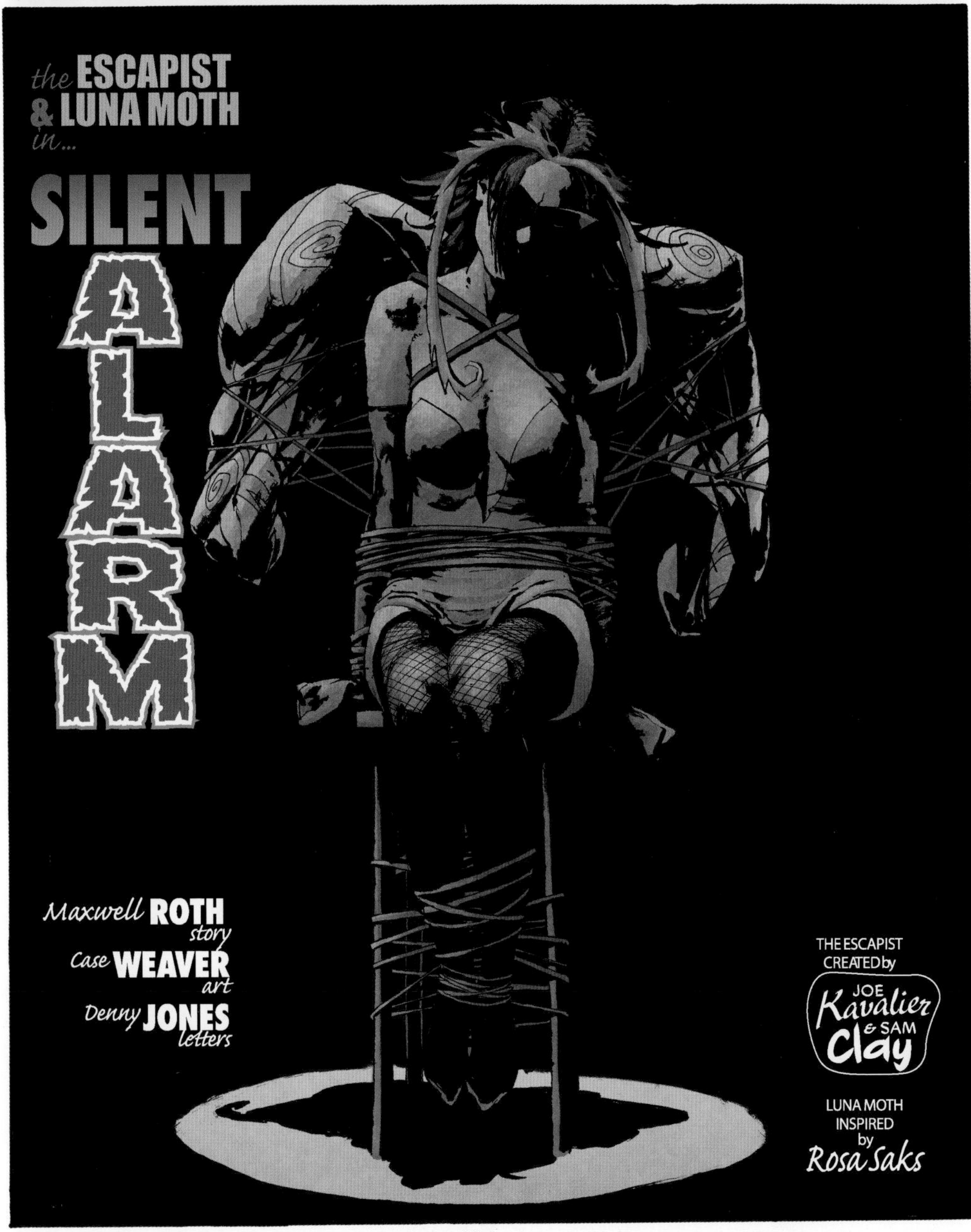
the ESCAPIST
& LUNA MOTH
in...
SILENT
ALARM
Maxwell ROTH
story
Case WEAVER
art
Denny JONES
letters
THE ESCAPIST
CREATED by
JOE
Kavalier
& SAM
Clay
LUNA MOTH
INSPIRED
by
Rosa Saks

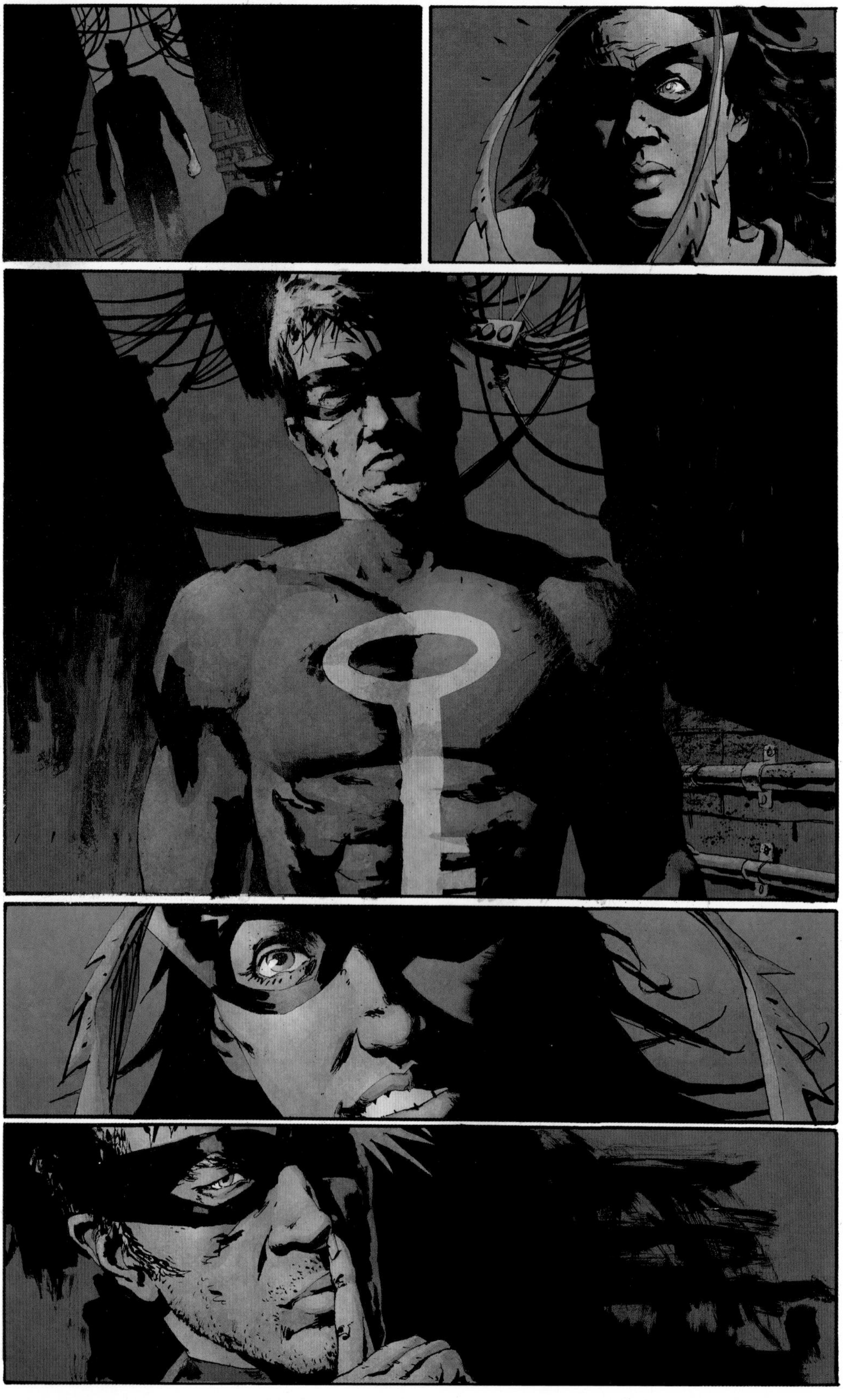

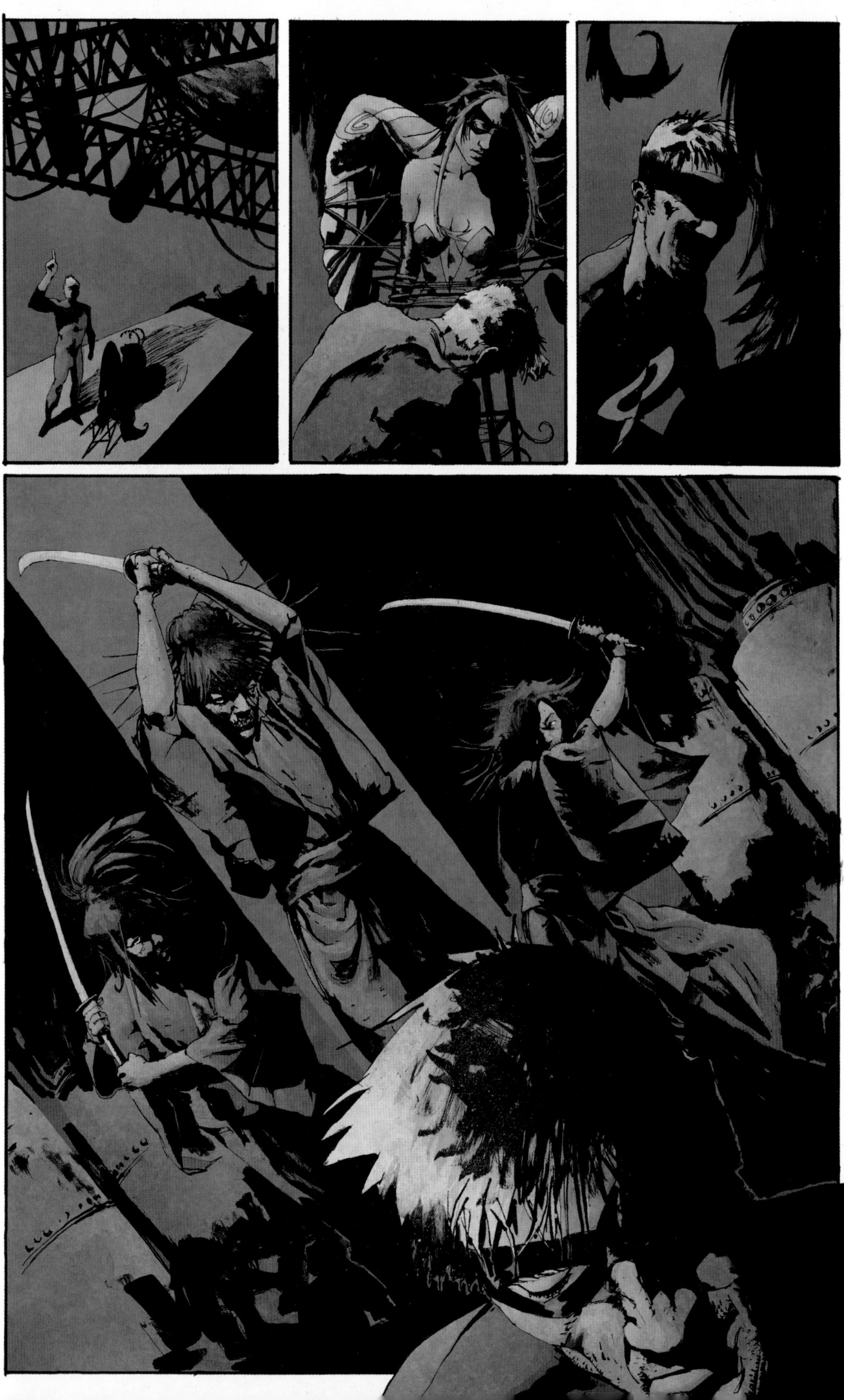

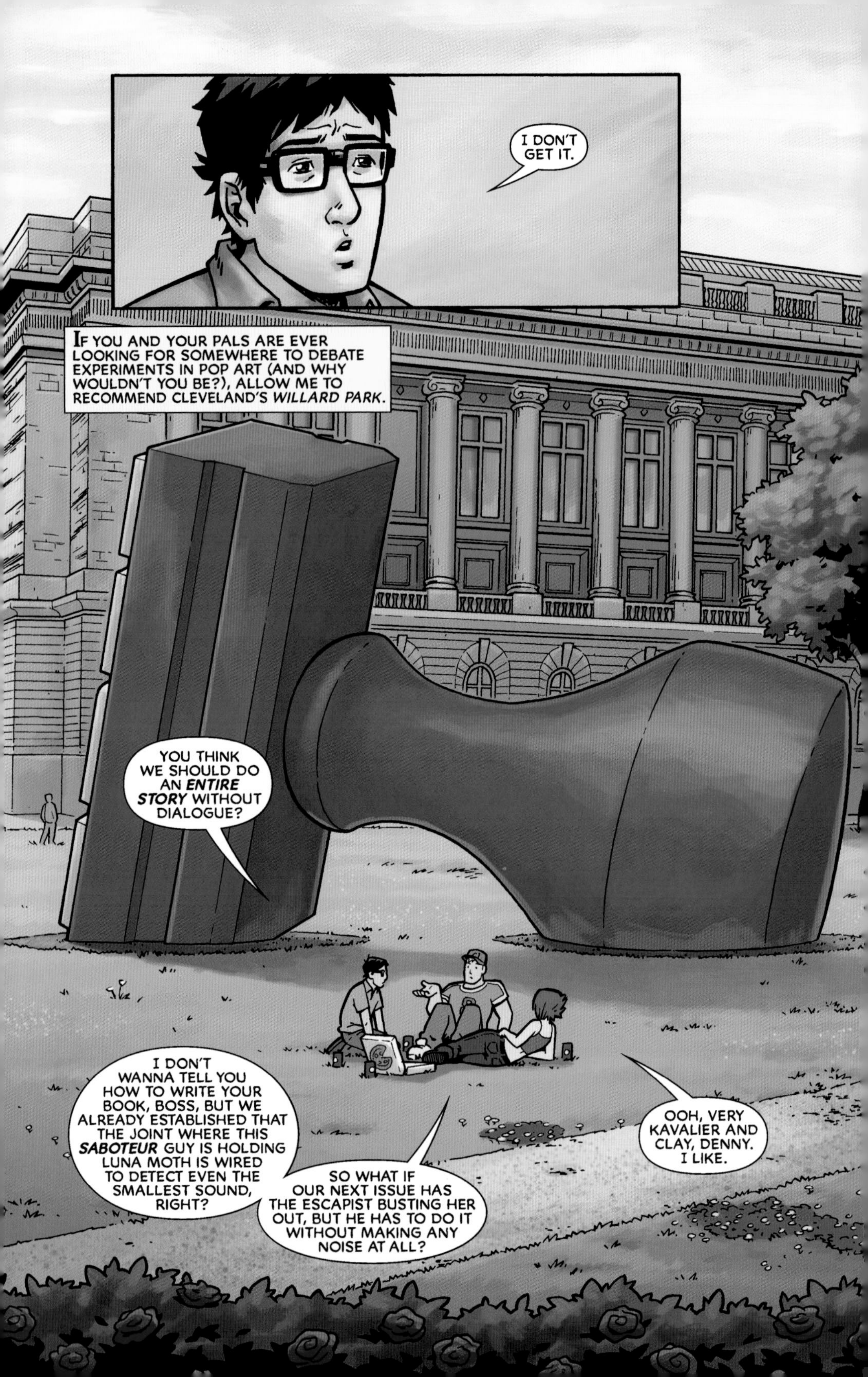
I DON'T GET IT.
IF YOU AND YOUR PALS ARE EVER LOOKING FOR SOMEWHERE TO DEBATE EXPERIMENTS IN POP ART (AND WHY WOULDN'T YOU BE?), ALLOW ME TO RECOMMEND CLEVELAND'S *WILLARD PARK*.
YOU THINK WE SHOULD DO AN *ENTIRE STORY* WITHOUT DIALOGUE?
I DON'T WANNA TELL YOU HOW TO WRITE YOUR BOOK, BOSS, BUT WE ALREADY ESTABLISHED THAT THE JOINT WHERE THIS *SABOTEUR* GUY IS HOLDING LUNA MOTH IS WIRED TO DETECT EVEN THE SMALLEST SOUND, RIGHT?
SO WHAT IF OUR NEXT ISSUE HAS THE ESCAPIST BUSTING HER OUT, BUT HE HAS TO DO IT WITHOUT MAKING ANY NOISE AT ALL?
OOH, VERY KAVALIER AND CLAY, DENNY. I LIKE.

CAN I AT LEAST USE *CAPTIONS?*

A FEW YEARS AGO, ARTISTS OLDENBURG AND VAN BRUGGEN WERE COMMISSIONED TO FILL A VACANT TRACT OF LAND WITH ONE OF THEIR INFAMOUS OVERSIZED REPLICAS OF EVERYDAY ITEMS.

EXCITED BY THE POSSIBILITIES THAT THIS OPEN "PAD" OF EARTH CREATED, THE DUO WENT TO WORK CONSTRUCTING A MASSIVE *RUBBER STAMP.*

WE HAVE TO KEEP PUSHING OURSELVES, MAX. WE CAN'T REST ON OUR LAURELS JUST BECAUSE OUR FIRST ISSUE *SOLD OUT.*

I DON'T KNOW, CASE. I'M AFRAID IT'S GONNA LOOK LIKE A *GIMMICK.* DIDN'T AN ISSUE OF *G.I. JOE* ALREADY DO THIS A MILLION YEARS AGO?

CONTROVERSIAL SINCE ITS UNVEILING, SOME CLEVELANDERS SEE THE MASSIVE STEEL WORK AS AN INSPIRING CELEBRATION OF THE CITY'S INDUSTRIAL ACHIEVEMENTS...

EISNER DID WORDLESS STORIES LONG BEFORE THAT, DIDN'T HE? AND YOU'RE THE ONE WHO ALWAYS SAYS THERE ARE NO NEW IDEAS, JUST NEW EXECUTIONS.

BESIDES, HAVING THE ESCAPIST AND LUNA SPEAK JUST THROUGH THEIR BODY LANGUAGE IS A COOL WAY TO SHOW HOW MUCH THEIR RELATIONSHIP HAS *EVOLVED.*

SORTA LIKE YOUR GUYS' *COLLABORATION.*

...BUT MOST SEE THE SCULPTURE AS JUST PLAIN *UGLY.*

DENNY, MAY I SIDEBAR WITH YOU FOR A SECOND?

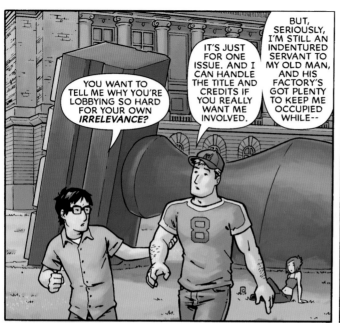

YOU WANT TO TELL ME WHY YOU'RE LOBBYING SO HARD FOR YOUR OWN *IRRELEVANCE?*

IT'S JUST FOR ONE ISSUE. AND I CAN HANDLE THE TITLE AND CREDITS IF YOU REALLY WANT ME INVOLVED.

BUT, SERIOUSLY, I'M STILL AN INDENTURED SERVANT TO MY OLD MAN, AND HIS FACTORY'S GOT PLENTY TO KEEP ME OCCUPIED WHILE--

SHUT UP. THIS HAS NOTHING TO DO WITH YOUR DAD OR...OR WHAT YOU THINK IS BEST FOR OUR BOOK.

THIS IS ABOUT ME AND *CASE,* RIGHT?

LOOK...

WHAT IS *WRONG* WITH YOU?

LOOK, IT'S OBVIOUS THE TWO OF YOU ARE INTO EACH OTHER, BUT YOU'RE BOTH EITHER TOO STUBBORN OR TOO STUPID TO MAKE THE FIRST MOVE.

BUT IF I LEAVE YOU GUYS *ALONE* IN THE STUDIO FOR A WHOLE MONTH...

WELL, YOU GET THE PICTURE.

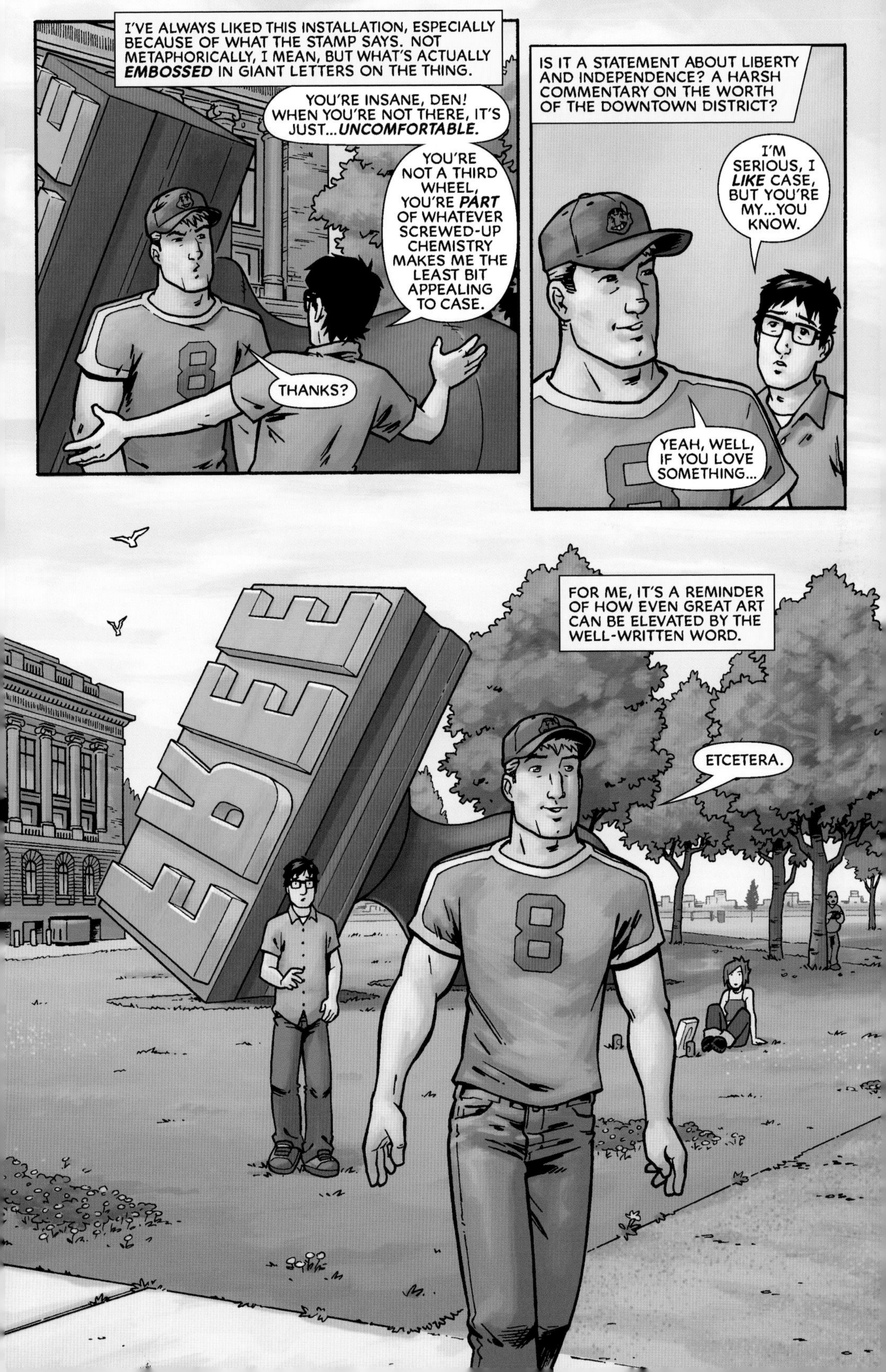
I'VE ALWAYS LIKED THIS INSTALLATION, ESPECIALLY BECAUSE OF WHAT THE STAMP SAYS. NOT METAPHORICALLY, I MEAN, BUT WHAT'S ACTUALLY *EMBOSSED* IN GIANT LETTERS ON THE THING.
YOU'RE INSANE, DEN! WHEN YOU'RE NOT THERE, IT'S JUST... *UNCOMFORTABLE*.
YOU'RE NOT A THIRD WHEEL, YOU'RE *PART* OF WHATEVER SCREWED-UP CHEMISTRY MAKES ME THE LEAST BIT APPEALING TO CASE.
THANKS?
IS IT A STATEMENT ABOUT LIBERTY AND INDEPENDENCE? A HARSH COMMENTARY ON THE WORTH OF THE DOWNTOWN DISTRICT?
I'M SERIOUS, I *LIKE* CASE, BUT YOU'RE MY... YOU KNOW.
YEAH, WELL, IF YOU LOVE SOMETHING...
FOR ME, IT'S A REMINDER OF HOW EVEN GREAT ART CAN BE ELEVATED BY THE WELL-WRITTEN WORD.
ETCETERA.

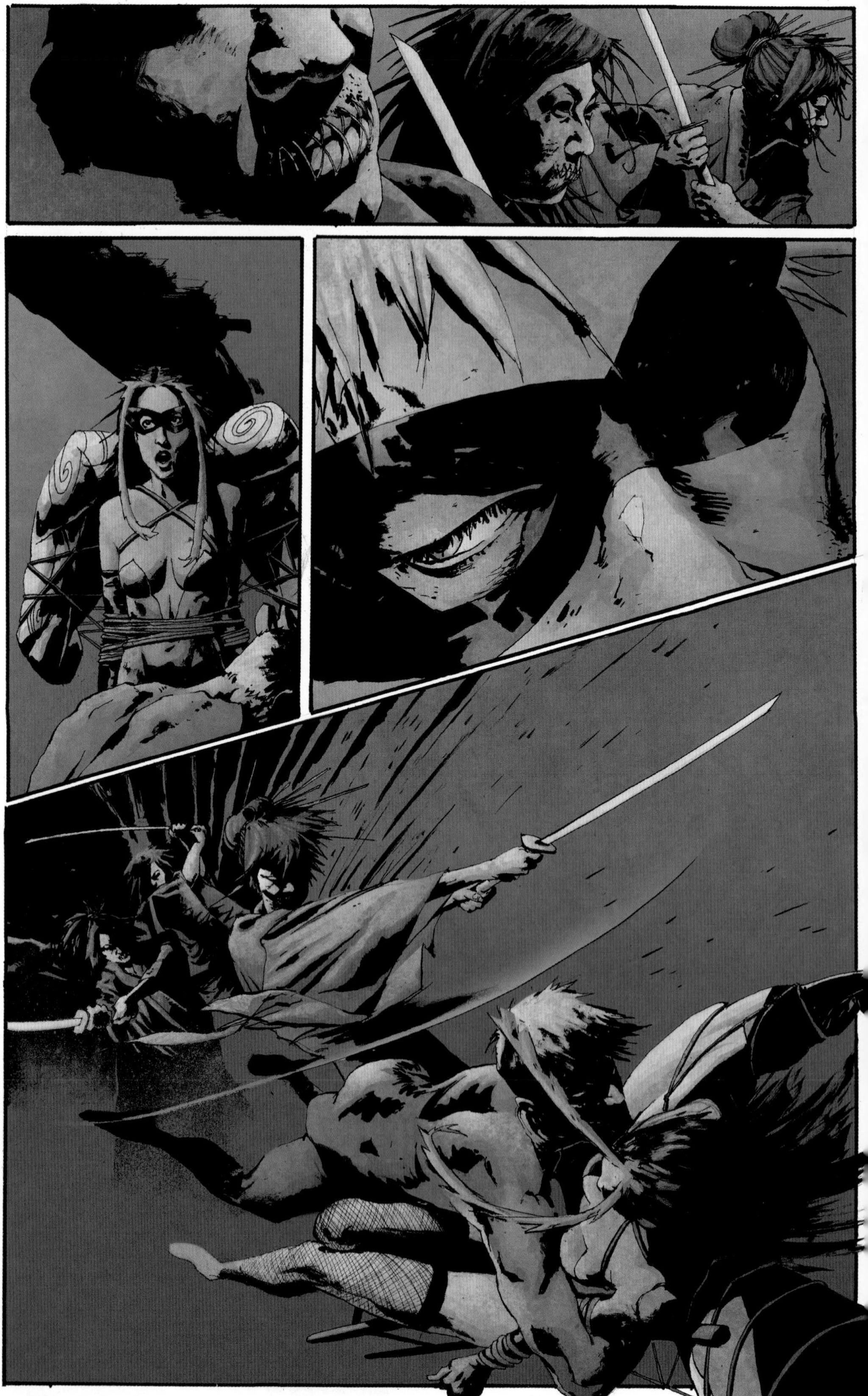

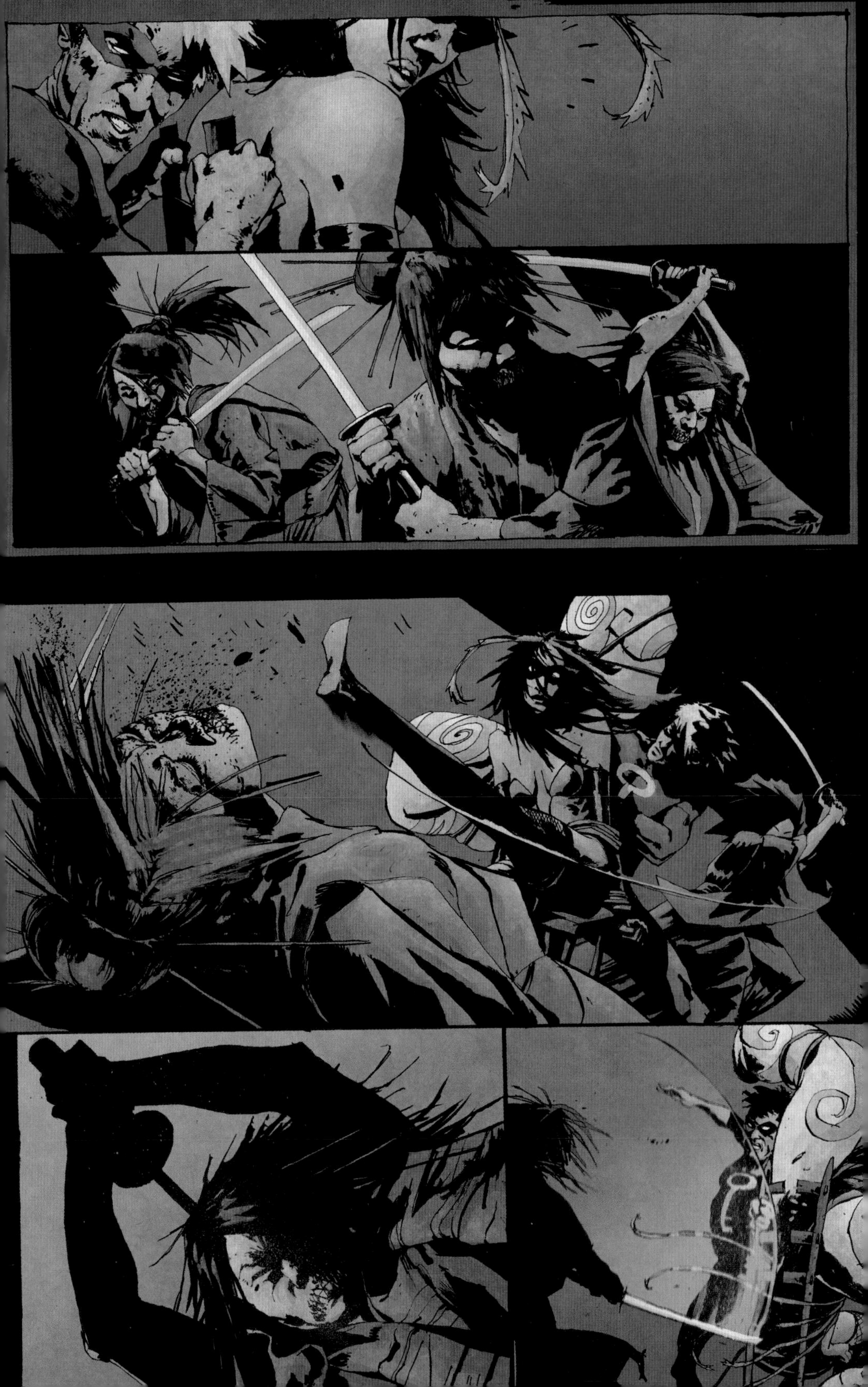

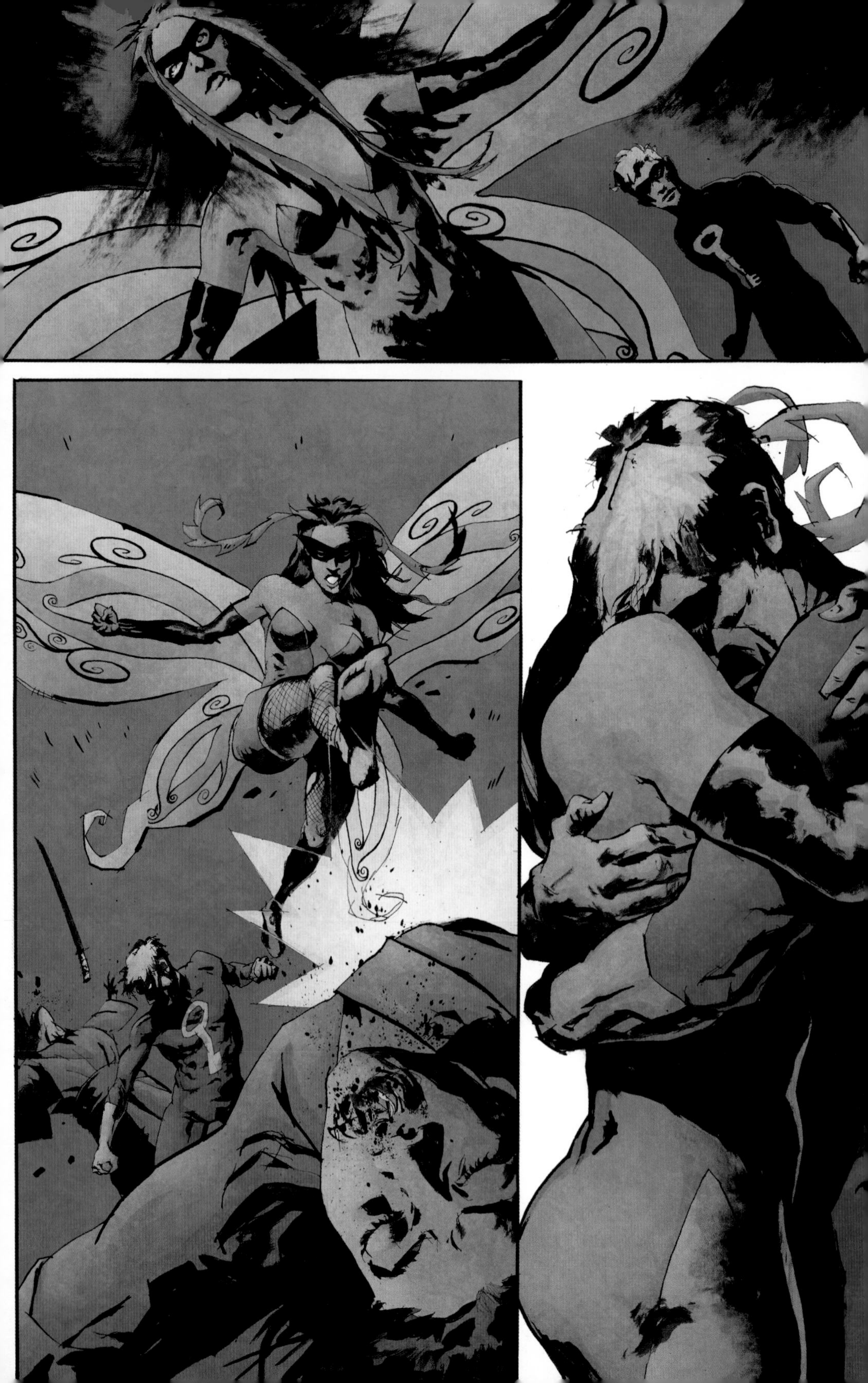

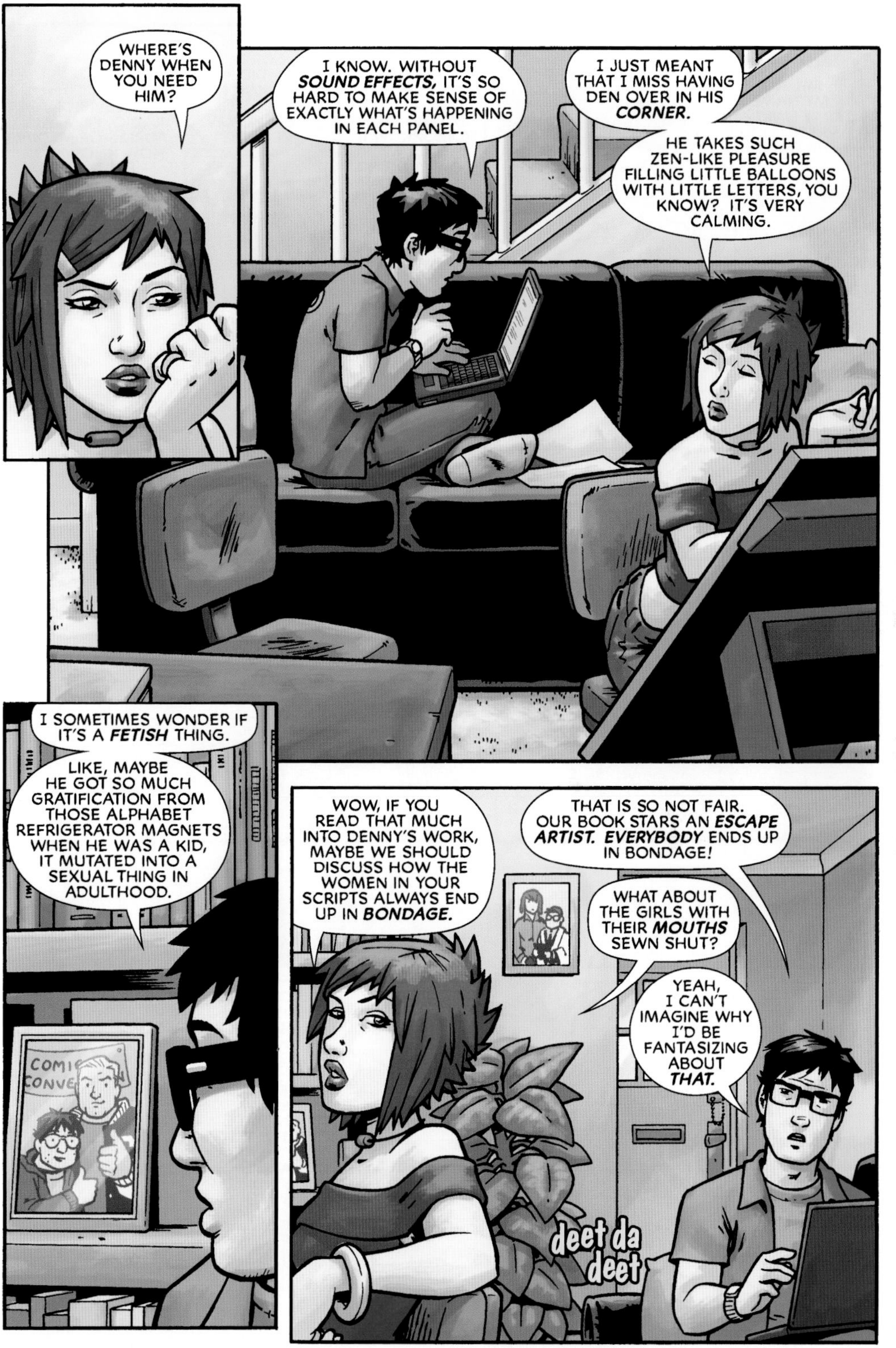
WHERE'S DENNY WHEN YOU NEED HIM?
I KNOW. WITHOUT *SOUND EFFECTS,* IT'S SO HARD TO MAKE SENSE OF EXACTLY WHAT'S HAPPENING IN EACH PANEL.
I JUST MEANT THAT I MISS HAVING DEN OVER IN HIS *CORNER.*
HE TAKES SUCH ZEN-LIKE PLEASURE FILLING LITTLE BALLOONS WITH LITTLE LETTERS, YOU KNOW? IT'S VERY CALMING.
I SOMETIMES WONDER IF IT'S A *FETISH* THING.
LIKE, MAYBE HE GOT SO MUCH GRATIFICATION FROM THOSE ALPHABET REFRIGERATOR MAGNETS WHEN HE WAS A KID, IT MUTATED INTO A SEXUAL THING IN ADULTHOOD.
WOW, IF YOU READ THAT MUCH INTO DENNY'S WORK, MAYBE WE SHOULD DISCUSS HOW THE WOMEN IN YOUR SCRIPTS ALWAYS END UP IN *BONDAGE.*
THAT IS SO NOT FAIR. OUR BOOK STARS AN *ESCAPE ARTIST. EVERYBODY* ENDS UP IN BONDAGE!
WHAT ABOUT THE GIRLS WITH THEIR *MOUTHS* SEWN SHUT?
YEAH, I CAN'T IMAGINE WHY I'D BE FANTASIZING ABOUT *THAT.*
deet da deet

WHAT?

MR. ROTH, MY NAME IS *TERRY LINKLATER.* PRESIDENT OF THE OMNIGRIP CORPORATION HERE IN L.A.?

LOVE WHAT YOU'RE DOING. I WANTED YOU TO KNOW THAT I'D BE AT YOUR BIG *SIGNING* TOMORROW IF ONLY MY BOARD DIDN'T FROWN ON PERSONAL USE OF OUR *GULFSTREAM.*

SORRY, DID...DID YOU SAY *OMNIGRIP?* AS IN...THE *TELEVISION* PEOPLE?

TELEVISION, RADIO, FILM, ALL FORMS OF MEDIA NOW KNOWN OR HERETOFORE DISCOVERED ANYWHERE IN THE UNIVERSE. EXCEPT THEATER. Heh.

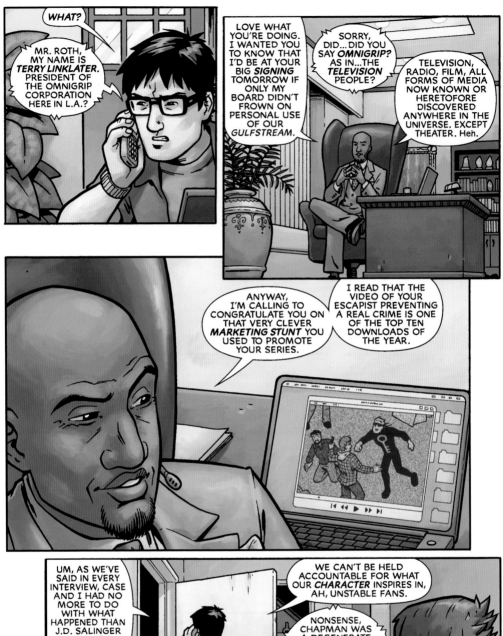

ANYWAY, I'M CALLING TO CONGRATULATE YOU ON THAT VERY CLEVER *MARKETING STUNT* YOU USED TO PROMOTE YOUR SERIES.

I READ THAT THE VIDEO OF YOUR ESCAPIST PREVENTING A REAL CRIME IS ONE OF THE TOP TEN DOWNLOADS OF THE YEAR.

UM, AS WE'VE SAID IN EVERY INTERVIEW, CASE AND I HAD NO MORE TO DO WITH WHAT HAPPENED THAN J.D. SALINGER DID WITH JOHN LENNON GETTING SHOT.

WE CAN'T BE HELD ACCOUNTABLE FOR WHAT OUR *CHARACTER* INSPIRES IN, AH, UNSTABLE FANS.

NONSENSE, CHAPMAN WAS A DEGENERATE MURDERER. BUT YOUR BOY WAS A *HERO* THAT NIGHT, AND THE WORLD KNOWS IT.

BUT REGARDLESS OF *WHO* WAS BEHIND THE ESCAPIST BREAKING THROUGH THE FOURTH WALL, THERE'S NOW CONSIDERABLE INTEREST IN THE PROPERTY FROM MULTIPLE SECTORS.

MY PEOPLE TELL ME THAT YOU PURCHASED THE RIGHTS TO THE ESCAPIST FOR A *SONG* FROM THE SUNSHINE ESTATE, AND I'D LIKE TO *REWARD* YOU FOR YOUR PRESCIENT INVESTMENT.

IT WAS HARDLY A "SONG." I USED MY ENTIRE *INHERITANCE* TO BUY THOSE RIGHTS. HE'S...THEY AREN'T FOR SALE.

I WON'T LIE TO YOU, MAXWELL. I'M OBVIOUSLY A BUSINESSMAN, BUT I GREW UP WITH THE ESCAPIST, AND I LOVE HIM ALMOST AS MUCH AS YOU.

YOU'VE BEEN DOING SOME IMPRESSIVE WORK WITH THE CHARACTER, BUT RIGHT NOW HE'S REACHING THOUSANDS OF PEOPLE, WHEN HE DESERVES AN AUDIENCE OF *MILLIONS*.

MORE TOYS

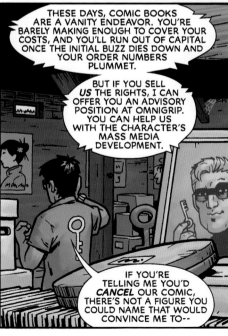

THESE DAYS, COMIC BOOKS ARE A VANITY ENDEAVOR. YOU'RE BARELY MAKING ENOUGH TO COVER YOUR COSTS, AND YOU'LL RUN OUT OF CAPITAL ONCE THE INITIAL BUZZ DIES DOWN AND YOUR ORDER NUMBERS PLUMMET.

BUT IF YOU SELL *US* THE RIGHTS, I CAN OFFER YOU AN ADVISORY POSITION AT OMNIGRIP. YOU CAN HELP US WITH THE CHARACTER'S MASS MEDIA DEVELOPMENT.

IF YOU'RE TELLING ME YOU'D *CANCEL* OUR COMIC, THERE'S NOT A FIGURE YOU COULD NAME THAT WOULD CONVINCE ME TO--

IF ONE FIGURE WON'T DO... HOW ABOUT *SEVEN?*

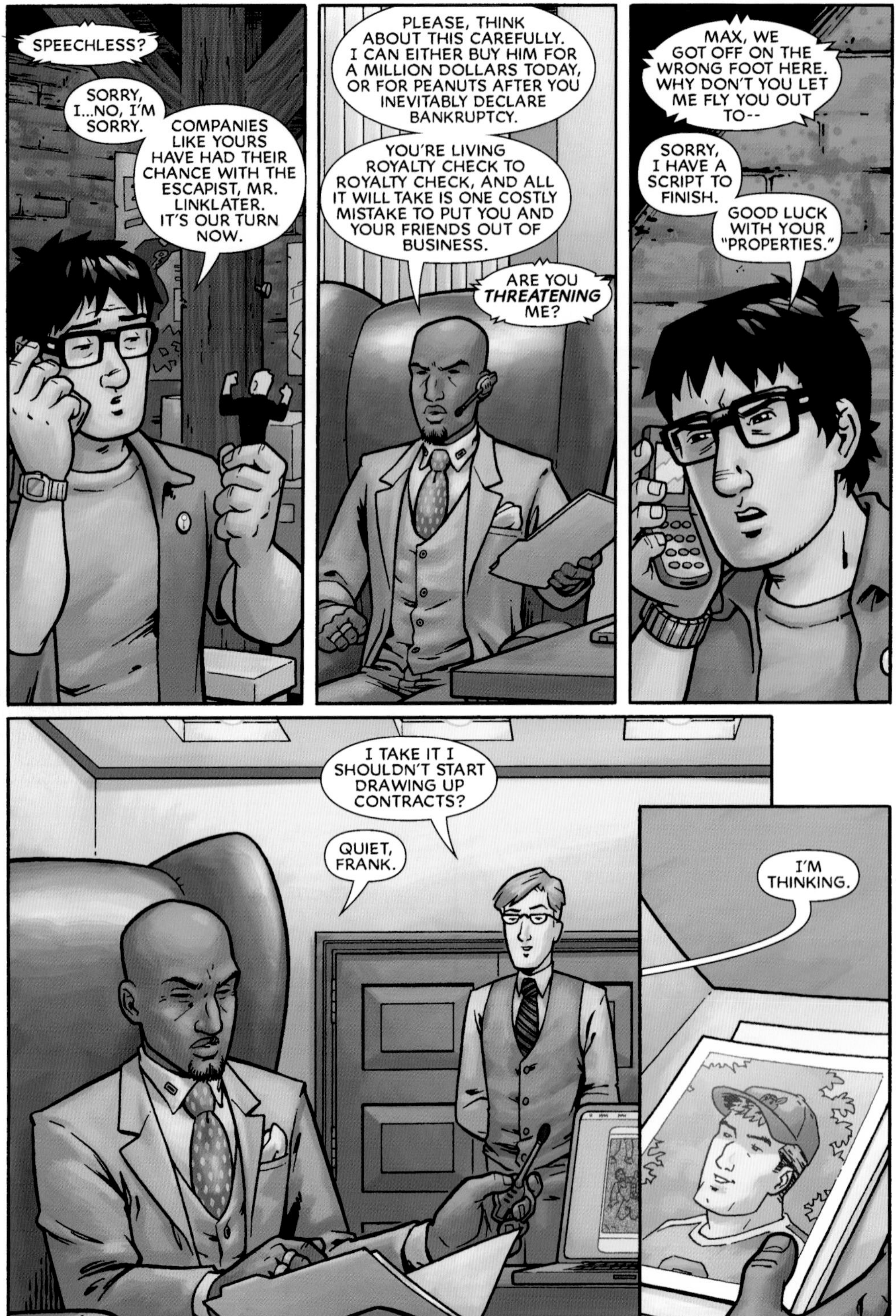
SPEECHLESS?
SORRY, I...NO, I'M SORRY.
COMPANIES LIKE YOURS HAVE HAD THEIR CHANCE WITH THE ESCAPIST, MR. LINKLATER. IT'S OUR TURN NOW.
PLEASE, THINK ABOUT THIS CAREFULLY. I CAN EITHER BUY HIM FOR A MILLION DOLLARS TODAY, OR FOR PEANUTS AFTER YOU INEVITABLY DECLARE BANKRUPTCY.
YOU'RE LIVING ROYALTY CHECK TO ROYALTY CHECK, AND ALL IT WILL TAKE IS ONE COSTLY MISTAKE TO PUT YOU AND YOUR FRIENDS OUT OF BUSINESS.
ARE YOU *THREATENING* ME?
MAX, WE GOT OFF ON THE WRONG FOOT HERE. WHY DON'T YOU LET ME FLY YOU OUT TO--
SORRY, I HAVE A SCRIPT TO FINISH.
GOOD LUCK WITH YOUR "PROPERTIES."
I TAKE IT I SHOULDN'T START DRAWING UP CONTRACTS?
QUIET, FRANK.
I'M THINKING.

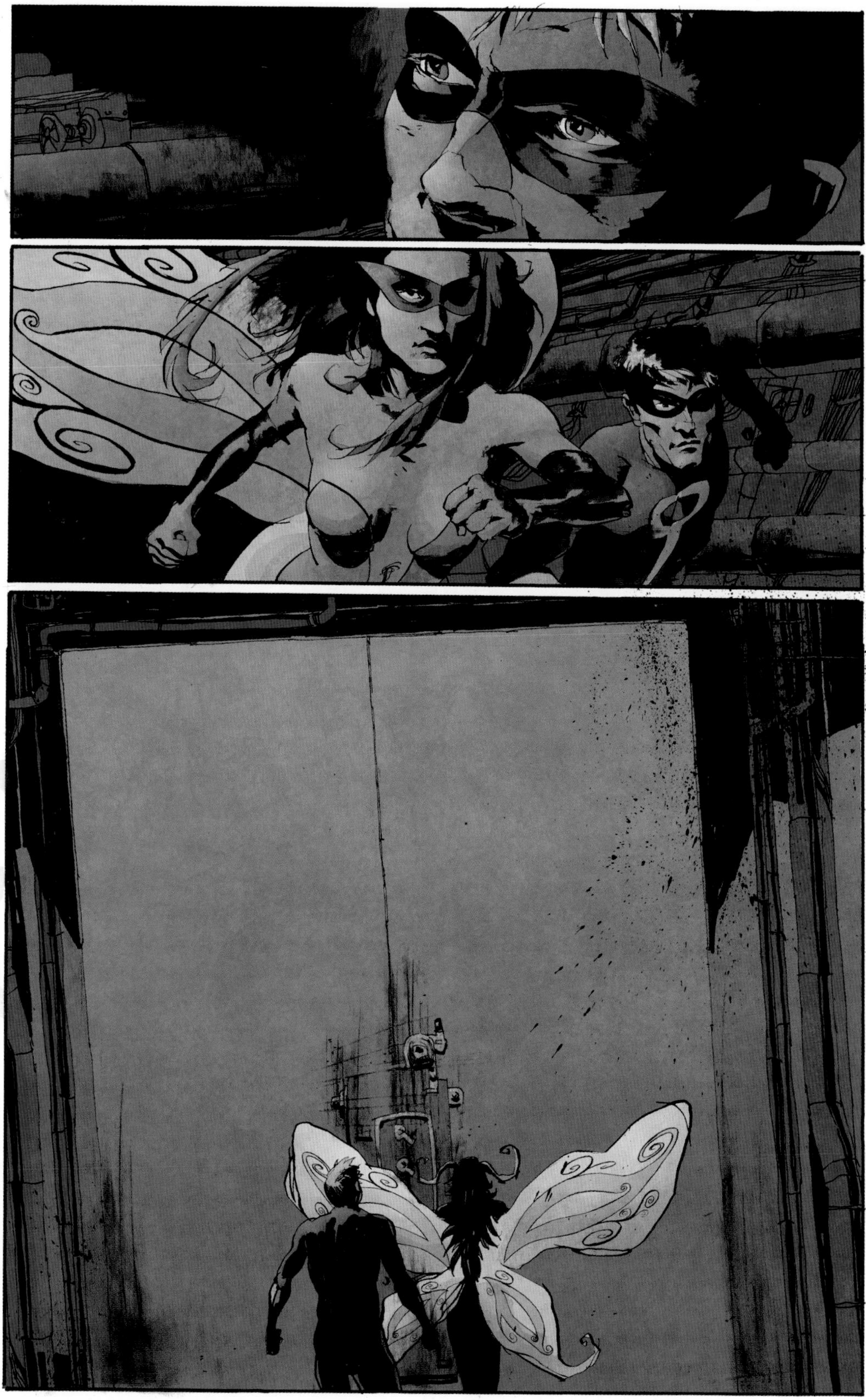

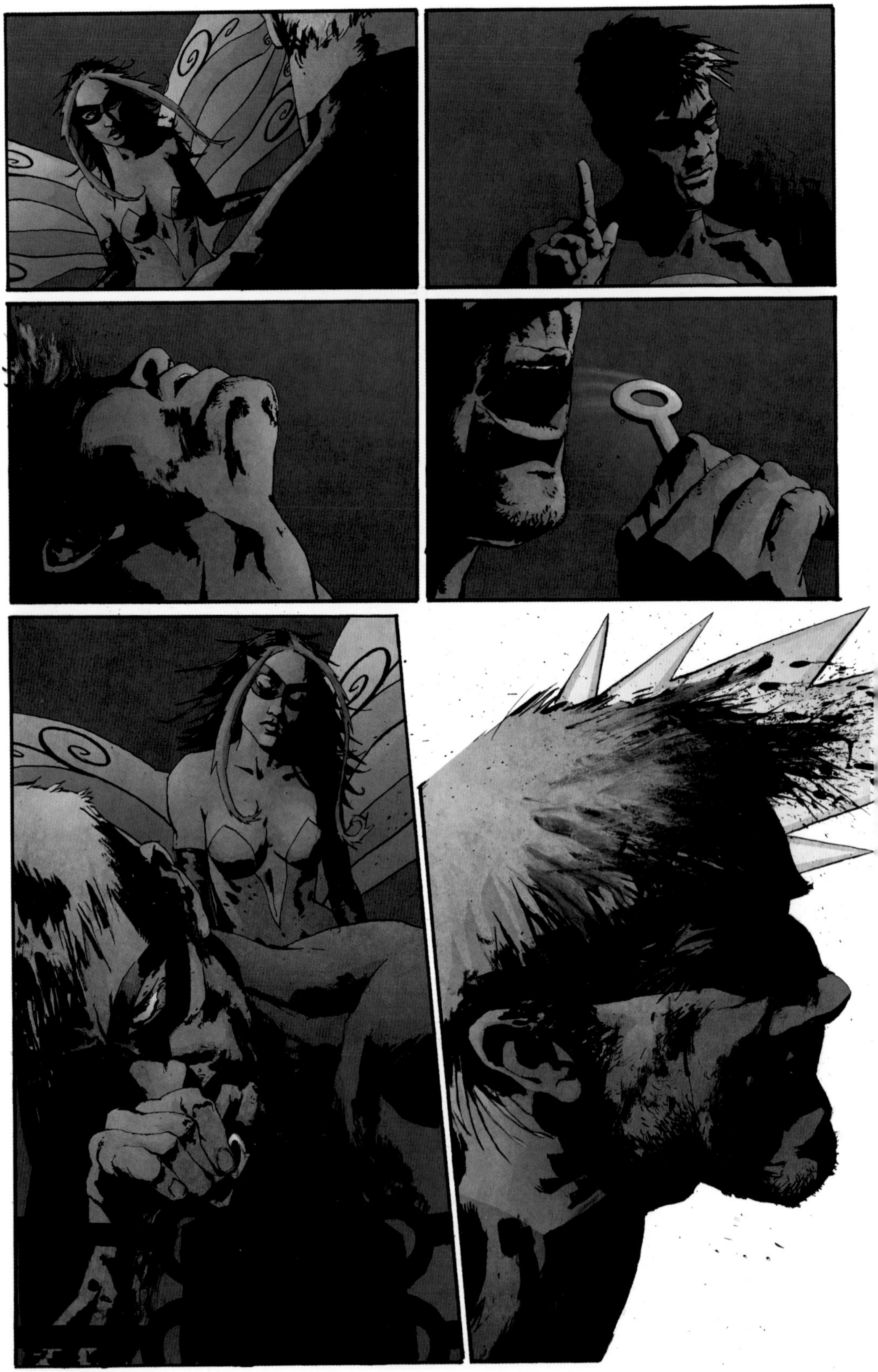

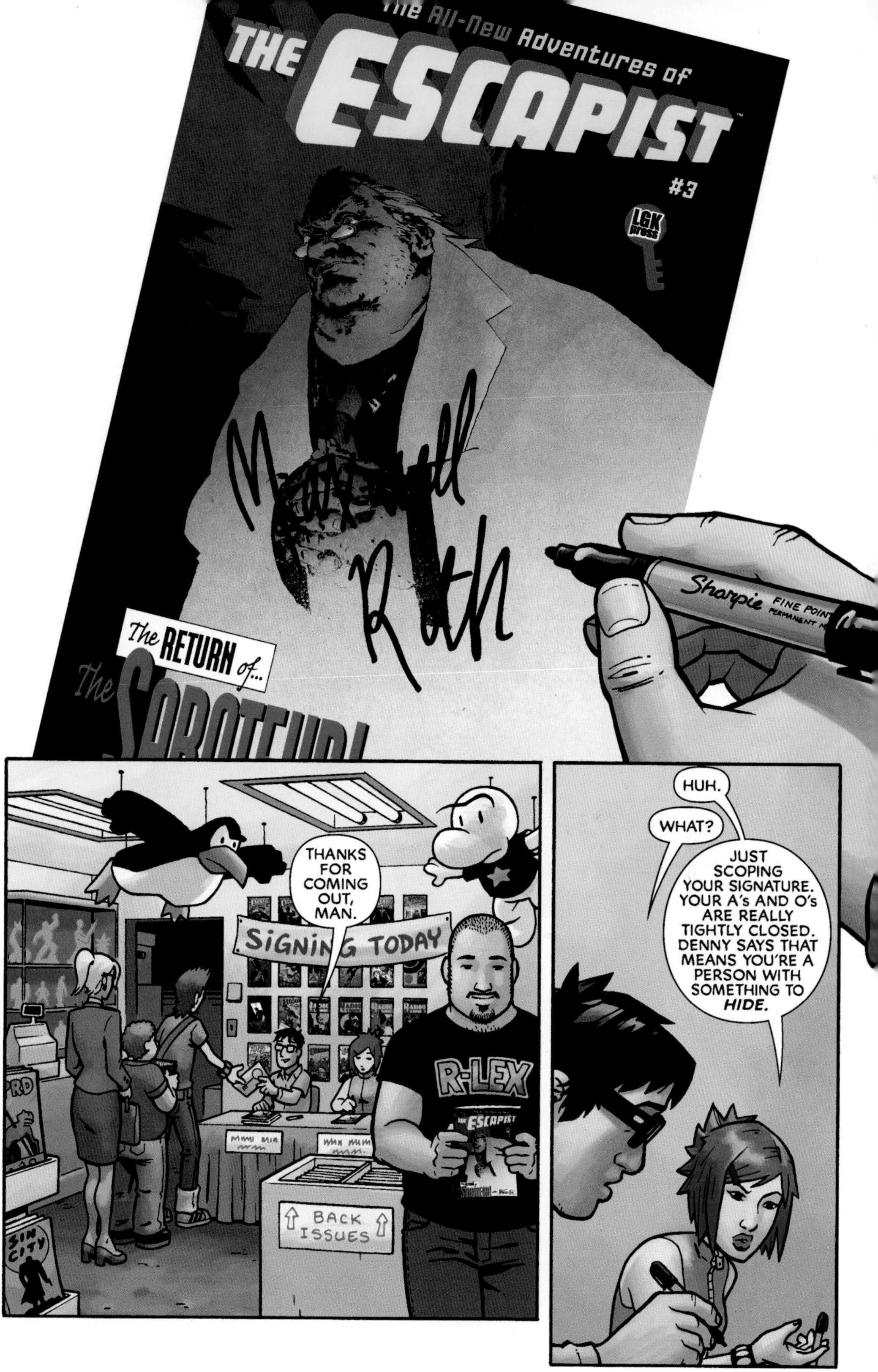

The All-New Adventures of
THE ESCAPIST
#3
LGK press
Sharpie FINE POINT
The RETURN of...
The
THANKS FOR COMING OUT, MAN.
SIGNING TODAY
R-LEX
THE ESCAPIST
BACK ISSUES
SIN CITY
HUH.
WHAT?
JUST SCOPING YOUR SIGNATURE. YOUR A's AND O's ARE REALLY TIGHTLY CLOSED. DENNY SAYS THAT MEANS YOU'RE A PERSON WITH SOMETHING TO *HIDE.*

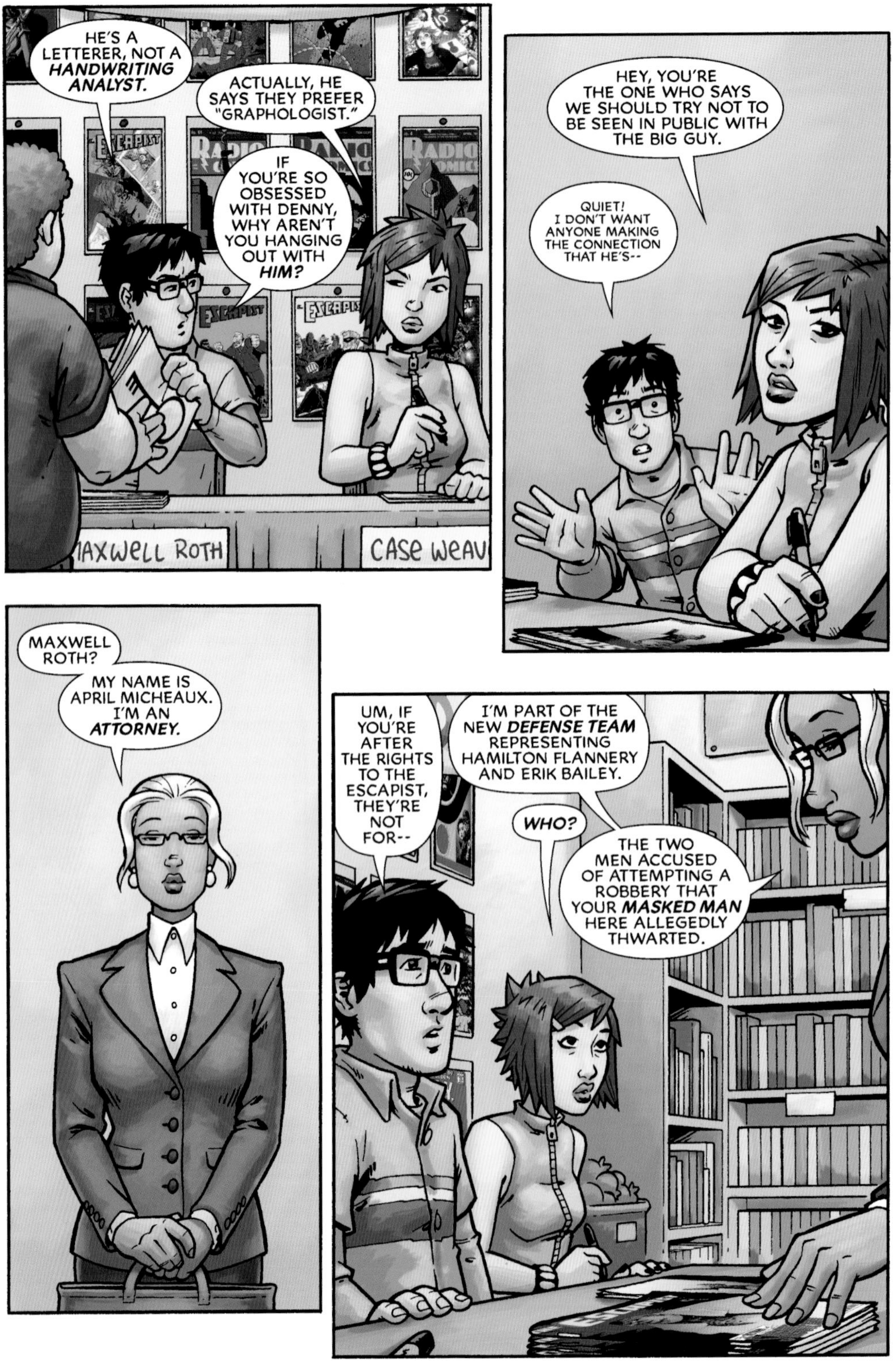
HE'S A LETTERER, NOT A ***HANDWRITING ANALYST.***
ACTUALLY, HE SAYS THEY PREFER "GRAPHOLOGIST."
IF YOU'RE SO OBSESSED WITH DENNY, WHY AREN'T YOU HANGING OUT WITH ***HIM?***
MAXWELL ROTH
CASE WEAV
HEY, YOU'RE THE ONE WHO SAYS WE SHOULD TRY NOT TO BE SEEN IN PUBLIC WITH THE BIG GUY.
QUIET! I DON'T WANT ANYONE MAKING THE CONNECTION THAT HE'S--
MAXWELL ROTH?
MY NAME IS APRIL MICHEAUX. I'M AN ***ATTORNEY.***
UM, IF YOU'RE AFTER THE RIGHTS TO THE ESCAPIST, THEY'RE NOT FOR--
I'M PART OF THE NEW ***DEFENSE TEAM*** REPRESENTING HAMILTON FLANNERY AND ERIK BAILEY.
WHO?
THE TWO MEN ACCUSED OF ATTEMPTING A ROBBERY THAT YOUR ***MASKED MAN*** HERE ALLEGEDLY THWARTED.

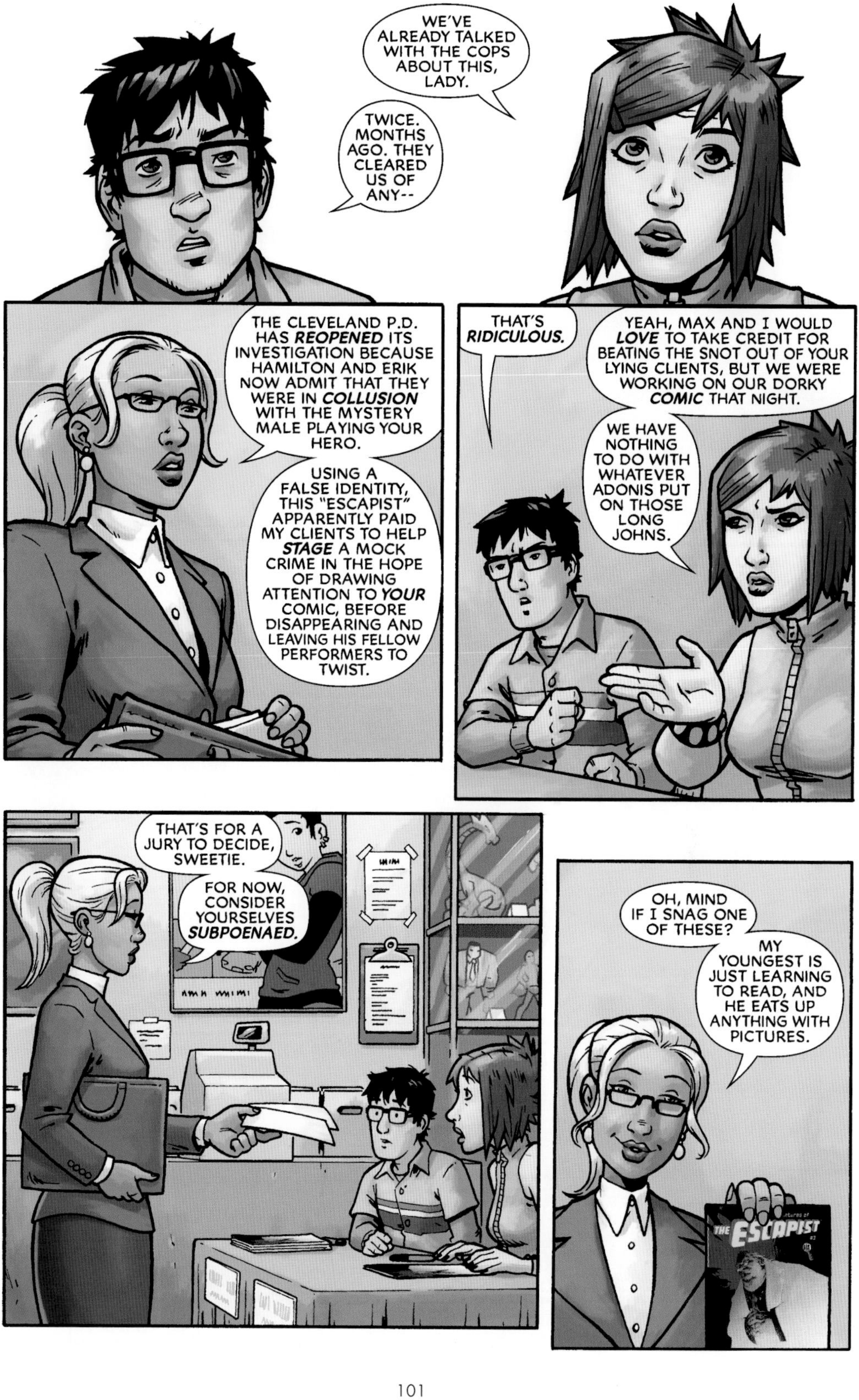
WE'VE ALREADY TALKED WITH THE COPS ABOUT THIS, LADY.
TWICE. MONTHS AGO. THEY CLEARED US OF ANY--
THE CLEVELAND P.D. HAS *REOPENED* ITS INVESTIGATION BECAUSE HAMILTON AND ERIK NOW ADMIT THAT THEY WERE IN *COLLUSION* WITH THE MYSTERY MALE PLAYING YOUR HERO.
USING A FALSE IDENTITY, THIS "ESCAPIST" APPARENTLY PAID MY CLIENTS TO HELP *STAGE* A MOCK CRIME IN THE HOPE OF DRAWING ATTENTION TO *YOUR* COMIC, BEFORE DISAPPEARING AND LEAVING HIS FELLOW PERFORMERS TO TWIST.
THAT'S *RIDICULOUS.*
YEAH, MAX AND I WOULD *LOVE* TO TAKE CREDIT FOR BEATING THE SNOT OUT OF YOUR LYING CLIENTS, BUT WE WERE WORKING ON OUR DORKY *COMIC* THAT NIGHT.
WE HAVE NOTHING TO DO WITH WHATEVER ADONIS PUT ON THOSE LONG JOHNS.
THAT'S FOR A JURY TO DECIDE, SWEETIE.
FOR NOW, CONSIDER YOURSELVES *SUBPOENAED.*
OH, MIND IF I SNAG ONE OF THESE?
MY YOUNGEST IS JUST LEARNING TO READ, AND HE EATS UP ANYTHING WITH PICTURES.
THE ESCAPIST

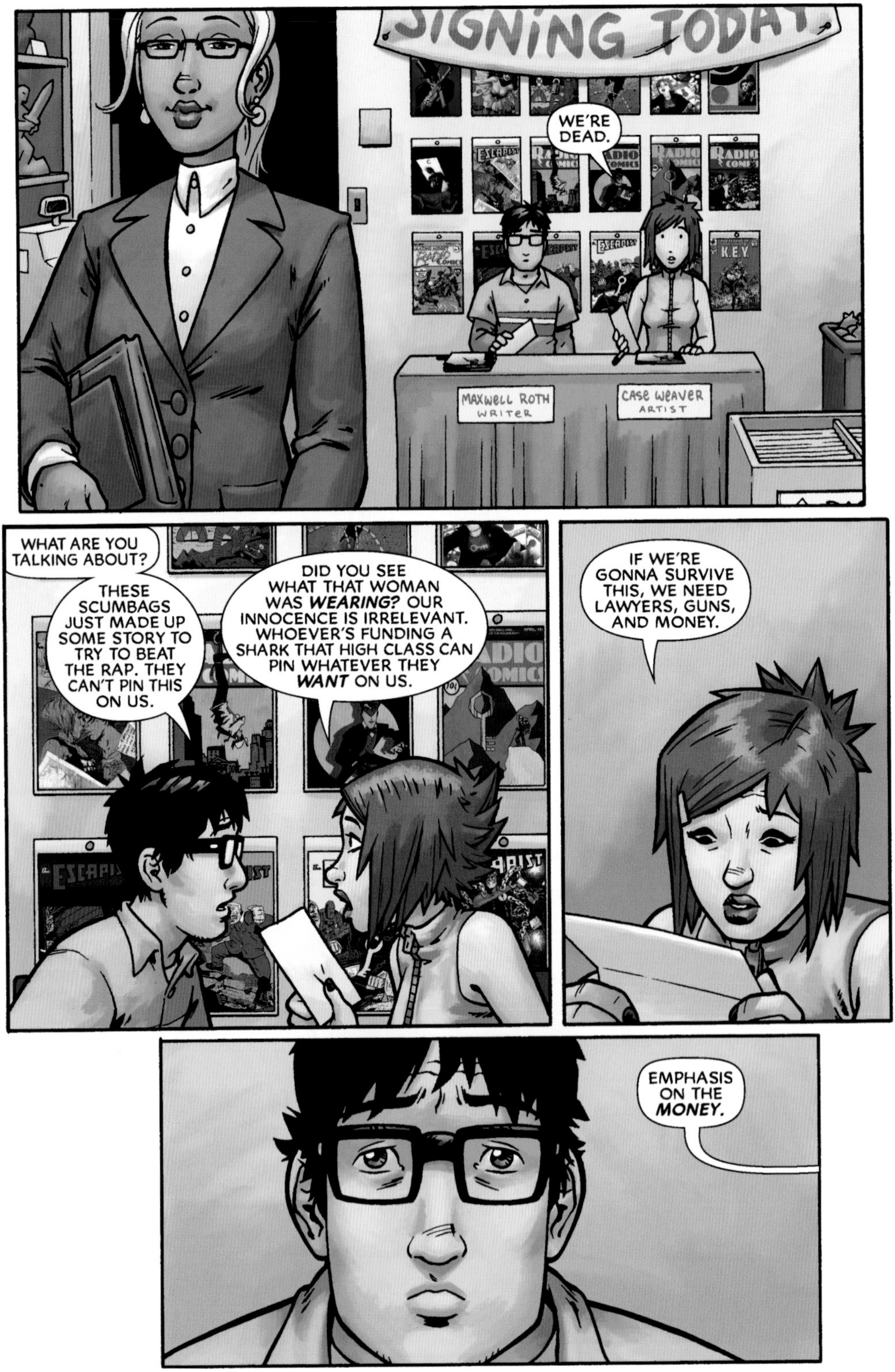
SIGNING TODAY
WE'RE DEAD.
MAXWELL ROTH
WRITER
CASE WEAVER
ARTIST
WHAT ARE YOU TALKING ABOUT?
THESE SCUMBAGS JUST MADE UP SOME STORY TO TRY TO BEAT THE RAP. THEY CAN'T PIN THIS ON US.
DID YOU SEE WHAT THAT WOMAN WAS ***WEARING?*** OUR INNOCENCE IS IRRELEVANT. WHOEVER'S FUNDING A SHARK THAT HIGH CLASS CAN PIN WHATEVER THEY ***WANT*** ON US.
IF WE'RE GONNA SURVIVE THIS, WE NEED LAWYERS, GUNS, AND MONEY.
EMPHASIS ON THE ***MONEY.***

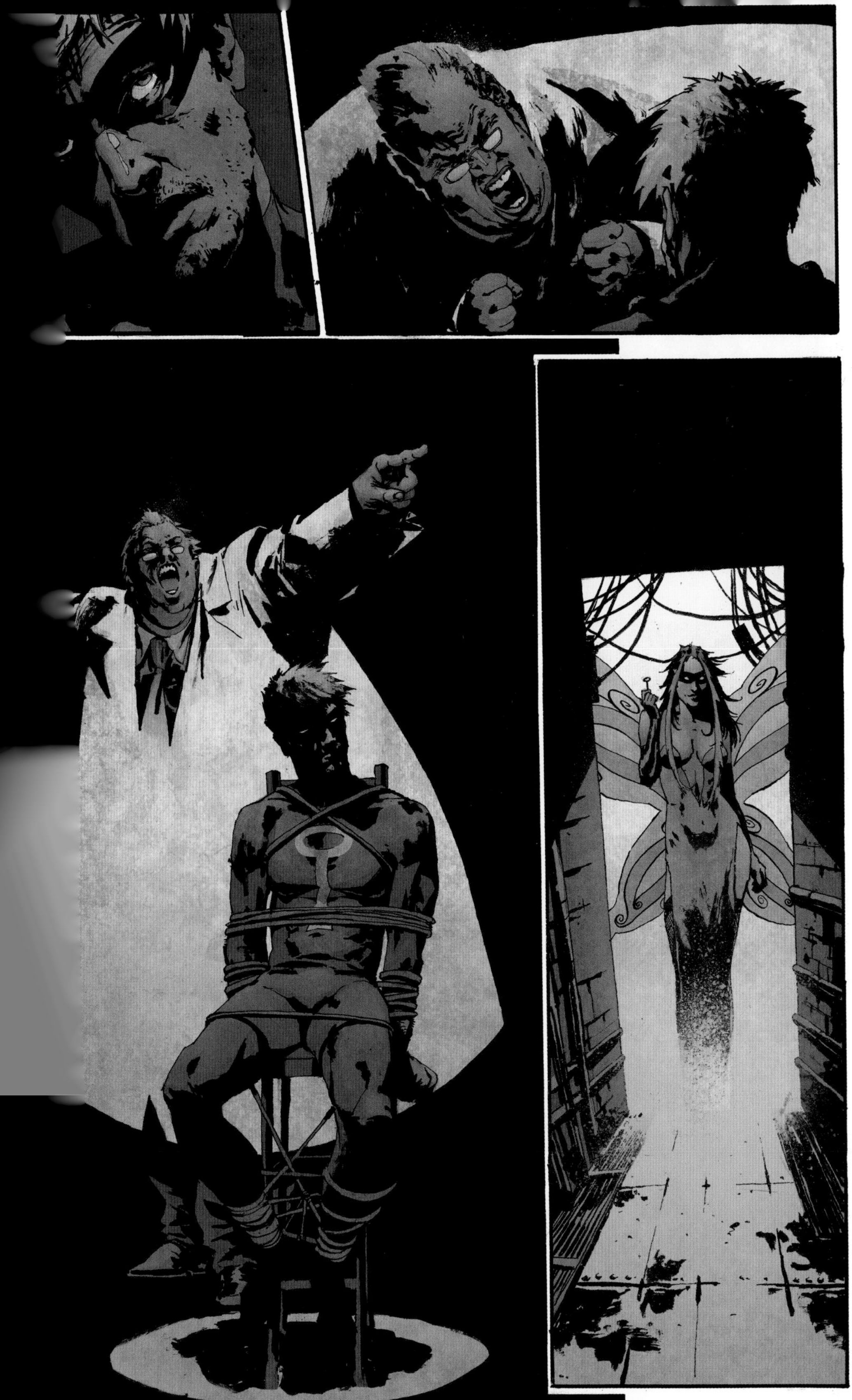

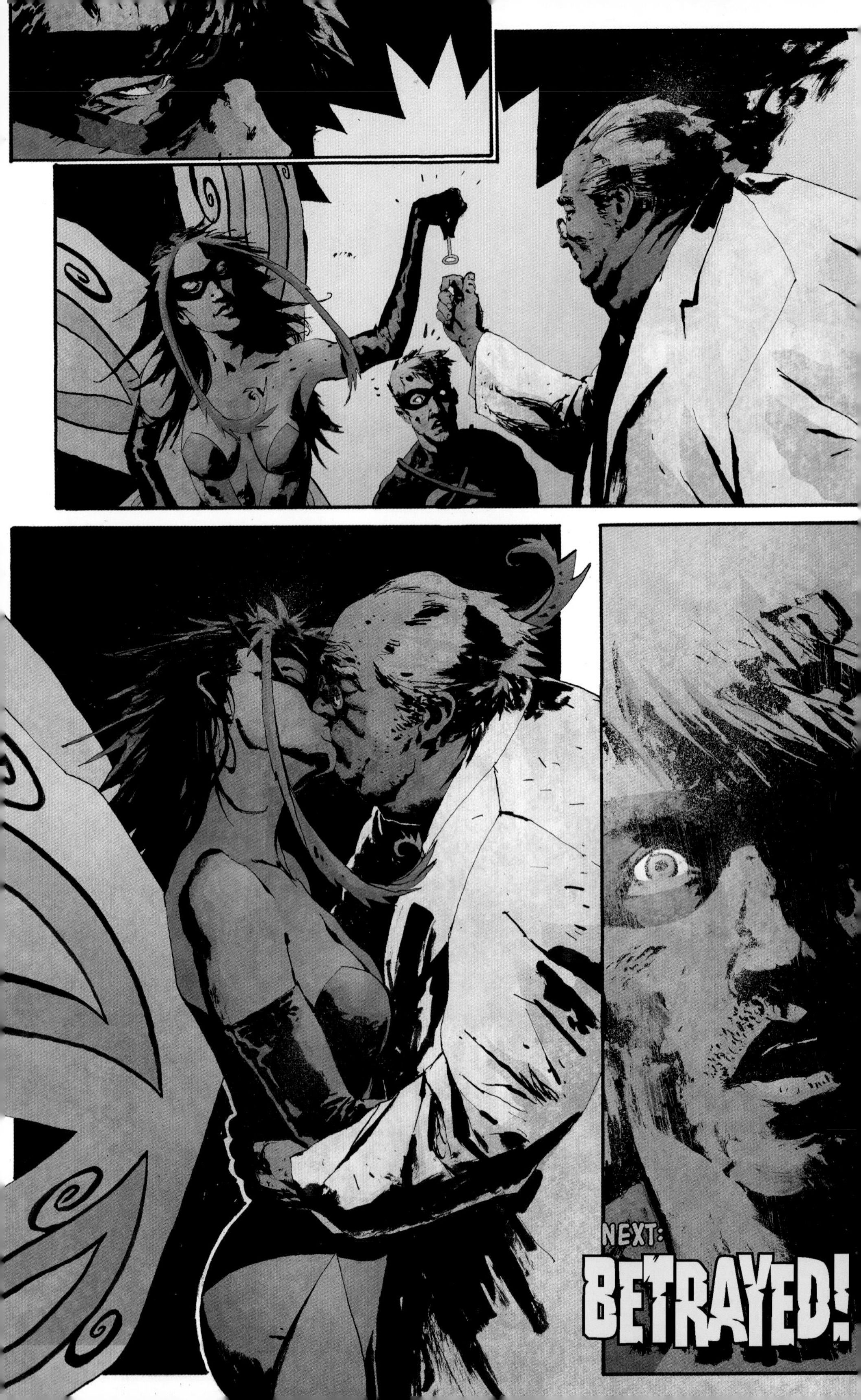
NEXT:
BETRAYED!

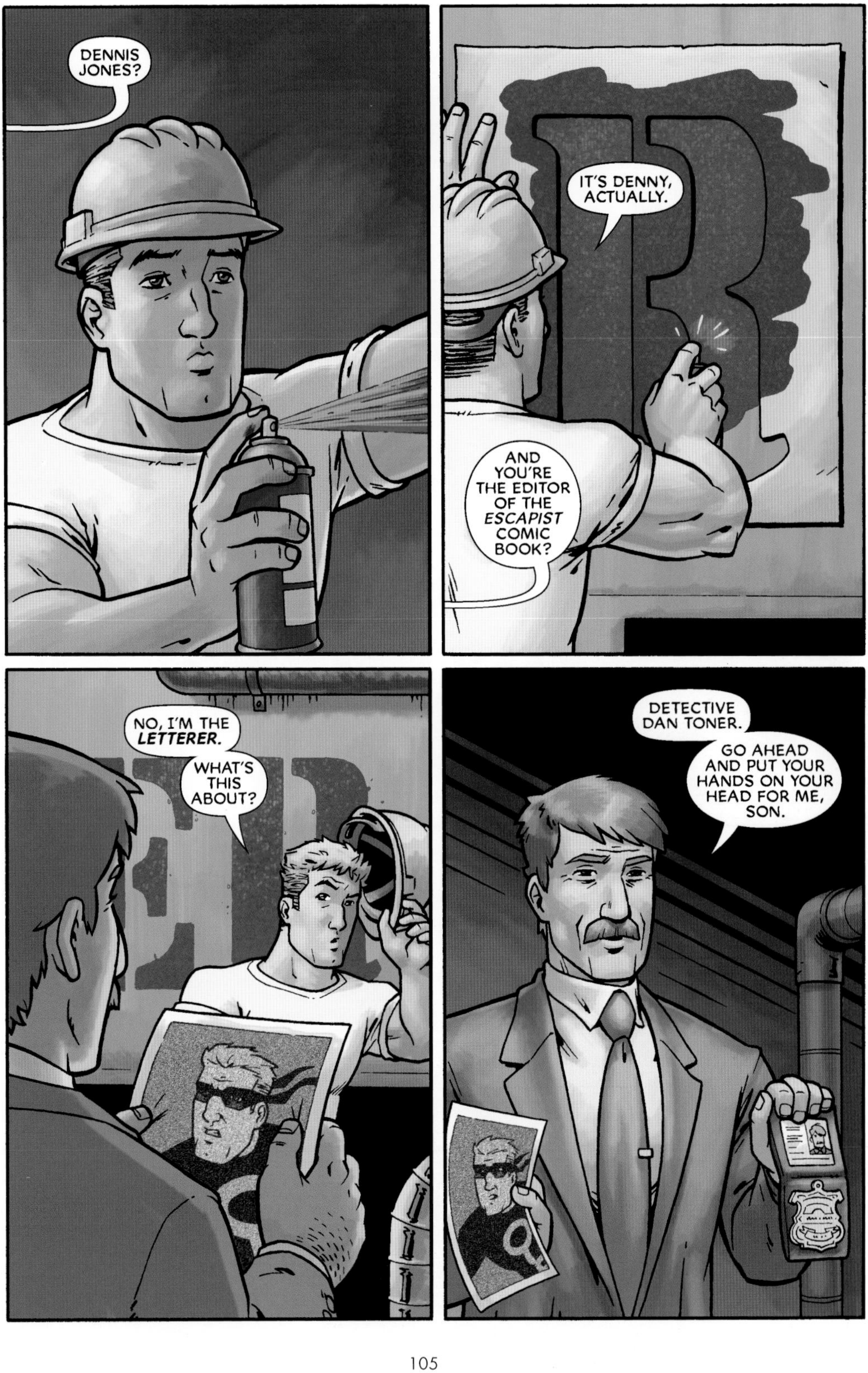
DENNIS JONES?
IT'S DENNY, ACTUALLY.
AND YOU'RE THE EDITOR OF THE *ESCAPIST* COMIC BOOK?
NO, I'M THE ***LETTERER.***
WHAT'S THIS ABOUT?
DETECTIVE DAN TONER.
GO AHEAD AND PUT YOUR HANDS ON YOUR HEAD FOR ME, SON.

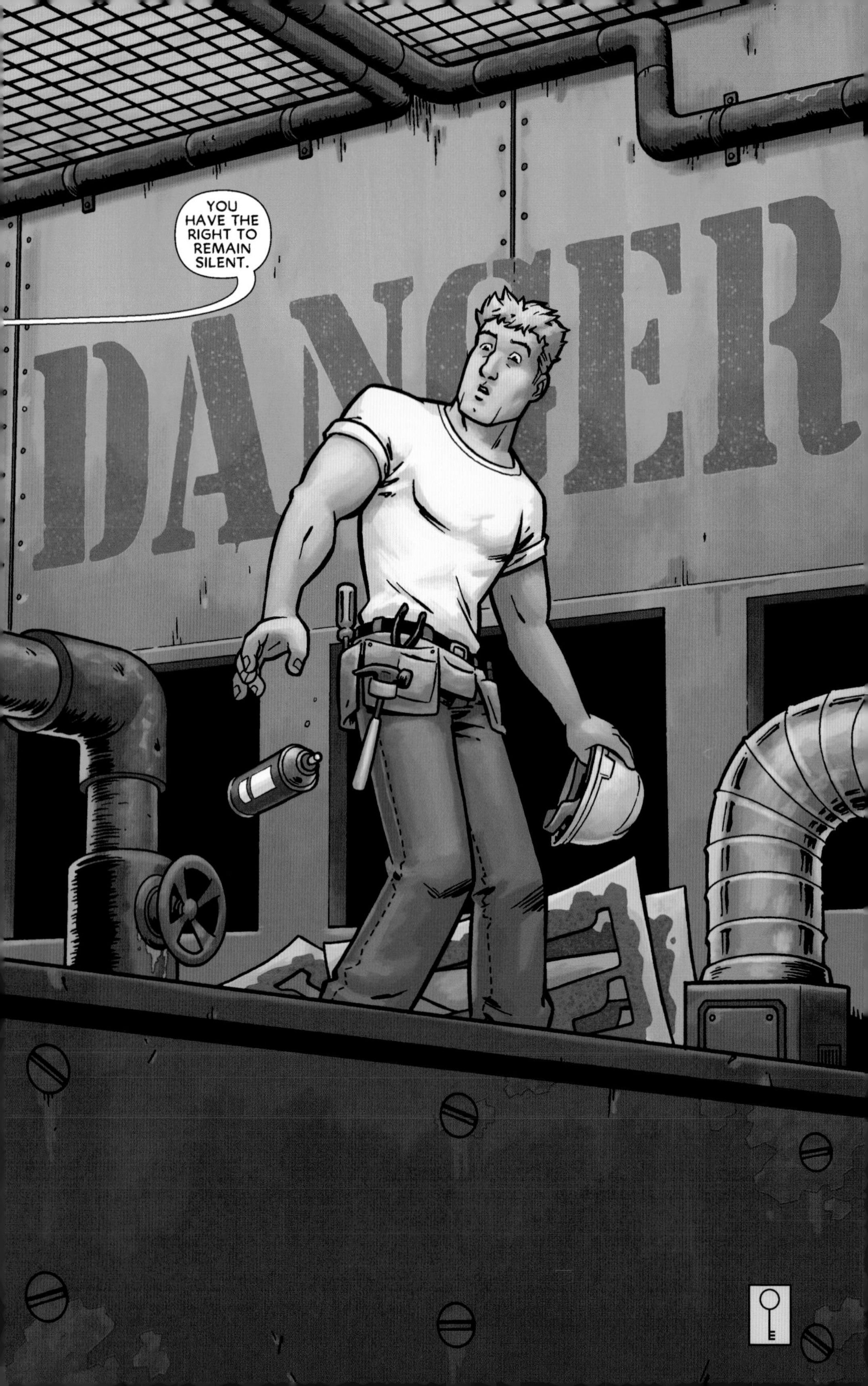
YOU HAVE THE RIGHT TO REMAIN SILENT.
DANGER

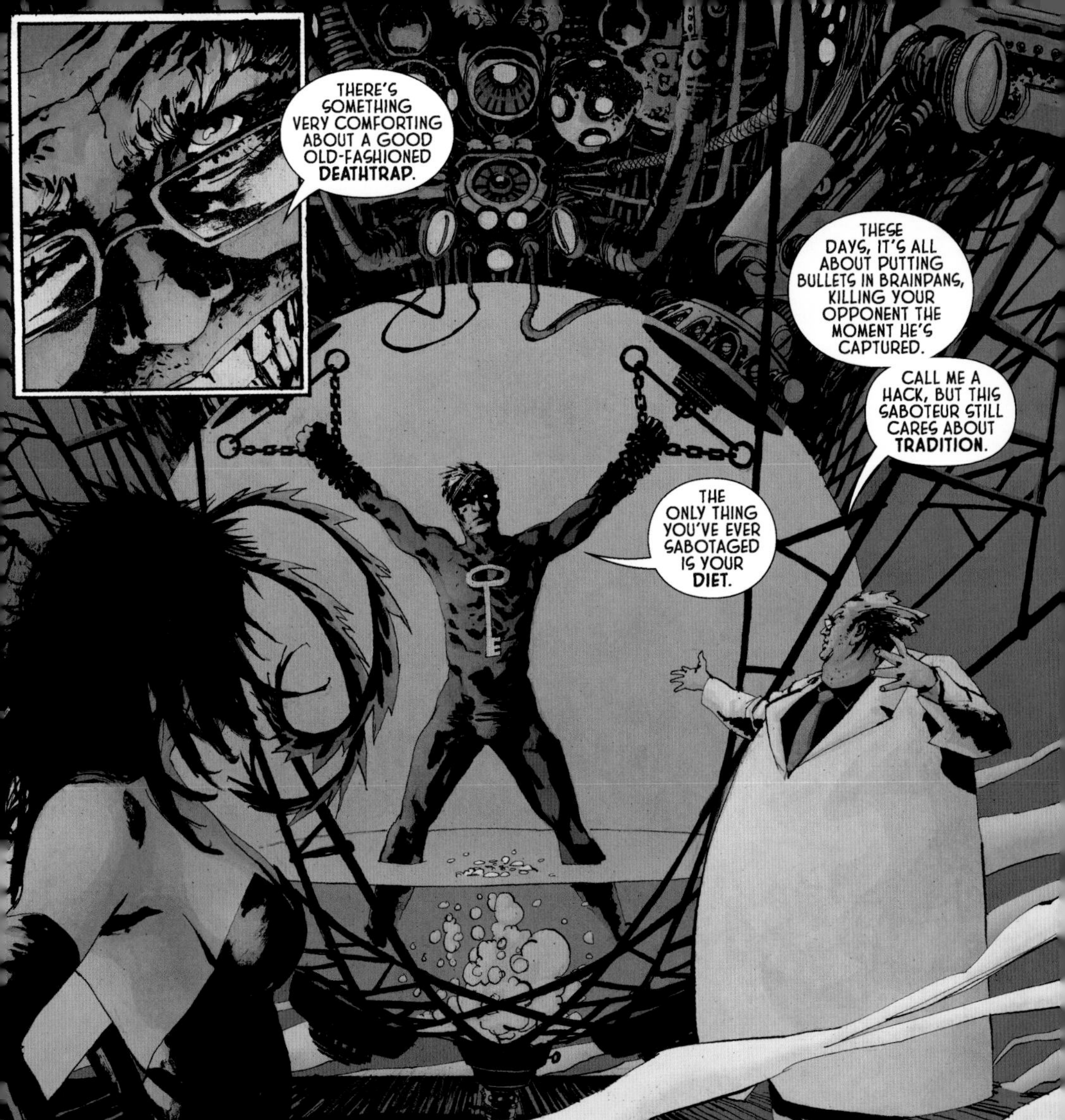
THERE'S SOMETHING VERY COMFORTING ABOUT A GOOD OLD-FASHIONED DEATHTRAP.
THESE DAYS, IT'S ALL ABOUT PUTTING BULLETS IN BRAINPANS, KILLING YOUR OPPONENT THE MOMENT HE'S CAPTURED.
CALL ME A HACK, BUT THIS SABOTEUR STILL CARES ABOUT TRADITION.
THE ONLY THING YOU'VE EVER SABOTAGED IS YOUR DIET.

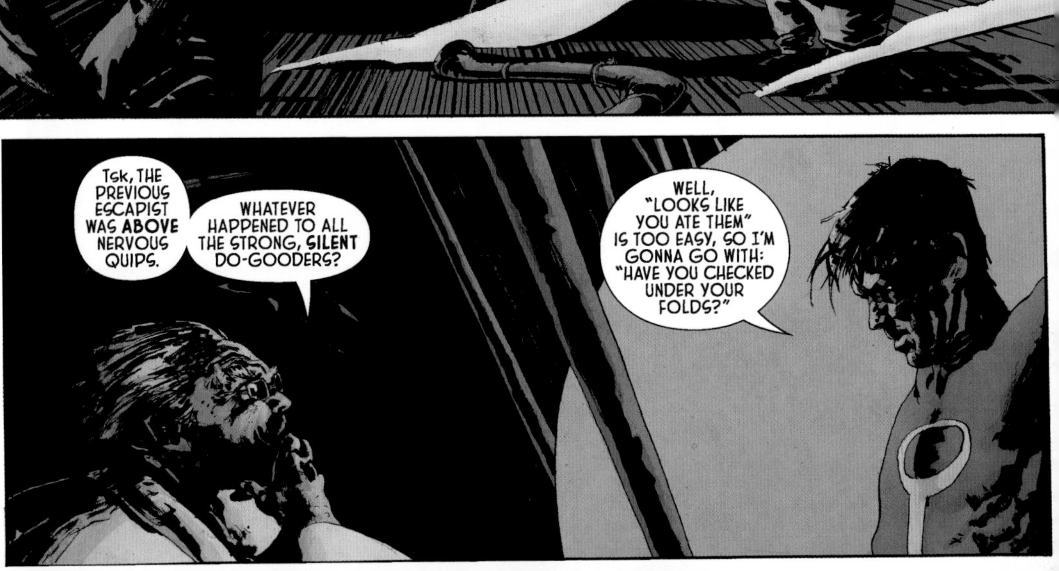
Tsk, THE PREVIOUS ESCAPIST WAS ABOVE NERVOUS QUIPS.
WHATEVER HAPPENED TO ALL THE STRONG, SILENT DO-GOODERS?
WELL, "LOOKS LIKE YOU ATE THEM" IS TOO EASY, SO I'M GONNA GO WITH: "HAVE YOU CHECKED UNDER YOUR FOLDS?"

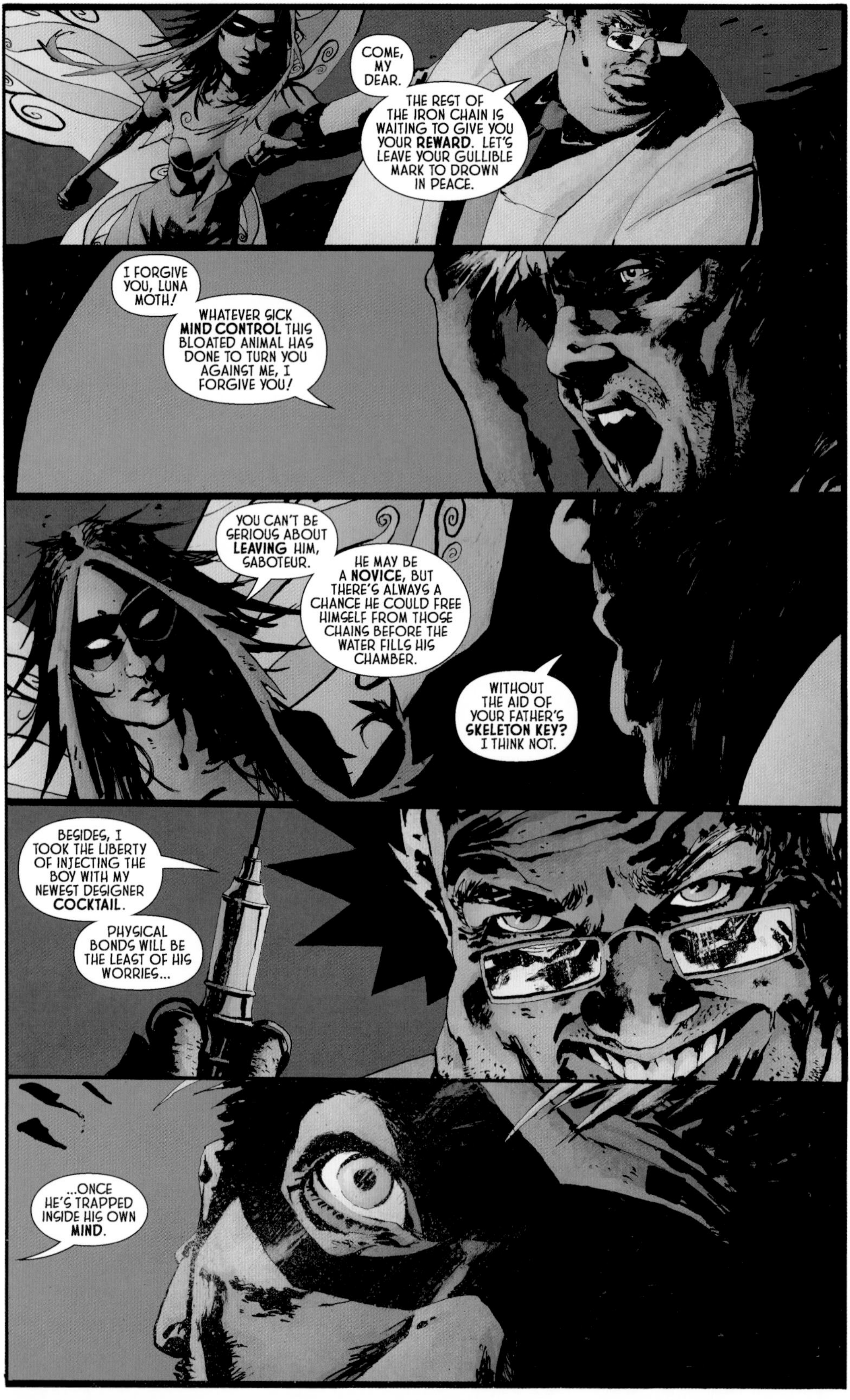
COME, MY DEAR.
THE REST OF THE IRON CHAIN IS WAITING TO GIVE YOU YOUR REWARD. LET'S LEAVE YOUR GULLIBLE MARK TO DROWN IN PEACE.
I FORGIVE YOU, LUNA MOTH!
WHATEVER SICK MIND CONTROL THIS BLOATED ANIMAL HAS DONE TO TURN YOU AGAINST ME, I FORGIVE YOU!
YOU CAN'T BE SERIOUS ABOUT LEAVING HIM, SABOTEUR.
HE MAY BE A NOVICE, BUT THERE'S ALWAYS A CHANCE HE COULD FREE HIMSELF FROM THOSE CHAINS BEFORE THE WATER FILLS HIS CHAMBER.
WITHOUT THE AID OF YOUR FATHER'S SKELETON KEY? I THINK NOT.
BESIDES, I TOOK THE LIBERTY OF INJECTING THE BOY WITH MY NEWEST DESIGNER COCKTAIL.
PHYSICAL BONDS WILL BE THE LEAST OF HIS WORRIES...
...ONCE HE'S TRAPPED INSIDE HIS OWN MIND.

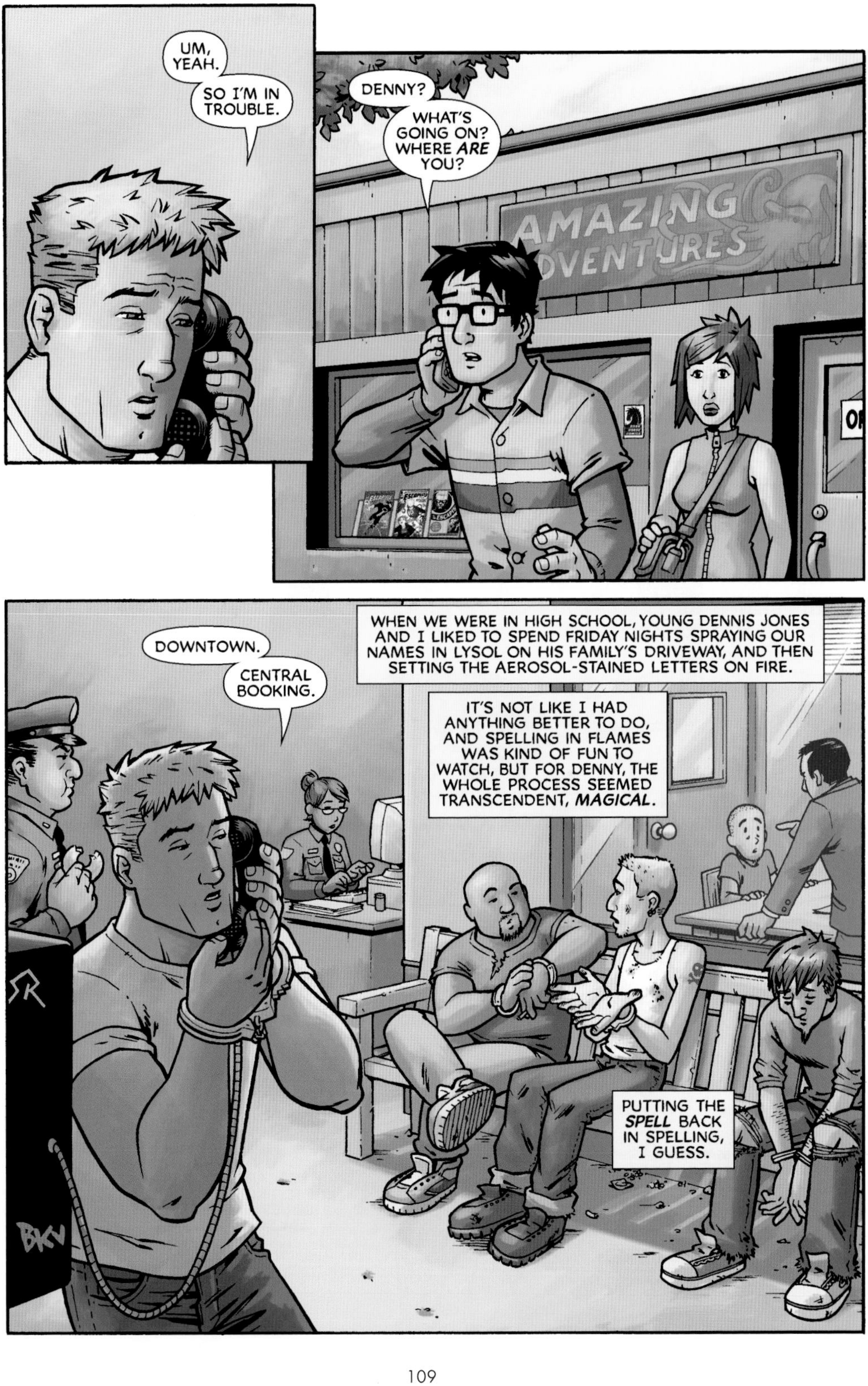
UM, YEAH.
SO I'M IN TROUBLE.
DENNY?
WHAT'S GOING ON? WHERE *ARE* YOU?
AMAZING ADVENTURES
DOWNTOWN.
CENTRAL BOOKING.
WHEN WE WERE IN HIGH SCHOOL, YOUNG DENNIS JONES AND I LIKED TO SPEND FRIDAY NIGHTS SPRAYING OUR NAMES IN LYSOL ON HIS FAMILY'S DRIVEWAY, AND THEN SETTING THE AEROSOL-STAINED LETTERS ON FIRE.
IT'S NOT LIKE I HAD ANYTHING BETTER TO DO, AND SPELLING IN FLAMES WAS KIND OF FUN TO WATCH, BUT FOR DENNY, THE WHOLE PROCESS SEEMED TRANSCENDENT, *MAGICAL*.
PUTTING THE *SPELL* BACK IN SPELLING, I GUESS.
BKV

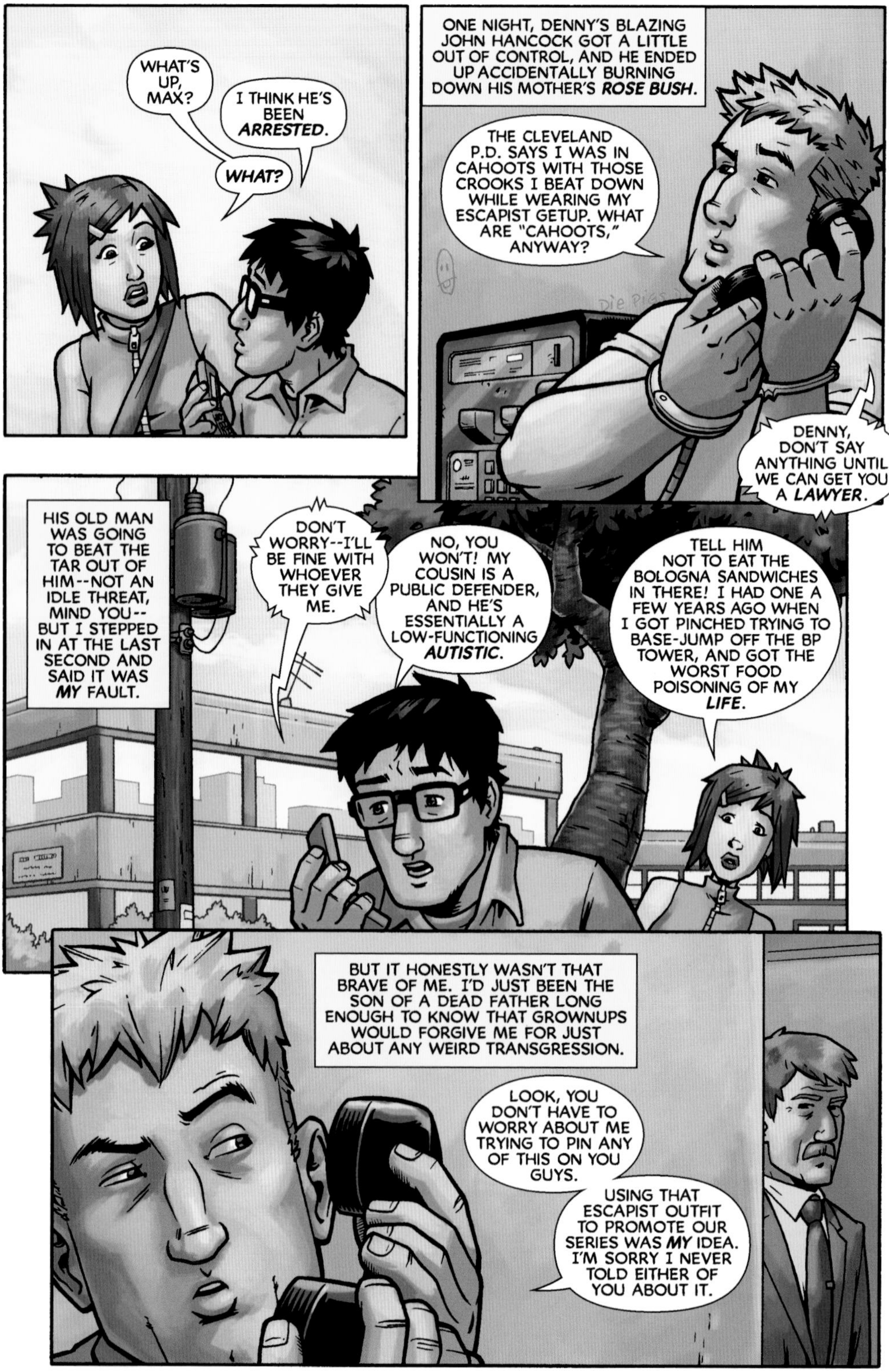
WHAT'S UP, MAX?
I THINK HE'S BEEN ARRESTED.
WHAT?
ONE NIGHT, DENNY'S BLAZING JOHN HANCOCK GOT A LITTLE OUT OF CONTROL, AND HE ENDED UP ACCIDENTALLY BURNING DOWN HIS MOTHER'S ROSE BUSH.
THE CLEVELAND P.D. SAYS I WAS IN CAHOOTS WITH THOSE CROOKS I BEAT DOWN WHILE WEARING MY ESCAPIST GETUP. WHAT ARE "CAHOOTS," ANYWAY?
DENNY, DON'T SAY ANYTHING UNTIL WE CAN GET YOU A LAWYER.
HIS OLD MAN WAS GOING TO BEAT THE TAR OUT OF HIM--NOT AN IDLE THREAT, MIND YOU--BUT I STEPPED IN AT THE LAST SECOND AND SAID IT WAS MY FAULT.
DON'T WORRY--I'LL BE FINE WITH WHOEVER THEY GIVE ME.
NO, YOU WON'T! MY COUSIN IS A PUBLIC DEFENDER, AND HE'S ESSENTIALLY A LOW-FUNCTIONING AUTISTIC.
TELL HIM NOT TO EAT THE BOLOGNA SANDWICHES IN THERE! I HAD ONE A FEW YEARS AGO WHEN I GOT PINCHED TRYING TO BASE-JUMP OFF THE BP TOWER, AND GOT THE WORST FOOD POISONING OF MY LIFE.
BUT IT HONESTLY WASN'T THAT BRAVE OF ME. I'D JUST BEEN THE SON OF A DEAD FATHER LONG ENOUGH TO KNOW THAT GROWNUPS WOULD FORGIVE ME FOR JUST ABOUT ANY WEIRD TRANSGRESSION.
LOOK, YOU DON'T HAVE TO WORRY ABOUT ME TRYING TO PIN ANY OF THIS ON YOU GUYS.
USING THAT ESCAPIST OUTFIT TO PROMOTE OUR SERIES WAS MY IDEA. I'M SORRY I NEVER TOLD EITHER OF YOU ABOUT IT.

DENNY HAD SAVED ME FROM COUNTLESS HORDES OF ANTI-SEMITIC BULLIES, SO I CONSIDERED THE WHOLE "BURNING BUSH" DEBACLE A SMALL REPAYMENT.

WHAT THE HELL ARE YOU TALKING ABOUT?

I'M THE ONE WHO THOUGHT UP THIS STUPID PUBLICITY STUNT!

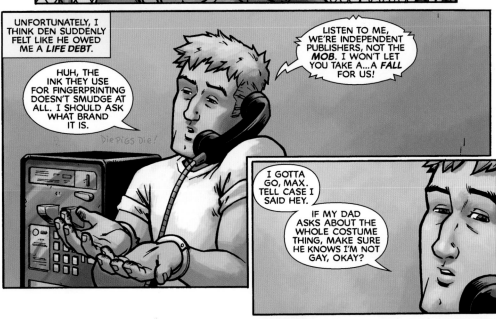

UNFORTUNATELY, I THINK DEN SUDDENLY FELT LIKE HE OWED ME A *LIFE DEBT.*

HUH, THE INK THEY USE FOR FINGERPRINTING DOESN'T SMUDGE AT ALL. I SHOULD ASK WHAT BRAND IT IS.

LISTEN TO ME, WE'RE INDEPENDENT PUBLISHERS, NOT THE *MOB.* I WON'T LET YOU TAKE A...A *FALL* FOR US!

Die PiGS Die!

I GOTTA GO, MAX. TELL CASE I SAID HEY.

IF MY DAD ASKS ABOUT THE WHOLE COSTUME THING, MAKE SURE HE KNOWS I'M NOT GAY, OKAY?

DENNY, WAIT!

DENNY? *HELLO...?*

HE SAVED THOSE PEOPLE'S LIVES! WHY ARE THE COPS SUDDENLY TREATING HIM LIKE PUBLIC ENEMY #1?

CUSTOMER PARKING ONLY

I'M PRETTY SURE THEY'RE NOT THE BAD GUYS HERE.

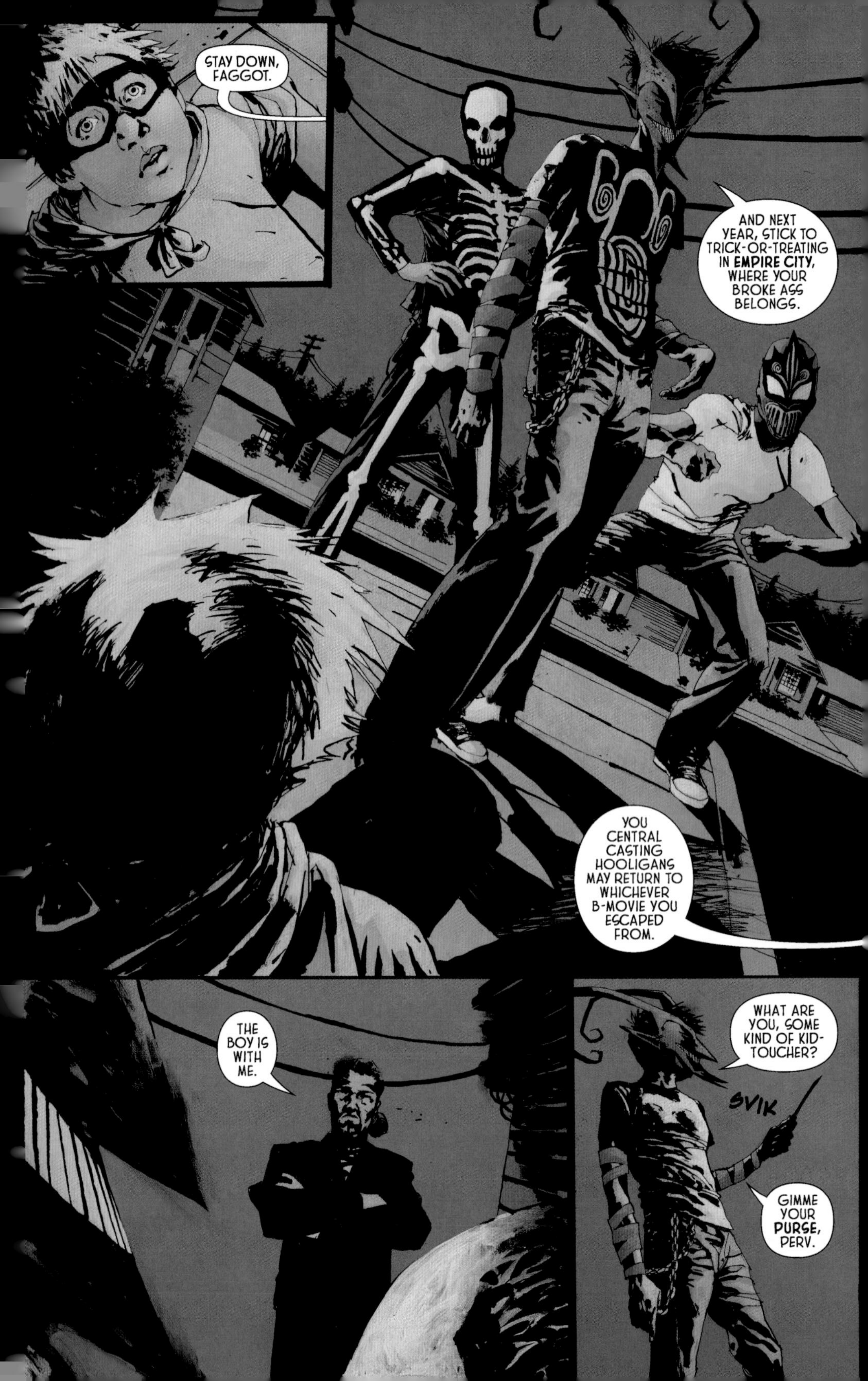
STAY DOWN, FAGGOT.
AND NEXT YEAR, STICK TO TRICK-OR-TREATING IN EMPIRE CITY, WHERE YOUR BROKE ASS BELONGS.
YOU CENTRAL CASTING HOOLIGANS MAY RETURN TO WHICHEVER B-MOVIE YOU ESCAPED FROM.
THE BOY IS WITH ME.
WHAT ARE YOU, SOME KIND OF KID-TOUCHER?
SVIK
GIMME YOUR PURSE, PERV.

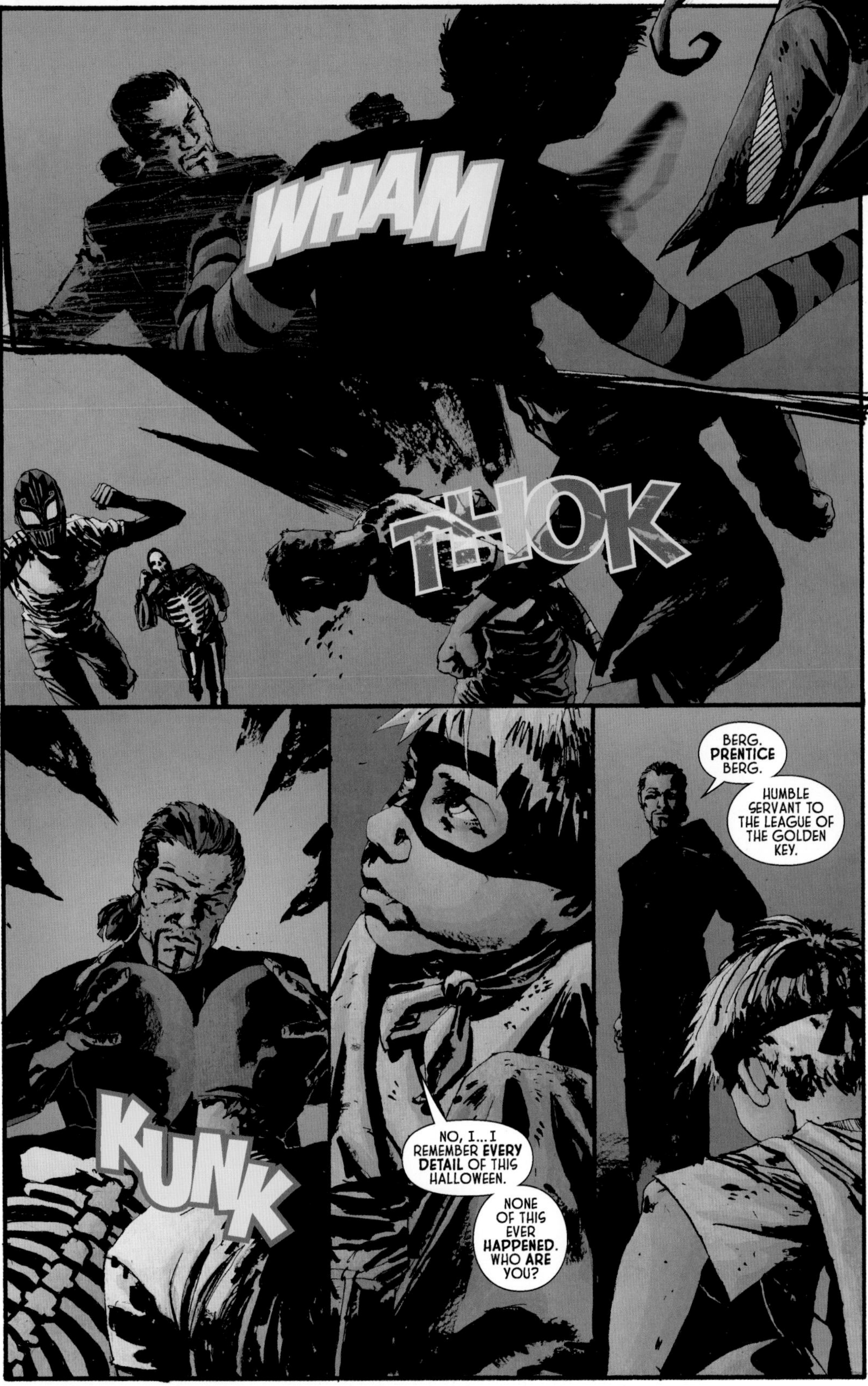
WHAM
THOK
KUNK
NO, I... I REMEMBER EVERY DETAIL OF THIS HALLOWEEN.
NONE OF THIS EVER HAPPENED. WHO ARE YOU?
BERG. PRENTICE BERG.
HUMBLE SERVANT TO THE LEAGUE OF THE GOLDEN KEY.

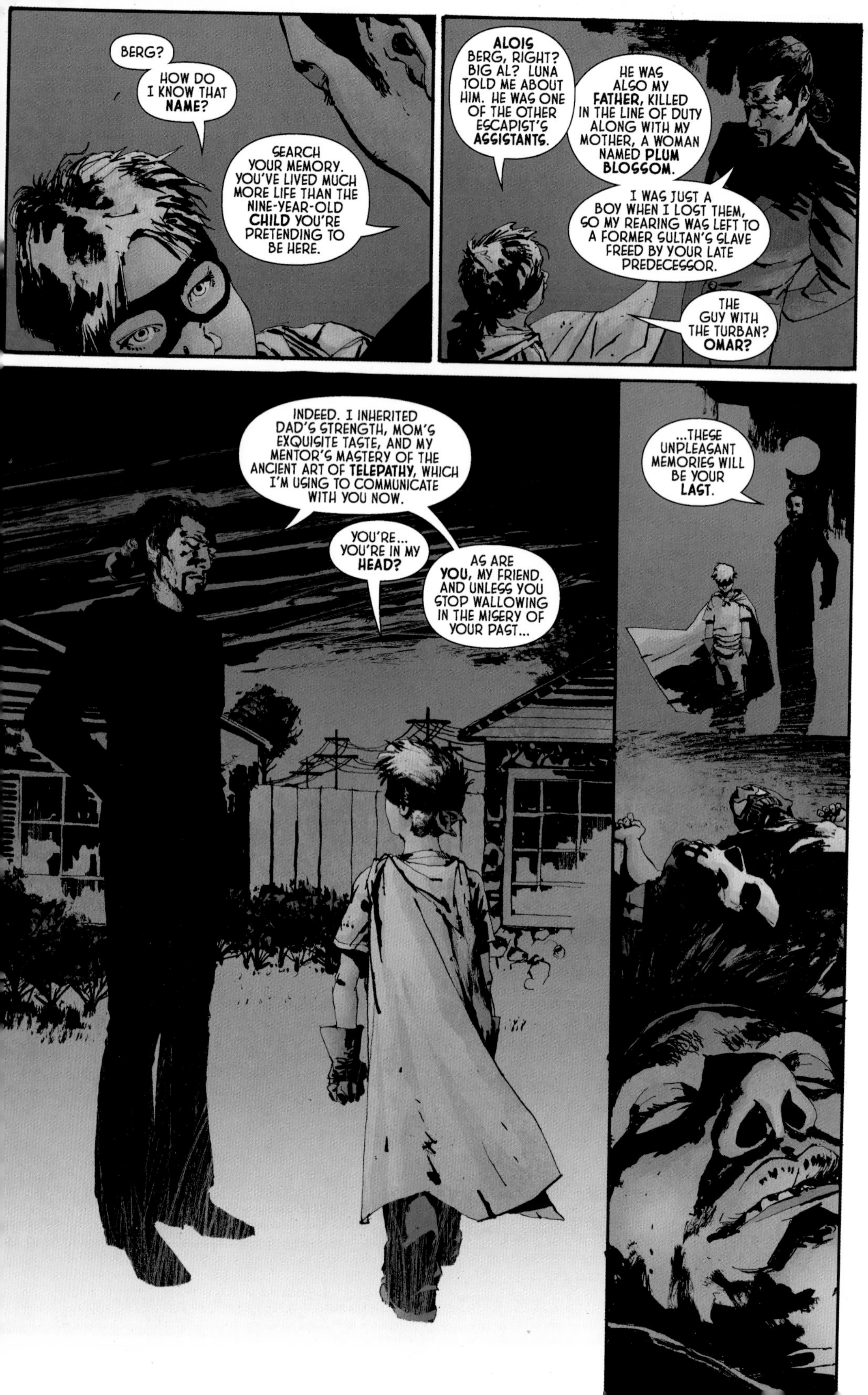
BERG?
HOW DO I KNOW THAT **NAME?**
SEARCH YOUR MEMORY. YOU'VE LIVED MUCH MORE LIFE THAN THE NINE-YEAR-OLD **CHILD** YOU'RE PRETENDING TO BE HERE.
ALOIS BERG, RIGHT? BIG AL? LUNA TOLD ME ABOUT HIM. HE WAS ONE OF THE OTHER ESCAPIST'S **ASSISTANTS.**
HE WAS ALSO MY **FATHER,** KILLED IN THE LINE OF DUTY ALONG WITH MY MOTHER, A WOMAN NAMED **PLUM BLOSSOM.**
I WAS JUST A BOY WHEN I LOST THEM, SO MY REARING WAS LEFT TO A FORMER SULTAN'S SLAVE FREED BY YOUR LATE PREDECESSOR.
THE GUY WITH THE TURBAN? **OMAR?**
INDEED. I INHERITED DAD'S STRENGTH, MOM'S EXQUISITE TASTE, AND MY MENTOR'S MASTERY OF THE ANCIENT ART OF **TELEPATHY,** WHICH I'M USING TO COMMUNICATE WITH YOU NOW.
YOU'RE... YOU'RE IN MY **HEAD?**
AS ARE **YOU,** MY FRIEND. AND UNLESS YOU STOP WALLOWING IN THE MISERY OF YOUR PAST...
...THESE UNPLEASANT MEMORIES WILL BE YOUR **LAST.**

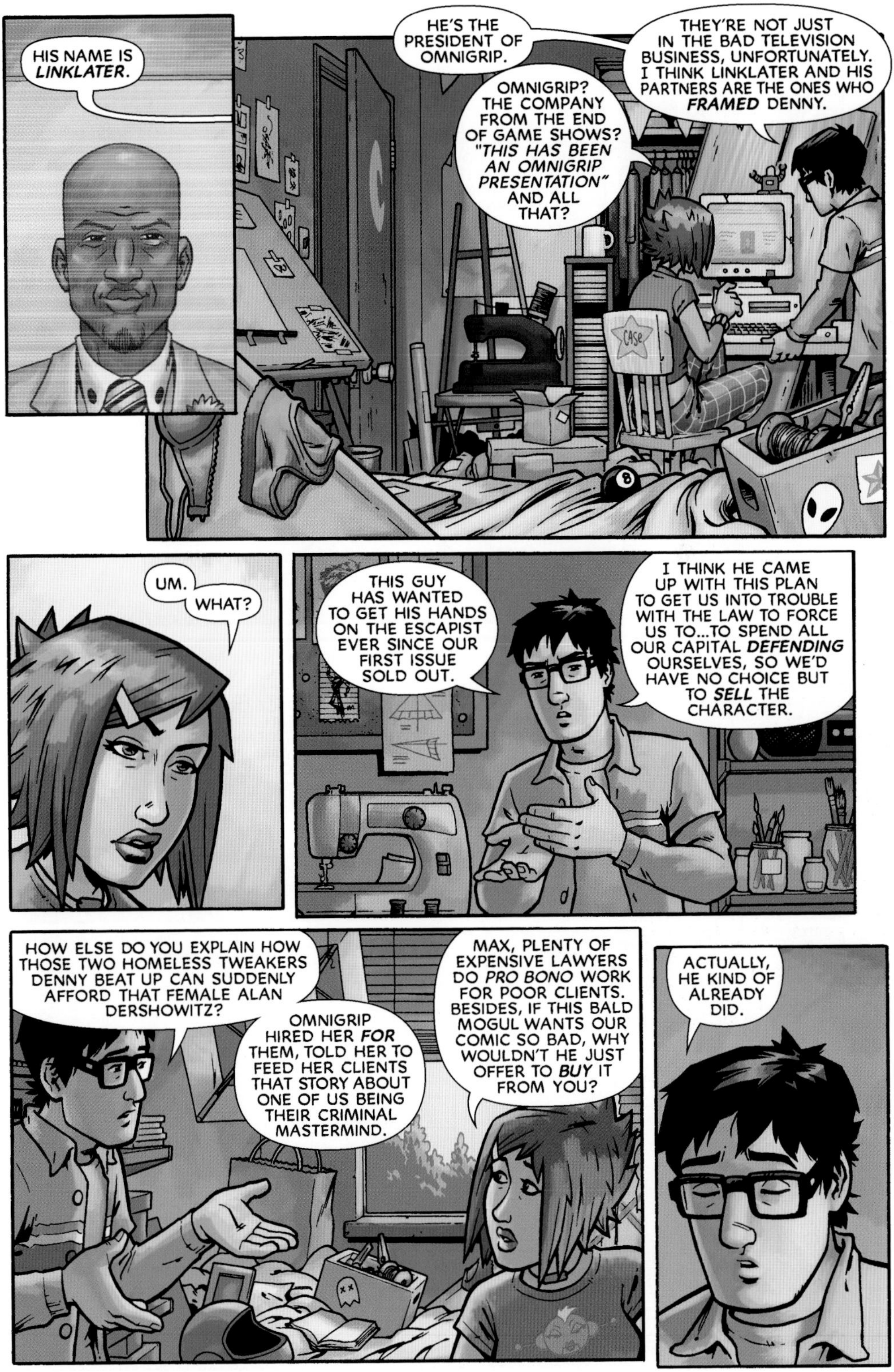
HIS NAME IS *LINKLATER*.
HE'S THE PRESIDENT OF OMNIGRIP.
OMNIGRIP? THE COMPANY FROM THE END OF GAME SHOWS? *"THIS HAS BEEN AN OMNIGRIP PRESENTATION"* AND ALL THAT?
THEY'RE NOT JUST IN THE BAD TELEVISION BUSINESS, UNFORTUNATELY. I THINK LINKLATER AND HIS PARTNERS ARE THE ONES WHO *FRAMED* DENNY.
UM.
WHAT?
THIS GUY HAS WANTED TO GET HIS HANDS ON THE ESCAPIST EVER SINCE OUR FIRST ISSUE SOLD OUT.
I THINK HE CAME UP WITH THIS PLAN TO GET US INTO TROUBLE WITH THE LAW TO FORCE US TO...TO SPEND ALL OUR CAPITAL *DEFENDING* OURSELVES, SO WE'D HAVE NO CHOICE BUT TO *SELL* THE CHARACTER.
HOW ELSE DO YOU EXPLAIN HOW THOSE TWO HOMELESS TWEAKERS DENNY BEAT UP CAN SUDDENLY AFFORD THAT FEMALE ALAN DERSHOWITZ?
OMNIGRIP HIRED HER *FOR* THEM, TOLD HER TO FEED HER CLIENTS THAT STORY ABOUT ONE OF US BEING THEIR CRIMINAL MASTERMIND.
MAX, PLENTY OF EXPENSIVE LAWYERS DO *PRO BONO* WORK FOR POOR CLIENTS. BESIDES, IF THIS BALD MOGUL WANTS OUR COMIC SO BAD, WHY WOULDN'T HE JUST OFFER TO *BUY* IT FROM YOU?
ACTUALLY, HE KIND OF ALREADY DID.

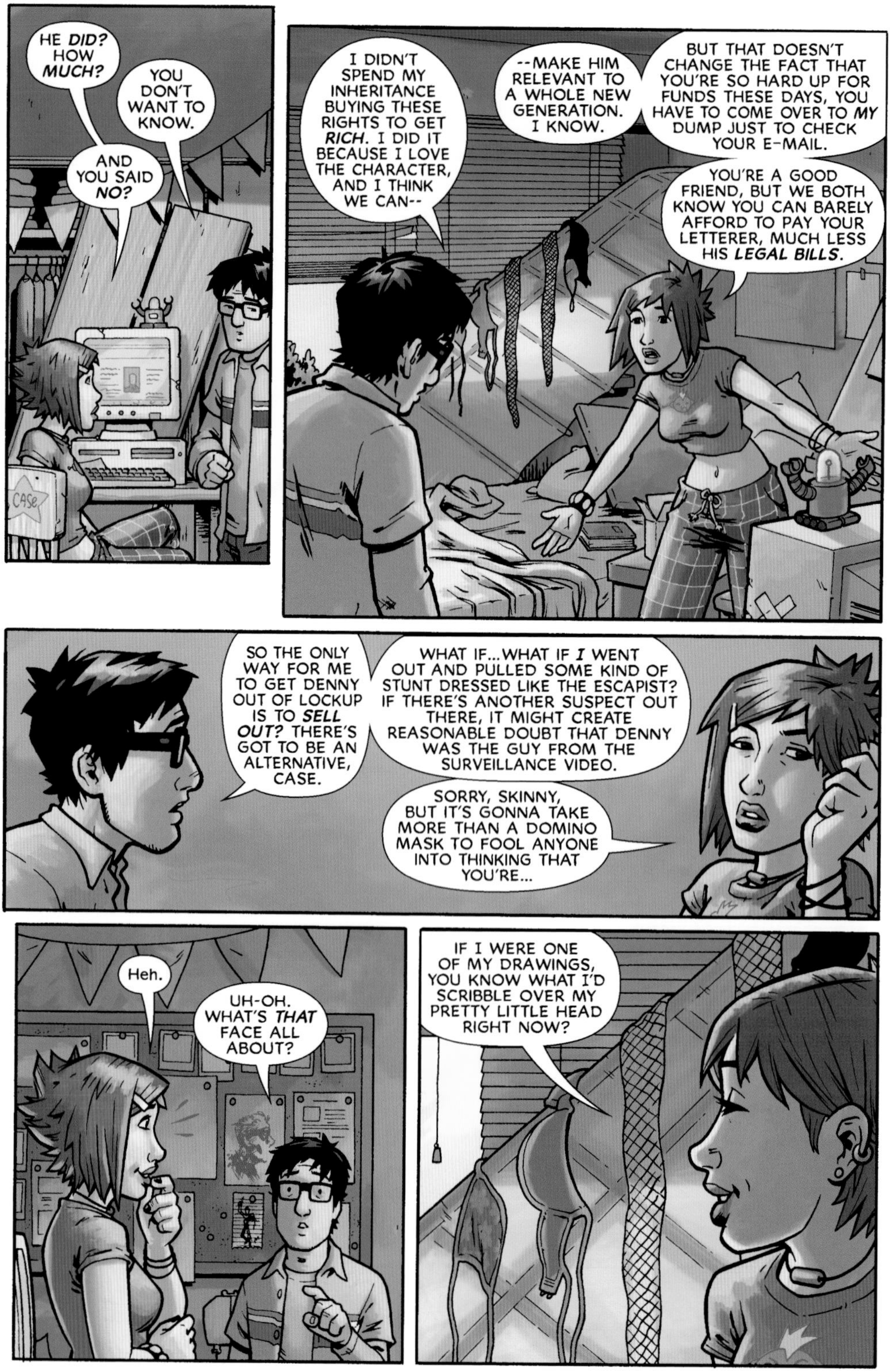

HE DID? HOW MUCH?
YOU DON'T WANT TO KNOW.
AND YOU SAID NO?
I DIDN'T SPEND MY INHERITANCE BUYING THESE RIGHTS TO GET RICH. I DID IT BECAUSE I LOVE THE CHARACTER, AND I THINK WE CAN--
--MAKE HIM RELEVANT TO A WHOLE NEW GENERATION. I KNOW.
BUT THAT DOESN'T CHANGE THE FACT THAT YOU'RE SO HARD UP FOR FUNDS THESE DAYS, YOU HAVE TO COME OVER TO MY DUMP JUST TO CHECK YOUR E-MAIL.
YOU'RE A GOOD FRIEND, BUT WE BOTH KNOW YOU CAN BARELY AFFORD TO PAY YOUR LETTERER, MUCH LESS HIS LEGAL BILLS.
CASE
SO THE ONLY WAY FOR ME TO GET DENNY OUT OF LOCKUP IS TO SELL OUT? THERE'S GOT TO BE AN ALTERNATIVE, CASE.
WHAT IF...WHAT IF I WENT OUT AND PULLED SOME KIND OF STUNT DRESSED LIKE THE ESCAPIST? IF THERE'S ANOTHER SUSPECT OUT THERE, IT MIGHT CREATE REASONABLE DOUBT THAT DENNY WAS THE GUY FROM THE SURVEILLANCE VIDEO.
SORRY, SKINNY, BUT IT'S GONNA TAKE MORE THAN A DOMINO MASK TO FOOL ANYONE INTO THINKING THAT YOU'RE...
Heh.
UH-OH. WHAT'S THAT FACE ALL ABOUT?
IF I WERE ONE OF MY DRAWINGS, YOU KNOW WHAT I'D SCRIBBLE OVER MY PRETTY LITTLE HEAD RIGHT NOW?

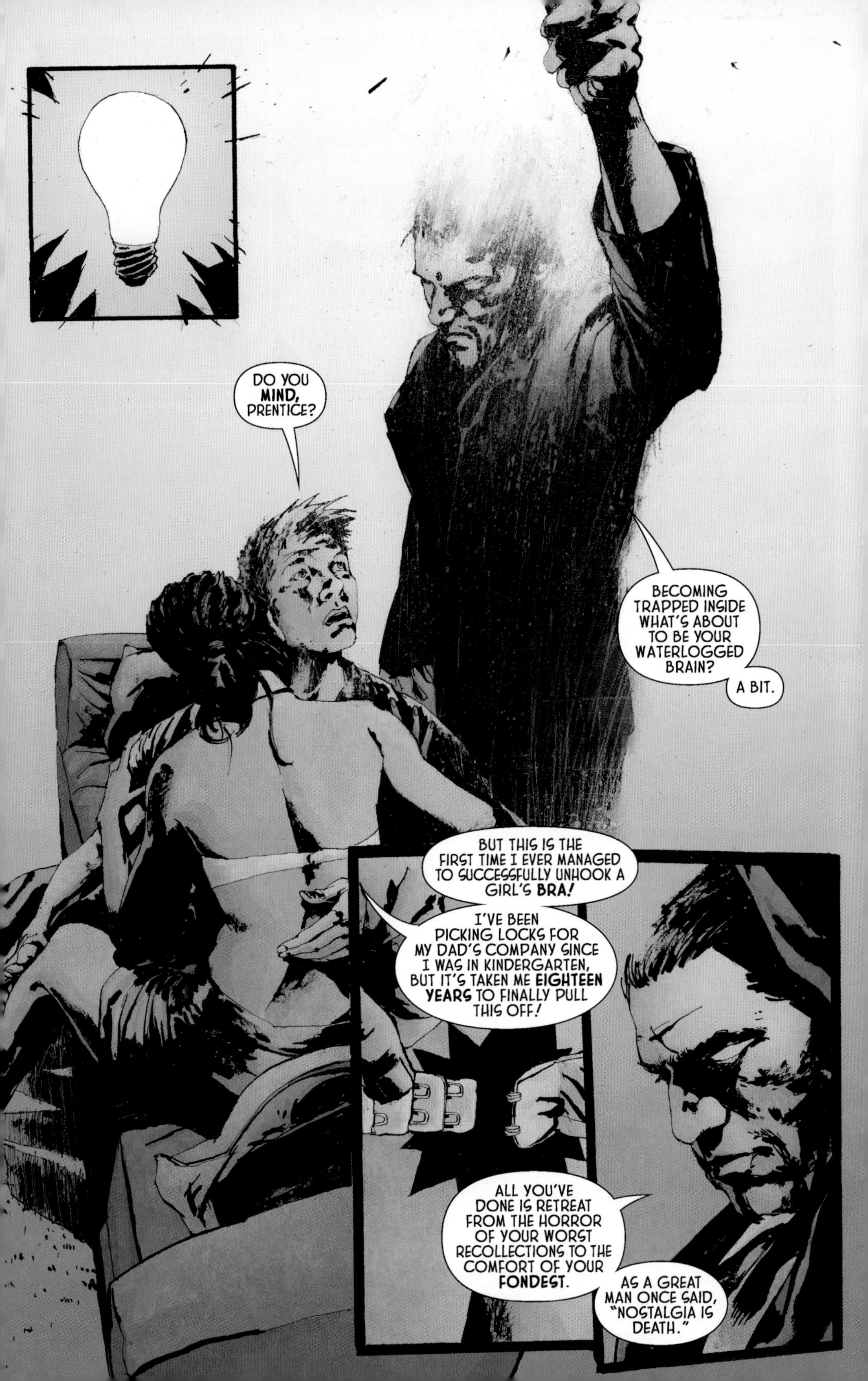
DO YOU MIND, PRENTICE?
BECOMING TRAPPED INSIDE WHAT'S ABOUT TO BE YOUR WATERLOGGED BRAIN?
A BIT.
BUT THIS IS THE FIRST TIME I EVER MANAGED TO SUCCESSFULLY UNHOOK A GIRL'S BRA!
I'VE BEEN PICKING LOCKS FOR MY DAD'S COMPANY SINCE I WAS IN KINDERGARTEN, BUT IT'S TAKEN ME EIGHTEEN YEARS TO FINALLY PULL THIS OFF!
ALL YOU'VE DONE IS RETREAT FROM THE HORROR OF YOUR WORST RECOLLECTIONS TO THE COMFORT OF YOUR FONDEST.
AS A GREAT MAN ONCE SAID, "NOSTALGIA IS DEATH."

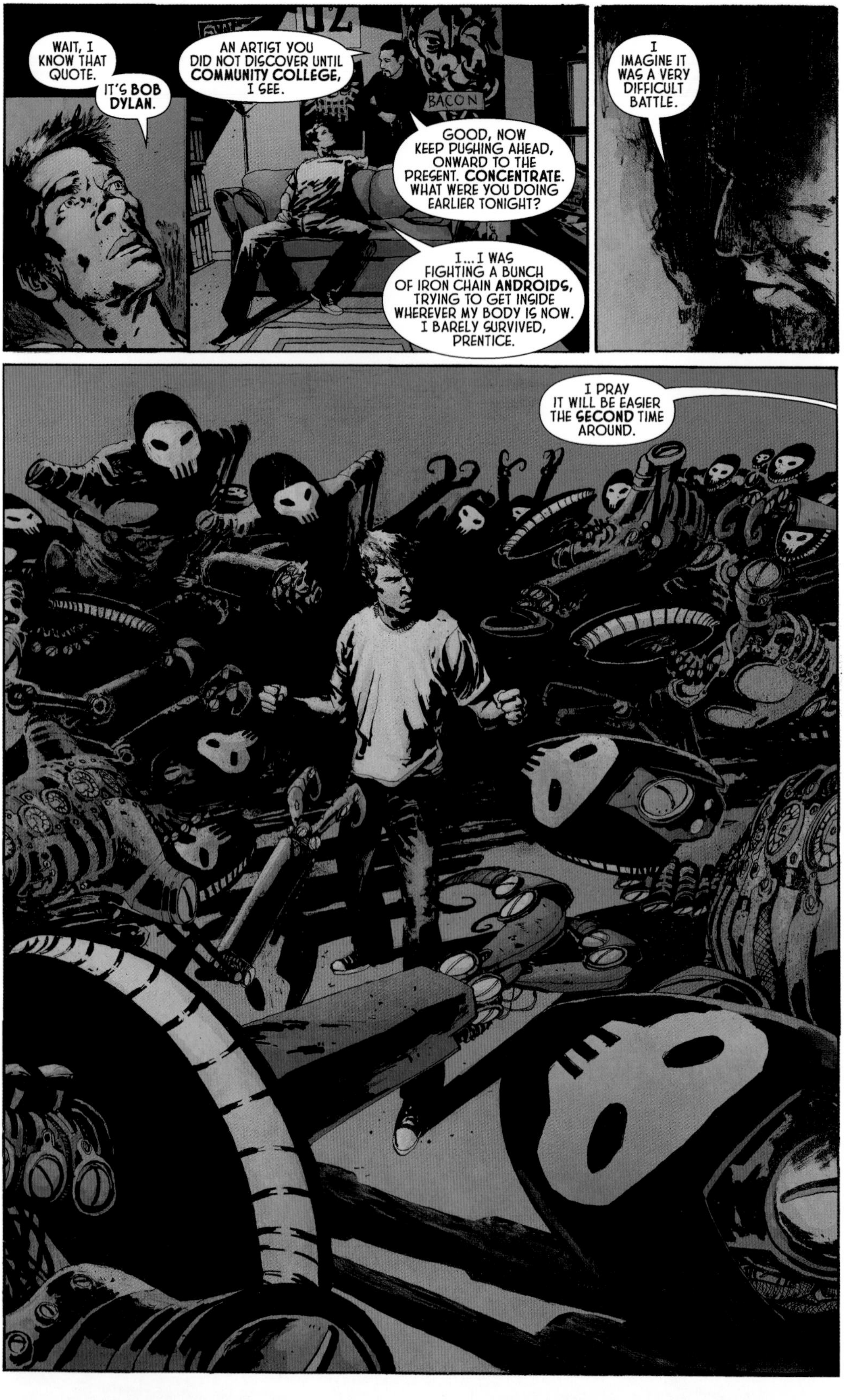
WAIT, I KNOW THAT QUOTE.
IT'S **BOB DYLAN.**
AN ARTIST YOU DID NOT DISCOVER UNTIL **COMMUNITY COLLEGE,** I SEE.
BACON
GOOD, NOW KEEP PUSHING AHEAD, ONWARD TO THE PRESENT. **CONCENTRATE.** WHAT WERE YOU DOING EARLIER TONIGHT?
I... I WAS FIGHTING A BUNCH OF IRON CHAIN **ANDROIDS,** TRYING TO GET INSIDE WHEREVER MY BODY IS NOW. I BARELY SURVIVED, PRENTICE.
I IMAGINE IT WAS A VERY DIFFICULT BATTLE.
I PRAY IT WILL BE EASIER THE **SECOND** TIME AROUND.

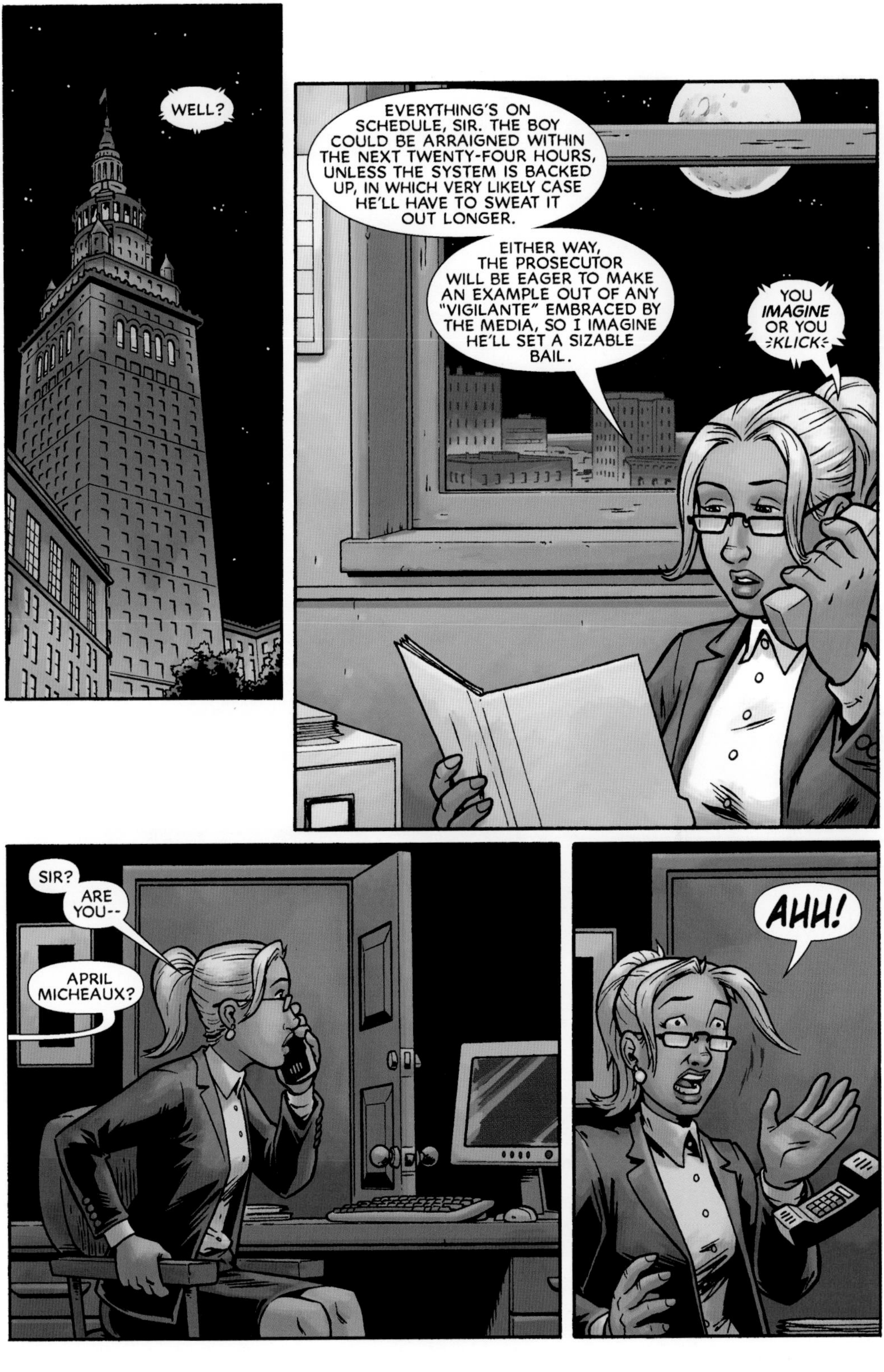
WELL?
EVERYTHING'S ON SCHEDULE, SIR. THE BOY COULD BE ARRAIGNED WITHIN THE NEXT TWENTY-FOUR HOURS, UNLESS THE SYSTEM IS BACKED UP, IN WHICH VERY LIKELY CASE HE'LL HAVE TO SWEAT IT OUT LONGER.
EITHER WAY, THE PROSECUTOR WILL BE EAGER TO MAKE AN EXAMPLE OUT OF ANY "VIGILANTE" EMBRACED BY THE MEDIA, SO I IMAGINE HE'LL SET A SIZABLE BAIL.
YOU *IMAGINE* OR YOU *KLICK*
SIR?
ARE YOU--
APRIL MICHEAUX?
AHH!

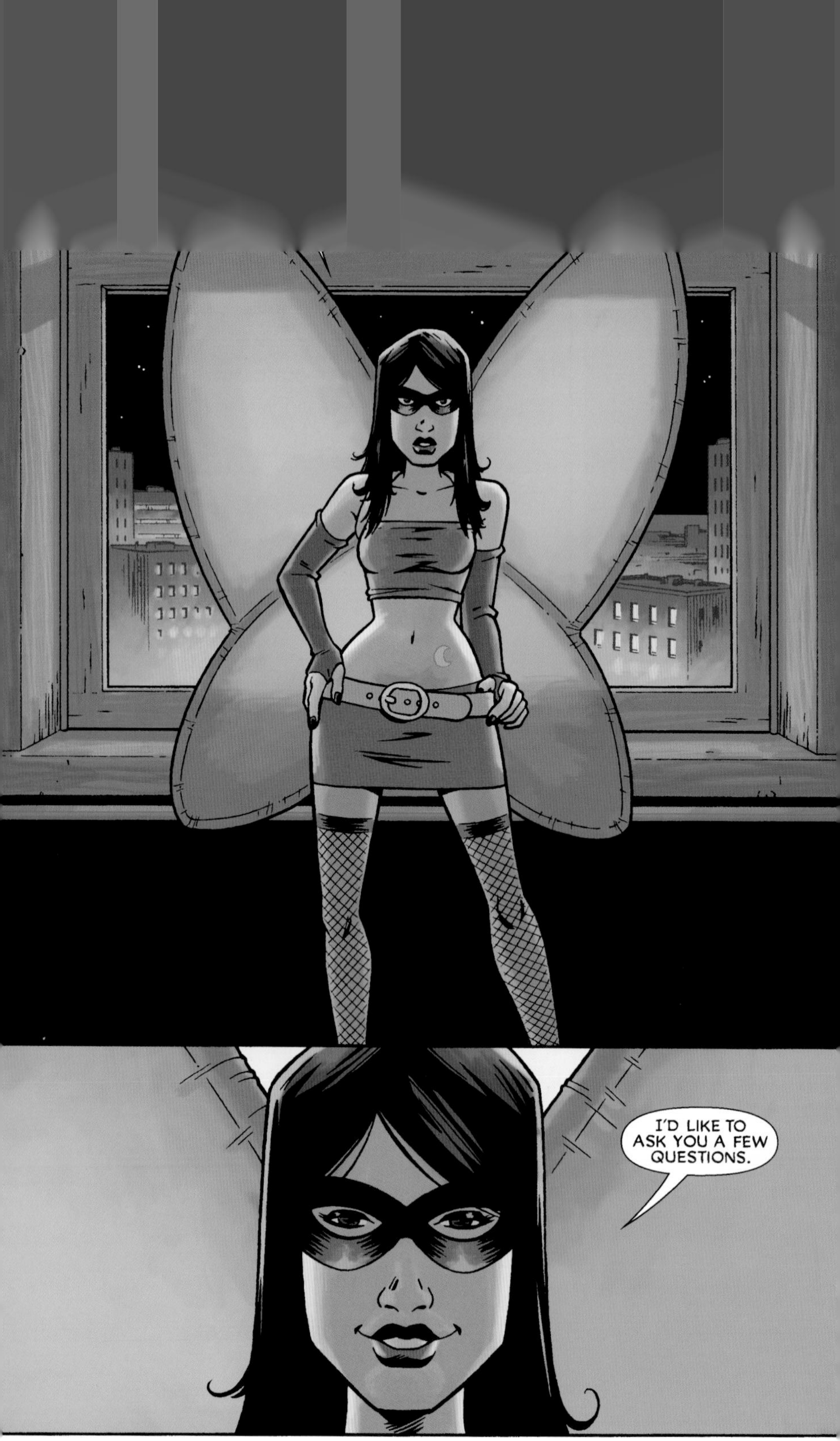
I'D LIKE TO ASK YOU A FEW QUESTIONS.

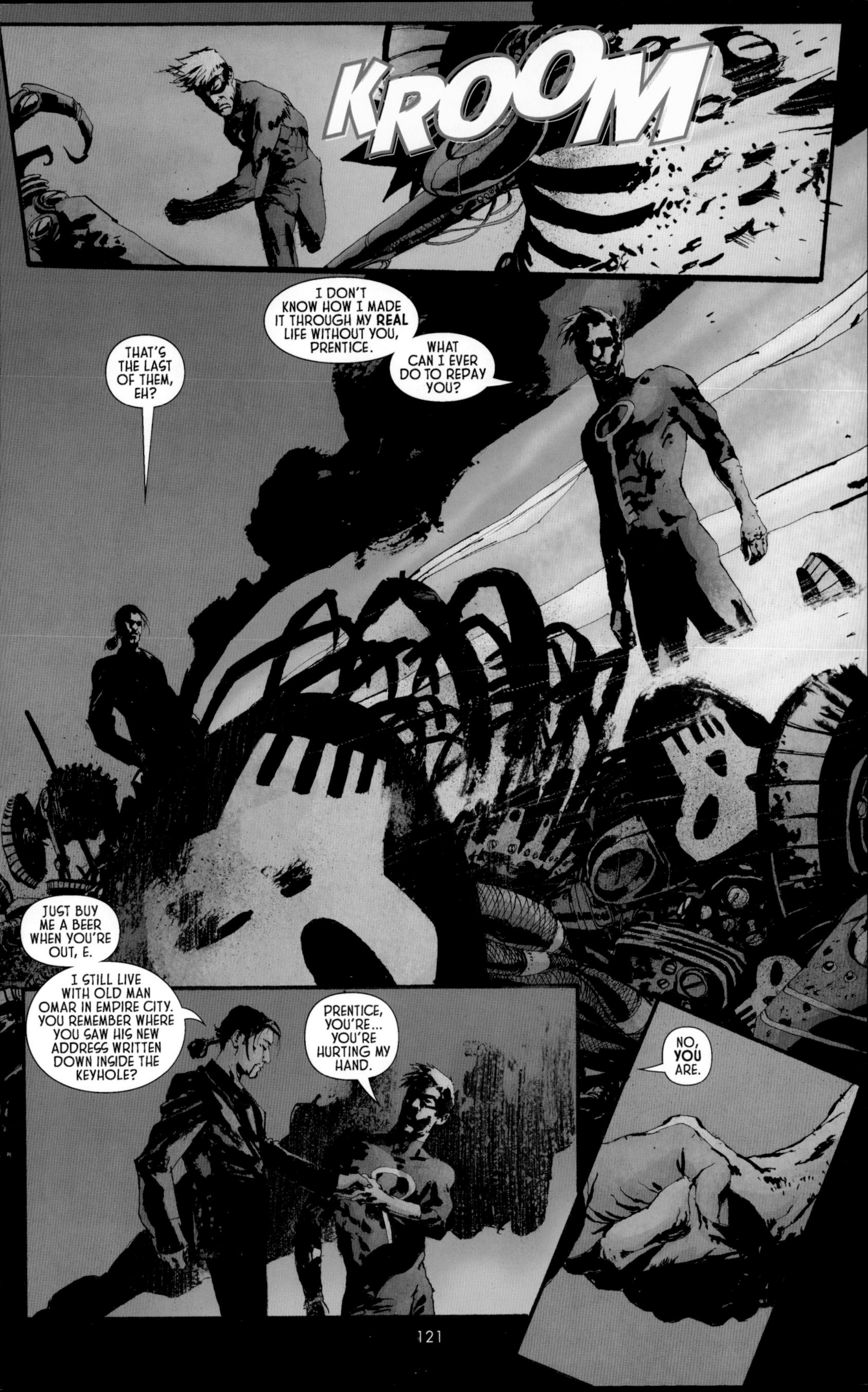
KROOM
THAT'S THE LAST OF THEM, EH?
I DON'T KNOW HOW I MADE IT THROUGH MY REAL LIFE WITHOUT YOU, PRENTICE.
WHAT CAN I EVER DO TO REPAY YOU?
JUST BUY ME A BEER WHEN YOU'RE OUT, E.
I STILL LIVE WITH OLD MAN OMAR IN EMPIRE CITY. YOU REMEMBER WHERE YOU SAW HIS NEW ADDRESS WRITTEN DOWN INSIDE THE KEYHOLE?
PRENTICE, YOU'RE... YOU'RE HURTING MY HAND.
NO, YOU ARE.

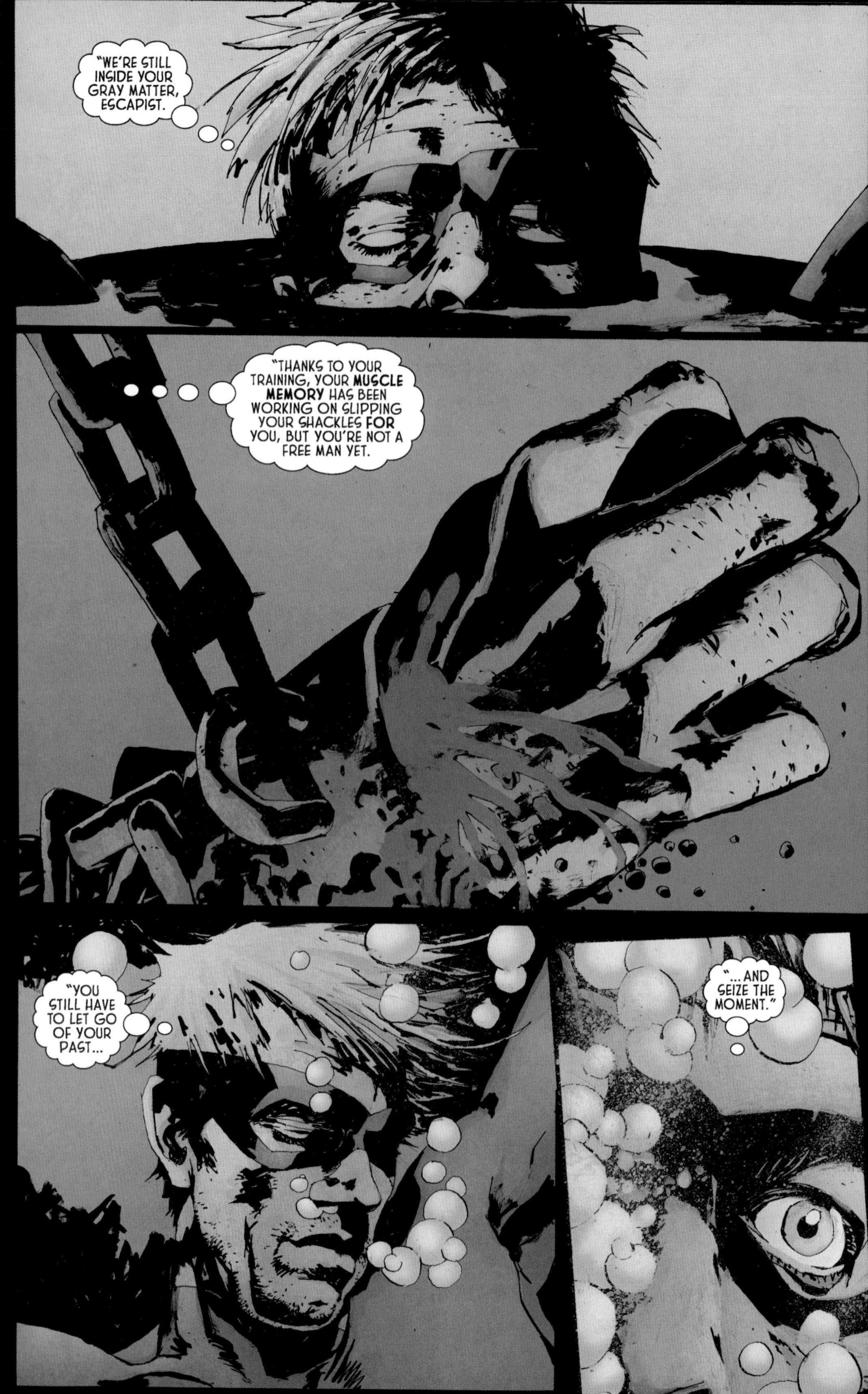
"WE'RE STILL INSIDE YOUR GRAY MATTER, ESCAPIST.
"THANKS TO YOUR TRAINING, YOUR MUSCLE MEMORY HAS BEEN WORKING ON SLIPPING YOUR SHACKLES FOR YOU, BUT YOU'RE NOT A FREE MAN YET.
"YOU STILL HAVE TO LET GO OF YOUR PAST...
"...AND SEIZE THE MOMENT."

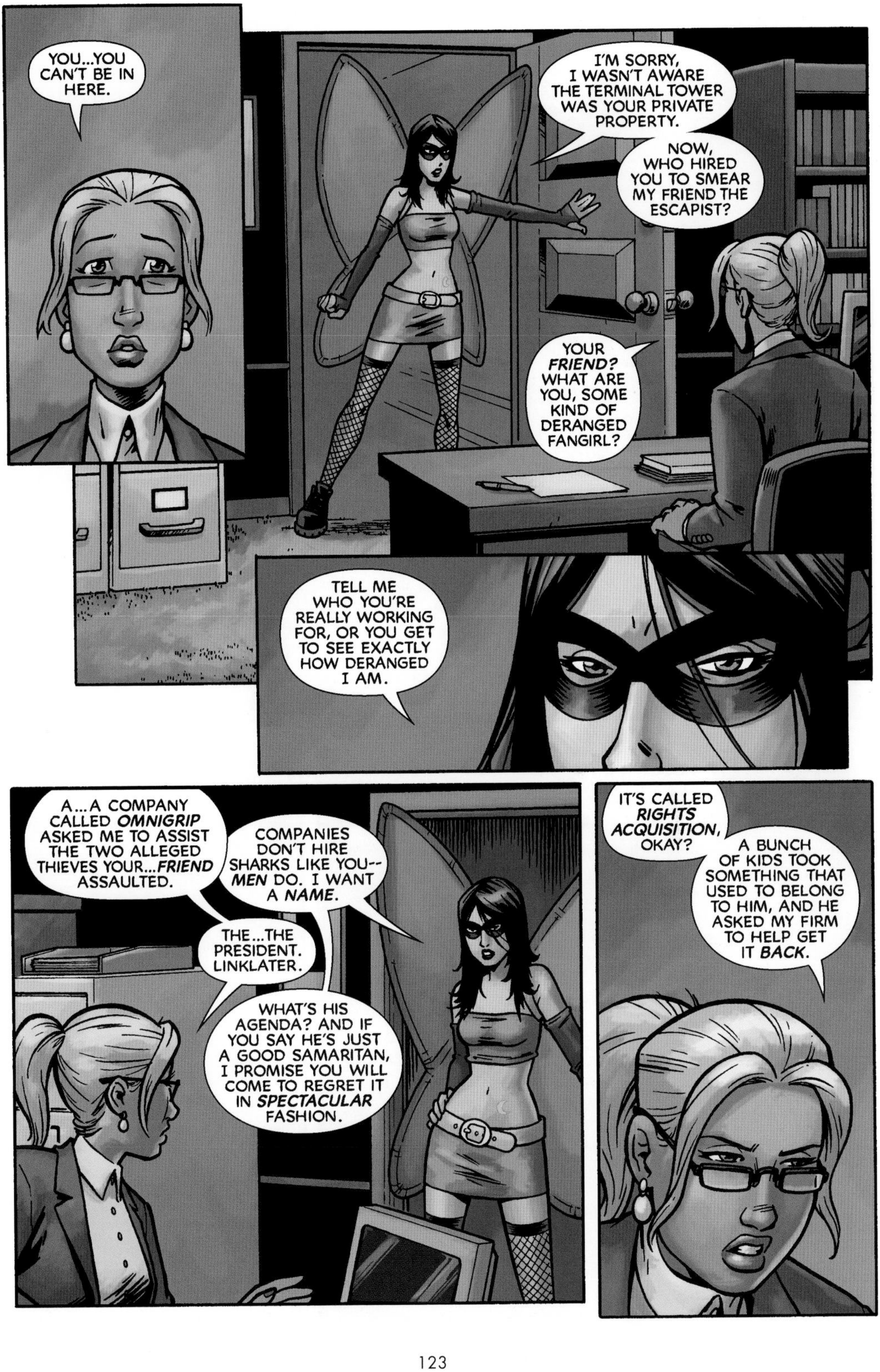
YOU...YOU CAN'T BE IN HERE.
I'M SORRY, I WASN'T AWARE THE TERMINAL TOWER WAS YOUR PRIVATE PROPERTY.
NOW, WHO HIRED YOU TO SMEAR MY FRIEND THE ESCAPIST?
YOUR FRIEND? WHAT ARE YOU, SOME KIND OF DERANGED FANGIRL?
TELL ME WHO YOU'RE REALLY WORKING FOR, OR YOU GET TO SEE EXACTLY HOW DERANGED I AM.
A...A COMPANY CALLED OMNIGRIP ASKED ME TO ASSIST THE TWO ALLEGED THIEVES YOUR...FRIEND ASSAULTED.
COMPANIES DON'T HIRE SHARKS LIKE YOU-- MEN DO. I WANT A NAME.
THE...THE PRESIDENT. LINKLATER.
WHAT'S HIS AGENDA? AND IF YOU SAY HE'S JUST A GOOD SAMARITAN, I PROMISE YOU WILL COME TO REGRET IT IN SPECTACULAR FASHION.
IT'S CALLED RIGHTS ACQUISITION, OKAY?
A BUNCH OF KIDS TOOK SOMETHING THAT USED TO BELONG TO HIM, AND HE ASKED MY FIRM TO HELP GET IT BACK.

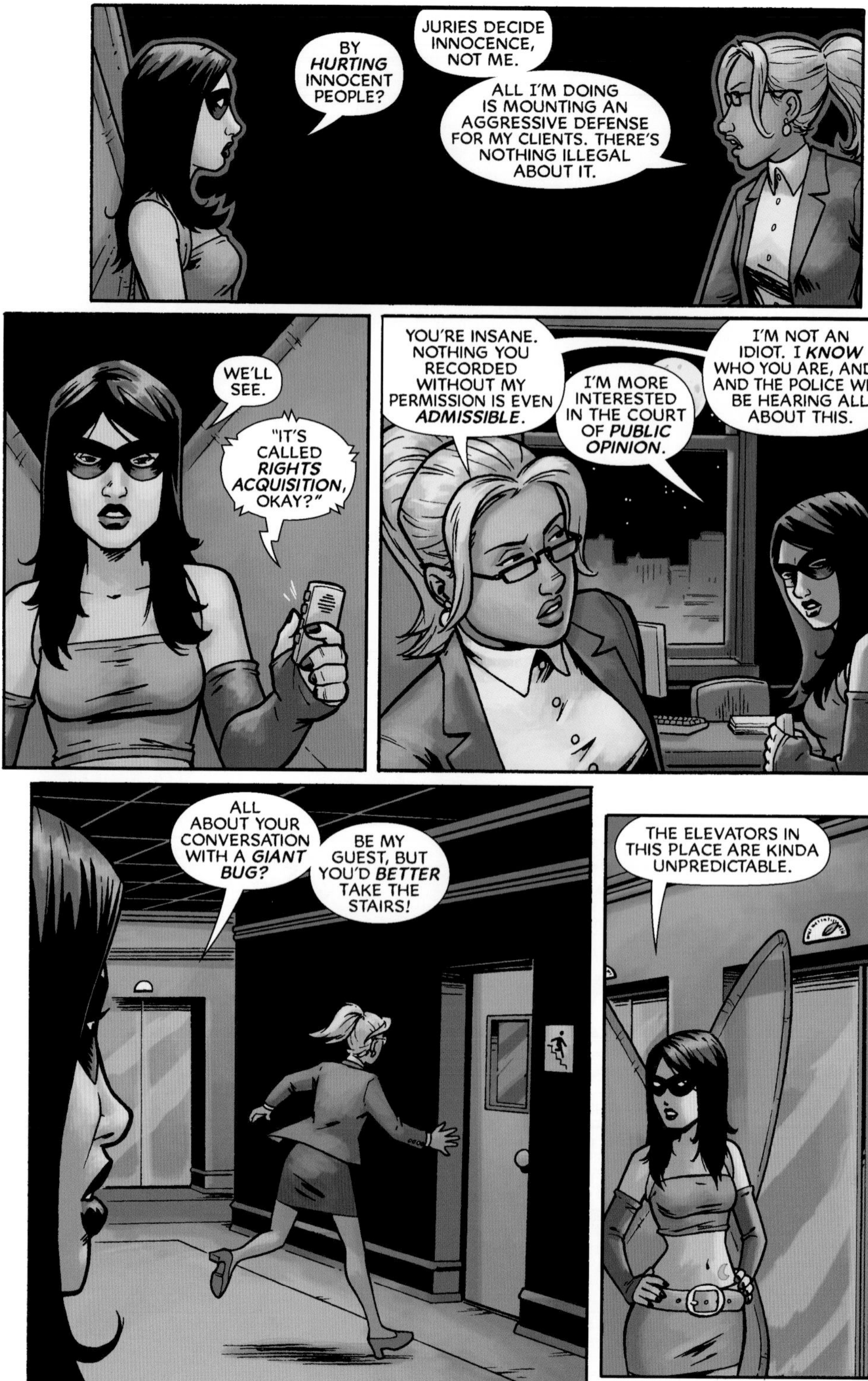
BY *HURTING* INNOCENT PEOPLE?
JURIES DECIDE INNOCENCE, NOT ME.
ALL I'M DOING IS MOUNTING AN AGGRESSIVE DEFENSE FOR MY CLIENTS. THERE'S NOTHING ILLEGAL ABOUT IT.
WE'LL SEE.
"IT'S CALLED *RIGHTS ACQUISITION*, OKAY?"
YOU'RE INSANE. NOTHING YOU RECORDED WITHOUT MY PERMISSION IS EVEN *ADMISSIBLE*.
I'M MORE INTERESTED IN THE COURT OF *PUBLIC OPINION*.
I'M NOT AN IDIOT. I *KNOW* WHO YOU ARE, AND... AND THE POLICE WILL BE HEARING ALL ABOUT THIS.
ALL ABOUT YOUR CONVERSATION WITH A *GIANT BUG*?
BE MY GUEST, BUT YOU'D *BETTER* TAKE THE STAIRS!
THE ELEVATORS IN THIS PLACE ARE KINDA UNPREDICTABLE.

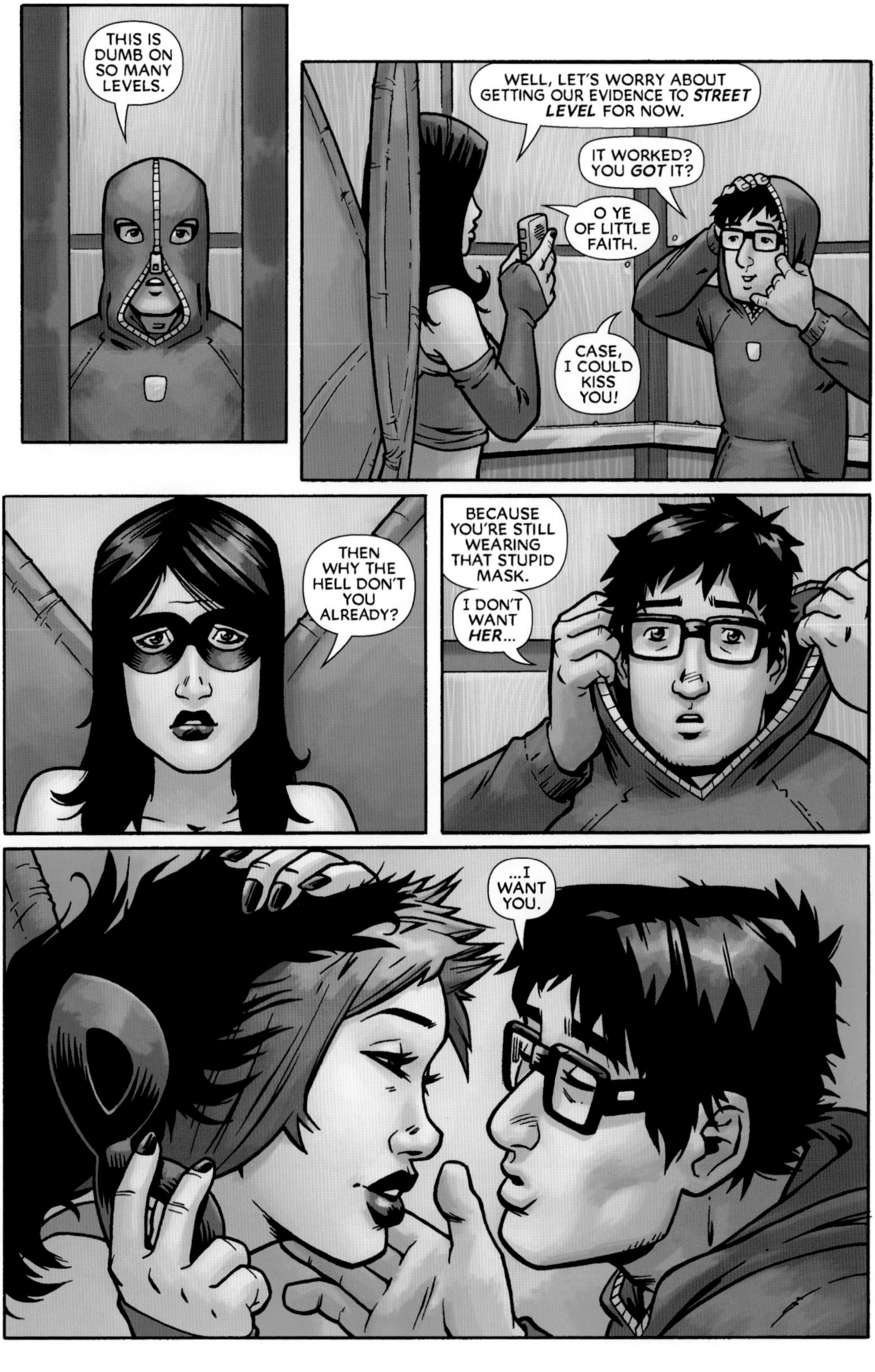
THIS IS DUMB ON SO MANY LEVELS.
WELL, LET'S WORRY ABOUT GETTING OUR EVIDENCE TO *STREET LEVEL* FOR NOW.
IT WORKED? YOU *GOT* IT?
O YE OF LITTLE FAITH.
CASE, I COULD KISS YOU!
THEN WHY THE HELL DON'T YOU ALREADY?
BECAUSE YOU'RE STILL WEARING THAT STUPID MASK.
I DON'T WANT *HER*...
...I WANT YOU.

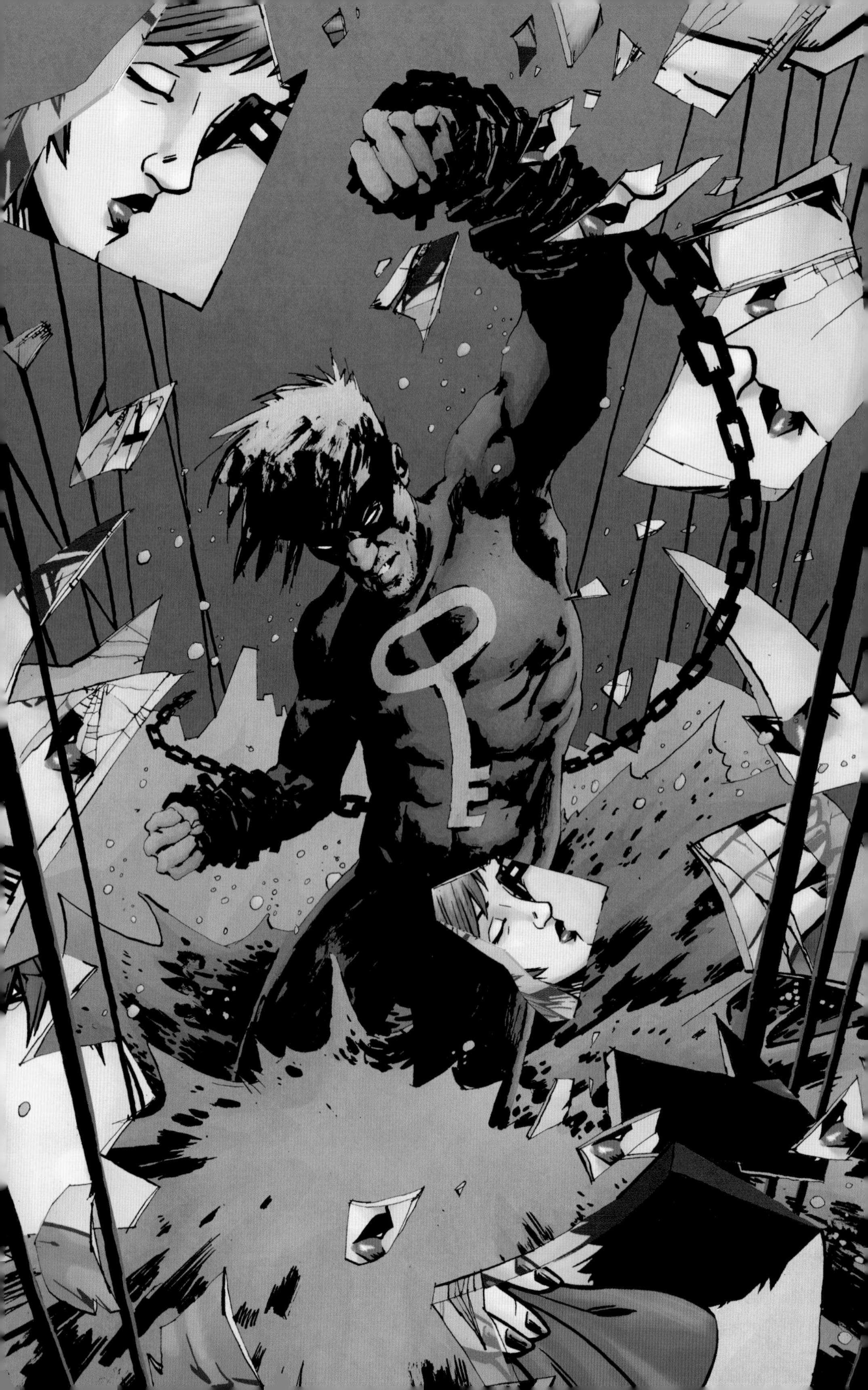

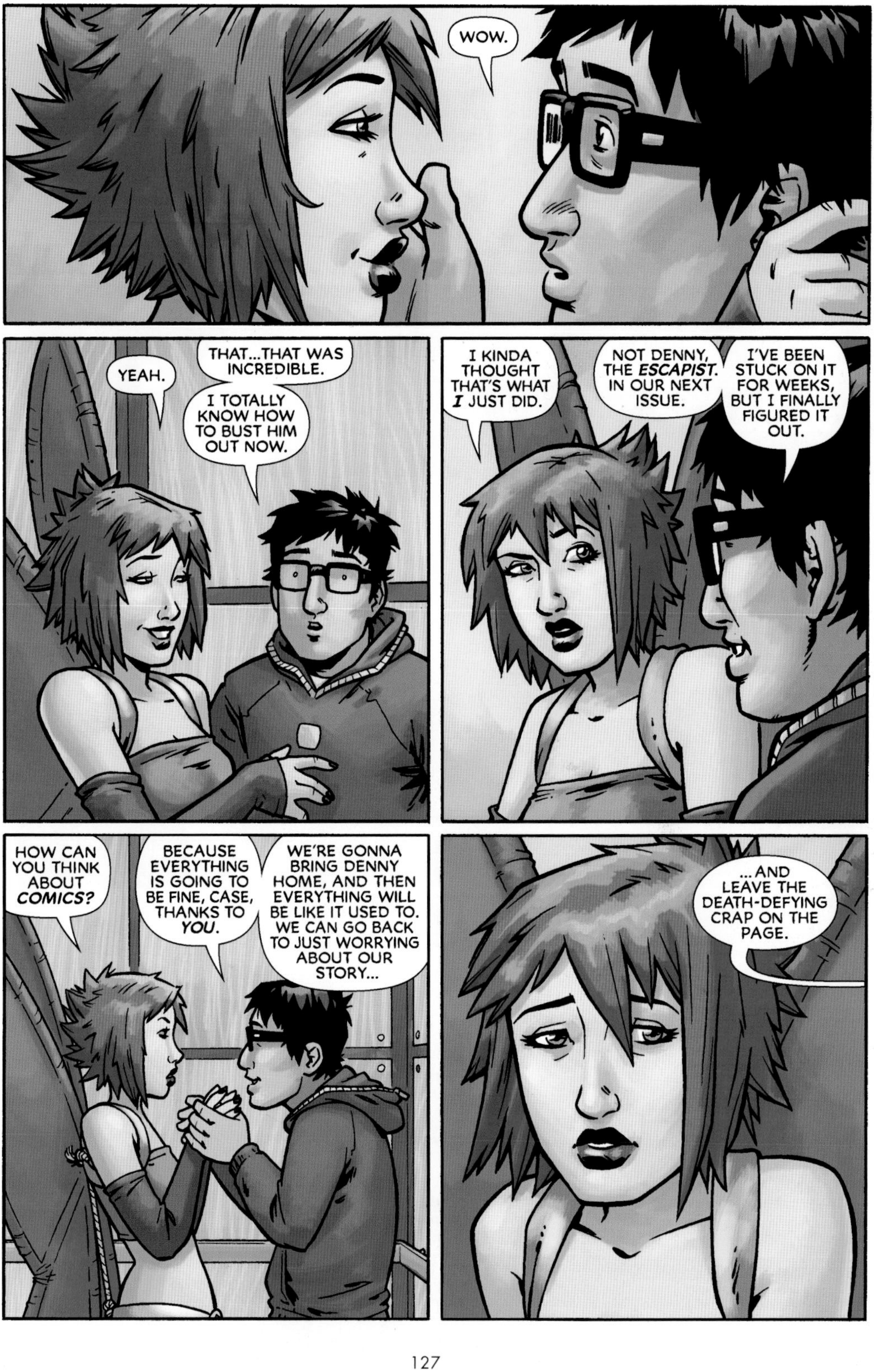
WOW.
YEAH.
THAT...THAT WAS INCREDIBLE.
I TOTALLY KNOW HOW TO BUST HIM OUT NOW.
I KINDA THOUGHT THAT'S WHAT *I* JUST DID.
NOT DENNY, THE *ESCAPIST*. IN OUR NEXT ISSUE.
I'VE BEEN STUCK ON IT FOR WEEKS, BUT I FINALLY FIGURED IT OUT.
HOW CAN YOU THINK ABOUT *COMICS?*
BECAUSE EVERYTHING IS GOING TO BE FINE, CASE, THANKS TO *YOU*.
WE'RE GONNA BRING DENNY HOME, AND THEN EVERYTHING WILL BE LIKE IT USED TO. WE CAN GO BACK TO JUST WORRYING ABOUT OUR STORY...
...AND LEAVE THE DEATH-DEFYING CRAP ON THE PAGE.

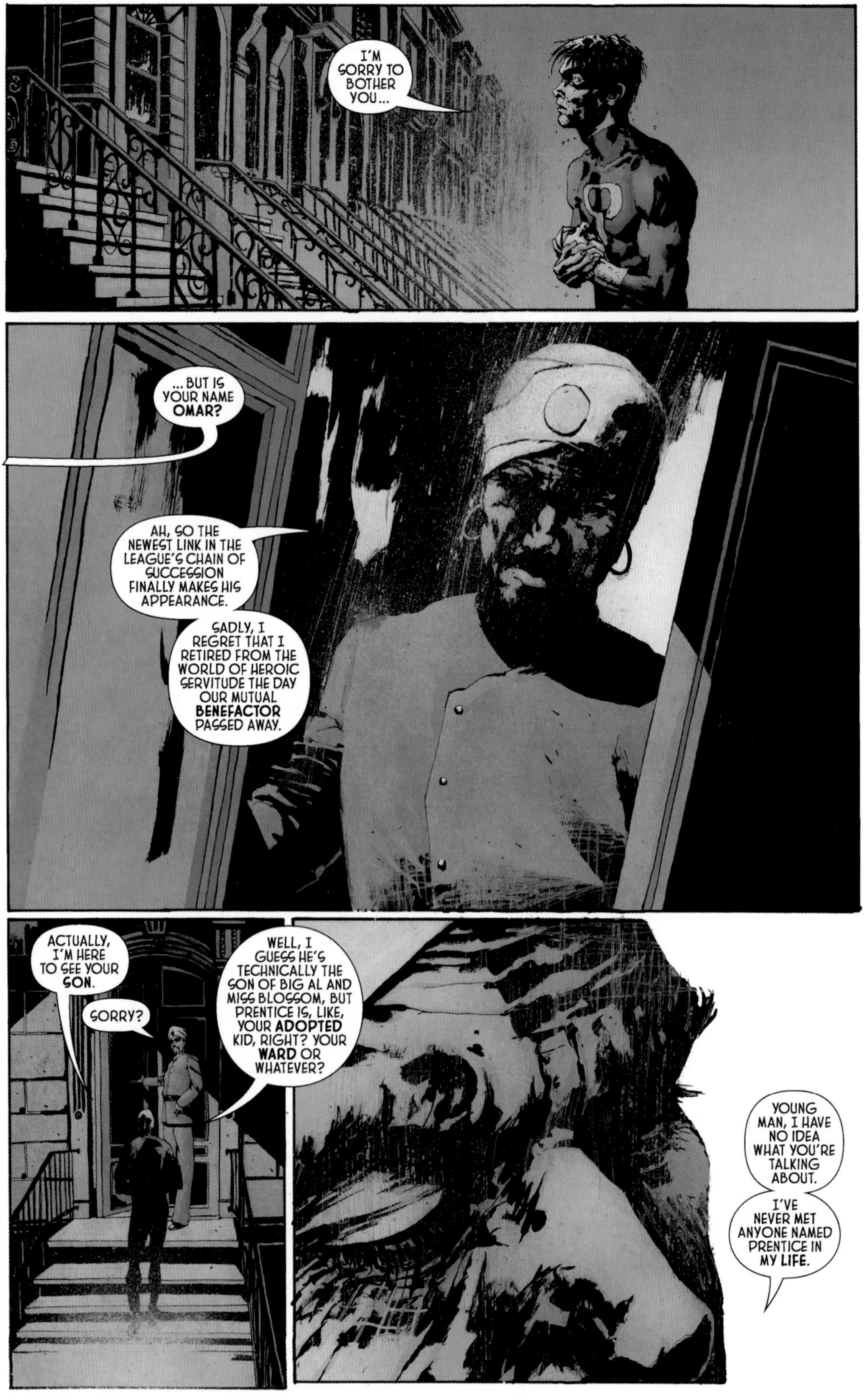
I'M SORRY TO BOTHER YOU...
...BUT IS YOUR NAME **OMAR?**
AH, SO THE NEWEST LINK IN THE LEAGUE'S CHAIN OF SUCCESSION FINALLY MAKES HIS APPEARANCE.
SADLY, I REGRET THAT I RETIRED FROM THE WORLD OF HEROIC SERVITUDE THE DAY OUR MUTUAL **BENEFACTOR** PASSED AWAY.
ACTUALLY, I'M HERE TO SEE YOUR **SON**.
SORRY?
WELL, I GUESS HE'S TECHNICALLY THE SON OF BIG AL AND MISS BLOSSOM, BUT PRENTICE IS, LIKE, YOUR **ADOPTED** KID, RIGHT? YOUR **WARD** OR WHATEVER?
YOUNG MAN, I HAVE NO IDEA WHAT YOU'RE TALKING ABOUT.
I'VE NEVER MET ANYONE NAMED PRENTICE IN **MY LIFE**.

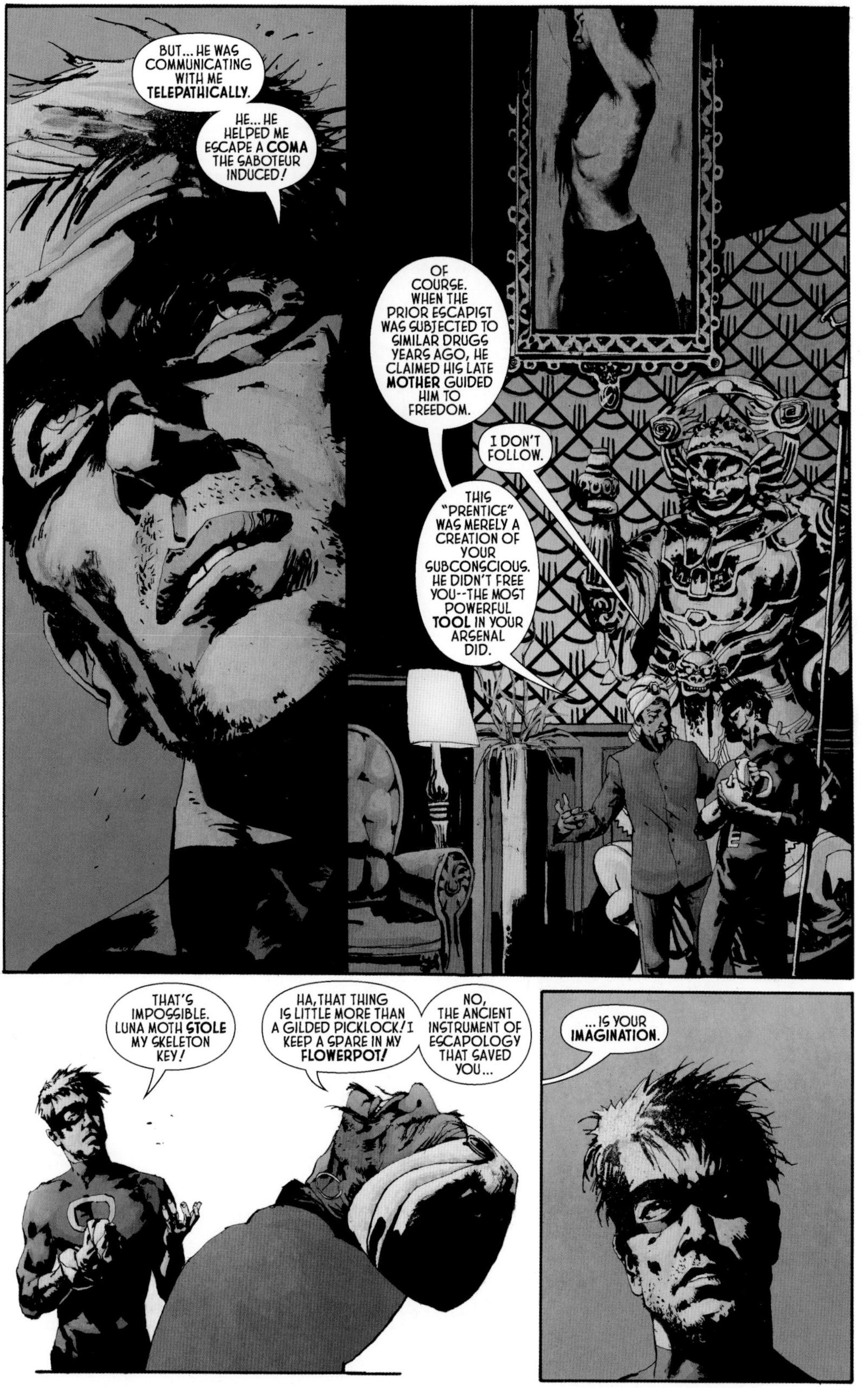
BUT... HE WAS COMMUNICATING WITH ME TELEPATHICALLY.
HE... HE HELPED ME ESCAPE A COMA THE SABOTEUR INDUCED!
OF COURSE. WHEN THE PRIOR ESCAPIST WAS SUBJECTED TO SIMILAR DRUGS YEARS AGO, HE CLAIMED HIS LATE MOTHER GUIDED HIM TO FREEDOM.
I DON'T FOLLOW.
THIS "PRENTICE" WAS MERELY A CREATION OF YOUR SUBCONSCIOUS. HE DIDN'T FREE YOU--THE MOST POWERFUL TOOL IN YOUR ARSENAL DID.
THAT'S IMPOSSIBLE. LUNA MOTH STOLE MY SKELETON KEY!
HA, THAT THING IS LITTLE MORE THAN A GILDED PICKLOCK! I KEEP A SPARE IN MY FLOWERPOT!
NO, THE ANCIENT INSTRUMENT OF ESCAPOLOGY THAT SAVED YOU...
...IS YOUR IMAGINATION.

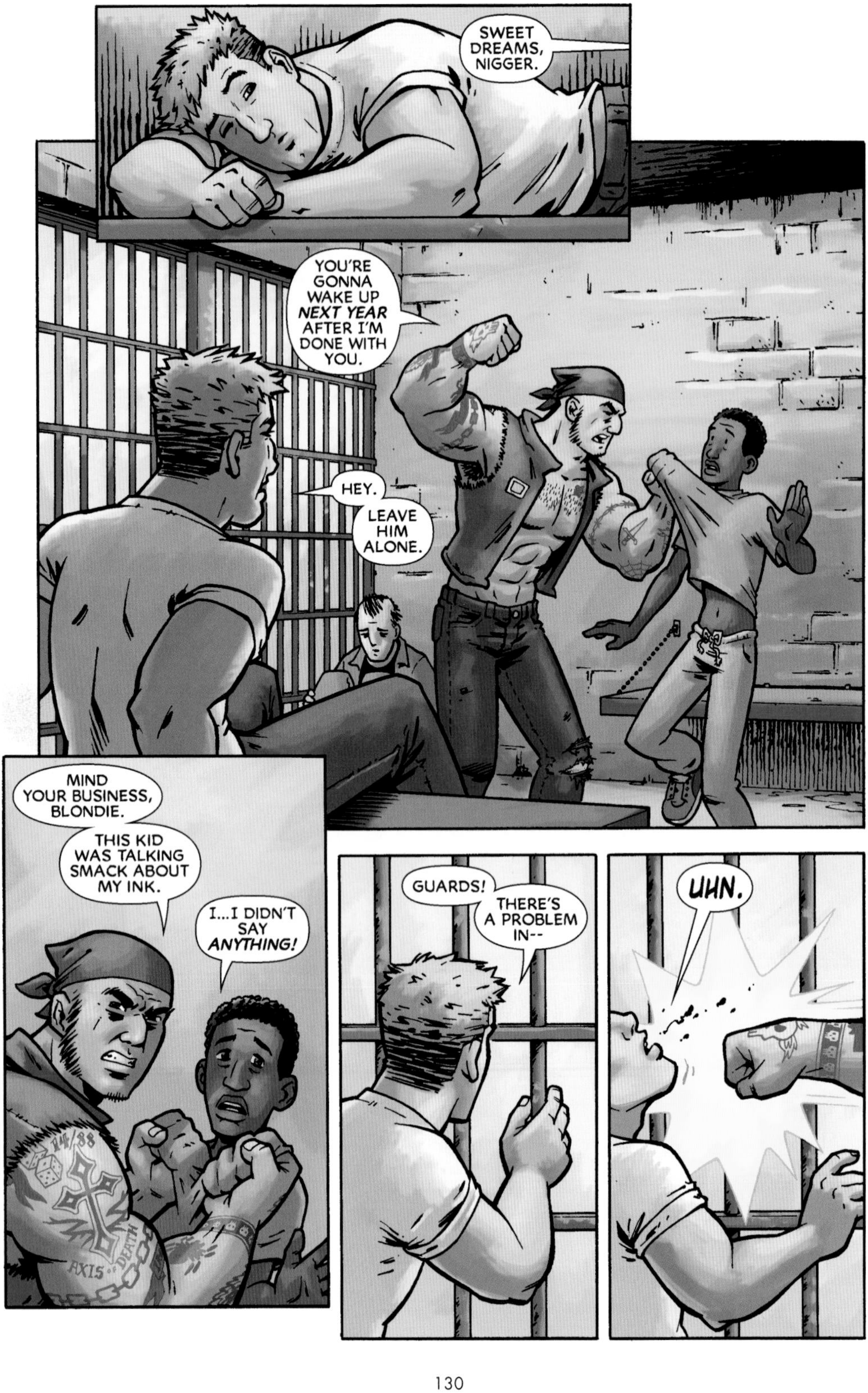

SWEET DREAMS, NIGGER.
YOU'RE GONNA WAKE UP *NEXT YEAR* AFTER I'M DONE WITH YOU.
HEY.
LEAVE HIM ALONE.
MIND YOUR BUSINESS, BLONDIE.
THIS KID WAS TALKING SMACK ABOUT MY INK.
I...I DIDN'T SAY *ANYTHING!*
GUARDS!
THERE'S A PROBLEM IN--
UHN.

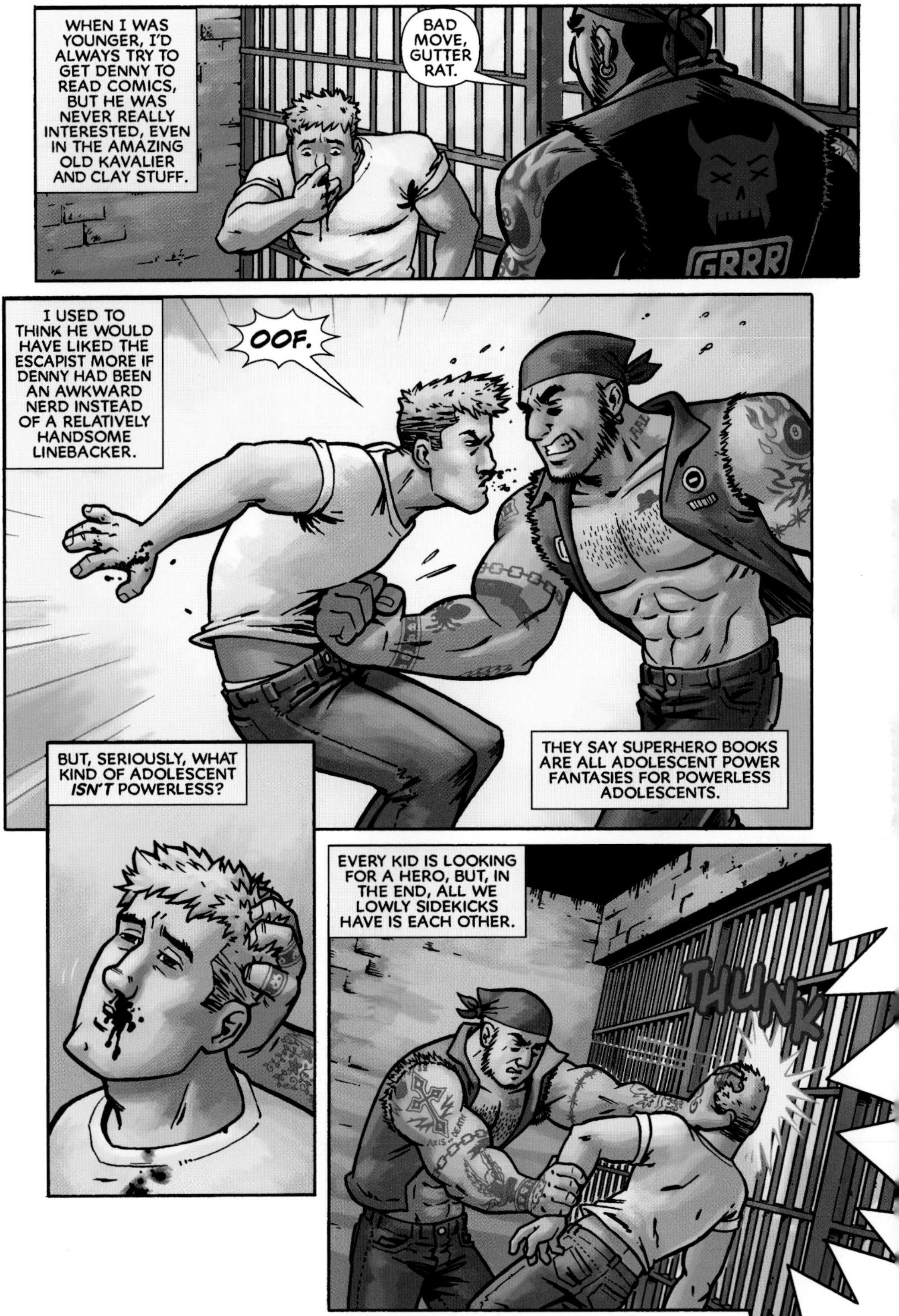
WHEN I WAS YOUNGER, I'D ALWAYS TRY TO GET DENNY TO READ COMICS, BUT HE WAS NEVER REALLY INTERESTED, EVEN IN THE AMAZING OLD KAVALIER AND CLAY STUFF.
BAD MOVE, GUTTER RAT.
GRRR
I USED TO THINK HE WOULD HAVE LIKED THE ESCAPIST MORE IF DENNY HAD BEEN AN AWKWARD NERD INSTEAD OF A RELATIVELY HANDSOME LINEBACKER.
OOF.
THEY SAY SUPERHERO BOOKS ARE ALL ADOLESCENT POWER FANTASIES FOR POWERLESS ADOLESCENTS.
BUT, SERIOUSLY, WHAT KIND OF ADOLESCENT *ISN'T* POWERLESS?
EVERY KID IS LOOKING FOR A HERO, BUT, IN THE END, ALL WE LOWLY SIDEKICKS HAVE IS EACH OTHER.
THUNK

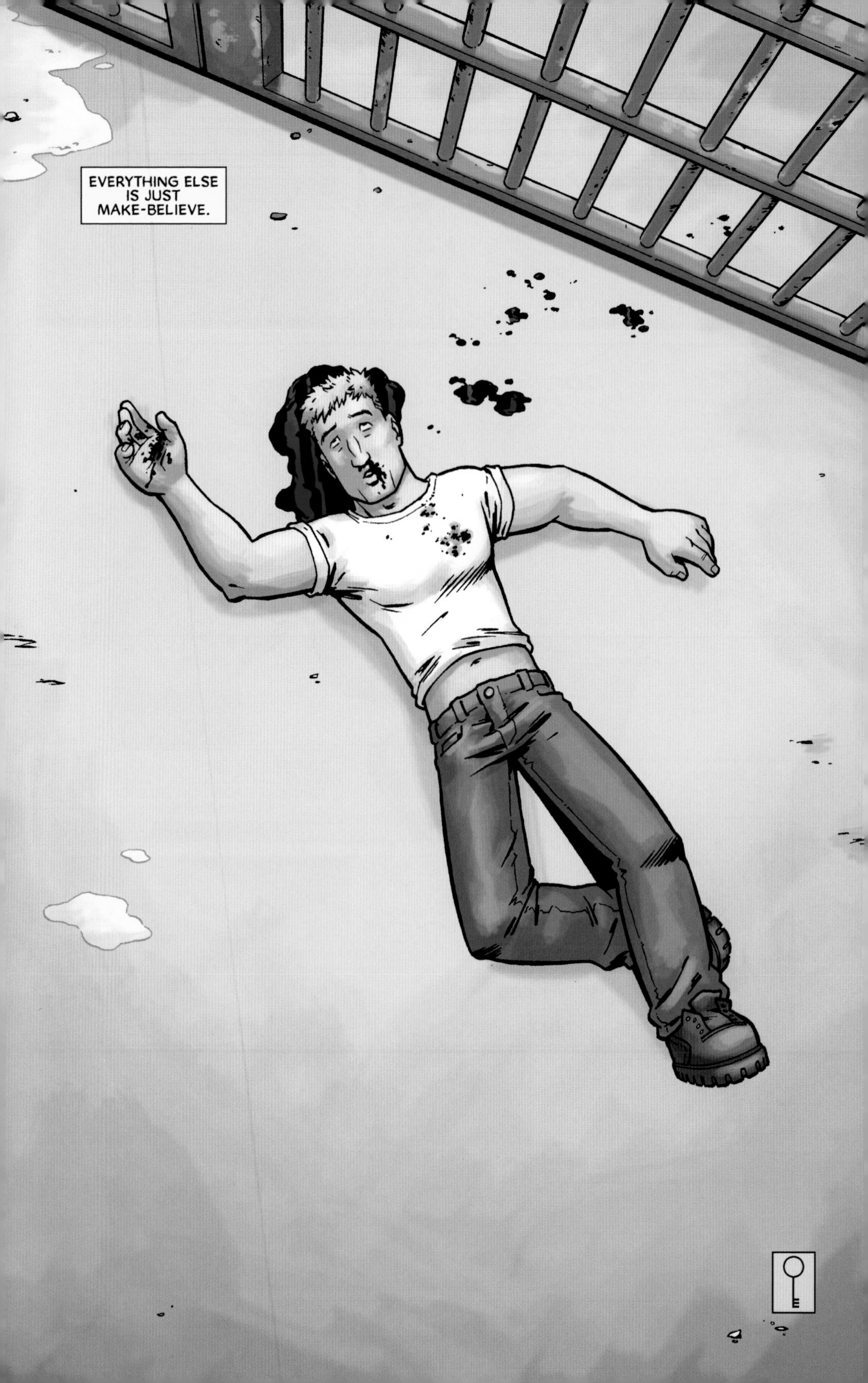
EVERYTHING ELSE IS JUST MAKE-BELIEVE.

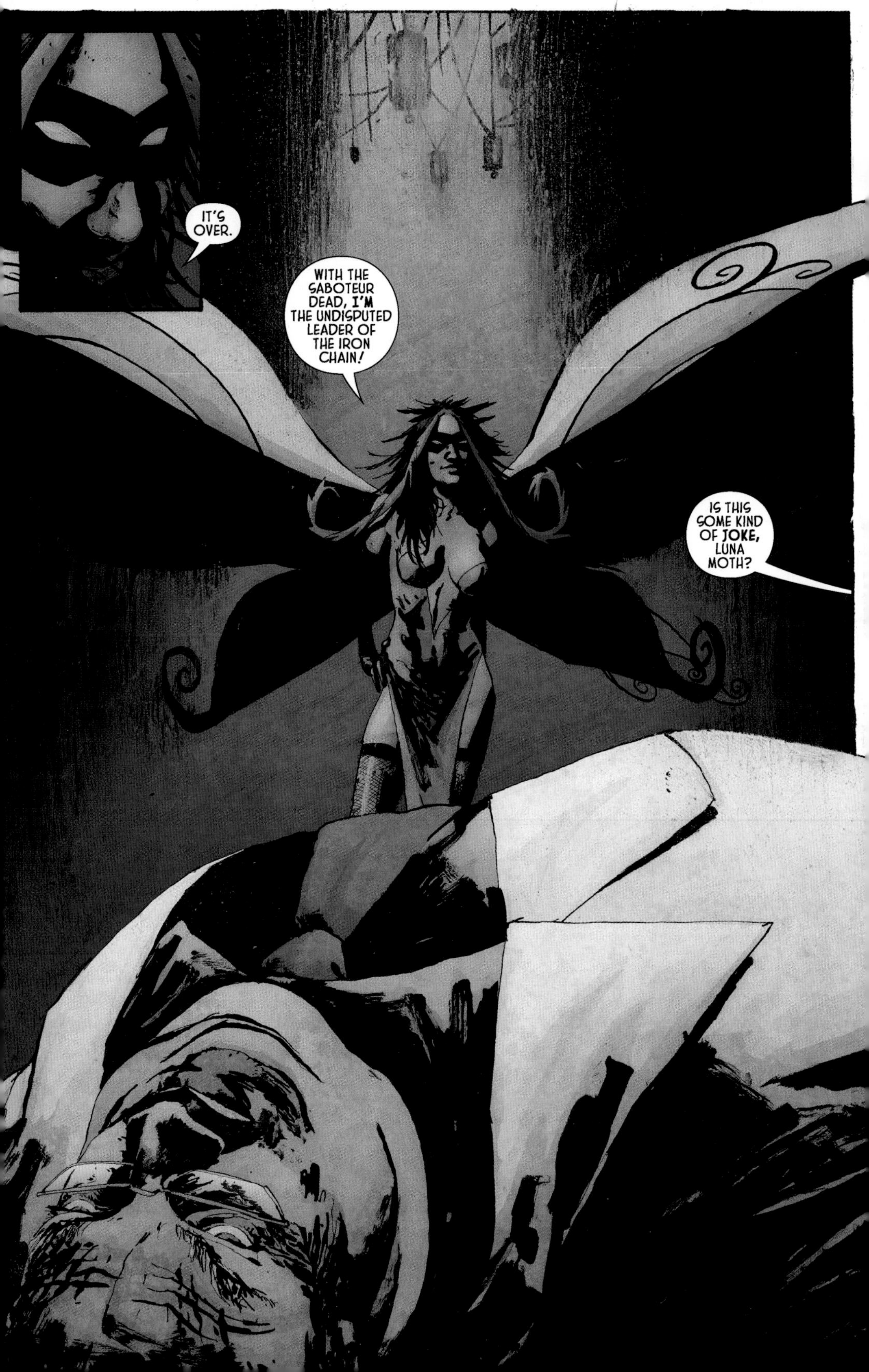
IT'S OVER.
WITH THE SABOTEUR DEAD, I'M THE UNDISPUTED LEADER OF THE IRON CHAIN!
IS THIS SOME KIND OF JOKE, LUNA MOTH?

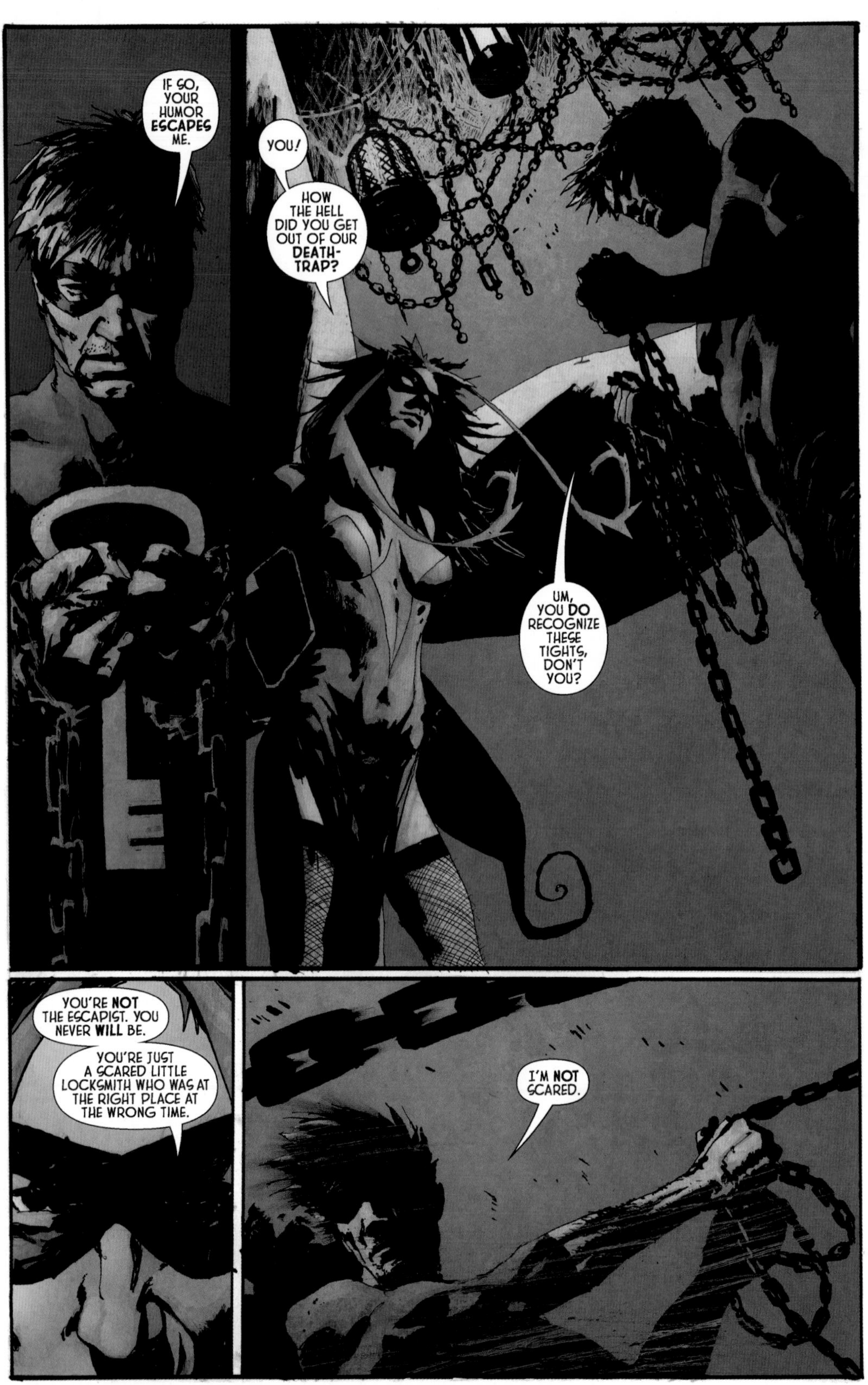
IF SO, YOUR HUMOR ESCAPES ME.
YOU!
HOW THE HELL DID YOU GET OUT OF OUR DEATH-TRAP?
UM, YOU DO RECOGNIZE THESE TIGHTS, DON'T YOU?
YOU'RE NOT THE ESCAPIST. YOU NEVER WILL BE.
YOU'RE JUST A SCARED LITTLE LOCKSMITH WHO WAS AT THE RIGHT PLACE AT THE WRONG TIME.
I'M NOT SCARED.

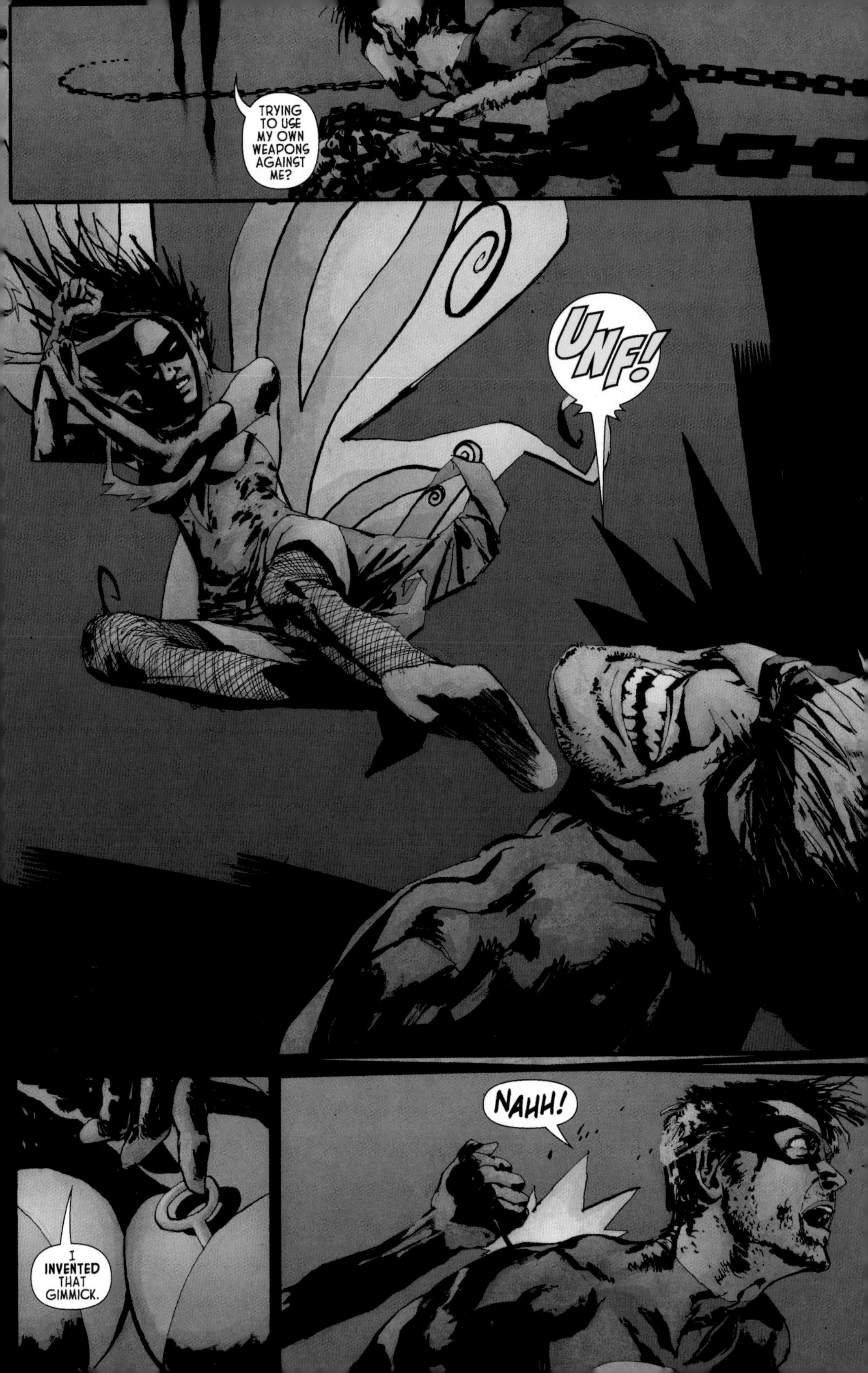
TRYING TO USE MY OWN WEAPONS AGAINST ME?
UNF!
I INVENTED THAT GIMMICK.
NAHH!

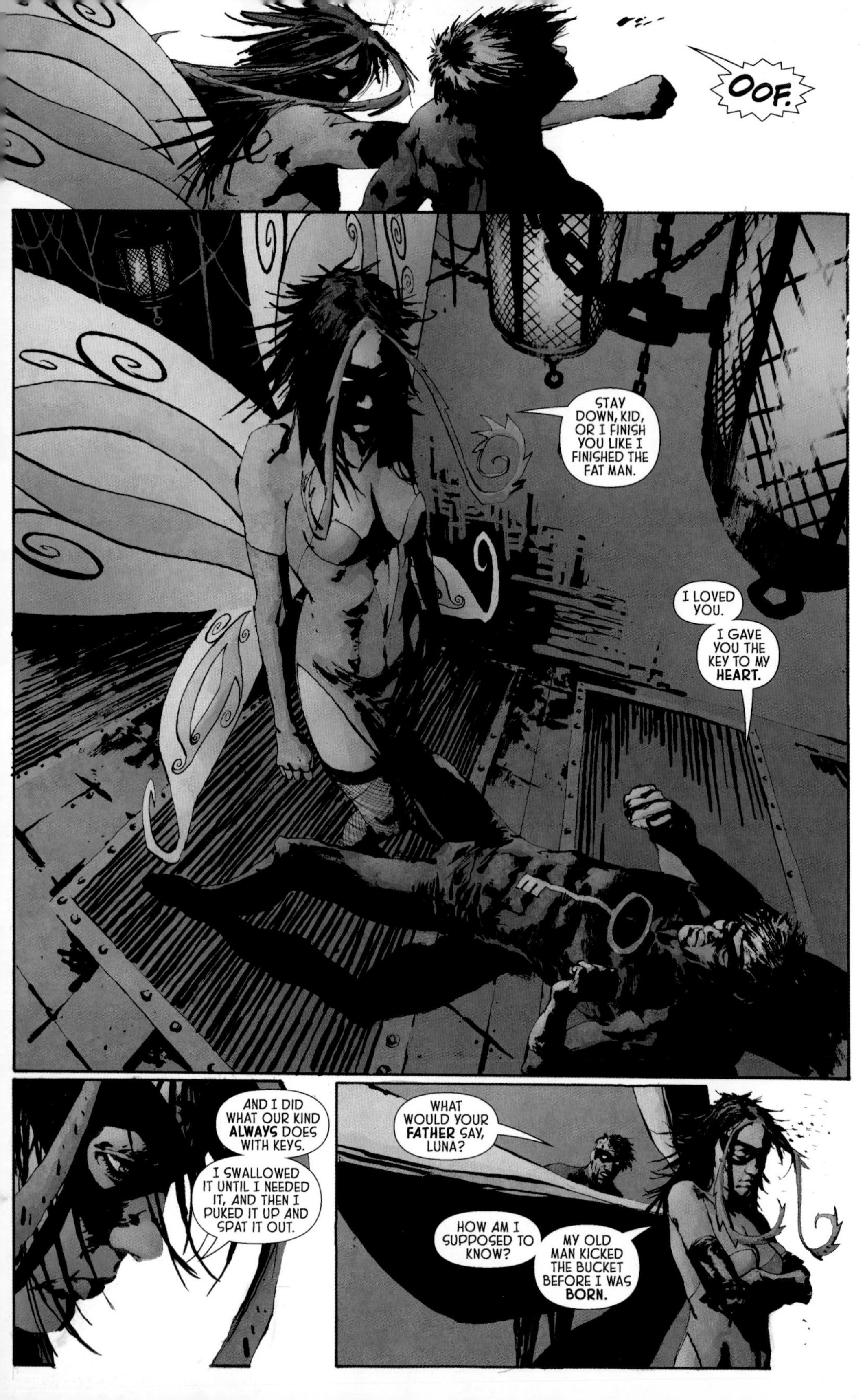
OOF.
STAY DOWN, KID, OR I FINISH YOU LIKE I FINISHED THE FAT MAN.
I LOVED YOU.
I GAVE YOU THE KEY TO MY **HEART.**
AND I DID WHAT OUR KIND **ALWAYS** DOES WITH KEYS.
I SWALLOWED IT UNTIL I NEEDED IT, AND THEN I PUKED IT UP AND SPAT IT OUT.
WHAT WOULD YOUR **FATHER** SAY, LUNA?
HOW AM I SUPPOSED TO KNOW?
MY OLD MAN KICKED THE BUCKET BEFORE I WAS **BORN.**

THAT'S. IMPOSSIBLE. THE ORIGINAL ESCAPIST DIED IN MY ARMS JUST A FEW **MONTHS** AGO.

YOU MEAN, YOU'RE **NOT** REALLY HIS DAUGHTER?

THE LAST PERSON YOU'D EVER EXPECT.

THAT'S JUST A STORY I MADE UP THE NIGHT I RAN INTO YOU. I HAD BROKEN INTO THE KEYHOLE TO STEAL LUNA MOTH'S OLD **WINGS**.

I'M NOT **HER** DAUGHTER EITHER, BY THE WAY.

THEN... WHO **ARE** YOU?

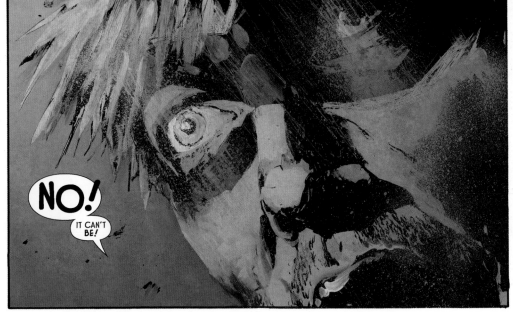

NO! IT CAN'T BE!

137

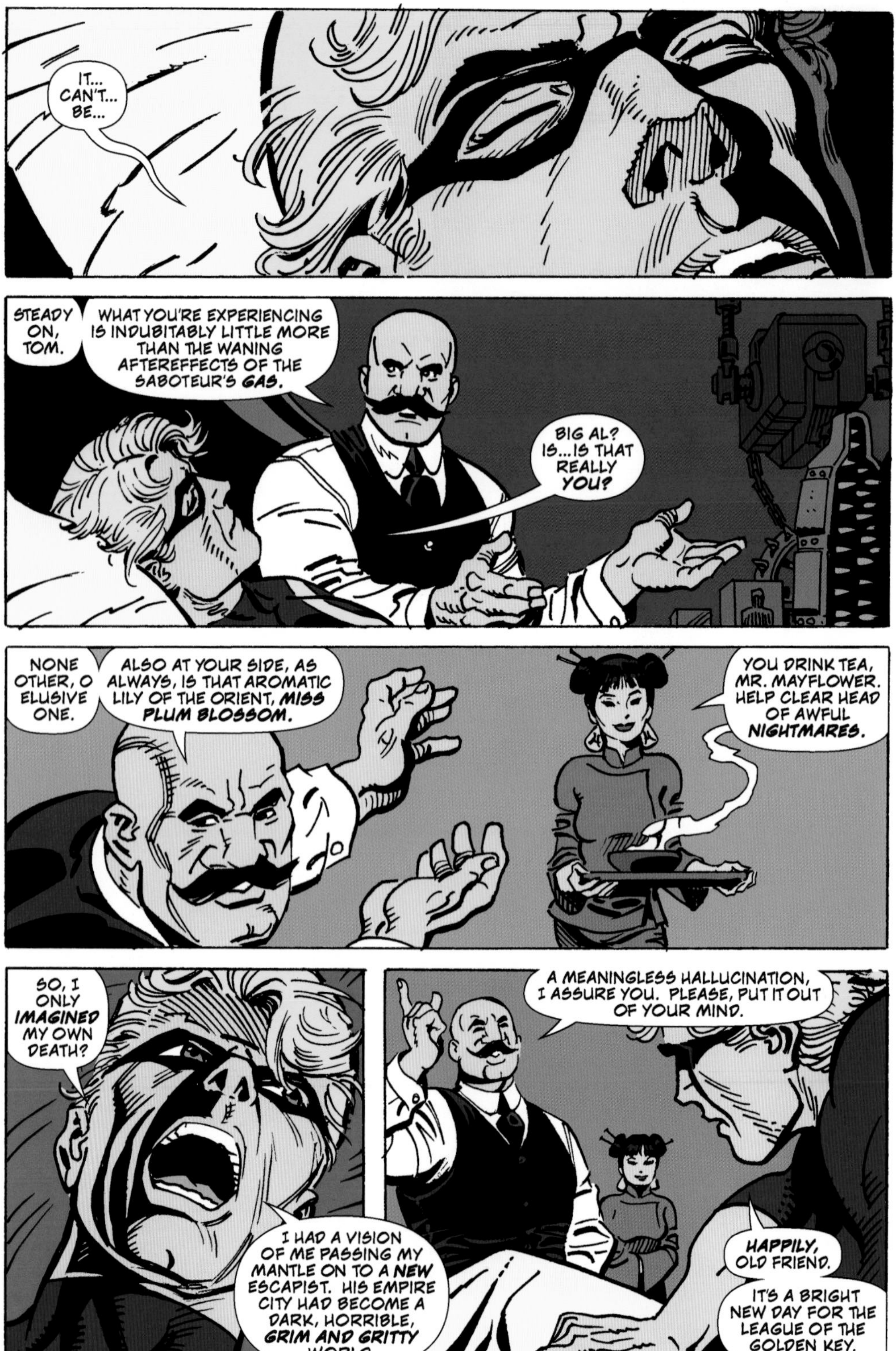
IT... CAN'T... BE...
STEADY ON, TOM.
WHAT YOU'RE EXPERIENCING IS INDUBITABLY LITTLE MORE THAN THE WANING AFTEREFFECTS OF THE SABOTEUR'S GAS.
BIG AL? IS...IS THAT REALLY YOU?
NONE OTHER, O ELUSIVE ONE.
ALSO AT YOUR SIDE, AS ALWAYS, IS THAT AROMATIC LILY OF THE ORIENT, MISS PLUM BLOSSOM.
YOU DRINK TEA, MR. MAYFLOWER. HELP CLEAR HEAD OF AWFUL NIGHTMARES.
SO, I ONLY IMAGINED MY OWN DEATH?
I HAD A VISION OF ME PASSING MY MANTLE ON TO A NEW ESCAPIST. HIS EMPIRE CITY HAD BECOME A DARK, HORRIBLE, GRIM AND GRITTY WORLD.
A MEANINGLESS HALLUCINATION, I ASSURE YOU. PLEASE, PUT IT OUT OF YOUR MIND.
HAPPILY, OLD FRIEND.
IT'S A BRIGHT NEW DAY FOR THE LEAGUE OF THE GOLDEN KEY.

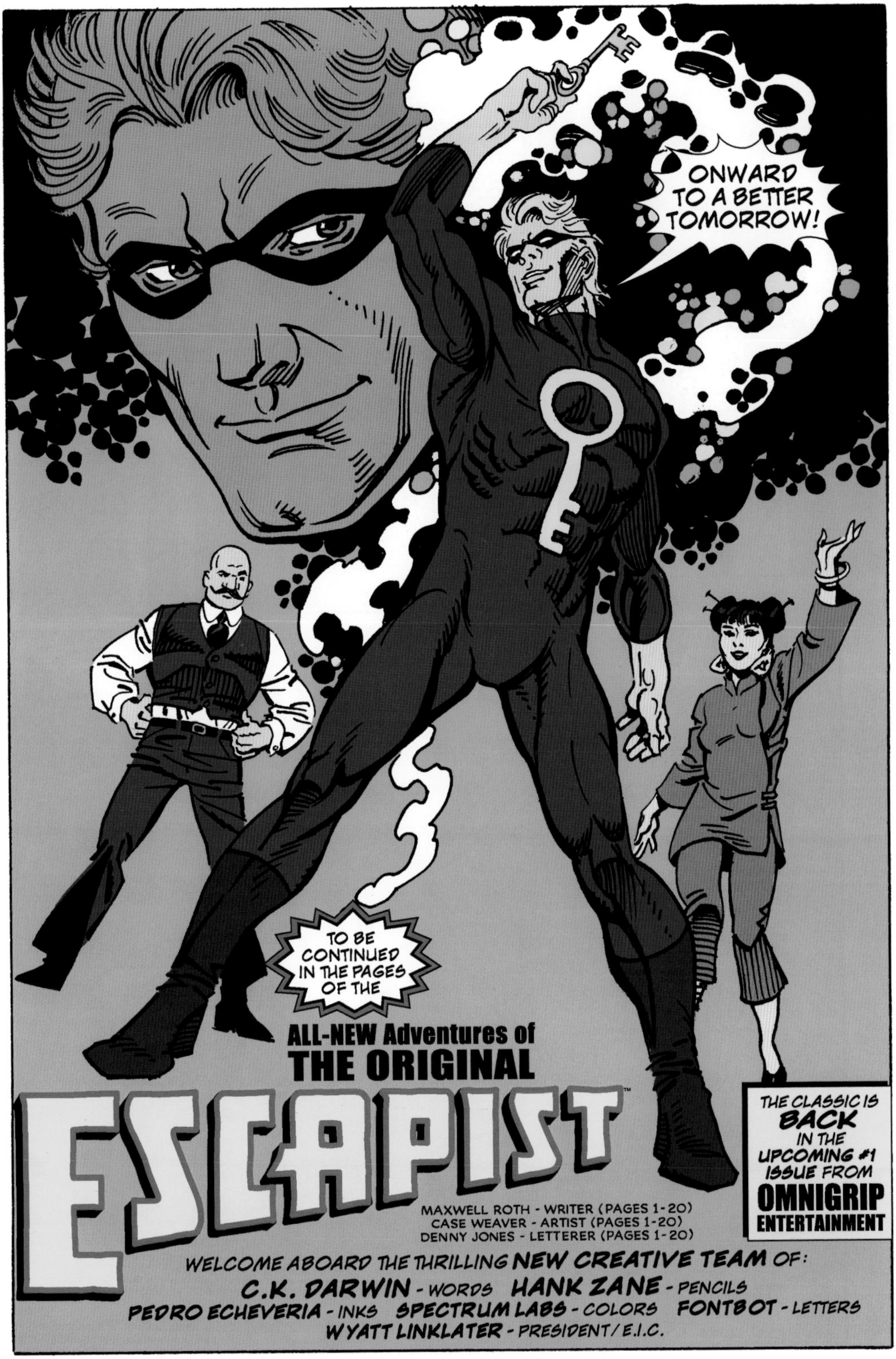
ONWARD TO A BETTER TOMORROW!
TO BE CONTINUED IN THE PAGES OF THE
ALL-NEW Adventures of THE ORIGINAL
ESCAPIST™
THE CLASSIC IS BACK IN THE UPCOMING #1 ISSUE FROM OMNIGRIP ENTERTAINMENT
MAXWELL ROTH - WRITER (PAGES 1-20)
CASE WEAVER - ARTIST (PAGES 1-20)
DENNY JONES - LETTERER (PAGES 1-20)
WELCOME ABOARD THE THRILLING NEW CREATIVE TEAM OF:
C.K. DARWIN - WORDS HANK ZANE - PENCILS
PEDRO ECHEVERIA - INKS SPECTRUM LABS - COLORS FONTBOT - LETTERS
WYATT LINKLATER - PRESIDENT/E.I.C.

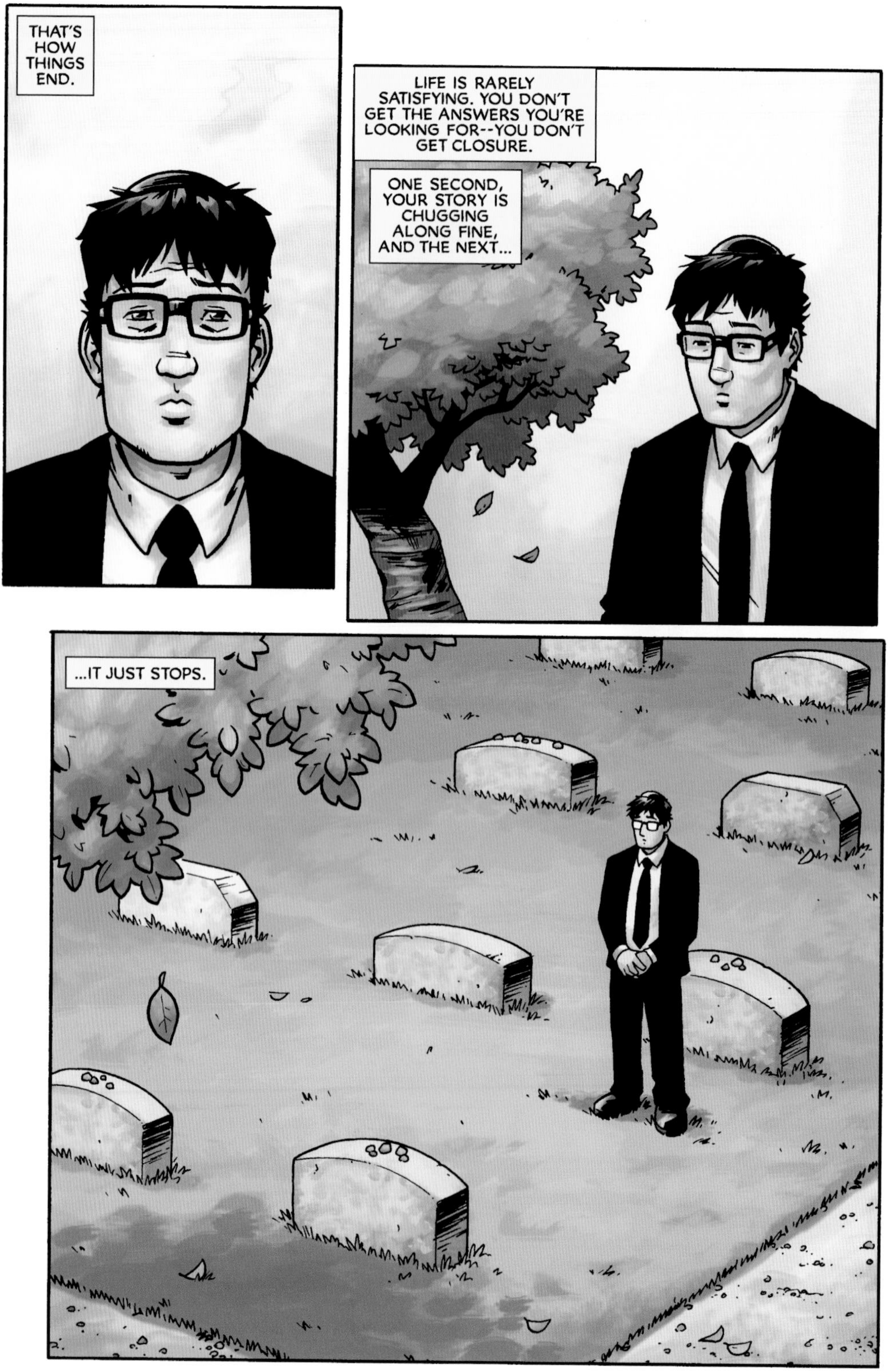
THAT'S HOW THINGS END.
LIFE IS RARELY SATISFYING. YOU DON'T GET THE ANSWERS YOU'RE LOOKING FOR--YOU DON'T GET CLOSURE.
ONE SECOND, YOUR STORY IS CHUGGING ALONG FINE, AND THE NEXT...
...IT JUST STOPS.

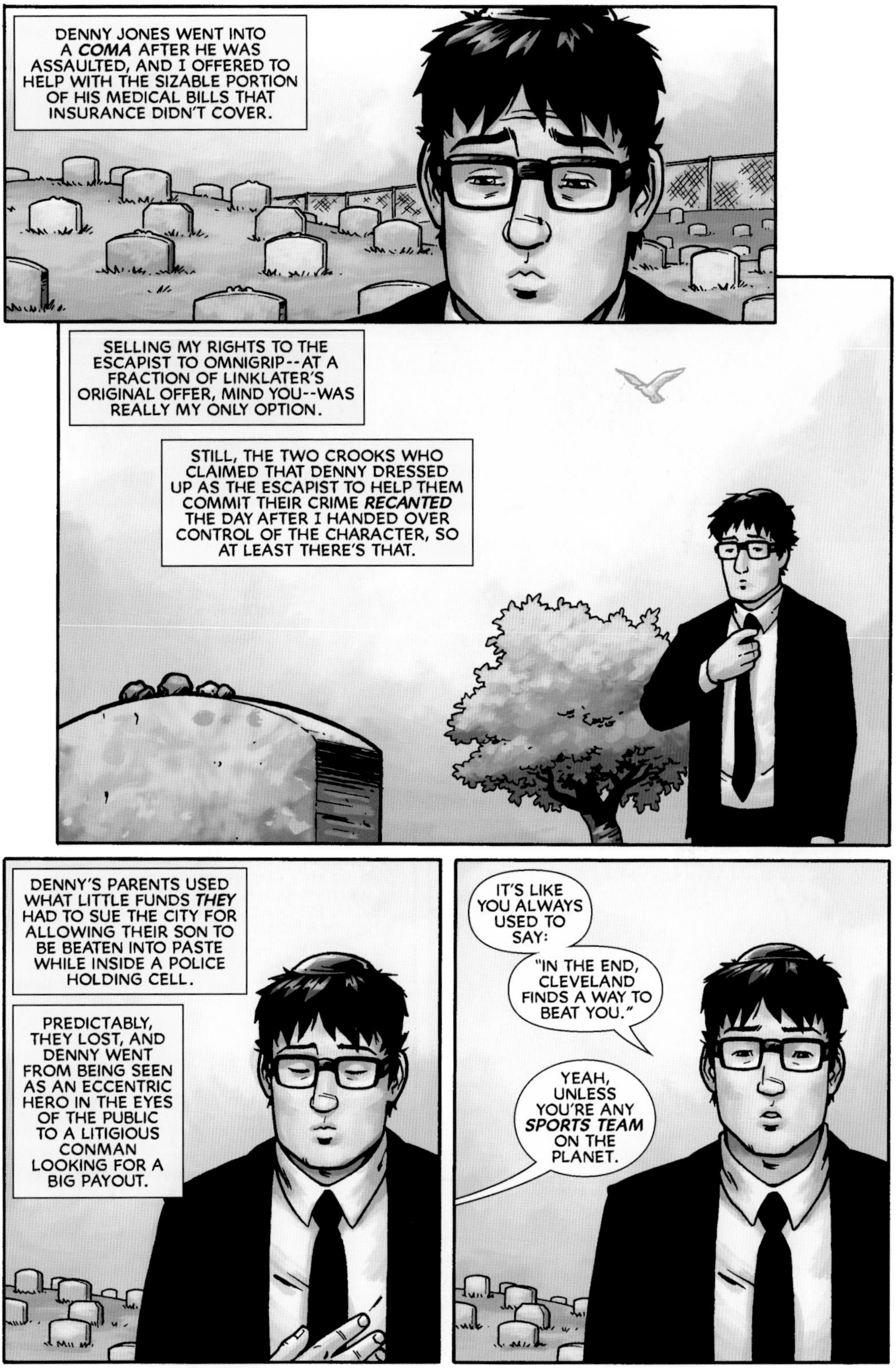
DENNY JONES WENT INTO A COMA AFTER HE WAS ASSAULTED, AND I OFFERED TO HELP WITH THE SIZABLE PORTION OF HIS MEDICAL BILLS THAT INSURANCE DIDN'T COVER.
SELLING MY RIGHTS TO THE ESCAPIST TO OMNIGRIP--AT A FRACTION OF LINKLATER'S ORIGINAL OFFER, MIND YOU--WAS REALLY MY ONLY OPTION.
STILL, THE TWO CROOKS WHO CLAIMED THAT DENNY DRESSED UP AS THE ESCAPIST TO HELP THEM COMMIT THEIR CRIME RECANTED THE DAY AFTER I HANDED OVER CONTROL OF THE CHARACTER, SO AT LEAST THERE'S THAT.
DENNY'S PARENTS USED WHAT LITTLE FUNDS THEY HAD TO SUE THE CITY FOR ALLOWING THEIR SON TO BE BEATEN INTO PASTE WHILE INSIDE A POLICE HOLDING CELL.
PREDICTABLY, THEY LOST, AND DENNY WENT FROM BEING SEEN AS AN ECCENTRIC HERO IN THE EYES OF THE PUBLIC TO A LITIGIOUS CONMAN LOOKING FOR A BIG PAYOUT.
IT'S LIKE YOU ALWAYS USED TO SAY:
"IN THE END, CLEVELAND FINDS A WAY TO BEAT YOU."
YEAH, UNLESS YOU'RE ANY SPORTS TEAM ON THE PLANET.

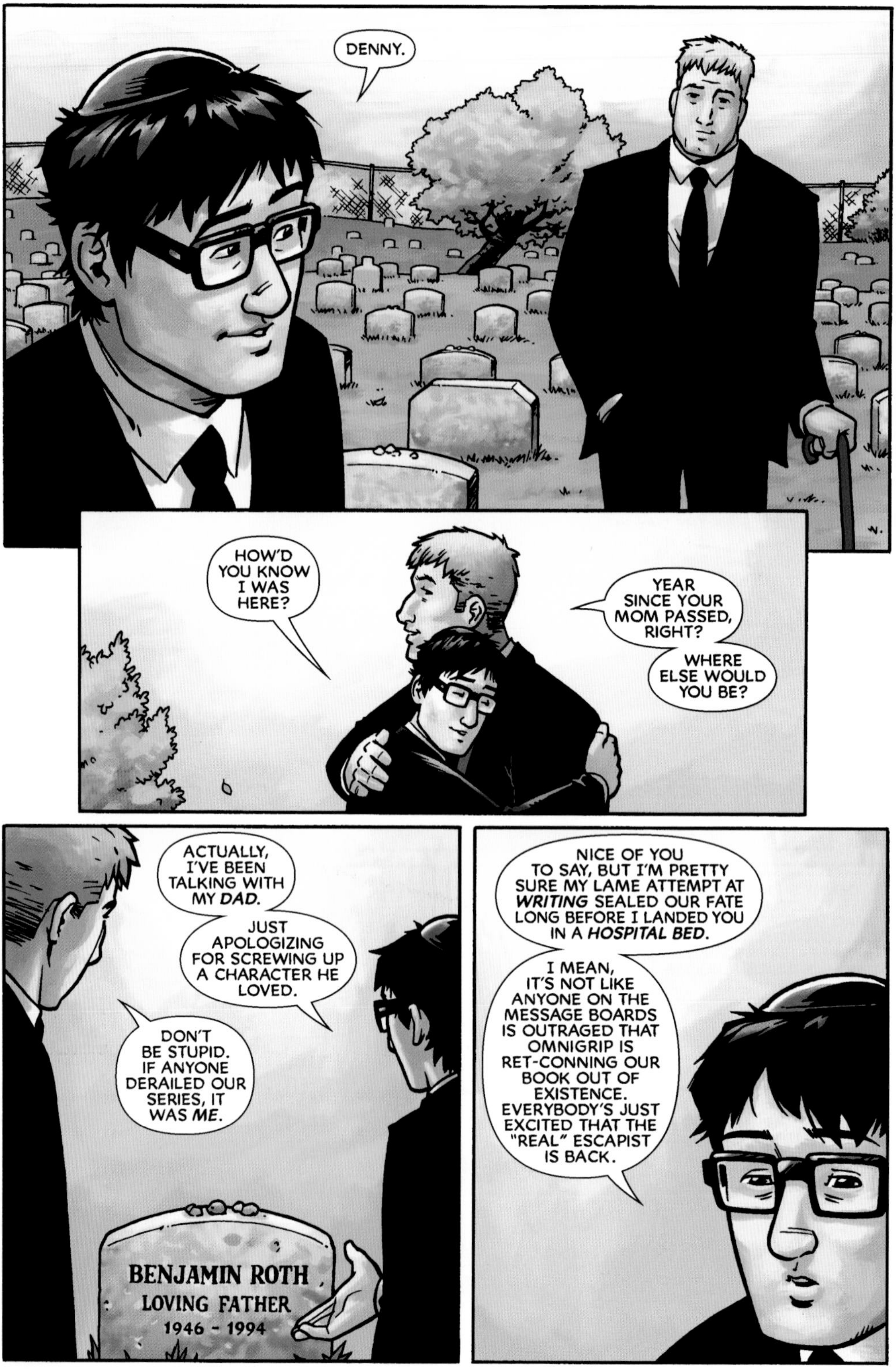
DENNY.
HOW'D YOU KNOW I WAS HERE?
YEAR SINCE YOUR MOM PASSED, RIGHT?
WHERE ELSE WOULD YOU BE?
ACTUALLY, I'VE BEEN TALKING WITH MY *DAD*.
JUST APOLOGIZING FOR SCREWING UP A CHARACTER HE LOVED.
DON'T BE STUPID. IF ANYONE DERAILED OUR SERIES, IT WAS *ME*.
BENJAMIN ROTH
LOVING FATHER
1946 - 1994
NICE OF YOU TO SAY, BUT I'M PRETTY SURE MY LAME ATTEMPT AT ***WRITING*** SEALED OUR FATE LONG BEFORE I LANDED YOU IN A ***HOSPITAL BED***.
I MEAN, IT'S NOT LIKE ANYONE ON THE MESSAGE BOARDS IS OUTRAGED THAT OMNIGRIP IS RET-CONNING OUR BOOK OUT OF EXISTENCE. EVERYBODY'S JUST EXCITED THAT THE "REAL" ESCAPIST IS BACK.

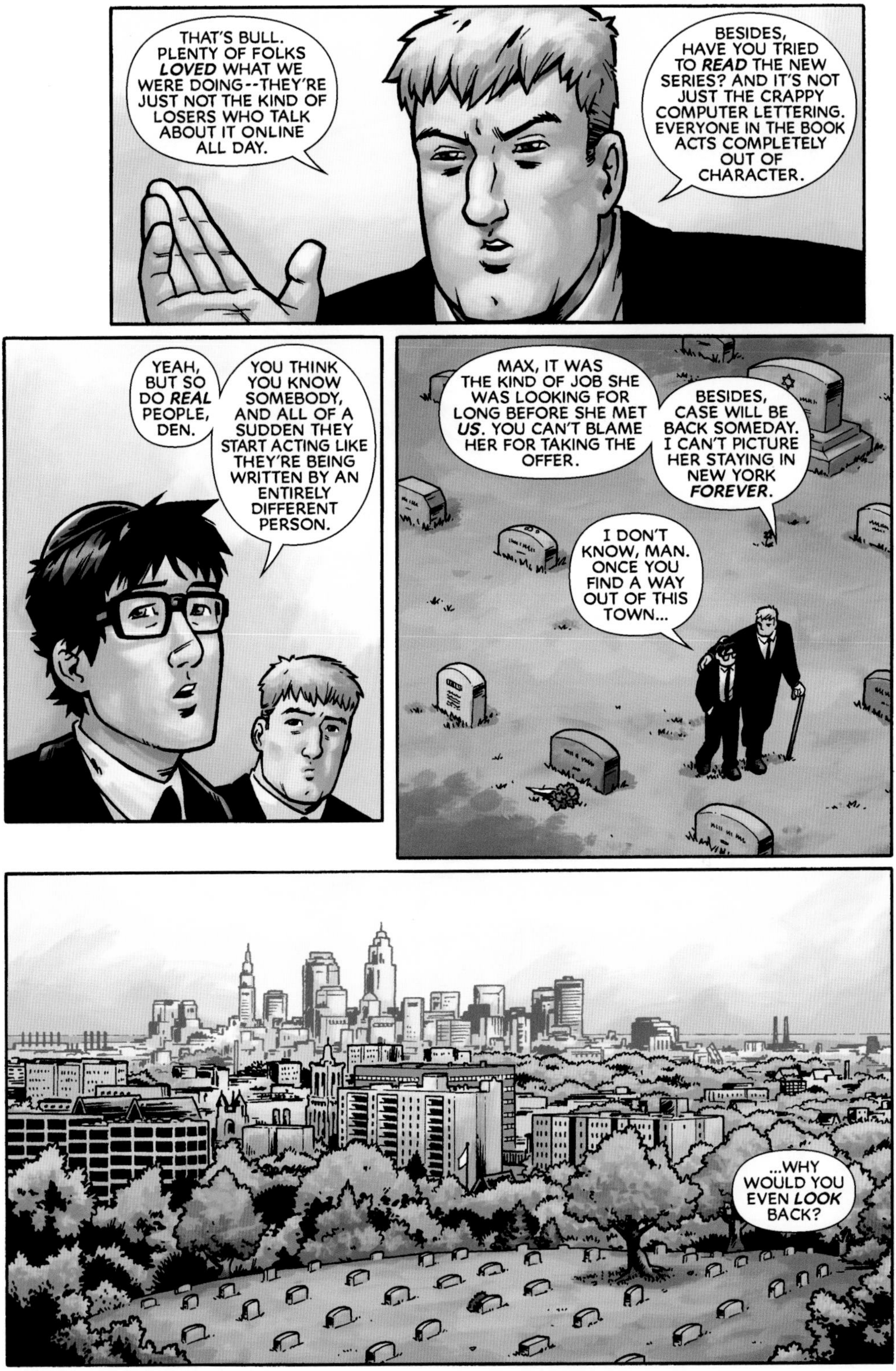
THAT'S BULL. PLENTY OF FOLKS LOVED WHAT WE WERE DOING--THEY'RE JUST NOT THE KIND OF LOSERS WHO TALK ABOUT IT ONLINE ALL DAY.
BESIDES, HAVE YOU TRIED TO READ THE NEW SERIES? AND IT'S NOT JUST THE CRAPPY COMPUTER LETTERING. EVERYONE IN THE BOOK ACTS COMPLETELY OUT OF CHARACTER.
YEAH, BUT SO DO REAL PEOPLE, DEN.
YOU THINK YOU KNOW SOMEBODY, AND ALL OF A SUDDEN THEY START ACTING LIKE THEY'RE BEING WRITTEN BY AN ENTIRELY DIFFERENT PERSON.
MAX, IT WAS THE KIND OF JOB SHE WAS LOOKING FOR LONG BEFORE SHE MET US. YOU CAN'T BLAME HER FOR TAKING THE OFFER.
BESIDES, CASE WILL BE BACK SOMEDAY. I CAN'T PICTURE HER STAYING IN NEW YORK FOREVER.
I DON'T KNOW, MAN. ONCE YOU FIND A WAY OUT OF THIS TOWN...
...WHY WOULD YOU EVEN LOOK BACK?

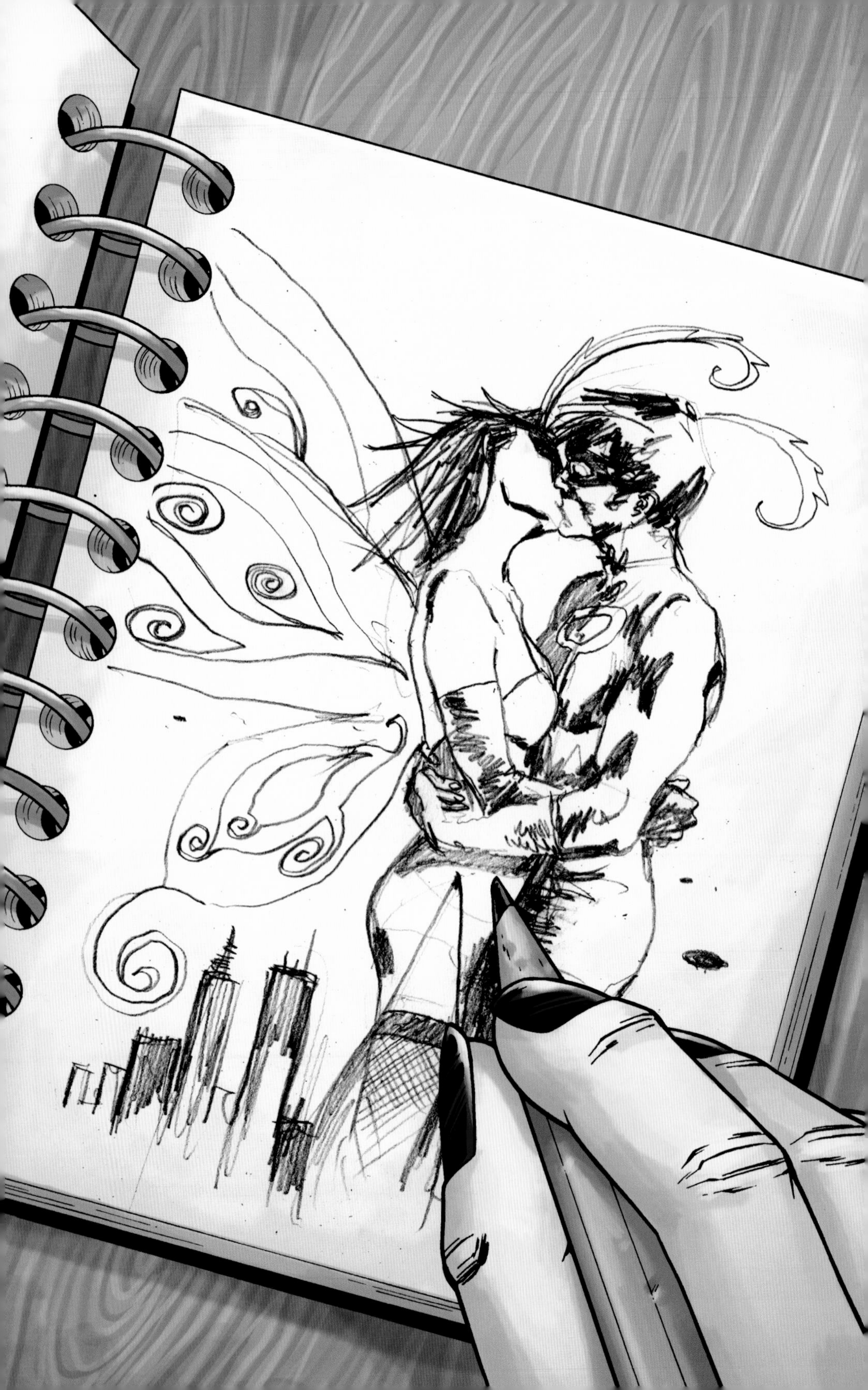

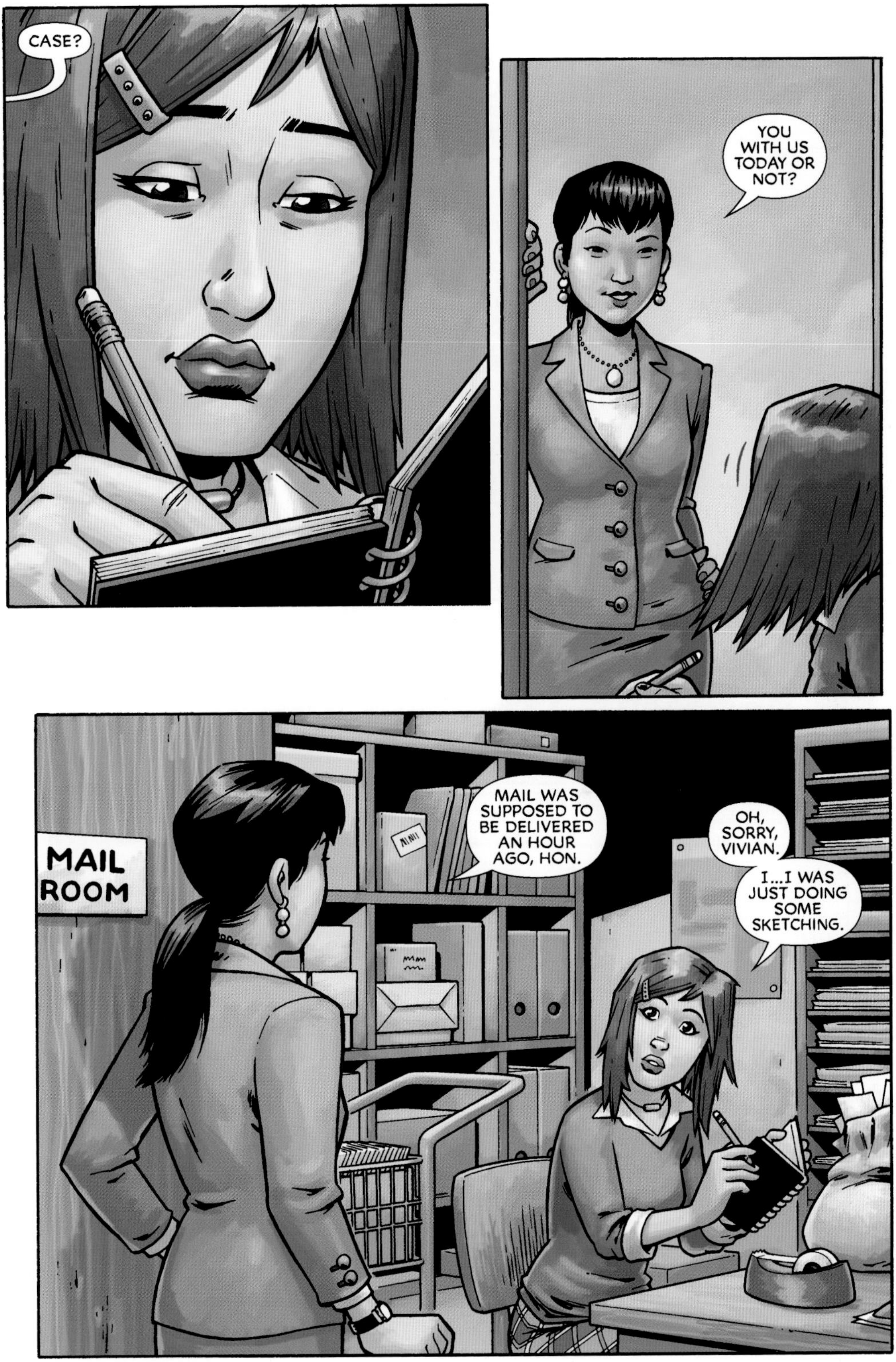
CASE?
YOU WITH US TODAY OR NOT?
MAIL ROOM
MAIL WAS SUPPOSED TO BE DELIVERED AN HOUR AGO, HON.
OH, SORRY, VIVIAN.
I...I WAS JUST DOING SOME SKETCHING.

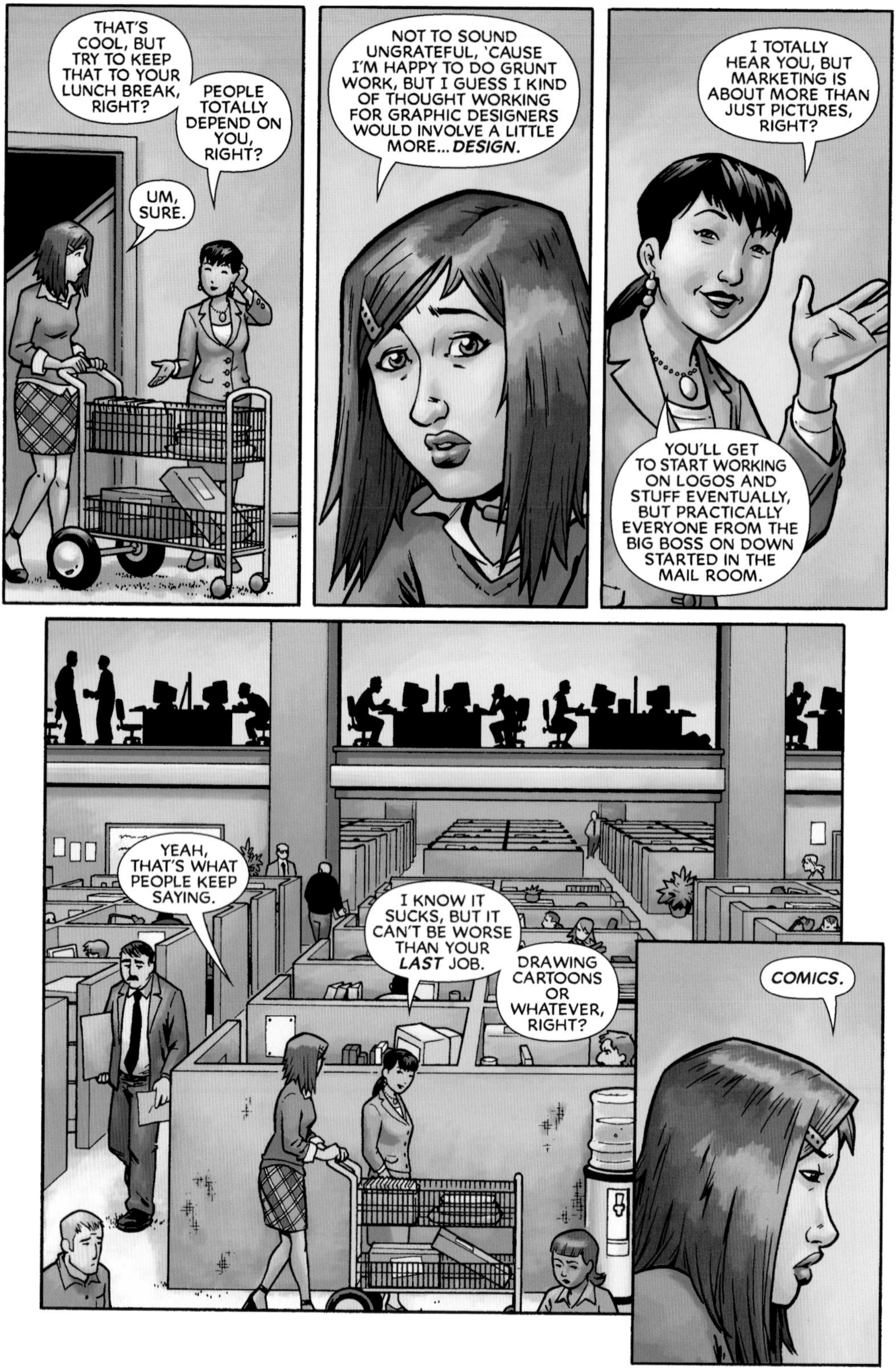
THAT'S COOL, BUT TRY TO KEEP THAT TO YOUR LUNCH BREAK, RIGHT?
PEOPLE TOTALLY DEPEND ON YOU, RIGHT?
UM, SURE.
NOT TO SOUND UNGRATEFUL, 'CAUSE I'M HAPPY TO DO GRUNT WORK, BUT I GUESS I KIND OF THOUGHT WORKING FOR GRAPHIC DESIGNERS WOULD INVOLVE A LITTLE MORE... *DESIGN*.
I TOTALLY HEAR YOU, BUT MARKETING IS ABOUT MORE THAN JUST PICTURES, RIGHT?
YOU'LL GET TO START WORKING ON LOGOS AND STUFF EVENTUALLY, BUT PRACTICALLY EVERYONE FROM THE BIG BOSS ON DOWN STARTED IN THE MAIL ROOM.
YEAH, THAT'S WHAT PEOPLE KEEP SAYING.
I KNOW IT SUCKS, BUT IT CAN'T BE WORSE THAN YOUR *LAST* JOB.
DRAWING CARTOONS OR WHATEVER, RIGHT?
COMICS.

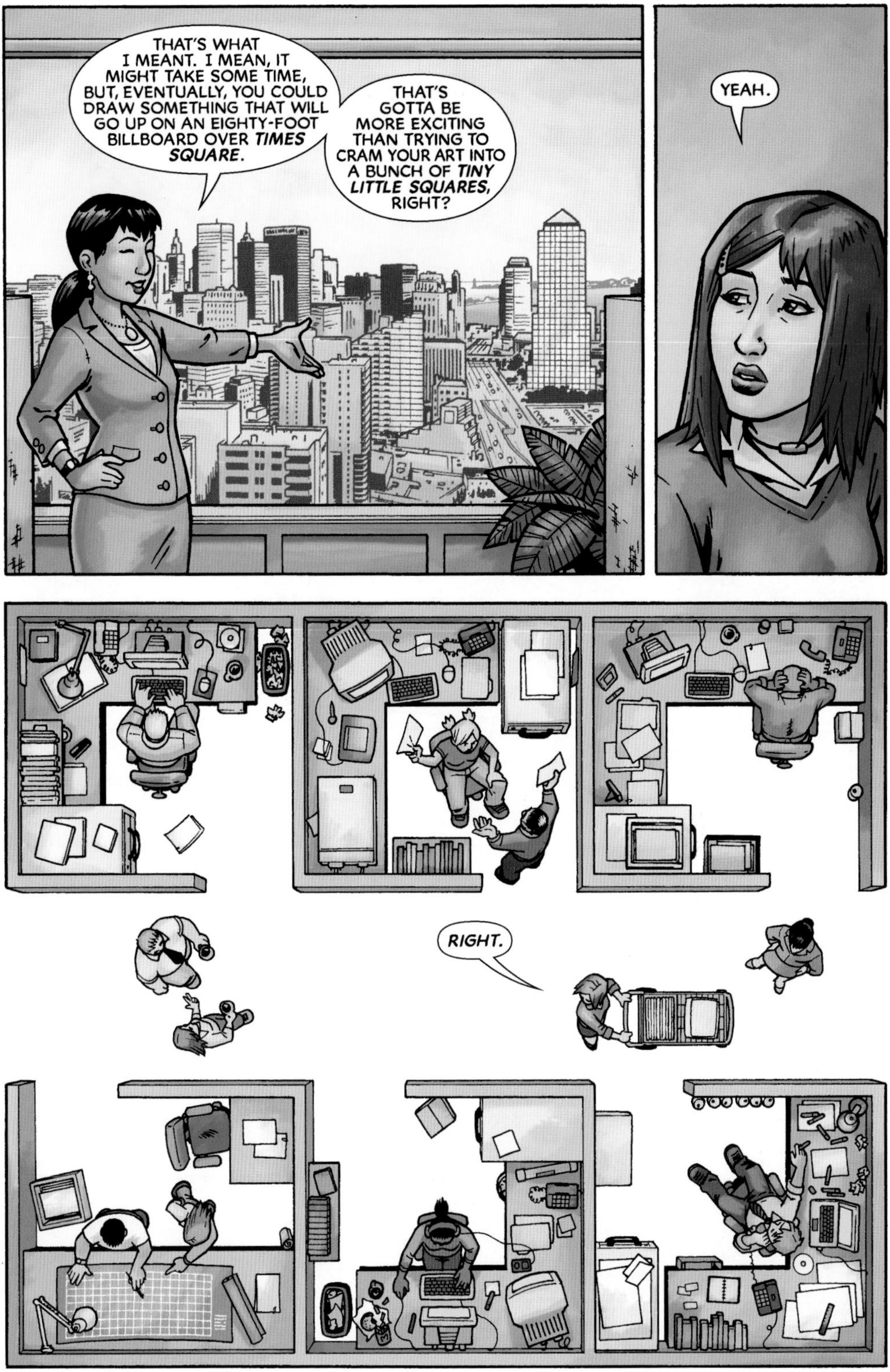

THAT'S WHAT I MEANT. I MEAN, IT MIGHT TAKE SOME TIME, BUT, EVENTUALLY, YOU COULD DRAW SOMETHING THAT WILL GO UP ON AN EIGHTY-FOOT BILLBOARD OVER *TIMES SQUARE*.
THAT'S GOTTA BE MORE EXCITING THAN TRYING TO CRAM YOUR ART INTO A BUNCH OF *TINY LITTLE SQUARES*, RIGHT?
YEAH.
RIGHT.

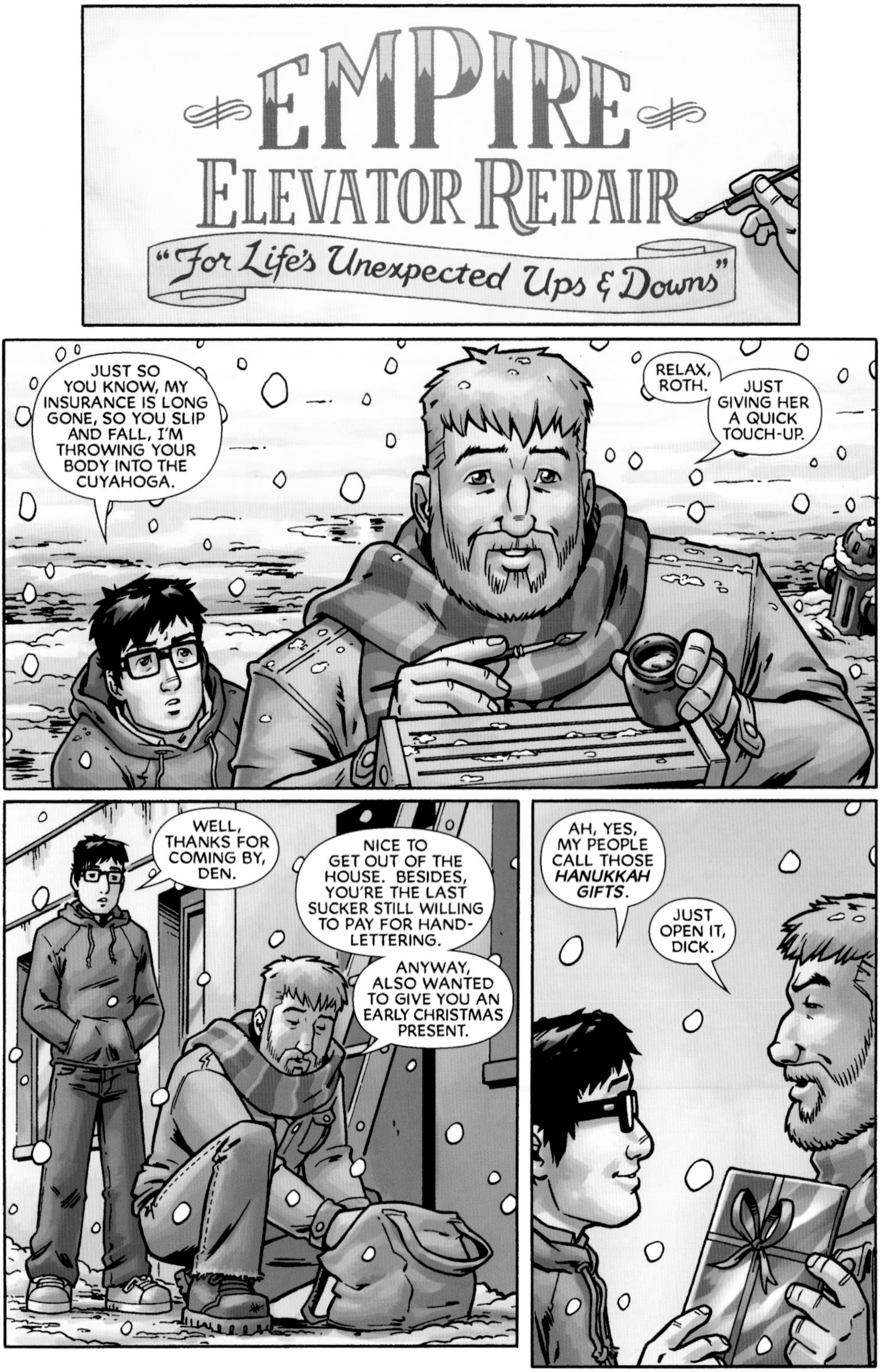
EMPIRE
ELEVATOR REPAIR
"For Life's Unexpected Ups & Downs"
JUST SO YOU KNOW, MY INSURANCE IS LONG GONE, SO YOU SLIP AND FALL, I'M THROWING YOUR BODY INTO THE CUYAHOGA.
RELAX, ROTH.
JUST GIVING HER A QUICK TOUCH-UP.
WELL, THANKS FOR COMING BY, DEN.
NICE TO GET OUT OF THE HOUSE. BESIDES, YOU'RE THE LAST SUCKER STILL WILLING TO PAY FOR HAND-LETTERING.
ANYWAY, ALSO WANTED TO GIVE YOU AN EARLY CHRISTMAS PRESENT.
AH, YES, MY PEOPLE CALL THOSE *HANUKKAH GIFTS*.
JUST OPEN IT, DICK.

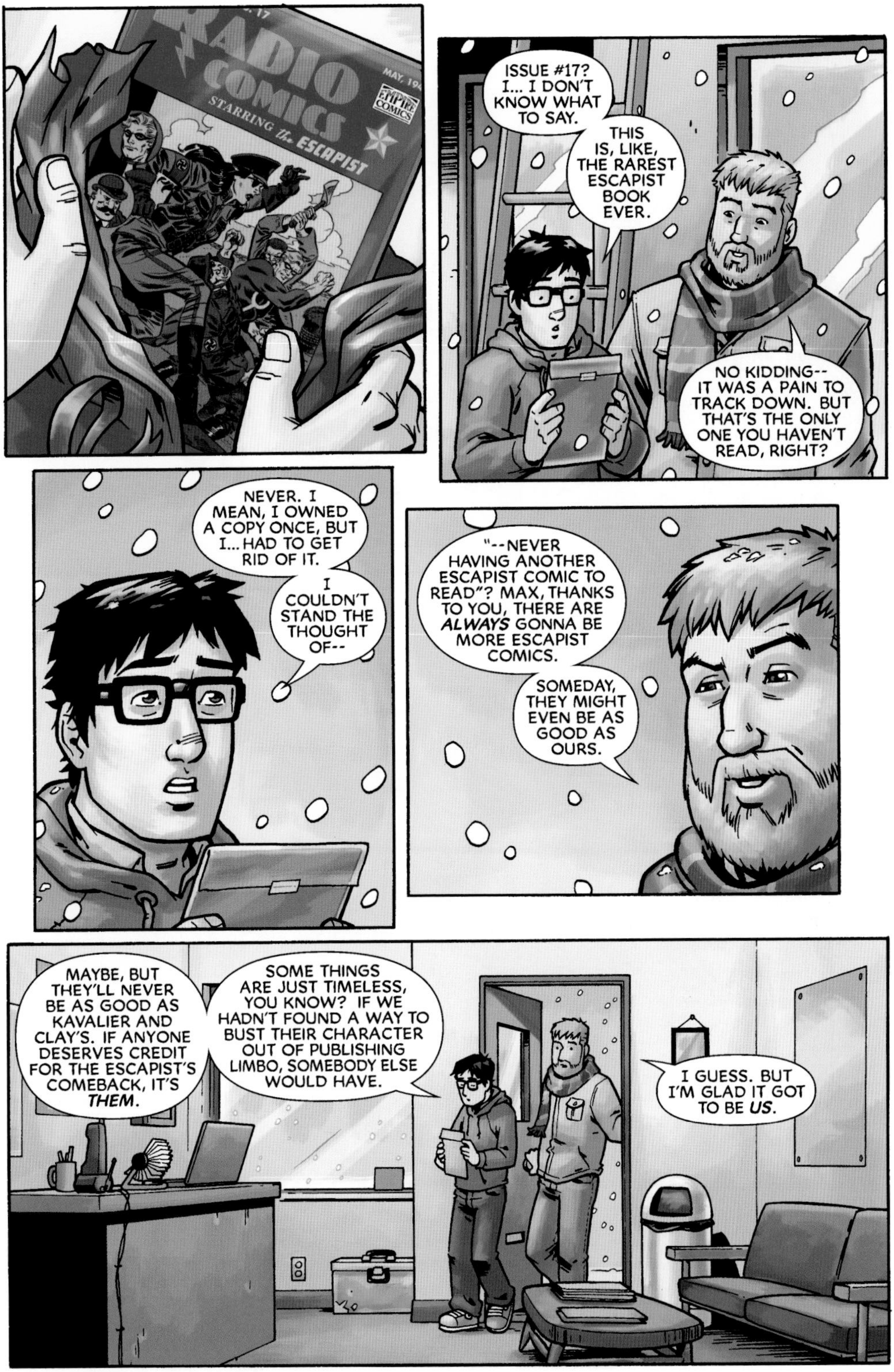
RADIO COMICS
MAY, 194
EMPIRE COMICS
STARRING the ESCAPIST
ISSUE #17? I... I DON'T KNOW WHAT TO SAY.
THIS IS, LIKE, THE RAREST ESCAPIST BOOK EVER.
NO KIDDING-- IT WAS A PAIN TO TRACK DOWN. BUT THAT'S THE ONLY ONE YOU HAVEN'T READ, RIGHT?
NEVER. I MEAN, I OWNED A COPY ONCE, BUT I... HAD TO GET RID OF IT.
I COULDN'T STAND THE THOUGHT OF--
"--NEVER HAVING ANOTHER ESCAPIST COMIC TO READ"? MAX, THANKS TO YOU, THERE ARE *ALWAYS* GONNA BE MORE ESCAPIST COMICS.
SOMEDAY, THEY MIGHT EVEN BE AS GOOD AS OURS.
MAYBE, BUT THEY'LL NEVER BE AS GOOD AS KAVALIER AND CLAY'S. IF ANYONE DESERVES CREDIT FOR THE ESCAPIST'S COMEBACK, IT'S *THEM*.
SOME THINGS ARE JUST TIMELESS, YOU KNOW? IF WE HADN'T FOUND A WAY TO BUST THEIR CHARACTER OUT OF PUBLISHING LIMBO, SOMEBODY ELSE WOULD HAVE.
I GUESS. BUT I'M GLAD IT GOT TO BE *US*.

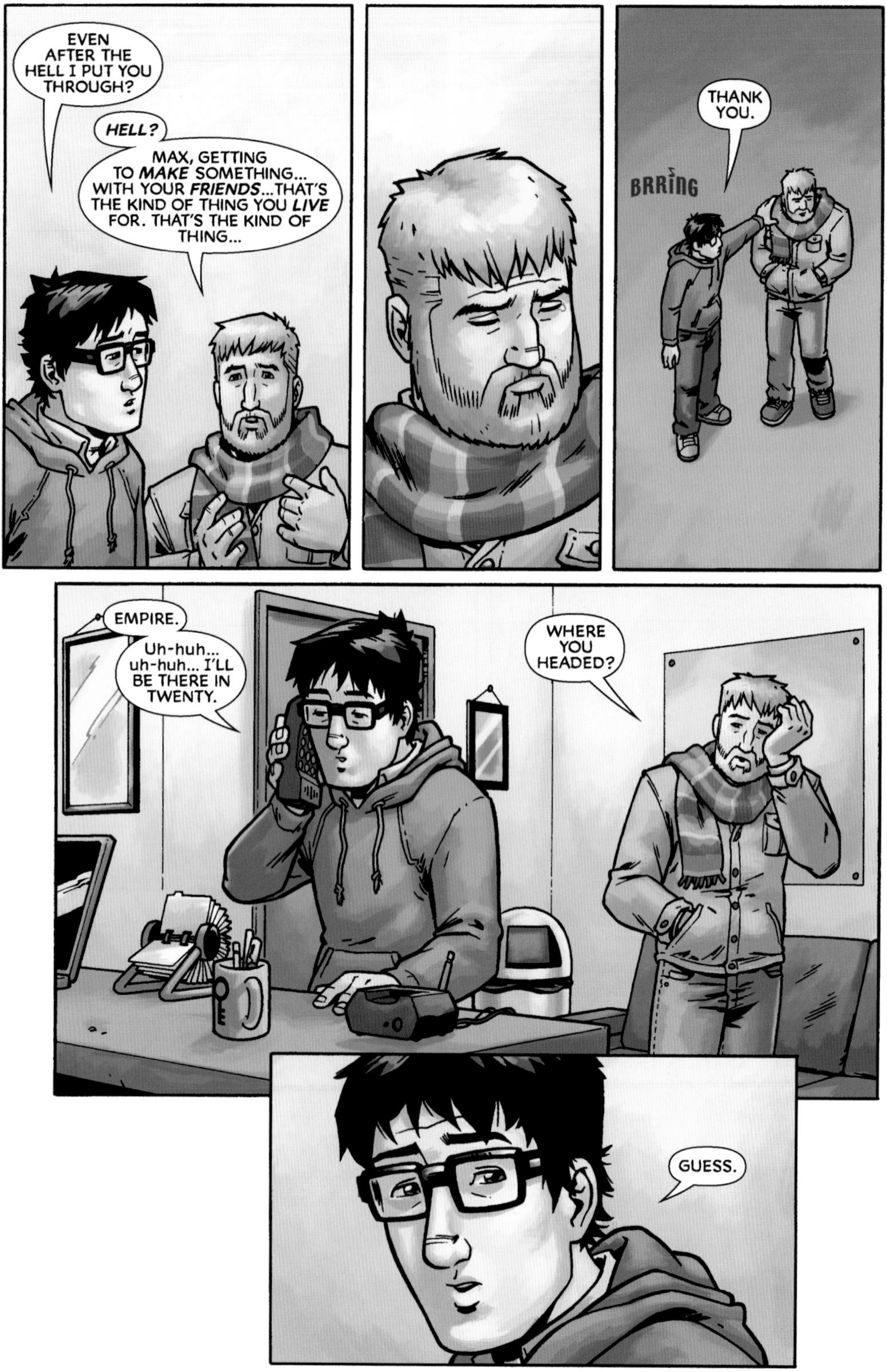
EVEN AFTER THE HELL I PUT YOU THROUGH?
HELL?
MAX, GETTING TO MAKE SOMETHING... WITH YOUR FRIENDS...THAT'S THE KIND OF THING YOU LIVE FOR. THAT'S THE KIND OF THING...
THANK YOU.
BRRING
EMPIRE.
Uh-huh... uh-huh... I'LL BE THERE IN TWENTY.
WHERE YOU HEADED?
GUESS.

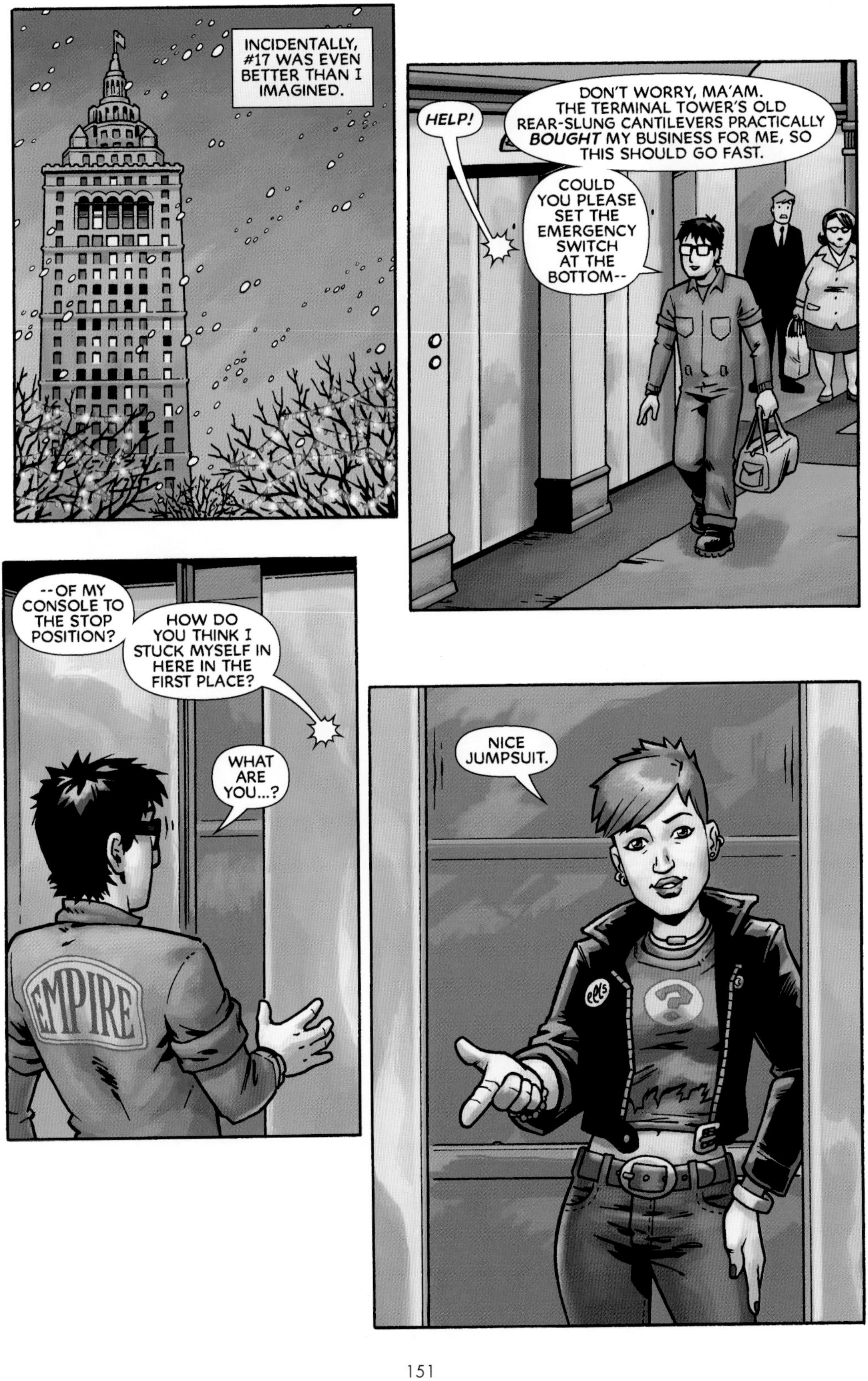
INCIDENTALLY, #17 WAS EVEN BETTER THAN I IMAGINED.
HELP!
DON'T WORRY, MA'AM. THE TERMINAL TOWER'S OLD REAR-SLUNG CANTILEVERS PRACTICALLY *BOUGHT* MY BUSINESS FOR ME, SO THIS SHOULD GO FAST.
COULD YOU PLEASE SET THE EMERGENCY SWITCH AT THE BOTTOM--
--OF MY CONSOLE TO THE STOP POSITION?
HOW DO YOU THINK I STUCK MYSELF IN HERE IN THE FIRST PLACE?
WHAT ARE YOU...?
EMPIRE
NICE JUMPSUIT.

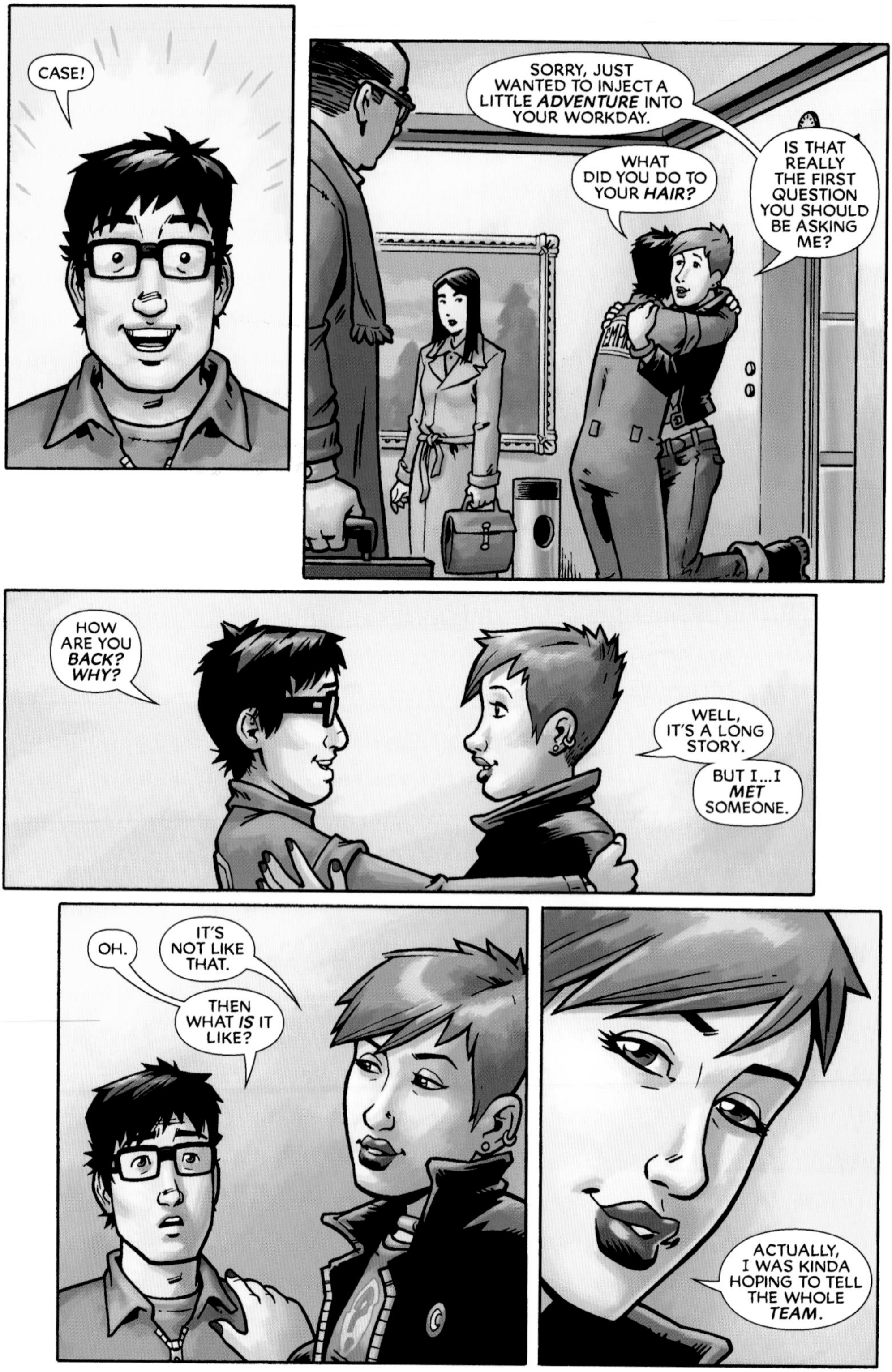
CASE!
SORRY, JUST WANTED TO INJECT A LITTLE *ADVENTURE* INTO YOUR WORKDAY.
WHAT DID YOU DO TO YOUR *HAIR?*
IS THAT REALLY THE FIRST QUESTION YOU SHOULD BE ASKING ME?
HOW ARE YOU *BACK? WHY?*
WELL, IT'S A LONG STORY.
BUT I...I *MET* SOMEONE.
OH.
IT'S NOT LIKE THAT.
THEN WHAT *IS* IT LIKE?
ACTUALLY, I WAS KINDA HOPING TO TELL THE WHOLE *TEAM*.

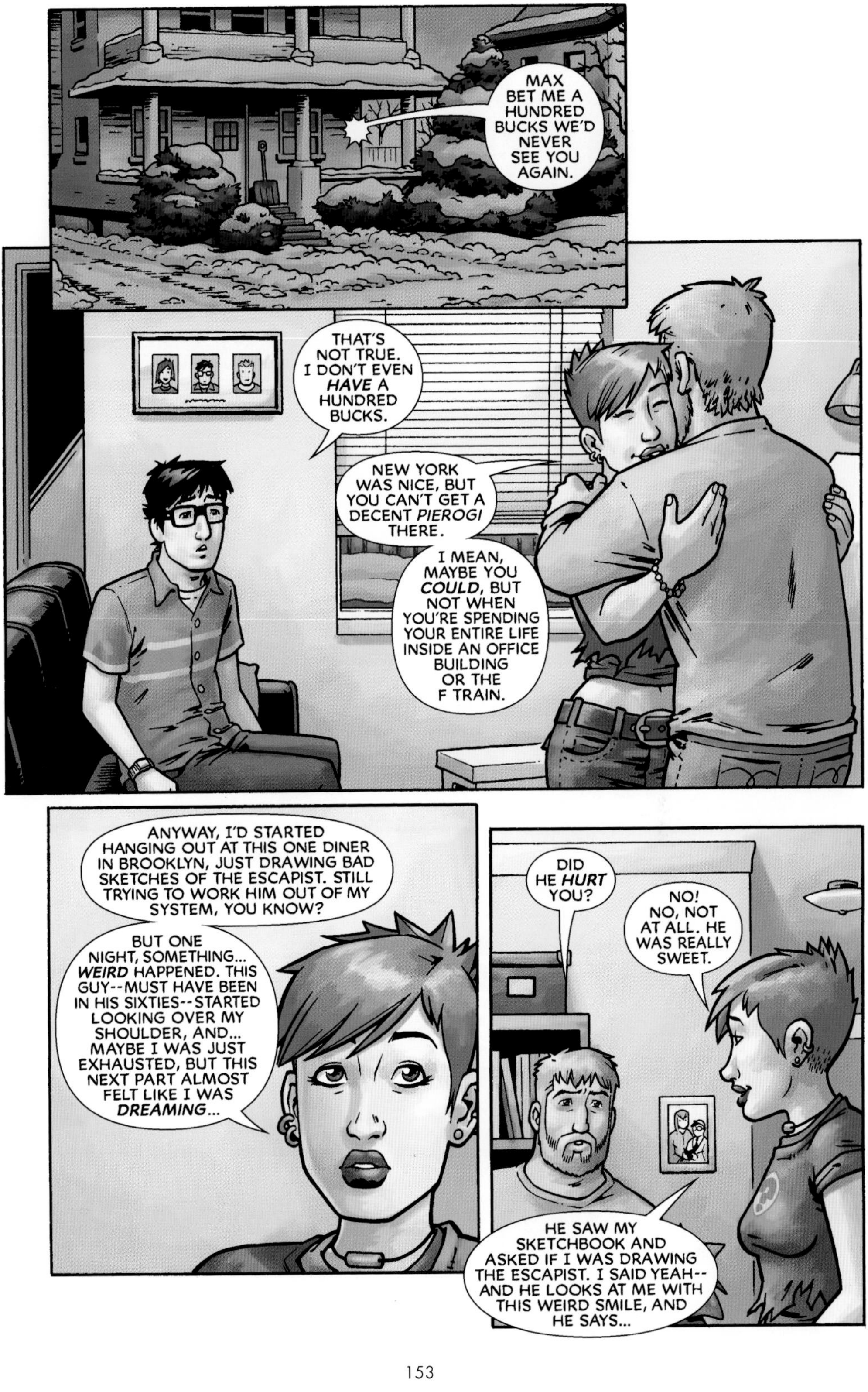
MAX BET ME A HUNDRED BUCKS WE'D NEVER SEE YOU AGAIN.
THAT'S NOT TRUE. I DON'T EVEN *HAVE* A HUNDRED BUCKS.
NEW YORK WAS NICE, BUT YOU CAN'T GET A DECENT *PIEROGI* THERE.
I MEAN, MAYBE YOU *COULD*, BUT NOT WHEN YOU'RE SPENDING YOUR ENTIRE LIFE INSIDE AN OFFICE BUILDING OR THE F TRAIN.
ANYWAY, I'D STARTED HANGING OUT AT THIS ONE DINER IN BROOKLYN, JUST DRAWING BAD SKETCHES OF THE ESCAPIST. STILL TRYING TO WORK HIM OUT OF MY SYSTEM, YOU KNOW?
BUT ONE NIGHT, SOMETHING... *WEIRD* HAPPENED. THIS GUY--MUST HAVE BEEN IN HIS SIXTIES--STARTED LOOKING OVER MY SHOULDER, AND... MAYBE I WAS JUST EXHAUSTED, BUT THIS NEXT PART ALMOST FELT LIKE I WAS *DREAMING*...
DID HE *HURT* YOU?
NO! NO, NOT AT ALL. HE WAS REALLY SWEET.
HE SAW MY SKETCHBOOK AND ASKED IF I WAS DRAWING THE ESCAPIST. I SAID YEAH-- AND HE LOOKS AT ME WITH THIS WEIRD SMILE, AND HE SAYS...

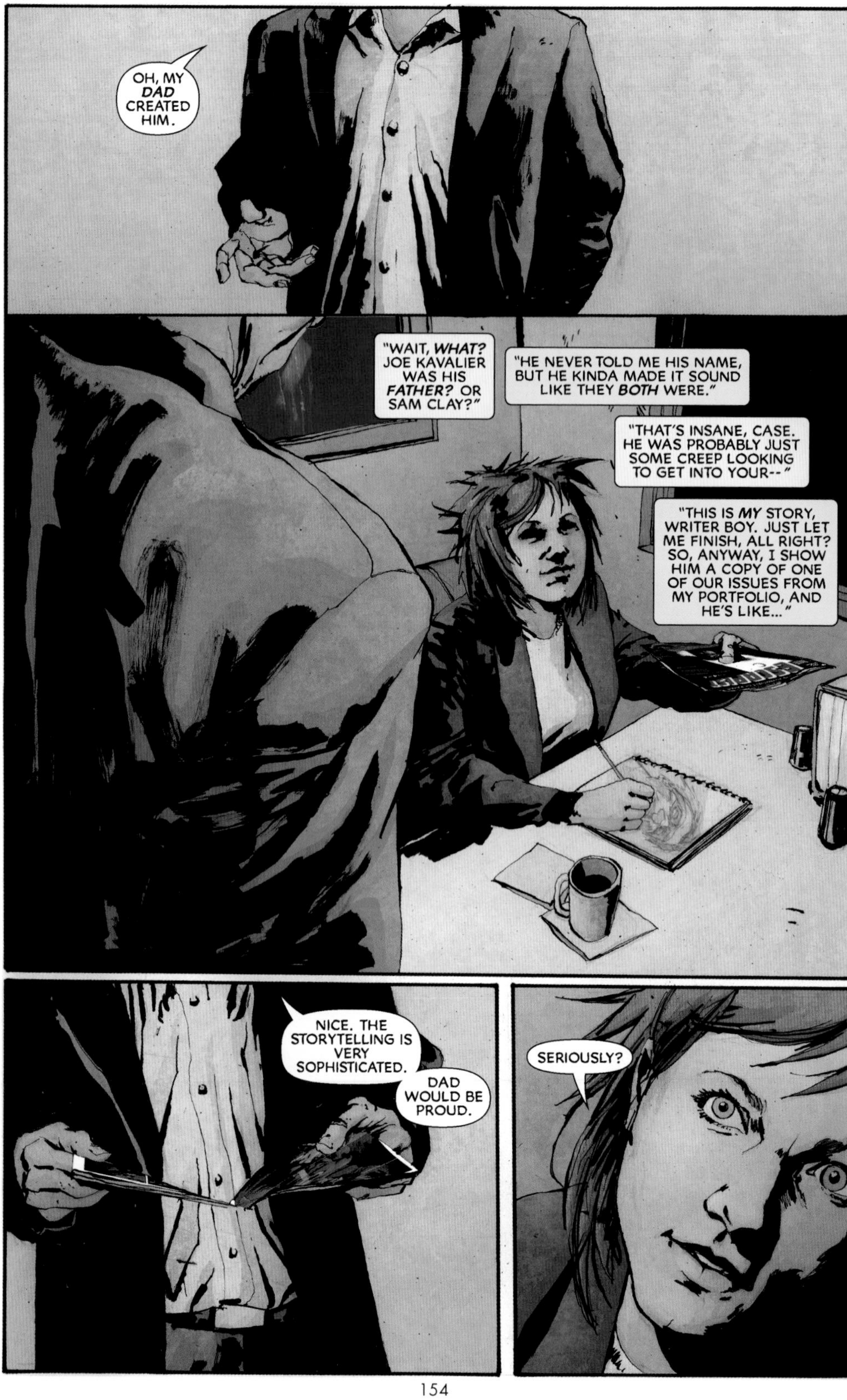
OH, MY DAD CREATED HIM.
"WAIT, WHAT? JOE KAVALIER WAS HIS FATHER? OR SAM CLAY?"
"HE NEVER TOLD ME HIS NAME, BUT HE KINDA MADE IT SOUND LIKE THEY BOTH WERE."
"THAT'S INSANE, CASE. HE WAS PROBABLY JUST SOME CREEP LOOKING TO GET INTO YOUR--"
"THIS IS MY STORY, WRITER BOY. JUST LET ME FINISH, ALL RIGHT? SO, ANYWAY, I SHOW HIM A COPY OF ONE OF OUR ISSUES FROM MY PORTFOLIO, AND HE'S LIKE..."
NICE. THE STORYTELLING IS VERY SOPHISTICATED.
DAD WOULD BE PROUD.
SERIOUSLY?

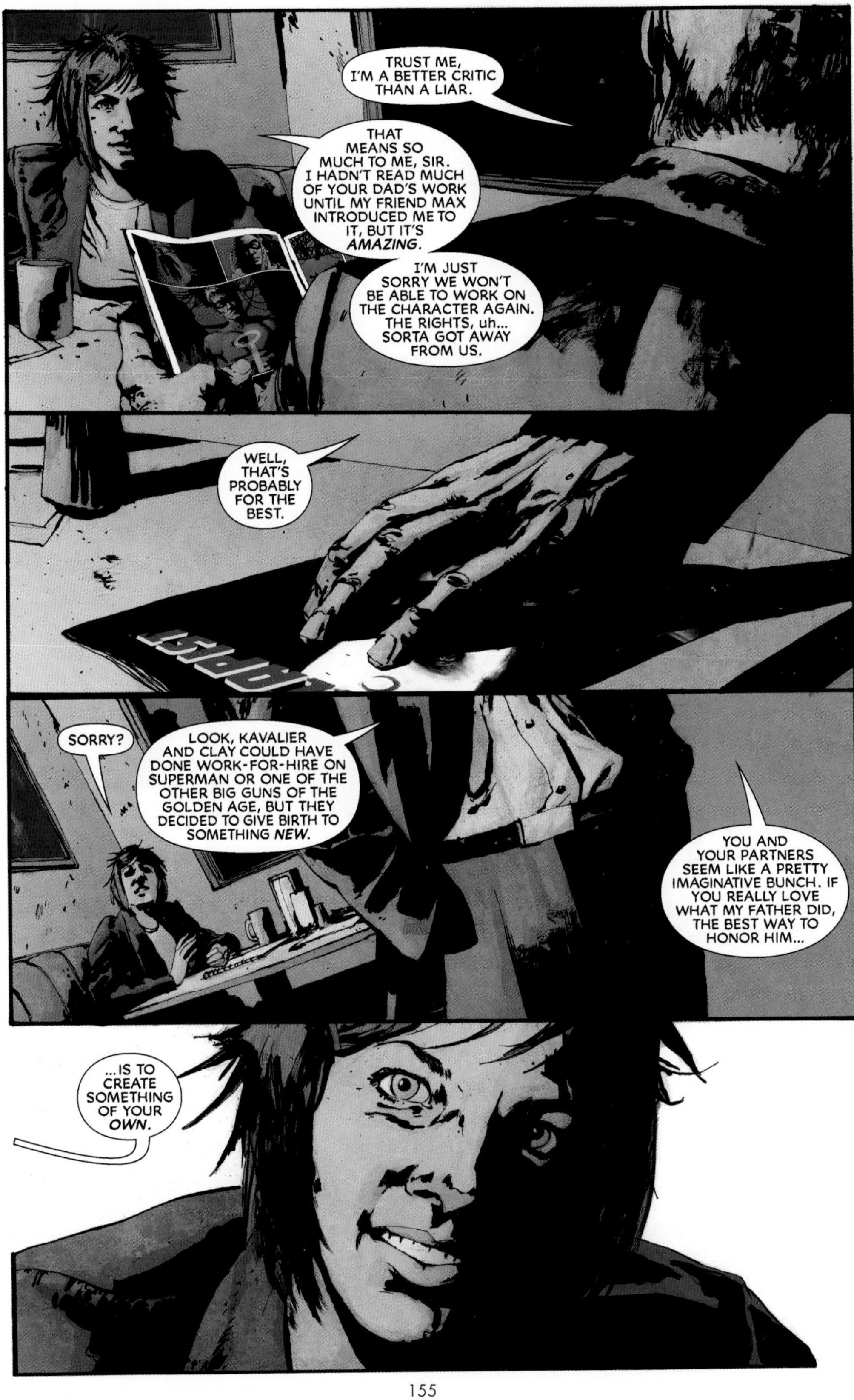
TRUST ME, I'M A BETTER CRITIC THAN A LIAR.
THAT MEANS SO MUCH TO ME, SIR. I HADN'T READ MUCH OF YOUR DAD'S WORK UNTIL MY FRIEND MAX INTRODUCED ME TO IT, BUT IT'S *AMAZING*.
I'M JUST SORRY WE WON'T BE ABLE TO WORK ON THE CHARACTER AGAIN. THE RIGHTS, uh... SORTA GOT AWAY FROM US.
WELL, THAT'S PROBABLY FOR THE BEST.
SORRY?
LOOK, KAVALIER AND CLAY COULD HAVE DONE WORK-FOR-HIRE ON SUPERMAN OR ONE OF THE OTHER BIG GUNS OF THE GOLDEN AGE, BUT THEY DECIDED TO GIVE BIRTH TO SOMETHING *NEW*.
YOU AND YOUR PARTNERS SEEM LIKE A PRETTY IMAGINATIVE BUNCH. IF YOU REALLY LOVE WHAT MY FATHER DID, THE BEST WAY TO HONOR HIM...
...IS TO CREATE SOMETHING OF YOUR *OWN*.

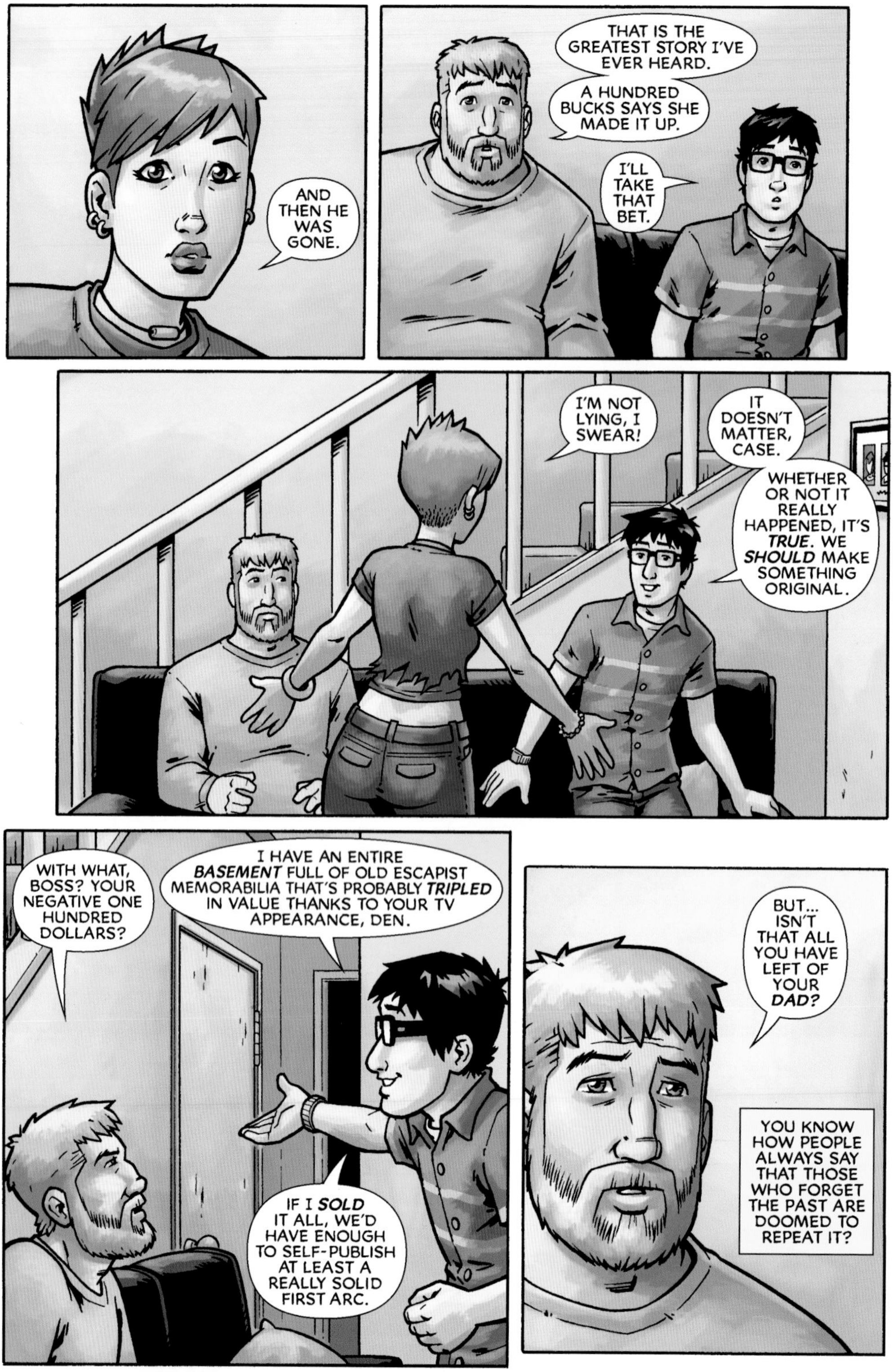
AND THEN HE WAS GONE.
THAT IS THE GREATEST STORY I'VE EVER HEARD.
A HUNDRED BUCKS SAYS SHE MADE IT UP.
I'LL TAKE THAT BET.
I'M NOT LYING, I SWEAR!
IT DOESN'T MATTER, CASE.
WHETHER OR NOT IT REALLY HAPPENED, IT'S ***TRUE***. WE ***SHOULD*** MAKE SOMETHING ORIGINAL.
WITH WHAT, BOSS? YOUR NEGATIVE ONE HUNDRED DOLLARS?
I HAVE AN ENTIRE ***BASEMENT*** FULL OF OLD ESCAPIST MEMORABILIA THAT'S PROBABLY ***TRIPLED*** IN VALUE THANKS TO YOUR TV APPEARANCE, DEN.
IF I ***SOLD*** IT ALL, WE'D HAVE ENOUGH TO SELF-PUBLISH AT LEAST A REALLY SOLID FIRST ARC.
BUT... ISN'T THAT ALL YOU HAVE LEFT OF YOUR ***DAD?***
YOU KNOW HOW PEOPLE ALWAYS SAY THAT THOSE WHO FORGET THE PAST ARE DOOMED TO REPEAT IT?

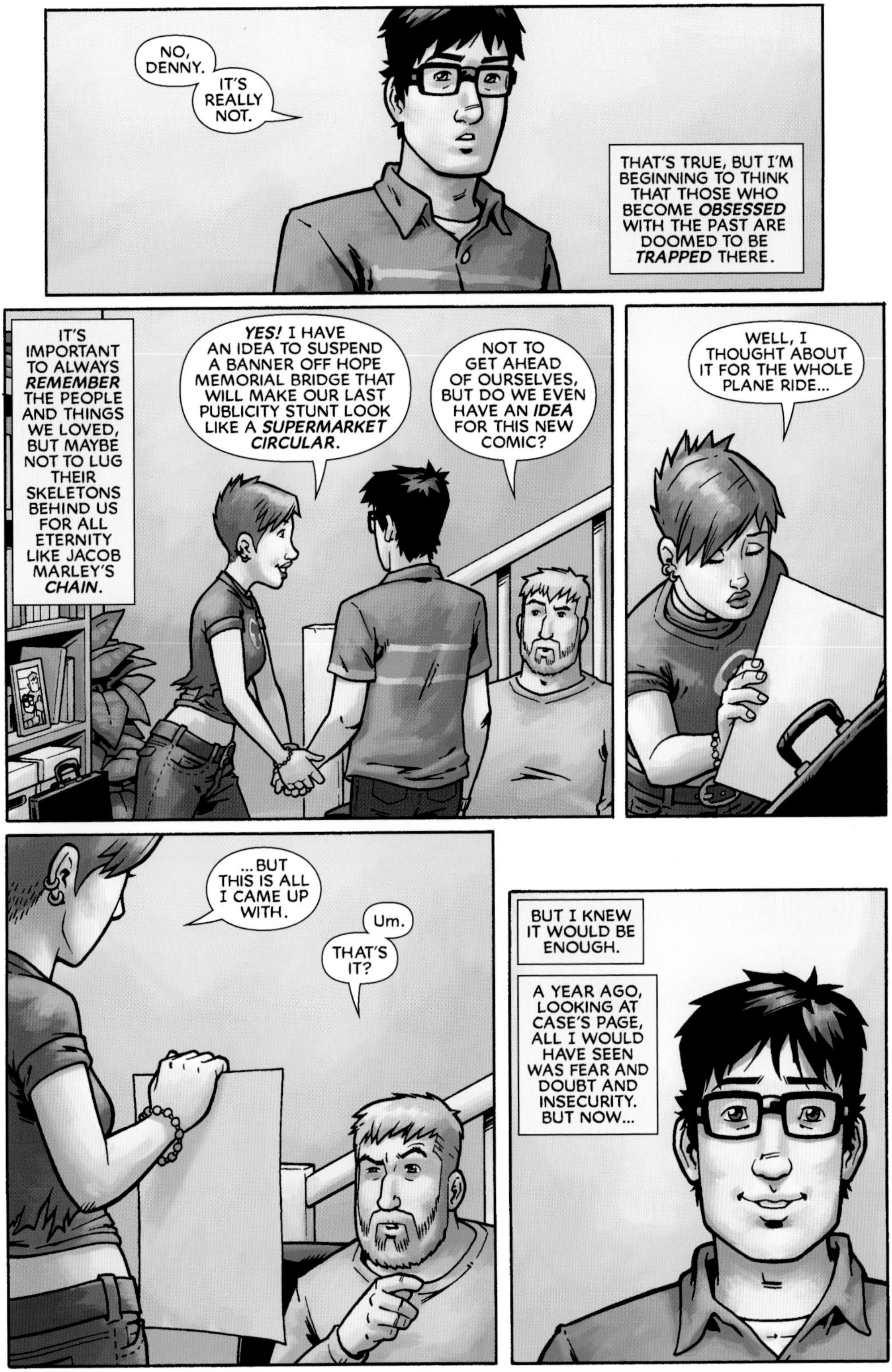
NO, DENNY.
IT'S REALLY NOT.
THAT'S TRUE, BUT I'M BEGINNING TO THINK THAT THOSE WHO BECOME *OBSESSED* WITH THE PAST ARE DOOMED TO BE *TRAPPED* THERE.
IT'S IMPORTANT TO ALWAYS *REMEMBER* THE PEOPLE AND THINGS WE LOVED, BUT MAYBE NOT TO LUG THEIR SKELETONS BEHIND US FOR ALL ETERNITY LIKE JACOB MARLEY'S *CHAIN*.
YES! I HAVE AN IDEA TO SUSPEND A BANNER OFF HOPE MEMORIAL BRIDGE THAT WILL MAKE OUR LAST PUBLICITY STUNT LOOK LIKE A *SUPERMARKET CIRCULAR*.
NOT TO GET AHEAD OF OURSELVES, BUT DO WE EVEN HAVE AN *IDEA* FOR THIS NEW COMIC?
WELL, I THOUGHT ABOUT IT FOR THE WHOLE PLANE RIDE...
...BUT THIS IS ALL I CAME UP WITH.
Um.
THAT'S IT?
BUT I KNEW IT WOULD BE ENOUGH.
A YEAR AGO, LOOKING AT CASE'S PAGE, ALL I WOULD HAVE SEEN WAS FEAR AND DOUBT AND INSECURITY. BUT NOW...

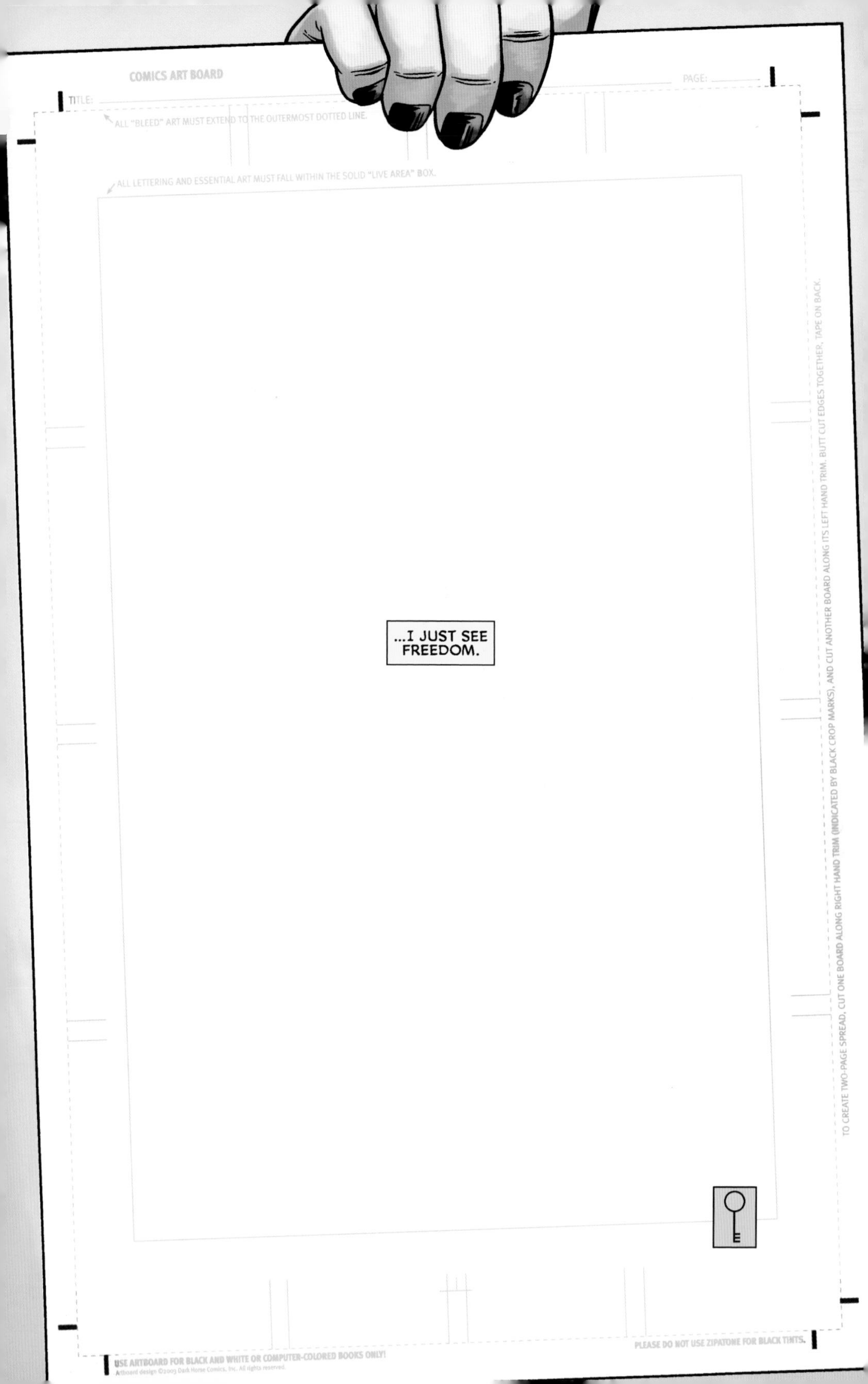
COMICS ART BOARD
TITLE:
PAGE:
ALL "BLEED" ART MUST EXTEND TO THE OUTERMOST DOTTED LINE.
ALL LETTERING AND ESSENTIAL ART MUST FALL WITHIN THE SOLID "LIVE AREA" BOX.
...I JUST SEE FREEDOM.
E
TO CREATE TWO-PAGE SPREAD, CUT ONE BOARD ALONG RIGHT HAND TRIM (INDICATED BY BLACK CROP MARKS), AND CUT ANOTHER BOARD ALONG ITS LEFT HAND TRIM. BUTT CUT EDGES TOGETHER, TAPE ON BACK.
PLEASE DO NOT USE ZIPATONE FOR BLACK TINTS.
USE ARTBOARD FOR BLACK AND WHITE OR COMPUTER-COLORED BOOKS ONLY!
Artboard design ©2003 Dark Horse Comics, Inc. All rights reserved.

COVER GALLERY

THE FOLLOWING PAGES feature the front cover artwork from issue eight of *Michael Chabon Presents the Amazing Adventures of The Escapist* and issues one through six of *The Escapists* comic book series.

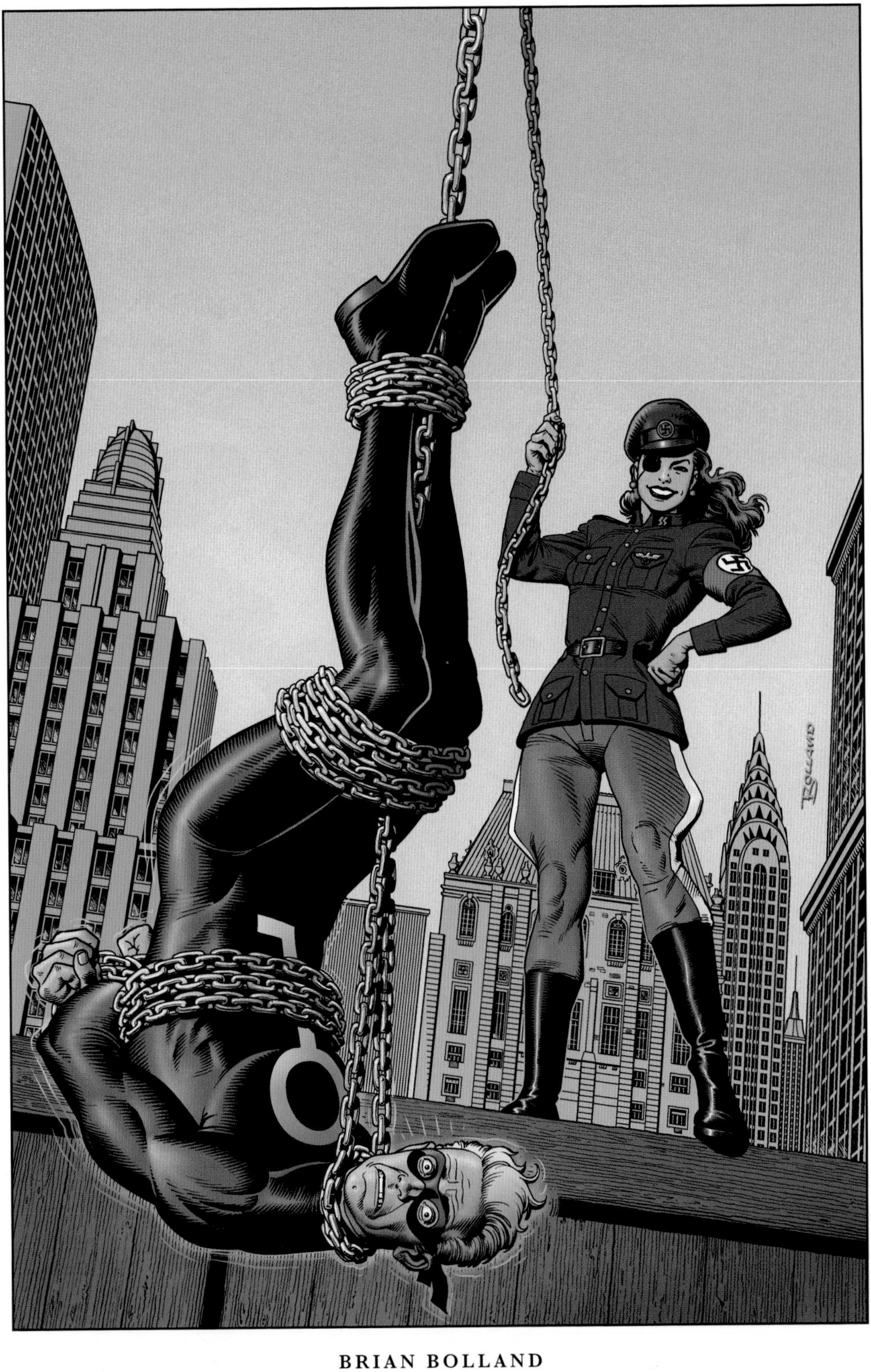
BOLLAND

BRIAN BOLLAND

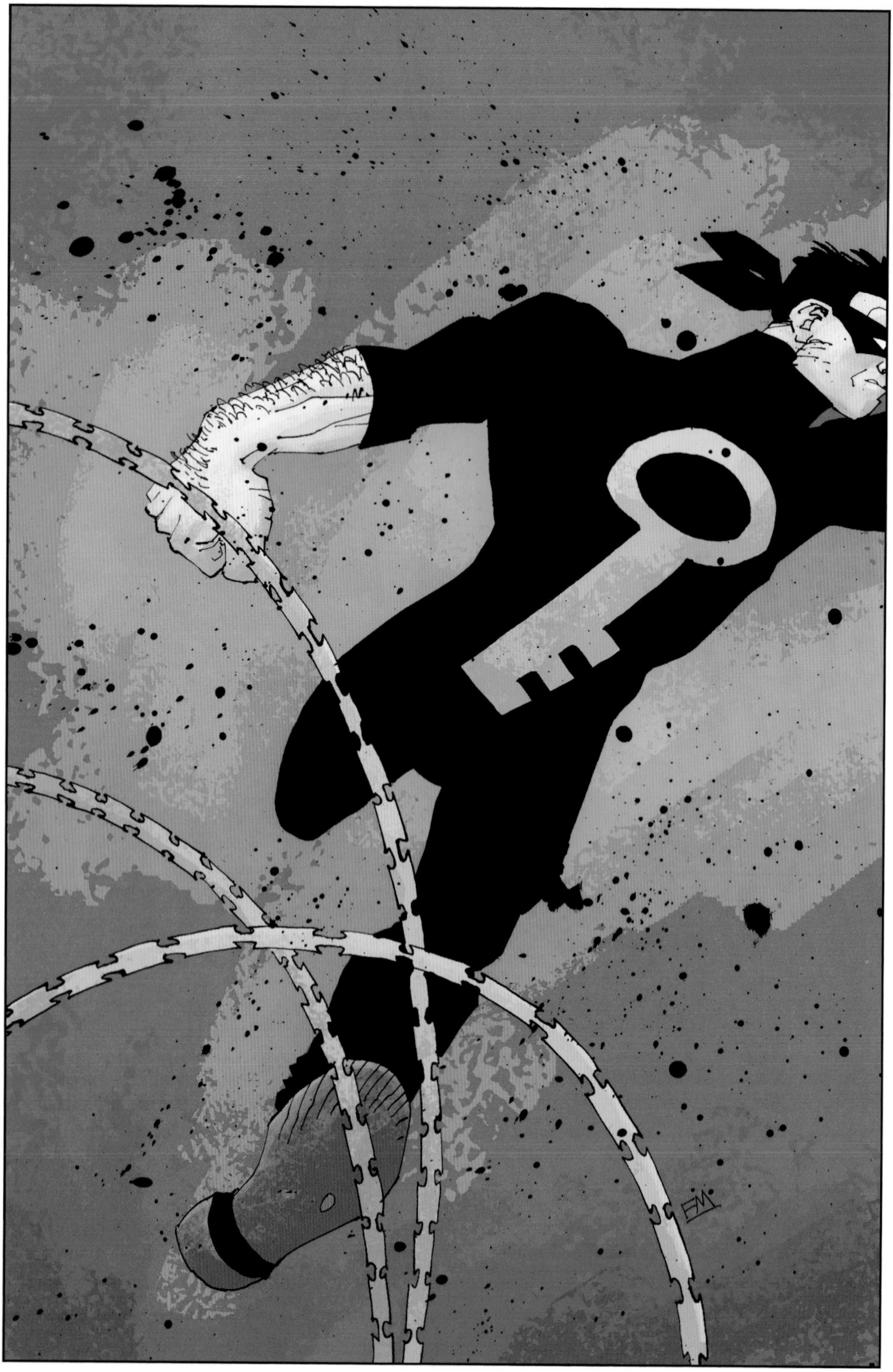

FRANK MILLER • Color by Dave Stewart

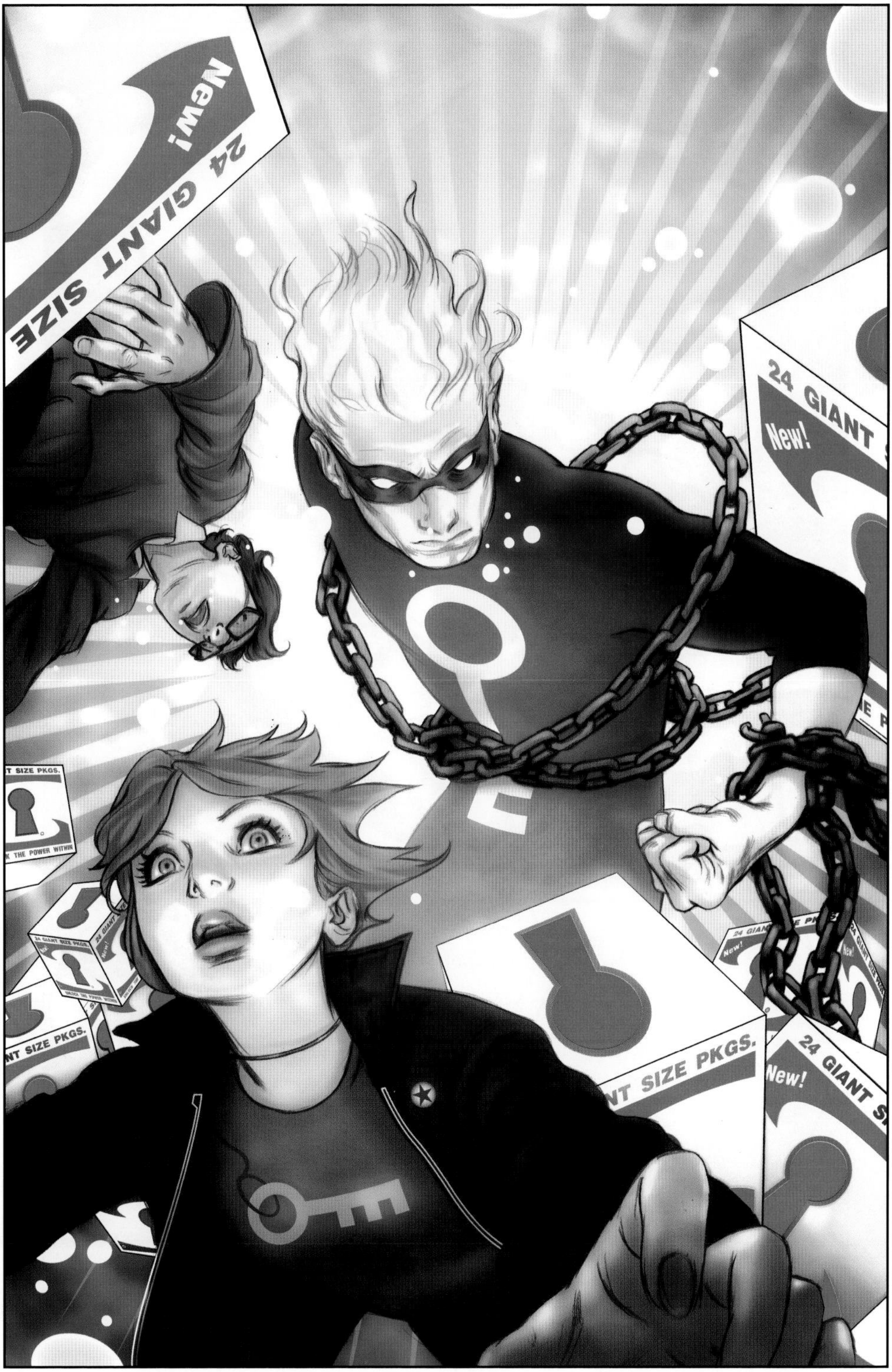
24 GIANT SIZE
New!
24 GIANT
New!
GIANT SIZE PKGS.
NT SIZE PKGS.
24 GIANT
New!

JAMES JEAN

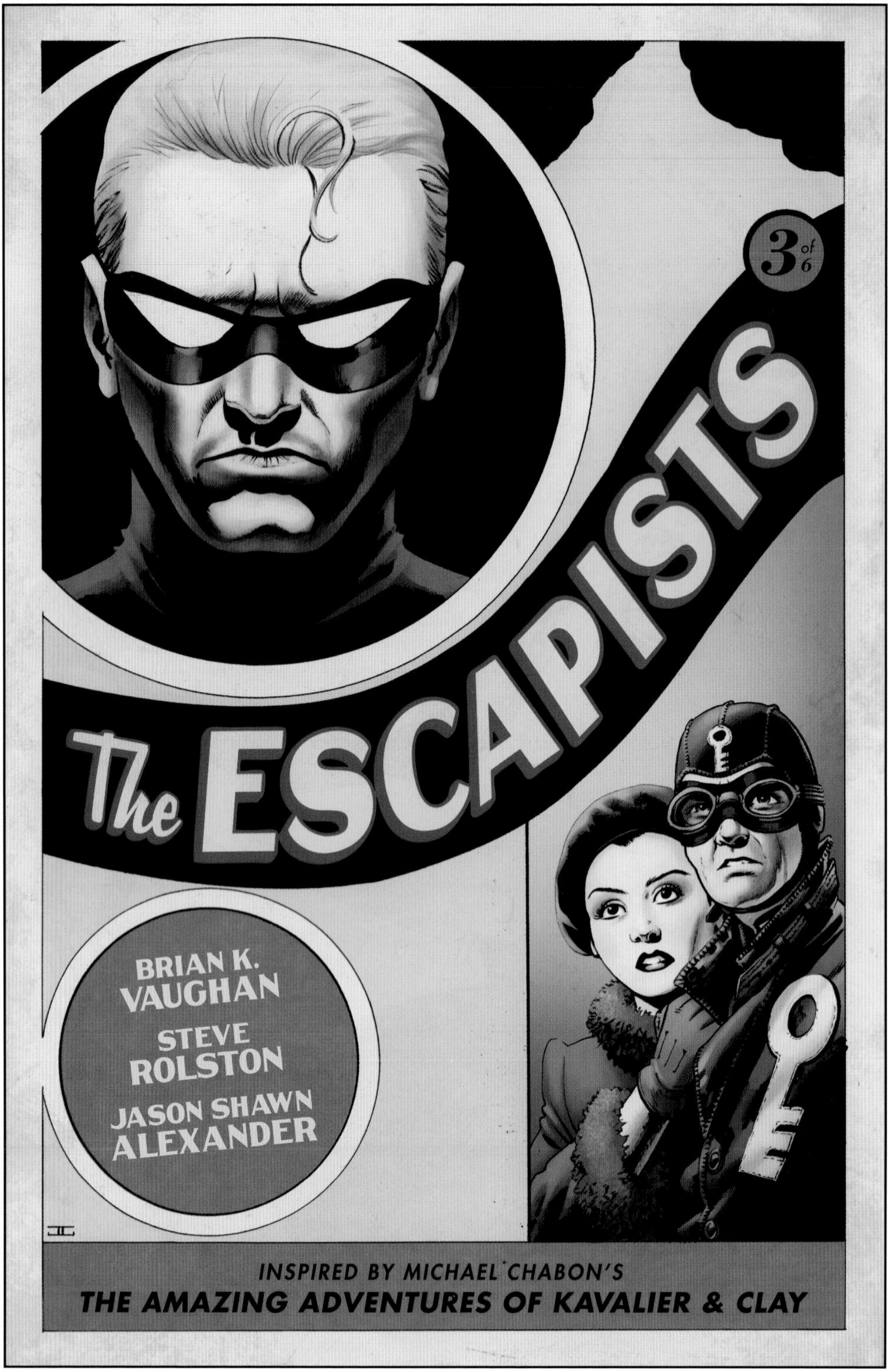
3 of 6
The ESCAPISTS
BRIAN K. VAUGHAN
STEVE ROLSTON
JASON SHAWN ALEXANDER
INSPIRED BY MICHAEL CHABON'S
THE AMAZING ADVENTURES OF KAVALIER & CLAY

JOHN CASSADAY • Color by Laura Martin

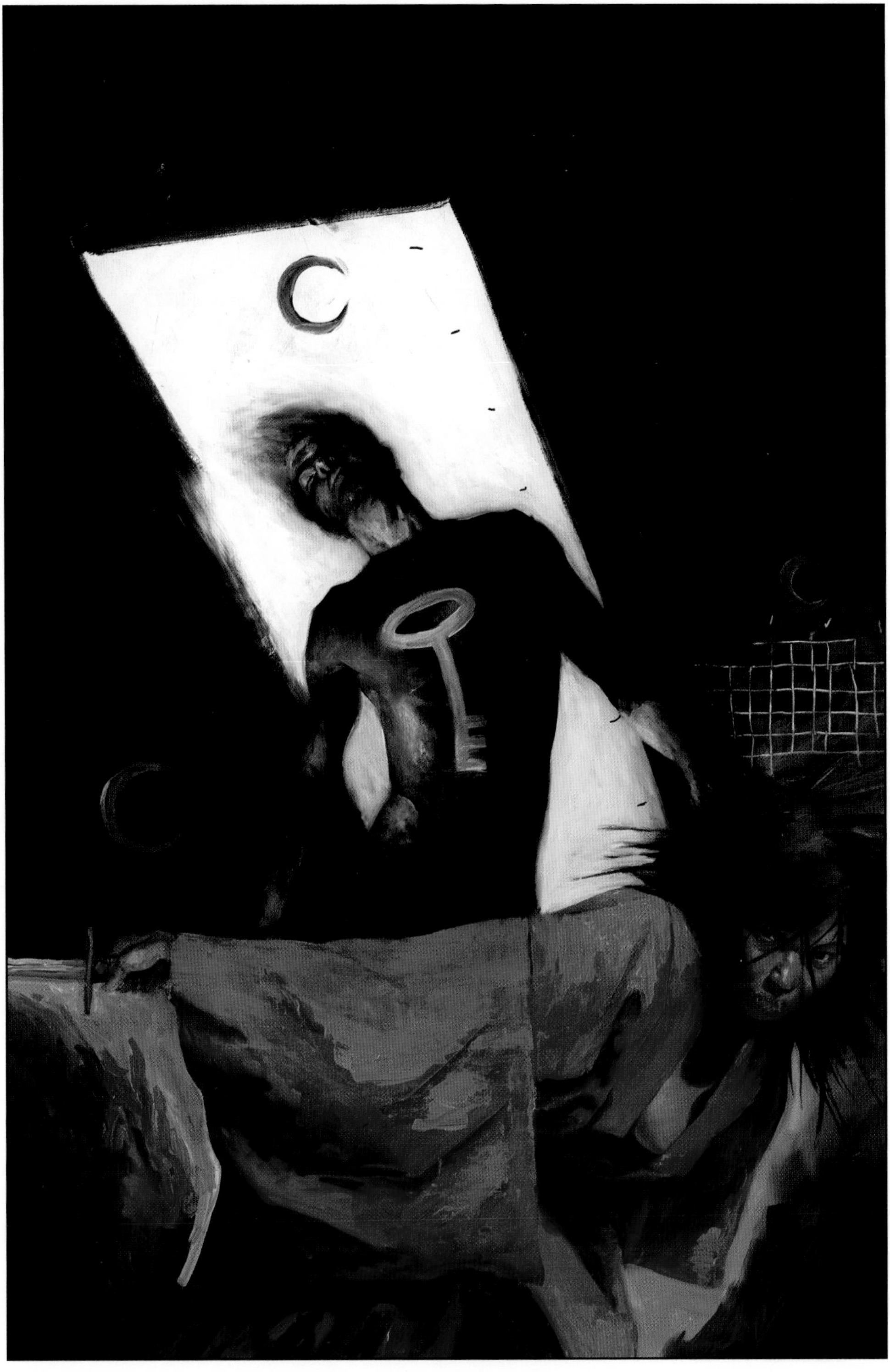

JASON SHAWN ALEXANDER

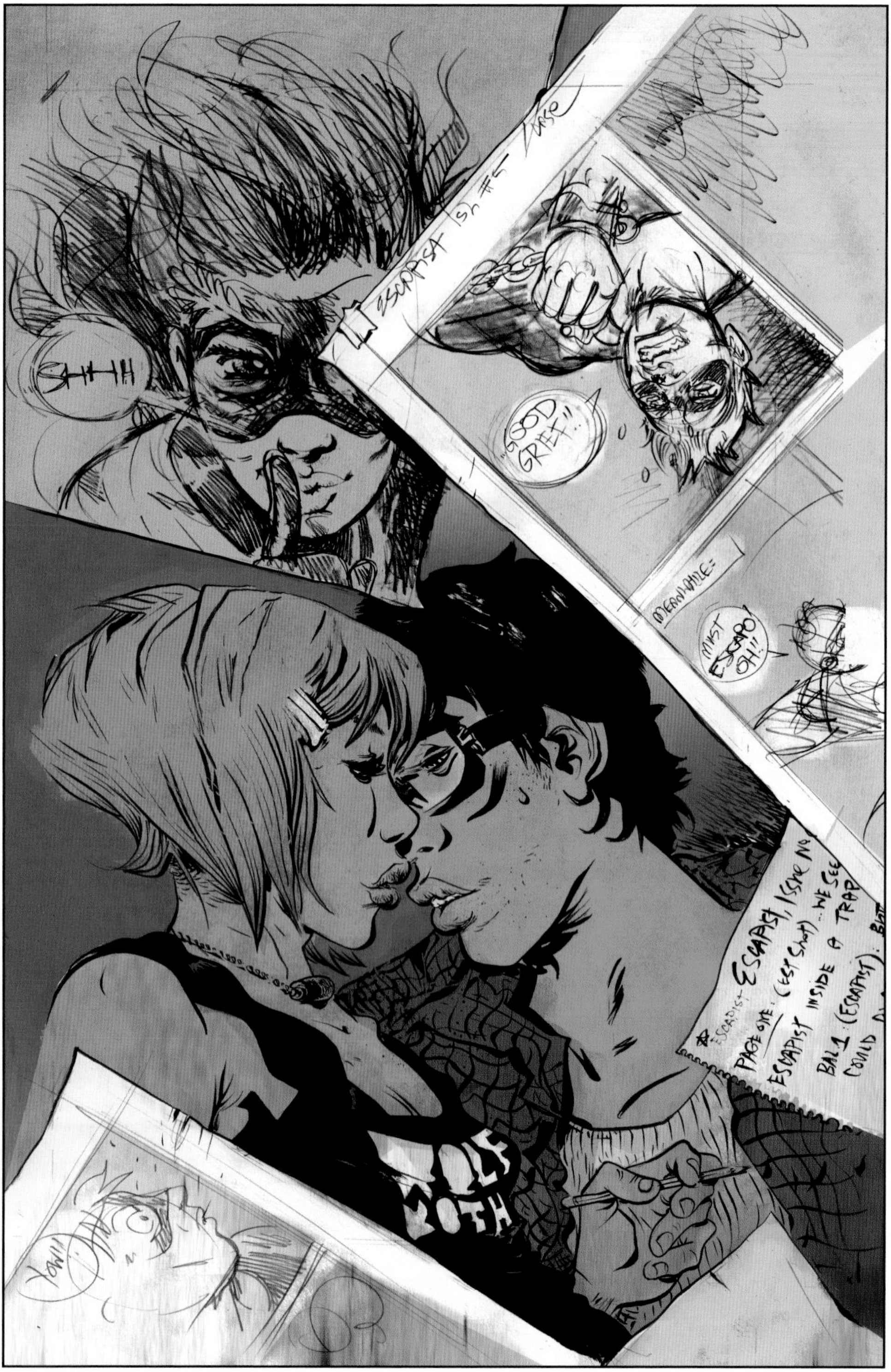
SHHH
GOOD GRIEF!!
MEANWHILE=
MUST ESCAPO OH!!
ESCAPIST– ESCAPIST, ISSUE NO
PAGE ONE: (EST SHOT)... WE SEE
ESCAPIST INSIDE A TRAP
BAL 1 (ESCAPIST):
COULD
YOW!!

PAUL POPE

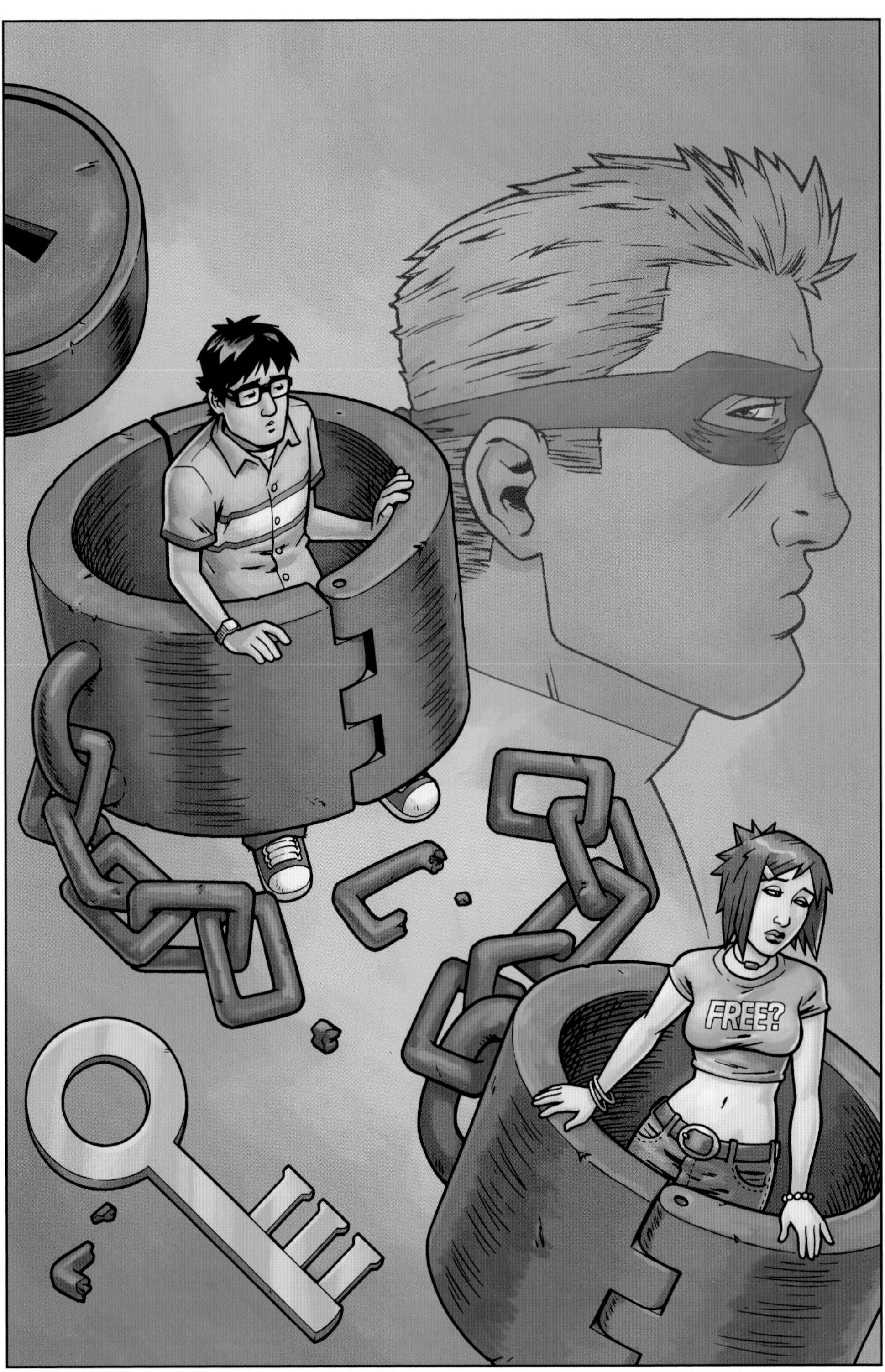
FREE?

STEVE ROLSTON • Color by Dave Stewart

ESCAPIST COVER GALLERY

THE FOLLOWING PAGES feature the three "faux" comics covers specially designed and used in the context of *The Escapists* story line.

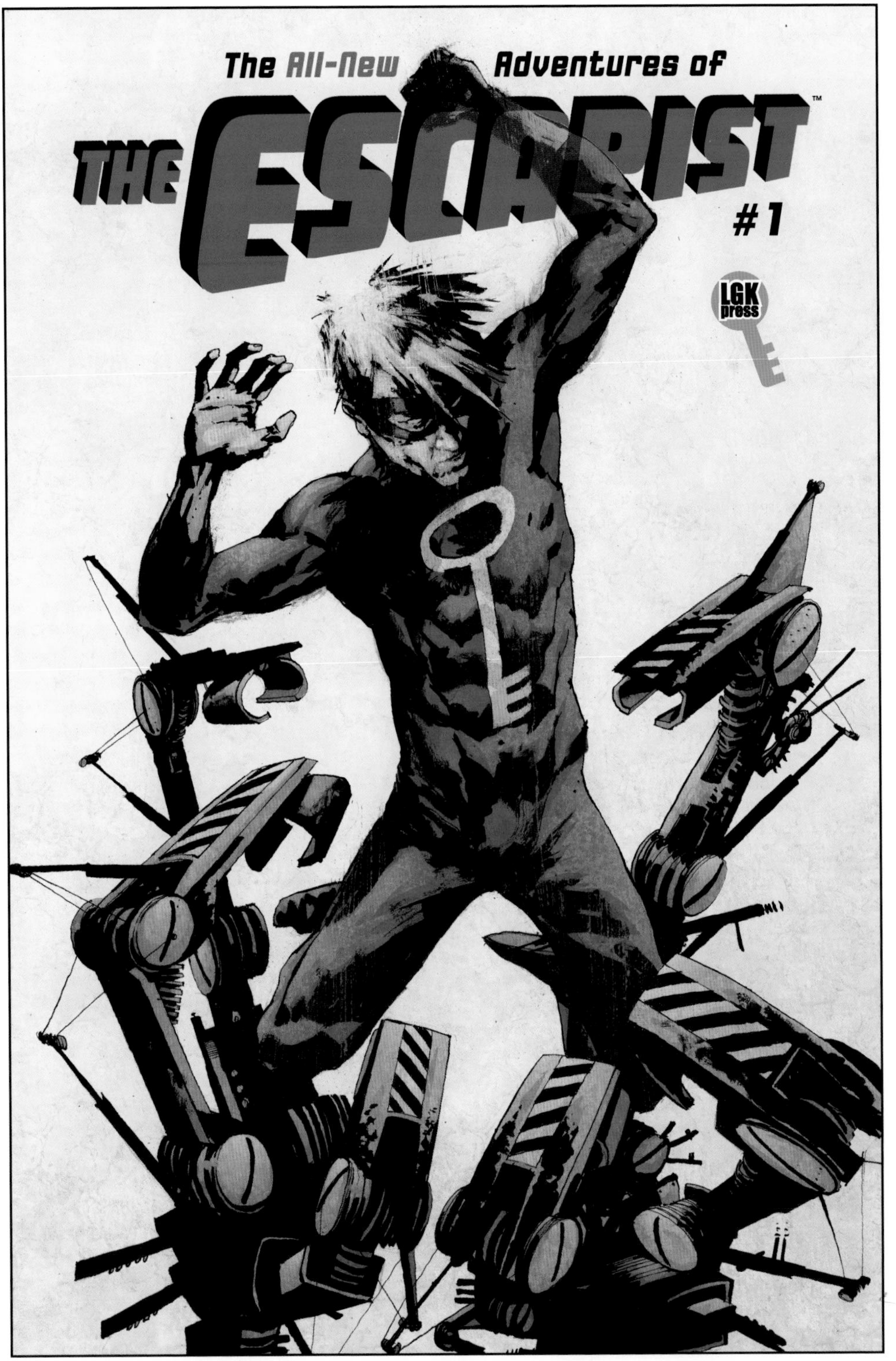
The All-New Adventures of
THE ESCAPIST
#1
LGK press

JASON SHAWN ALEXANDER • Color by Matthew Hollingsworth

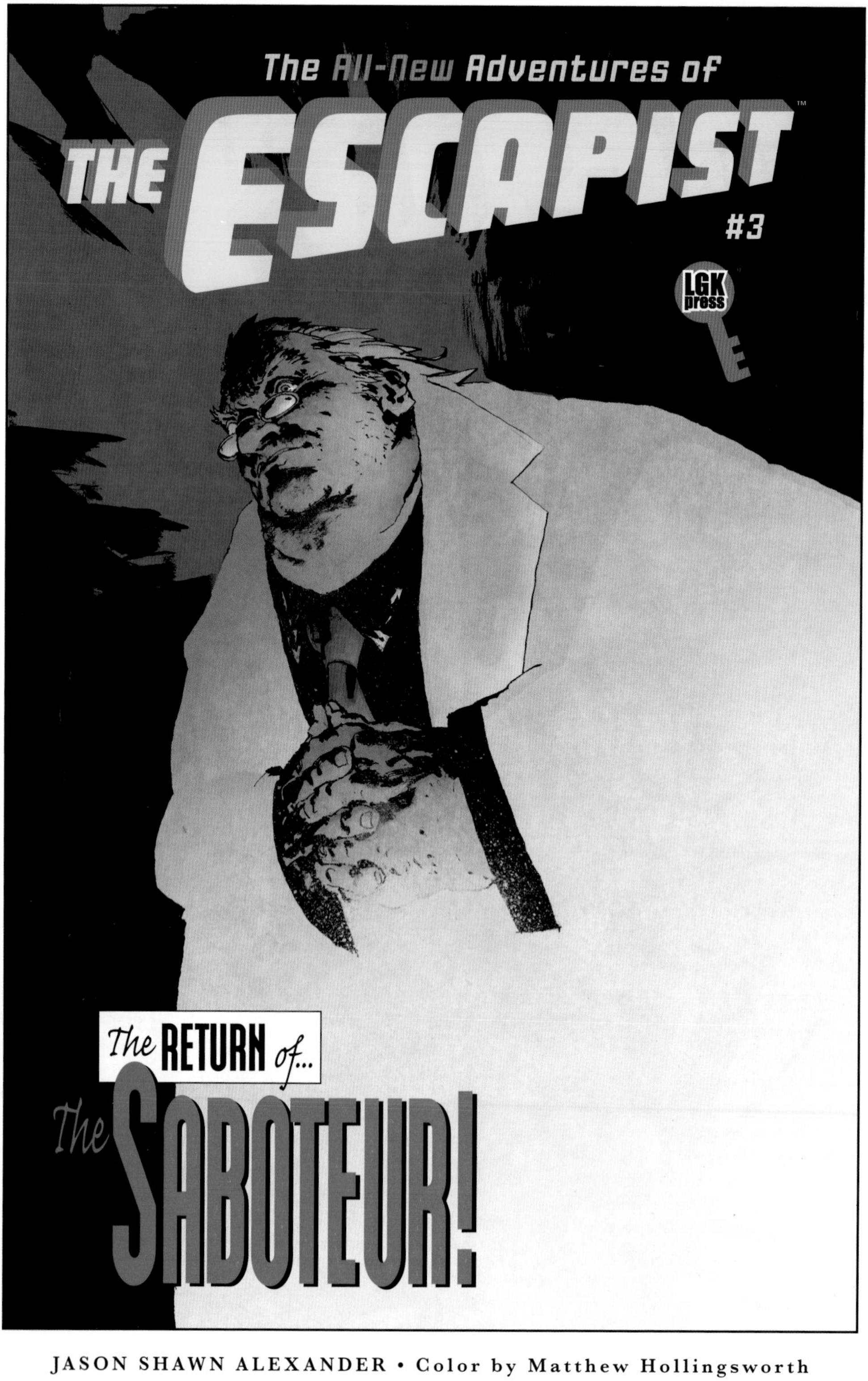
The All-New Adventures of
THE ESCAPIST™
#3
LGK press
The RETURN of...
The SABOTEUR!

JASON SHAWN ALEXANDER • Color by Matthew Hollingsworth

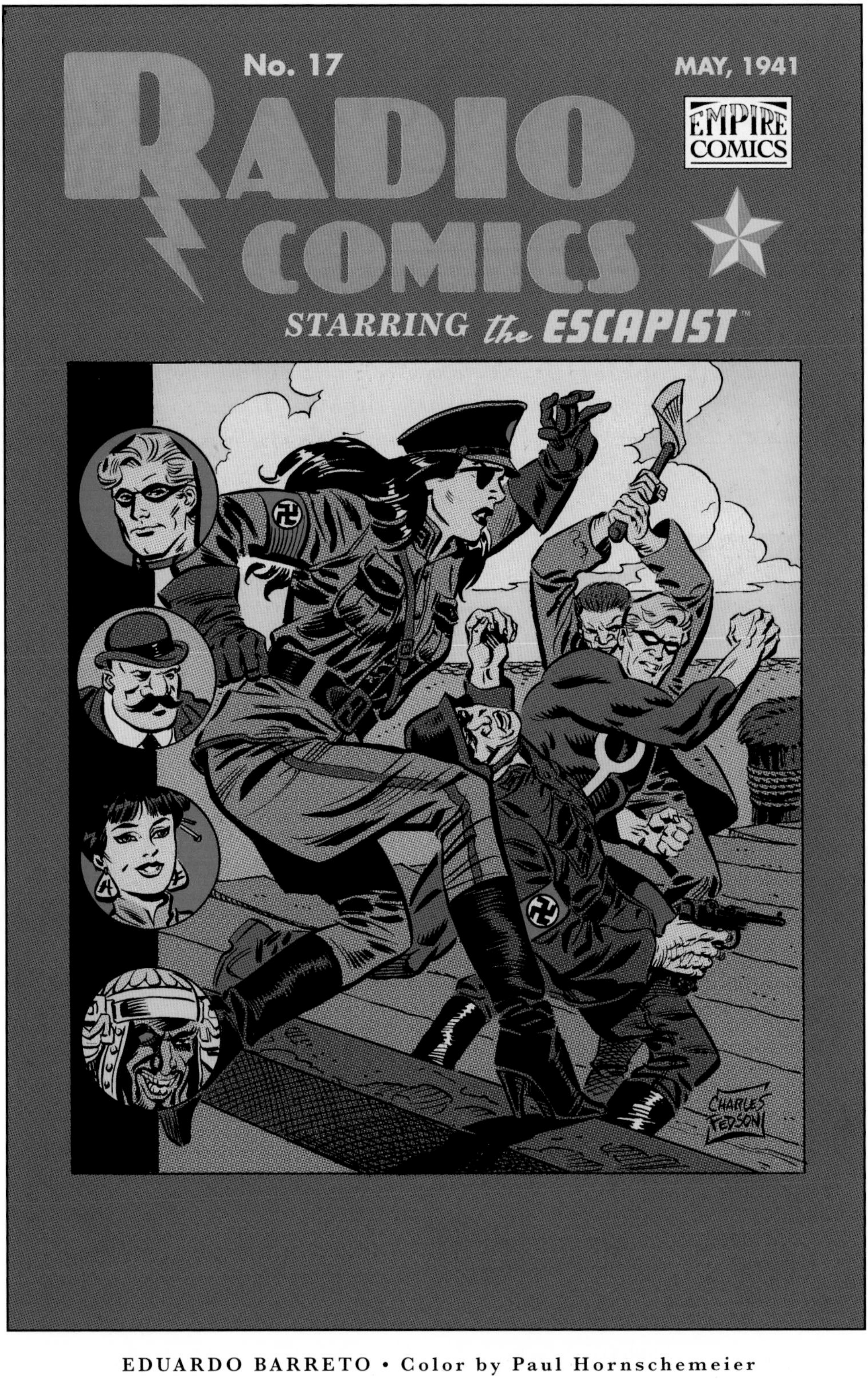
No. 17
MAY, 1941
EMPIRE COMICS
RADIO COMICS
STARRING the ESCAPIST
CHARLES PEDSON

EDUARDO BARRETO • Color by Paul Hornschemeier

CREATOR BIOGRAPHIES

JASON SHAWN ALEXANDER's art is primarily rooted in illustration and comics work, though his personal paintings are gathering gallery attention. He's completed several collections for Dark Horse, including *Abe Sapien: The Drowning*, *The Escapists*, and *The Secret*. He received two Eisner Award nominations for his run on Oni Press's *Queen & Country* as well as a silver medal from the Society of Illustrators West for his cover work on Dark Horse's *Damn Nation*. He lives in Los Angeles.

Uruguayan EDUARDO BARRETO enjoys international notoriety as the artist behind such high-profile titles as *Batman*, *Superman*, *Star Wars*, *Green Arrow*, *Daredevil*, and *Aliens/Predator*. Over the course of his career he has worked for DC, Marvel, Archie Comics, Western Publishing, Dark Horse, Oni Press, and a variety of newspaper and advertising companies. Since 2006, he has been illustrating the long-running *Judge Parker* newspaper strip for King Features. *Photo by Diana Schutz.*

Eisner, Harvey, and Inkpot Award-winning artist BRIAN BOLLAND began his comics career in a variety of underground U.K. magazines. His first regular work was *Powerman*, with Dave Gibbons, which was distributed in Nigeria from 1975 to 1977. Bolland is perhaps best known for his work on *The Killing Joke* with Alan Moore, recently re-released as a deluxe hardcover, and on *Judge Dredd*, as well as for his covers to such titles as *The Invisibles*, *Animal Man*, *Wonder Woman*, *Batman*, and *Tank Girl*. His latest collections are *Bolland Strips!* from Knockabout and *The Art of Brian Bolland* from Desperado/Image.

PHILIP BOND first gained a fan following through his creation *Wired World*, which began with the first issue of *Deadline*, the landmark U.K. comics magazine. He has since gone on to draw *Tank Girl; Kill Your Boyfriend; The Invisibles; Hellblazer: Bad Blood;* and *Vertigo Pop: London*, among others. In addition to cover art for *The Exterminators* and *American Splendor*, his most recent work is *Vimanarama* with Grant Morrison and *Red Herring* with David Tischman. Bond lives in New Jersey with his family.

In addition to his comics art, multiple Eisner Award winner JOHN CASSADAY has also designed works for Ringling Bros. and Barnum & Bailey Circus, Levi's Blue Jeans, and German hip-hop band Die Firma. His art has been exhibited in Hong Kong, New York City, and the Smithsonian Institute in Washington, DC. John lives in New York City and recently completed acclaimed runs on *Planetary* with Warren Ellis and *Astonishing X-Men* with Joss Whedon.

MATT HOLLINGSWORTH is great at brewing his own beer, but he makes a living as one of the most prolific and talented colorists working in comics today. He attended the Joe Kubert School of Cartoon Art before moving on to color such books as *Preacher, Hellboy, Catwoman, Grendel Tales: Devils and Deaths, The Eternals, Daredevil*, and *The Amazon*. He lives in Zagreb, Croatia, with his wife and two cats.

The Ignatz, Eisner, and Harvey Award-nominated cartoonist PAUL HORNSCHEMEIER lives in Chicago. His groundbreaking serial *Sequential* is collected in a hardcover of the same name, and his other critically acclaimed series, *Forlorn Funnies*, is collected in *Let Us Be Perfectly Clear* and the recently reissued *Mother, Come Home*, both from Fantagraphics Books, which also published Hornschemeier's *The Three Paradoxes* and *All and Sundry*. His most recent book is *Life with Mr. Dangerous* from Random House.

DAN JACKSON worked as an in-house digital production specialist at Dark Horse for over ten years before setting out on his own as a freelance colorist. He has lent his coloring talents to a variety of titles, including *Star Wars, The Amazing Adventures of the Escapist,* and *Werewolves on the Moon*, among many others. He lives in Portland, Oregon, with his wife and two daughters.

JAMES JEAN is an award-winning illustrator living in Los Angeles. He was born in Taiwan in 1979, raised in New Jersey, and educated at the School of Visual Arts in New York City. Upon graduating in 2001, he quickly became an acclaimed cover artist for DC Comics, garnering multiple Eisner and Harvey awards, and gold medals from the Society of Illustrators of both Los Angeles and New York. DC Comics recently published an art book of his *Fables* cover paintings. He has also created covers for *The Umbrella Academy* and contributed to many national and international publications, including *Time, The New York Times, Rolling Stone*, and *Playboy*, among others.

FRANK MILLER began his comics career in the '70s, revitalizing Marvel's *Daredevil*. He then took his talents to DC, where he reinvented Batman in 1986 with *Batman: The Dark Knight Returns*. Its sequel, *Batman: The Dark Knight Strikes Again*, published fifteen years later, broke all industry sales records. Prior to that, Miller developed a host of creator-owned projects: *Sin City*, *The Big Guy and Rusty the Boy Robot* with Geof Darrow, *Martha Washington* with Dave Gibbons, *Bad Boy* with Simon Bisley, and *300* with Lynn Varley. He has received many Eisner and Harvey awards, and his work has been adapted into the hit films *Sin City*, co-directed by Miller and Robert Rodriguez, and *300*, directed by Zack Snyder, on which Miller served as a consultant. Miller took the directing reins himself for *The Spirit*, his adaptation of Will Eisner's classic crime comic. *Photo by Diana Schutz.*

TOM ORZECHOWSKI has been associated with most of the publishers around. He lettered Marvel's *Uncanny X-Men* from the beginning, and stayed with it for eighteen years. At the same time (mid-'70s) he worked in the final true undergrounds. Since 1989, he's lettered manga for Viz, Eclipse, and Dark Horse, specializing in Masamune Shirow's books. His current work includes *Spawn*, *X-Men Forever*, and *Grendel: Behold the Devil*. *Photo by Lois Buhalis.*

PAUL POPE is the visionary cartoonist behind such titles as *THB*, *The One Trick Rip Off*, and *Batman Year 100*. Having begun his career as a self-publisher, in 1995 he became the first Western artist to be signed to a five-year contract with Kodansha, Japan's largest manga publisher. Since then, his works have included *Heavy Liquid* and *100%* at DC/Vertigo, as well as "Teenage Sidekick," a story in DC's *Solo*, which garnered him an Eisner Award. He lives and works in New York City. *Photo by Aliya Naumoff.*

STEVE ROLSTON is best known as the premier artist on the Eisner Award-winning espionage series *Queen & Country*. His other illustration credits include *Pounded, Jingle Belle, MEK,* and *Emiko Superstar*. With both his artist and writer hats on, he created the cartoony *Jack Spade & Tony Two-Fist* and the "slacker noir" graphic novel *One Bad Day*. Steve lives in Vancouver, Canada, and can be digitally located at www.steverolston.com.

ALEX ROSS revolutionized painting in comics with *Marvels* at Marvel in 1993, *Kingdom Come* at DC in 1996, and *Uncle Sam* at Vertigo in 1998. Between 1998 and 2003, Ross brought Superman, Batman, Captain Marvel, and Wonder Woman to life in a series of tabloid-sized comics celebrating the sixtieth anniversaries of these icons. Ross worked as character designer and co-plotter for the *Earth X* trilogy for Marvel, co-plotted and painted the series *Justice* for DC, designed the uniform for the new Captain America for Marvel, and co-masterminded *Project Superpowers* for Dynamite. Ross also painted the poster for the 2002 Academy Awards, the opening credits for *Spider-Man 2*, and multiple album and DVD covers.

DAVE STEWART started out as a design intern at Dark Horse, and is now the award-winning colorist of *Hellboy*, *Umbrella Academy*, *The Goon*, and many, many other books. In addition to coloring some of the best artists in comics, he practices kung fu, speaks Cherokee, and raises black cats, which makes him a cross-cultural triple threat in his native state of Idaho.

Multiple Eisner Award-winning writer BRIAN K. VAUGHAN is best known for penning the runaway hit *Y–The Last Man*. Co-creator of *Runaways*, *Ex Machina*, and the graphic novel *Pride of Baghdad*, Vaughan has also grappled with such characters as Batman, Spider-Man, Dr. Strange, the X-Men, and the castaways of TV's *Lost*. A former magician and president of his high school's "Circus Club," Brian used to perform a straitjacket routine that would make the Escapist cringe.

MICHAEL CHABON is a multiple award-winning writer and, according to his Dark Horse editor, a truly amazing person.

EDITOR
DIANA SCHUTZ

ASSOCIATE EDITOR
DAVE MARSHALL

BOOK DESIGN
AMY ARENDTS
TINA ALESSI

LOGO DESIGN
LIA RIBACCHI

DIGITAL PRODUCTION
DAN JACKSON
MATT DRYER

PUBLISHER
MIKE RICHARDSON

THE ESCAPISTS™

This volume collects issues one through six of the Dark Horse comic book series *The Escapists*, originally published in 2006 and collected as a hardcover edition in 2007.

Published by Dark Horse Books
A division of Dark Horse Comics, Inc.
10956 SE Main Street
Milwaukie, Oregon 97222
United States of America

darkhorse.com
barclayagency.com/chabon.html

Representation for Michael Chabon
by Mary Evans, Inc. Literary Agency
and Law Offices of Harris M. Miller II, P.C.

First Softcover Edition: December 2009
ISBN 978-1-59582-361-8

10 9 8 7 6 5 4 3 2 1

PRINTED IN CHINA